# Gerald Gardner and the Cauldron of Inspiration

## An Investigation into the Sources of Gardnerian Witchcraft

### By Philip Heselton

## www.capallbann.co.uk

R. H. Greenfield
28 Malwood Road
London
SW12 8EN
UK

# Gerald Gardner and the Cauldron of Inspiration

©Copyright Philip Heselton 2003

ISBN 186163 1642

**ALL RIGHTS RESERVED**

No part of this publication may be reproduced, stored in a retrieval system or transmitted in any form or by any means, electronic, mechanical, photocopying, scanning, recording or otherwise without the prior written permission of the author and the publisher.

Cover design by Paul Mason

Published by:

> Capall Bann Publishing
> Auton Farm
> Milverton
> Somerset
> TA4 1NE

# DEDICATION

In gratitude for the interest, encouragement and love by my partner Hilary and my fellow members of the Triple Horse Coven during the writing of this book.

And in memory of my father
Kenneth Yeaman Heselton
*(3rd April 1921 - 28th May 2003)*

and my aunt
Ruby Loiuse Jennings
*(8th December 1925 - 6th June 2003)*

from whom I discovered how to see and how to understand

## Picture Credits

John Belham-Payne: 39, 40. Ann Cook: 2. Jerry Cornelius: 30. Patricia Crowther: 24. Nicholas Culpeper: 29, 31. R.A. Gilbert: 9. Chris Hare: 16, 17. Hodder and Stoughton : 22. Lucas Mellinger: 26. Ian Stevenson: 3,7. The author: 4, 5, 6, 10, 11, 12, 14, 21, 23, 25, 48. All other illustrations in the collection of the author. The author has made every effort to identify copyright holders and to obtain their permission but would be glad to hear of any inadvertent errors or omissions.

# Contents

| | | |
|---|---|---|
| Foreword | | 11 |
| Introduction | | 13 |
| Chapter 1 | From The New Forest | 17 |
| Chapter 2 | Katherine Oldmeadow - Children's Author | 34 |
| Chapter 3 | Mother Sabine - Matriarch Of The Coven? | 64 |
| Chapter 4 | Druidry, Aunt Agatha and the Sword of Nuada | 79 |
| Chapter 5 | Gymnosophists And Dionysians | 101 |
| Chapter 6 | The Abbey Folk Park And The Ancient British Church | 135 |
| Chapter 7 | The Witches' Cottage In The Woods | 155 |
| Chapter 8 | Folk-Lore and Other Societies | 168 |
| Chapter 9 | Aleister Crowley and the O.T.O. | 179 |
| Chapter 10 | High Magic's Aid | 215 |
| Chapter 11 | Covens Old And New | 250 |
| Chapter 12 | The Book of Shadows | 273 |
| Chapter 13 | An Exercise In Creativity | 290 |
| Chapter 14 | The Cunning Man and the Temple of the Muses | 312 |
| Chapter 15 | The Witches' Mill | 322 |
| Chapter 16 | | 360 |
| Chapter 17 | "Witchcraft Today" | 374 |
| Chapter 18 | Heritage Of The Wica | 384 |
| Appendix A | Acknowledgements | 396 |
| Appendix B | References | 401 |
| Appendix C | Further Reading | 423 |
| Index | | 425 |

# By the Same Author

*Skyways and Landmarks Revisited* (with Jimmy Goddard and Paul Baines) (1985)

*Earth Mysteries - An Exploratory Introduction* (with Brian Larkman) (1985)

*Tony Wedd - New Age Pioneer* (1986)

*The Elements of Earth Mysteries* (1991)

*Secret Places of the Goddess* (1995)

*Earth Mysteries* (1995)

*Newland Avenue School - 1896-1996 - Our Past, Present and Future* (1996)

*Mirrors of Magic* (1997)

*Magical Guardians - Exploring the Spirit and Nature of Trees* (1998)

*Leylines - A Beginner's Guide* (1999)

*Wiccan Roots - Gerald Gardner and the Modern Witchcraft Revival* (2000)

*Gerald Gardner and the Witchcraft Revival - The Significance of His Life and Works to the Story of Modern Witchcraft* (2001)

# Illustrations

[1] Gardner in about 1936, at the time of his retirement, p17
[2] Edith Woodford-Grimes ('Dafo') in 1917, p 25
[3] Dorothy St. Quintin Fordham in about 1950, p25
[4] The Naked Man, p29
[5] A modern ritual site in the New Forest, p31
[6] The possible site of the New Forest Coven's rituals, p32
[7] Believed to be Katherine Oldmeadow, Highcliffe Castle 1942, p37
[8] "Oh, look" she whispered. "It's a baby!" Illustration by Rosa C. Petherick in Katharine L. Oldmeadow's "Princess Charming" , p42
[9] Rosamund Carnsew's application form for membership of the Order of the Morgen Rothe, p66
[10] The Bungalow, Sutton, Sussex - Rosamund Carnsew's home from 1903 to 1910, p71
[11] The garden of 'Whinchat' at the junction of Avenue Road and Chewton Farm Road, Walkford - Rosamund and George Sabine's home from 1924 to 1948, p74
[12] Highcliffe, Walkford and Chewton Common in 1939, p76
[13] Letterhead of the Church of the Universal Bond (An Druidh Uileach Braithreachas) showing the rose cross, p84
[14] 'The Sword of Nuada' showing the stages of its adaptation to Golden Dawn and Wiccan ritual, p92
[15] Harry 'Dion' Byngham at an Order of Woodcraft Chivalry ritual, p114
[16] The Sanctuary in about 1930, p118
[17] One of the Sanctuary's wooden bungalows, p119
[18] Ross Nichols outside his hut at Spielplatz, p128
[19] A consecration in the Catholic Apostolic Church. The figure in the centre of the front row is W.B. Crow., p139
[20] The Abbey Folk Park, p146
[21] The former Abbey Church at the Abbey Folk Park, p148
[22] J.S.M. Ward in the Witch's Cottage at the Abbey Folk Park, p149

[23] Part of Bricket Wood in about 1950 showing the sites of Fouracres, Five Acres and the Witches' Cottage, p156
[24] The Witches' Cottage (courtesy of Patricia Crowther), p162
[25] The Witches' Cottage in 1999, p167
[26] Aleister Crowley towards the end of his life, at Netherwood, Hastings, p181
[27] Netherwood, Crowley's last residence, in about 1905, p182
[28] Netherwood, Hastings, p183
[29] The Charter on display at the Museum of Magic and Witchcraft, p199
[30] A detail of the controversial signature on the Charter, p201
[31] Part of the Crowley exhibit at the Museum of Magic and Witchcraft, p212
[32] and [33] Endpapers to Gardner's "High Magic's Aid" (1949), 234 and p235
[34] and [35] Illustrations from Mathers' "Key of Solomon" (1888), p238 and p239
[36] The cover of the original edition of "High Magic's Aid", p247
[37] A ritual area (complete with cauldron) adjacent to the Witches' Cottage, p252
[38] The display case in the Museum of Magic and Witchcraft showing the items lent by the Southern Coven of British Witches, p269
[39] The highly ornate calligraphy of the ritual passages in 'Text A' intended to be read from a distance during rituals, p283
[40] A further extract from 'Text A', the upper four lines in neat writing have probably been copied from another witch's book. The lower passage has been added later by Gardner when the book was used as a notebook., p283
[41] Gerald Gardner in 1951, p316
[42] Cecil Williamson in the doorway of the Witches' Cottage in 1951, p324

[43] Castletown showing the Museum and Gardner's house, p331
[44] The Museum of Magic and Witchcraft, Castletown, p332
[45] Windmill Farm buildings in early 1951 before occupation by the Museum, p333
[46 The Witches' Kitchen daytime menu card, p336
[47] The Witches' Kitchen, p337
[48] 77 Malew Street, Castletown - Gardner's home from 1952 until his death in 1964, p344
[49] The Upper Gallery, Museum of Magic and Witchcraft, p354
[50] Witch's Cottage display at the Museum of Magic and Witchcraft, p355
[51] Gardner at the entrance to his Museum of Magic and Witchcraft, p369
[52] Gerald Gardner in 1954, p 382

# Foreword

by Ronald Hutton,
Professor of History at the University of Bristol

Philip Heselton is the most interesting, valuable and enjoyable author who has yet written on what is becoming one of the greatest riddles in the history of modern religion: the origins of pagan witchcraft. This is arguably the only fully-formed religion that England has ever given the world. It appeared in the 1950s and was already in existence by the previous decade, and nothing else of certainty can yet be said. We lack both a story and a cast of characters; but nobody has got further towards providing both than Mr Heselton.

His work satisfies both my head and my heart. The former is delighted and impressed by the manner in which he fulfils all three of the basic requirements of a good historian. First, he provides data, on a scale and with a depth that has never been known in this subject before. All the thrill of the chase, which makes historical research so challenging and engrossing, is manifested in the way in which he discovers and analyses new evidence. Second, he provides his own interpretation of it, fairly and clearly, telling a story that the records can sustain. Third, he leaves the way open for other people to make their own readings of the same material, laying it out plainly enough to enable this and admitting what is fact and what conjecture, and pointing to places at which other interpretations are especially possible, and needed.

The two qualities of his work that appeal to my emotions are those that have always won hearts most effectively: generosity and love. He is affectionate to the dead, whose writings he studies, and gallant to other scholars. In some measure this is a collaborative book, the product of many conversations and exchanges of correspondence. It is one that encourages co-operation among researchers, rather than breeds rivalry and riposte. Through every page of his work shines also a love of both a tradition and of the land that produced it. Whether or not his suggested reconstruction of the birth of Wicca is accurate in every detail - or can ever be proved to be such - the facts that he has revealed beyond doubt are a magnificent testimony to the sheer intellectual adventurousness of the English middle class in the early twentieth century. There could not have been found in the western world of the time communities more physically prosperous and cosy, and socially respectable, than Barnet, Bricket Wood and Highcliffe, and yet they manifested ideas and practices that challenged the public norms of their civilisation on virtually every level. Nobody has ever done more than Philip Heselton to reveal the world of magic, paganism, naturism and faerie that lay behind the garden gates of inter-war English suburban villas; and perhaps only he could have done it at all.

Ronald Hutton

# Introduction

In 1954, a book[1] was published which made some remarkable claims. Its author, one Gerald Brosseau Gardner, was described on the title page as being a "member of one of the ancient covens of the Witch Cult which still survive in England".

From this first public announcement much has been written about modern witchcraft, or "Wicca" as it is also known. It is a craft which works with the unseen world and the subtle realms that all witches, from their own experience, know to be real. It is also a religion, firmly rooted in Paganism - the religion of the earth and of the God and Goddess - archetypes of the energies which make up the universe. There is no doubt that Wicca is a thriving and fulfilling religion/craft with a growing number of members. Yet what are its origins?

This question has occupied my mind for several years: being a geographer and historian I like to know where I am in time and space. And the origins of Wicca are misty to say the least.

It is almost an article of faith that in 1939, following his retirement, Gardner was initiated into a witch coven that still survived in the New Forest. This fascinated me and I wanted to know more. I suppose it was really a desire to discover my roots, or rather the roots of the religion that I practised. Nothing I had read about it was really satisfying: I wanted to dig deeper.

This desire to know more led to the research which resulted in the publication of my book, *Wiccan Roots*[2]. The story which I uncovered was fascinating and I demonstrated to my own satisfaction that, contrary to commonly expressed opinion, Gardner did not make the whole thing up, that he did meet the people he said he met and that they considered themselves witches.

That well-known writer on modern witchcraft and one of Gardner's first High Priestesses, Doreen Valiente, in an interview with Michael Thorn in 1991, told him:

*If I was younger and had lots of money, I would make my basis down in the New Forest and try and do a bit of original research - try to hunt up some remnants of what really went on there.*[3]

I felt the same: I wanted to know more about the New Forest coven, if it existed, and to find out what was going on prior to Gardner. As a result, I have spent several years, if not living in the New Forest, then certainly getting to know the area and its people, finding material in the process which enabled me to put in place several pieces of the jigsaw.

My essential quest with the present book has been to explore the sources from which modern witchcraft has emerged. More light has been shed on the group into which Gardner was initiated, together with their friends and acquaintances, and I have traced them back to the early 1920s, finding out something of what they were involved in and where they met.

I have also looked into some of the main influences on Gardner, from the time he retired until the publication of *Witchcraft Today*. In the course of those 18 or so years he met some remarkable people and got involved in some rather unusual activities. What is intriguing is how those activities intertwined, with the same people cropping up in different contexts.

I hope in this book to show something of the development of the beliefs and practices of modern witchcraft and thus give a clearer idea of its character when Gardner first became involved. It seemed clear to me quite early in my researches that he had contributed a lot to the Craft, but I was equally clear that he had not invented it and indeed I found that I could identify those who taught him.

I hope that you will get a taste of the liveliness and enthusiasm which permeates the story of the Craft, not least originating in Gardner's own character. It is what Philip Carr-Gomm has called "creative synthesis" [4] and is truly a "cauldron of inspiration", the title I have chosen for this book. Some of the ingredients remain to be uncovered, but it is an exciting journey and I hope that you will read it in the spirit of exploration rather than as a set text - the situation is far too fluid for that yet!

My approach has been to investigate those individuals living in the New Forest area, and more specifically Highcliffe, in the late 1930s and early 1940s who may have been members of the "old coven" referred to by Gardner.

I then look at the wider influences on Gardner - the people he met, organisations he joined and movements whose ideas he espoused - drawing a picture of his various enthusiasms, which waxed and waned over time.

Gardner helped to create the form of modern witchcraft through his writings and personal contacts, so I explore his published and unpublished works, including the various versions of the Book of Shadows. Intertwined with this, I give a broad outline of Gardner's life during the post-war period, which is fascinating in itself and relevant to our understanding of the development of his thoughts.

Lastly, I attempt to draw these threads together and come to some preliminary conclusions about the possible origins of the Gardnerian Craft.

I have enjoyed researching and writing this book immensely: I hope you will enjoy reading it. I am still enthusiastic and hopeful that a fuller story will one day emerge. As I said in *Wiccan Roots* and will repeat here - the subject has not finished with me yet!

Philip Heselton
Hull
February 2003

# Chapter 1

# From The New Forest

It is one of the foundation myths of Gardnerian witchcraft that Gardner made contact with and was subsequently initiated into a surviving witch coven in the New Forest, probably in 1939.

But what was the reality? I've gradually pieced together the story and told some of it in my book *Wiccan Roots*[1]. In outline, it went something like this:

*1. Gardner in about 1936, at the time of his retirement*

Born in 1884 into a wealthy Liverpool family of hardwood timber importers, Gerald Gardner spent his working life in Ceylon, Borneo and Malaya as a tea and rubber planter and customs officer.

Retiring to England in 1936 [2], he and his wife, Donna, soon moved out of London because of the growing threat of war. They settled in Highcliffe, a village on the edge of the New Forest, in Hampshire.

Out of curiosity, Gardner started attending meetings of the Rosicrucian Crotona Fellowship, which had its headquarters in nearby Christchurch. Gardner soon got to know a small group of members with whom he seemed to be particularly in tune. They were the Mason family from Southampton and their friend, a teacher of elocution who had recently moved to Christchurch, Edith Woodford-Grimes.

Soon, Gardner learned the secret of this little group and, at the isolated Chewton Mill House, owned by local worthy, Dorothy St. Quintin Fordham (née Clutterbuck) he was initiated into what they called the Wica. It suddenly came to him what this was and he realised that witchcraft had survived all the persecutions - he described it as the most wonderful night of his life [3].

He soon met other members of the coven (for that is what they were) and Edith (better known by her witch name, Dafo) took him under her wing and taught him much about the Craft.

In 1940, the group carried out a magical working to influence the minds of Hitler and the German High Command who were threatening the invasion of England. The working took a lot out of the group, and at least two of them died a short time later: I have speculated that they included the editor of the local paper and the local blacksmith.

## Retirement

Gardner retired to England in 1936 at the age of 52. Later in this book I tell the story of some of the people he met and the various clubs and other organisations that he joined.

Gardner was a strong and unusual character. On his retirement he brought with him certain qualities which would help him in facing the challenges which lay ahead. He was self-educated and had the ability to find information in unusual ways - to study unconventional subjects in unconventional ways. He had a life-long interest in weapons, on which he was a recognised authority. He was always wanting to increase our perspective on things by looking at the historical dimension, and prominent in this would be archaeological techniques.

Gardner was always interested in the local people of an area, and in their beliefs and practices - and he found out what he could by making friends with them and talking to them - not a universal way of doing things at the time. And he was impressed by the way the native peoples that he came across accepted magic as a normal part of life - as something which worked. There was in Gardner an inbuilt awareness of the reality of the 'otherworlds' which was intensified and strengthened by his experiences 'out East'.

After two years in London, however, he and his wife moved down to Highcliffe, on the edge of the New Forest, in July 1938. The ostensible reason for this was to protect his collection of weapons and because their flat might be requisitioned by the authorities.

It is clear, however, that Gardner already knew people in the area: *The only place in England where he had friends was the region of the New Forest, and he managed to get a house there...*[4] We do not know who these friends were, presumably people whom he had met at one of the clubs he belonged to who either already lived in, or had subsequently moved to somewhere in the vicinity of, the New Forest.

I suspect that they were naturists (nudists) because, as I tell in Chapter 5, Gardner was a keen naturist and joined two naturist clubs in the London area soon after his return to England. And there was, bounding Christchurch Harbour, one of the very few naturist clubs to exist in those days: its name was the New Forest Club.

## The Crotona Fellowship

According to Gardner's account, it was through an organisation called the Crotona Fellowship that he first made contact with the witches. I suspect that this was not in fact the case and that the naturist clubs of which Gardner was a member played a significant role, as I shall suggest in Chapter 5. Anyway, the "official story" [5] is that Gardner was "on one of his long cycle rambles" when he came across a building the foundation stone of which indicated that it was "The First Rosicrucian Theatre in England".

He had heard of the Rosicrucians. They were an esoteric movement dating from the 17th Century, having roots in gnosticism, kabbalism and several other occult traditions. There were several different branches, of which this one in Christchurch seemed to be one of the smallest and most unusual. Gardner, ever keen to explore something new, started to go along to the theatrical performances and other meetings of what was officially known as the Rosicrucian Order Crotona Fellowship (R.O.C.F.). He gradually learned its story.

It had been founded in his own home town of Liverpool in 1911 by one George Alexander Sullivan (1890-1942). In 1935, at the invitation of Catherine Chalk, one of its members, the Fellowship's headquarters was moved to Christchurch where, in 1938, the theatre was built. Sullivan, using his "stage name" of Alex Mathews, wrote plays with an esoteric theme, illustrating such teachings as reincarnation. Gardner was not overly impressed with either Sullivan or his plays. He considered Sullivan to be a charlatan and the plays to be amateurish at best.

## "The Most Interesting Element ..."

But Gardner continued to attend meetings of the Crotona Fellowship for he thought that they might possess some knowledge about the Rosicrucian tradition.

The biography entitled *Gerald Gardner Witch*, formally attributed to Jack Bracelin but now strongly suspected to be by the Sufi scholar and mystic, Idries Shah, gives an account of what happened next:

*Now, at meetings, Gardner had noticed a group of people apart from the rest. They seemed rather brow-beaten by the others, kept themselves to themselves. They were the most interesting element, however. Unlike many of the others, they had to earn their livings, were cheerful and optimistic and had a real interest in the occult. They had carefully read many books on the subject: unlike the general mass, who were supposed to have read all but seemed to know nothing. Gardner always felt at home with them, was invited to their houses, and had many talks with them.* [6]

From other evidence in that book and elsewhere, I managed to identify some of the members of this group as Edith Woodford-Grimes, Ernie Mason and his sisters Susie Mason and Rosetta Fudge. The suggestion in the book that they were looked down on by the other members of the Fellowship is probably rather exaggerated. Edith Woodford-Grimes was a prominent member who took major roles in the theatrical productions, organised the members' training in elocution and wrote publicity articles for publication in the local paper! Ernie Mason seems to have been well-respected by Sullivan, and Susie Mason was one of the few members of the Fellowship to be a beneficiary of Catherine Chalk's will. So the idea that they were a downtrodden group who banded together for comfort must be viewed with a certain scepticism.

Nevertheless, Gardner clearly found their company congenial, for he says:

*... I was really very fond of them, and I knew that they had all sorts of magical beliefs ... And I would have gone through hell and high water even then for any of them.*[7]

### 'Old Dorothy'

It is one of the oft-repeated statements about Wiccan history that Gerald Gardner was initiated by a witch called Dorothy Clutterbuck. Dorothy herself was not a myth, as Doreen Valiente demonstrated back in 1984[8]. But who was Dorothy? Was she, as some claim, merely a decoy, chosen by Gardner to draw attention away from Dafo?[9]

To try to answer these questions, I delved into her history and devoted over three chapters of *Wiccan Roots* to a study of her life and beliefs.

Dorothy Clutterbuck was born in India in 1880, the daughter of Thomas St.Quintin Clutterbuck and Ellen Ann Clutterbuck. Thomas was a Lieutenant Colonel in the Indian Army, retiring in about 1889.

In 1908, the Clutterbucks bought Chewton Mill House, in Highcliffe. This was originally a watermill but had been converted to a "gentleman's residence" before the Clutterbucks moved in.

Thomas died in 1910 and Ellen in 1920, so Dorothy was left

alone in the house (except for her companion, Elizabeth Slatter, and the servants!). She became actively involved in various "good causes" in the village and organised the Mill House Players, a local operatic group which staged mostly Gilbert and Sullivan operas in local venues.

In about 1931, Dorothy met Rupert Oswald Fordham (1861-1939), heir to a brewing family, who, after selling his country house in Bedfordshire, came to live for a while in purpose-built accommodation in Mill House before purchasing Latimers, a large house in its own grounds on the opposite side of Highcliffe.

Dorothy and Rupert went through a marriage ceremony in 1935, which was invalid as his wife was still alive. Following his death in 1939 and the successful legal challenge to the Letters of Administration by a son from Rupert's first marriage, Dorothy changed her name by deed poll in 1941 to Dorothy St. Quintin-Fordham.

During the war years, Dorothy kept a diary, or commonplace book, which was illustrated with watercolours by her friend Christine Wells (1885-1969). Several volumes of these diaries have, by good fortune, survived and they tell us quite a lot about what Dorothy considered important and her beliefs about life in general.

It is clear on reading these that Dorothy was a pagan in all but name. There is hardly a mention of Jesus and it seems as if her deepest spiritual experiences came from nature and, particularly, her garden. There are many poems in the diaries which would not look out of place in the pages of a modern pagan magazine.

Yet Dorothy was undoubtedly a "pillar of the community", being an enthusiastic member of the local Conservative Association as well as such bodies as the local Horticultural

Society, NSPCC, RSPCA, the Red Cross, the local Bee-keepers' Association, etc.

The first mention of Dorothy in the context of witchcraft is in the book *Gerald Gardner Witch* published in 1960. Gardner was about to be initiated:

> ... *he was taken to a big house in the neighbourhood. This belonged to "Old Dorothy" - a lady of note in the district, "county" and very well-to-do. She invariably wore a pearl necklace, worth some £5,000 at the time.* [10]

I have argued elsewhere[11] that this wording suggests strongly that Dorothy was not actually present at the initiation. However, I am firmly of the opinion that the Mill House was the scene of Gardner's initiation, so Dorothy must have given her permission for such a ritual to take place in her 'second home' - a superb venue, out of sight and hearing of the public road, in its own secret valley, and somewhere that was not permanently occupied since Dorothy moved to Latimers in 1935.

Well-respected witch and author, Patricia Crowther, who was initiated by Gardner in 1960, tells me that he used to talk about "Aunt Agatha" and it has been assumed that this was a reference to Dorothy. However, I believe now that it was in fact someone else, whose name I shall reveal later in this book. It is clear, however, that Gardner did nothing to dispel the idea that Dorothy was the High Priestess and his initiator, perhaps because he enjoyed people getting the wrong idea about things without actually having to tell untruths.

On a personal note, it suddenly came to me that I might have met Dorothy myself. The main beneficiary of her will, Arthur Stuart Beazley, lived in the same village (Bethersden in Kent) as my grandmother and I used to visit her frequently. Dorothy

*2. Edith Woodford-Grimes ('Dafo') in 1917 (W. Hazel)*

*3. Dorothy St. Quintin Fordham in about 1950 (courtesy of Ian Stevenson)*

also used to visit Beazley, so it is at least possible that some time in 1949 or 1950 our paths may have crossed. I like to think so anyway!

## Dafo

I am now clear that Gardner did not invent the main elements of Wiccan belief and practice. He was taught them by someone whom he often referred to as 'the witch', showing the regard and significance that he placed in her. She, more than any other, was the one person from whom Gardner learnt the way of the witches, their rituals and magical techniques.

Her name was Edith Rose Woodford-Grimes (1887-1975), but she is better remembered under her magical name of Dafo. Her role was far greater than has hitherto been acknowledged. Her knowledge and abilities were such as to provide a solid foundation for the development of the modern Craft, which is not to say that she invented it: I shall show in subsequent chapters that she did not. Edith was the first witch that Gardner ever met; she initiated him into the 'witch cult' - the Wica; most of the information about the witches that Gardner put in his books came from her. She it was whose book of rituals and magical practices was copied by Gardner.

After their first meeting, probably in 1938 though possibly a year or two before, Gardner quickly became a close family friend, giving away Edith's daughter, Rosanne, at her wedding. He and Edith also very likely became lovers. I hinted at this in *Wiccan Roots* [12] but it was Adrian Bott [13] who first stated this unambiguously. I openly acknowledge this, although I do not agree with his conclusion that Wicca was invented by Gardner and Dafo as a cover for and justification of their amorous activities.

I understand that when Jack Bracelin and 'Dayonis' visited

and talked with Edith in the 1950s, they considered it "fairly obvious" that she and Gardner had had an affair [14]. Gardner was clearly attracted to her, and a friend who receives impressions of things told me that she felt that Edith rather liked the attention that Gardner was bestowing on her.

Despite the fact that she was only three years younger than him, and was 50 years old when they probably first met, he seems to have thought of her as a "girl". That this is so, we can present the evidence of Doreen Valiente's copy of *Gerald Gardner Witch*. In the context of a trick which Gardner was playing (or, as I suspect, thought about playing) on Sullivan, the author reports; "He [i.e. Gardner] gave a girl a bracelet ..." Beside the word "girl", Doreen Valiente has annotated the text with the word "Dafo".

Dafo was born Edith Rose Wray in the Yorkshire market town of Malton. I have found out little about her early life, apart from the fact that she seems to have been the only one of the family to move away from home. She must have trained in music, teaching and elocution at some stage. She seems to have been living in Hampshire by 1917 and in 1920 married Samuel William Woodford Grimes and set up home in Southampton. By coincidence or design this was in the same street as the Mason family's house.

The marriage does not appear to have been very successful, and by 1938 Edith was living with her daughter in Christchurch and taking an active part in the Crotona Fellowship activities. She was also one of the leading lights of witchcraft activity in Highcliffe and, for a period of perhaps seven years, from 1938 to 1945, Edith was Gardner's main source of information about the Craft.

I wrote at considerable length about Dorothy and Dafo in *Wiccan Roots*. But were there others involved? Certainly this is hinted at in Bracelin, who quotes Gardner as saying: *I found that Old Dorothy and some like her, plus a number of New Forest people, had kept the light shining.*[15]

Gardner said that he was told this by the people who initiated him who had found a surviving coven centred in Highcliffe, on the edge of the New Forest. This was a clue that I felt could be followed up. I took the phrase "some like her" to mean individuals of a similar social background, so I was generally looking at her friends and acquaintances to see whether there was anyone who stood out as a possibility.

As a result of my investigations, I have come to believe that there were two further residents of Highcliffe involved in or who knew about witchcraft activity in the 1920s and 1930s - Katherine Oldmeadow and Rosamund Sabine. Each deserves a chapter to themselves!

## A Walk in the Forest

But before we look further into the membership of the old coven, a breath of fresh air might be in order! My researches are usually carried out in libraries and archives, so it was refreshing for a change to take to the wide expanses of the New Forest: I was looking for the witches' meeting place.

Doreen Valiente left a series of notebooks, dating from the mid 1950s to the mid 1980s, which contain a wealth of information including some hints as to where the New Forest coven held their outdoor rituals. She indicates that Gardner told her that they met at the old tree-stump known as the Naked Man and then went to the ritual site from there, crossing two streams in the process. He had obviously also mentioned the Knightwood Oak and Mark Ash Wood.

I will quote from Doreen's notebooks because it gives an idea of her thinking.

*I found the Knightwood Oak, though not Mark Ash Wood.*

*The Naked Man*

*Also, the "two streams" and the Naked Man. But I am still not sure where the rituals used to take place. To have walked from the Naked Man to Mark Ash Wood is much too far to have been practical. And yet Gerald said that they crossed two streams. Did he mean "between two streams"? This would indicate Burley Old Enclosure. (Rhinefield House is the other way - they would surely wish to avoid this large house?)*

*On the other hand, we do not have to assume that they went on foot. If they assembled at the Naked Man, and then all proceeded by car to the meeting place, once they were 'all present and correct', then Mark Ash Wood is of course quite feasible. The ground by the Naked Man itself is much too open and windy; but it would make an excellent assembly point. Remember the old tradition of "the coven-tree", the assembly place. A convoy of cars out of Highcliffe would have been noticed, so they needed to meet outside the town - and Old Dorothy may have been the only person who knew precisely where the meeting was to take place.[16]*

On a separate occasion she wrote:

*Re the site of the New Forest rituals, suppose the first stream referred to by Old Gerald was the Avon Water, just before Wilverley Post? Then the second stream would be the Ober Water, and the likely working place would be Burley Old Enclosure.*

I decided to take Gardner's words at face value. First of all, would he (or indeed most people) have noticed, or mentioned, the crossing of two streams if they had gone by car? I doubt it. But, on foot, streams become a major topographical feature, either because you walk across a definite footbridge or you are liable to get your feet wet in the process! So, I took it that they parked their vehicles (some would have had cars, others bicycles) at the Naked Man and walked to the ritual site, crossing two streams to get there.

Looking at the 1:25000 Ordnance Survey map, I realised that there is only one direction in which one could reasonably walk from the Naked Man crossing two streams, and that is to the north-east, ending up in the vicinity of Ferny Knap Inclosure. So, in November 2001, I followed in their footsteps, striking out north-east from the Naked Man. Of course, a lot can change in 60 years, particularly footpaths, but the main form of the land will remain the same. I followed a definite path around the heads of some valleys (or rather, I should have done. In fact, I made my way across rather boggy ground. Luckily I had my Wellington boots on!) and came down into the valley of the first stream. This looked like a well-established crossing point, with a typical light timber footbridge common in the New Forest. This was clearly more recent than Gardner's time but it may well have replaced an older one. I remembered that the paintings by the local artist Heywood Sumner[17] showed some very similar in design.

*A modern ritual site in the New Forest*

The path continued up a slight rise and then down towards the next stream crossing, which I could see ahead was a shallow ford. To my left, I was attracted to a small circle of pines which seemed to be surrounding a pool of water. As I approached, I noticed, on the western bank of the pool, the remains of a small fire and certain other items which made it clear that a fertility ritual had been performed there not long previously. It made me feel that I was on the right track: the area was still being used as it had been over 60 years previously.

Crossing the stream I made for Ferny Knap Inclosure, which is a plantation with magnificent Scots Pines round the perimeter, but there was nowhere in that vicinity where I felt that rituals had been held.

After walking around the Inclosure, I did, however, find a possible site which, whilst it is in the open, does appear to have been originally surrounded by pines in a circle. I am making no claims about it, but it did have an exciting "feel" to it, with some fine old gnarled pines. It was approximately at Grid Reference SU 258032.

*6. The possible site of the New Forest Coven's rituals*

We need to keep a very open mind about the New Forest ritual sites. Probably they used several at different seasons of the year. I strongly suspect that more information will come to us in due course.

# Chapter 2

# Katherine Oldmeadow - Children's Author

When I heard that Dorothy's best friend, Katherine Oldmeadow, was a published author, having over 20 books to her name, mainly girls' school stories, it occurred to me that there might be some clues scattered amongst them. My hunch turned out to be correct!

According to her birth certificate, Katherine Oldmeadow was born on 10th June 1878. Dorothy, in her diaries, gives Katherine's birthday as 10th July. However, Dorothy could have been mistaken, as she often was. Katherine was born at 110 Foregate Street, Chester. Her parents were George Edward Oldmeadow, a Writing Clerk, and Annie Oldmeadow, formerly Shepherd. She dedicates one book to her mother, where she says: "This little book is inscribed in affectionate remembrance to my mother who loved "everything that's old; old friends, old times, old manners, old books." Kit." [1] The Oldmeadows had been married on 14th May 1855 at St. Paul's, Bedford, where Annie was born. George came from Camberwell, in London. By 1881, the Oldmeadows were living at 45 Queen Street, Chester, and George was a Chief Superintendent with the Cheshire Constabulary. He ended up as a Deputy Chief Constable.

Katherine was the youngest of nine children, three boys and six girls. She was not the only writer in the family as one of her brothers was Ernest James Oldmeadow (born Chester 31 October 1867; died London 11 September 1949). He had been a Nonconformist minister in Halifax, Nova Scotia, but converted to Catholicism at the age of 30 and became editor of *The Tablet*, the Catholic newspaper, for 12 years from 1923 to 1936. At the age of 42, he founded a highly successful wine business after he had published various books, including adventure stories such as *The North Sea Bubble* (1906) about a German invasion of England. He was also created a Knight Commander of the Order of St. Gregory the Great.

How it came about I do not know, but by about 1913, Katherine was living in Highcliffe, in The Glen House. This was situated at the corner of Lymington Road and Mill Lane, only a quarter of a mile or so from The Mill House, Dorothy Clutterbuck's home. She shared the house with her unmarried sister, Ann, another sister, Edith and Edith's husband, Arthur Lawrie.

She was friendly with a variety of people of different backgrounds, as Highcliffe local historian, Ian Stevenson, points out:

*Sipping tea from delicate china in Highcliffe Castle's elegant Drawing Room might seem a world away from a steaming brew in a tin mug beside a gypsy's shack just up the road at Thorney Hill. Yet ... Katherine Oldmeadow made many friends among the Thorney Hill gypsies and took an interest in them and their customs. They were able to help her with much information ...*[2]

It is clear that Dorothy held Katherine in high regard, so much so that she gave her and her family the diaries that she and Christine Wells had spent so many hours producing. There was certainly a strong bond of friendship between them, for Dorothy writes of her appreciation of Katherine being there in a time of need.

Her diary entry for 10th July 1942 states :

> *White Roses bloomed & held their sway*
> *When Katherine Oldmeadow came this way*
> *And clever fairies round her cradle*
> *Gave her a brilliant brain & able*
> *Keen, dainty wit, a charming mind*
> *And talents of outstanding kind*
> *For, with her pen how many a page*
> *She's made for folks of every age.*
> *She's made them cry, & made them smile*
> *With her inimitable style.*
> *She bids you listen, bids you hark*
> *To Ponies trotting in the dark.*
> *She says my Darling shut your eye,*
> *The Gentlemen are going by.*
> *Here's to your brilliance and your wit.*
> *Here's to your Health My clever Kit.*

Conversely, Katherine is clearly writing about Mill House when she says:

*The figure of St. Francis, with a bird nestling on his shoulder, stands on an ancient mill stone, looking at the house whose hospitality is truly Franciscan; for all in trouble, poverty or sickness come knocking at the door and are received with open arms.*[3]

Katherine lived at The Glen House for the rest of her life. She lost her sight in 1960, and died on 8 July 1963. The house was demolished in the 1970s, the site now being occupied by the Brearley Court flats.

## Her Books

Katherine Oldmeadow had some 23 books published between 1919 and 1958, including two under the name of Pamela

7. Believed to be Katherine Oldmeadow, Highcliffe Castle 1942 (courtesy of Ian Stevenson)

Grant. These were as follows. The dates given are those of first publication.

>  *Madcap Judy* [1919]
>  *Ragged Robin* [1920]
>  *Princess Candida* [1922]
>  *Next Door to Number Five* [1923]
>  *Princess Charming* [1923]
>  *Princess Pat* [1924]
>  *The Fortunes of Doria\** [1924]
>  *Castle Dune* [1925]
>  *The Pimpernel Patrol* [1925]
>  *The House in the Oak Tree* [1925]
>  *Princess Anne* [1925]
>  *The Fortunes of Billy\**[1925]
>  *Princess Elizabeth* [1926]
>  *Princess Prunella* [1928]

*Cuckoo Fair* [1931]
*When George III Was King* [1934]
*St. David's Diamonds* [1935]
*A Strange Adventure* [1936]
*The Three Mary Anns* [1948]
*Under the Mountain* [1952]
*The Fortunes of Jacky* [1957]
*Three Corners Camp* [1958]

[* published under the name of Pamela Grant]

In addition, there was one non-fiction book, 72 pages long, entitled *The Folklore of Herbs*. It was published by Cornish Bros., official publishers to the University of Birmingham, in 1946.

There were also various short stories in collections which included other writers. These included *'Cheery Chums'* [1930]; *'The Mermaids of the Red Rocks'* [1930]; *'The Witch of Whitestones'* [1926] and others.

But, despite being a prolific author, she is still largely unknown. *The Oxford Companion to Children's Literature* [4], for example, fails to mention her.

The books, all now out of print, are somewhat difficult to obtain. Fortunately, however, the Highcliffe historian, Ian Stevenson, has an almost complete collection, which he very kindly made available for me to look at, which was a fascinating exercise.

They were certainly well worth studying, for there is no need to look very hard for pagan content in Katherine Oldmeadow's books: it is there in abundance. I found certain repetitive themes which suggested to me a deep interest in many of the topics that witches would have been knowledgeable about.

Some books have far more of this material than others and these seem in general to be the early ones, published between 1919 and 1926. These early books were the school stories. They represent Katherine Oldmeadow at her best, writing truly from the heart. And certain themes emerge from these stories which are, to say the least, suggestive of a knowledge of something very similar to what we now know as the Craft.

## Awareness of Nature and Landscape

There is a rich appreciation of Nature and of its experience evoking deep feelings in her characters. Katherine Oldmeadow was very much aware of and appeared to have a very deep emotional response to the landscape around her, both Chewton Glen, which was close to her house, and the New Forest generally. For example:

*The quiet, open glades were rather different from the thick Forest of her fancy, but the scampering Forest ponies enchanted her, and far away in the distance were great belts of fairy blue pine-trees.*[5]

*Great deep glades, where the beech-leaves lay like a fairy carpet of magic colours, and scarlet and orange and yellow toadstools grew all ready to be spread for some elfin feast. The bracken was a baby forest of golden trees, and across the purple-brown, autumn-scented heather big spiders were spinning shining silver webs in the sunshine.*[6]

*Outside she could see the rabbits playing among the corn-sheaves in the moonlight, and away in the little pine-wood the owls were hooting.*[7]

*It was the greatest fun getting ready for the night; though it really was not like night at all with a moon swinging like a great silver lantern over the Forest, and the only darkness lying in the shadows of the holly trees, which stood round the caravan like armed soldiers, their sober, prickly old heads crowned with yellow-tinted wreaths of honeysuckle.* [8]

There is frequent mention of secret meeting-places and the difficulties getting there:

*"There's a lovely old herb-garden outside, and a bowling green surrounded by a yew hedge twelve feet thick..." ... The girls...were unanimous in thinking the Yew Arbour the best meeting place for the S.S.S....* [9]

*So Chloe led the way to the caves, which lay in a hollow at the very bottom of the hill. Upon the turf that roofed them there stood a huge and ancient oak-tree, looking like some old twisted genie, guarding the entrance to the caves. The sun was exactly opposite the cavern, and the vivid green mosses which covered it shone with all the jewelled splendour of Aladdin's cave, and, peeping in, the girls saw the floor of the caves strewn with sand, which gleamed like silver in the darkness, and arched pillars of the same silvery brightness jewelled where the sun touched them with shining emeralds.* [10]
*"Oh, I say!" groaned Mary, "these prickles are really awful." "Be thankful they are," said Chloe, "for if there were no prickles there would be no secret."* [11]

And the following is a very vivid description of what could be a ritual site in the heart of the New Forest:

*To see the Forest in all its fairy loveliness you must leave the king's highway and plunge boldly into the greenwood, or make friends with some tiny stream and let it lead you onward like a gay, singing comrade. It will show you the Forest's noblest trees, its most magical colours, and its rarest wild-flowers. Pandora and Rory knew this, and before they had gone many miles they left the forest road and plunged into a rough track through pine-woods. "We'll show you the King's Council Chamber," promised Rory. "Pan and I call this wood that - the old King is the darlingest pine-tree, and he's got twenty-four courtiers." They emerged suddenly into a wide clearing, where a ring of fine old pines surrounded an immense tree, covered with cones as big as babies' heads. They lay fallen among the scented pine-needles, too, and Rory called them the king's treasures and began to pick them up to burn with the Christmas log.* [12]

## Fairies and Nature Spirits

Closely linked to this feeling for Nature is an awareness of the existence of fairies. Katherine Oldmeadow definitely believed that fairies were real, although she couldn't see them. Ian Stevenson wrote to me: *I am now convinced that she believed in fairies, and probably elves and wood-nymphs. She regularly refers to fairies, or "they" as one of her characters always says! I'm not sure that she ever saw one - and this may have frustrated her. In writing once about all different kinds of doors, KLO says: "Doors are wonderful things...There is the Door into Fairyland - the most wonderful door of all - which one seeks and never finds..."* [13] *This is her own comment, not from one of her characters. ... She undoubtedly regarded Chewton Glen as a magical place, and she brings it into her books ...* [14]

And direct description by Katherine Oldmeadow, strongly suggesting that she herself had experienced water-pixies in woodland pools, and accepted their existence, is the following: *...her eyes had that queer, deep, browny-green look seen in dark woodland pools usually inhabited by water-pixies...* [15].

To take just one book, *Princess Charming* includes many references to fairies. There is also an extended passage which is the most vivid description of the spirit underlying Nature in any of Katherine Oldmeadow's writings. It is a story of girls setting up a school in somewhere very like Glen House, in the vicinity of the Glen. There is much vivid description about the natural environment of The Glen, and about the fairies there.

8. "Oh, look" she whispered. "It's a baby!" Illustration by Rosa C. Petherick in Katharine L. Oldmeadow's "Princess Charming"

As Ian Stevenson says: *Chewton Glen was a magical place to her. Whenever she brought it into her stories it seemed fairy folk lurked behind every tree.* [16] In striking pagan imagery redolent of themes of feminine fertility and the cycle of rebirth, a baby is found in the depths of the woods [see Illustration 6]. The book is full not only of vivid descriptions of nature and the experience of it but also of the spirits which lie behind nature.

*"Who on earth are Them?" Mary Ellen looked shocked. Rory would have known at once to whom she referred. "The Little People, Miss. Green's the colour that rightly belongs to the trees and the grass and the little folk that lives among them, and human beings didn't ought to offend the creatures by making their own dresses of it."* [17]

*"Is it a wood - I mean a proper wood, with moss pin-cushions and trees twisted like old witches, and bats, and primroses and rabbits?" asked Jill. "It's the Glen," said Rory; "and hardly anybody goes there except us at this time of the year. The rabbits play hide-and-seek in the moonlight there - Pan and I have seen them scores of times; and there are squirrels, too, and crowds of primroses, and it's knee-deep in bluebells; and later there'll be the darlingest toad-stools, all yellow and brown and scarlet and cream, growing round the pine-trees in rings. Mary Ellen says - " Rory stopped suddenly. She had been snubbed so often by girls of Jill's age during the last two days that she felt afraid Jill would be bored with her too. "What does she say?" "If I tell, you'll say I'm a kid - just like that Meg girl. But I don't care: Pandora's fourteen and she believes they're there too."*

*"Do tell me what Mary Ellen says are in the wood besides primroses and rabbits - or shall I guess?" "Oh, do; but I don't believe you can." "Yes, I can: listen - it's Them." Jill's face was perfectly serious, and Rory glowed with happiness; here at last was a person who understood.*

*For a moment Jill did not speak, for the wood was not only real, but the wood of her dreams. The dark pines, quiet and tall sentinels round the oaks, rising like kings wearing amber-gold crowns, the ground beneath them with its covering of scented pine-needles and the wood-anemones, pale and beautiful. Rabbits, waving their little white flags, scuttled into their burrows; a little stream sang and murmured silvery songs over gray, mossy stones, and the great elm-tree fallen across it was covered with ferns more delicate and lovely than a wood-nymph's hair.*

*"Now, shut your eyes again," ordered Rory, satisfied with Jill's silent understanding of a "real" wood, and she led her on again until she was giddy, and after a short climb cried, "Now!" once more.*

*The pines were all gone and the stream had suddenly found its way across yellow sands into deep, deep blue sea. Below them the Glen lay in a green cup, its sides covered with primroses, golden gorse bushes and baby birch trees like maidens shaking their silvery tresses over the singing stream. At the bottom of the cup there lay a lake of bluebells, bluer than the sea, bluer than heaven, bluer than anything Jill had ever seen in her life.*

*"Oh, how perfectly, perfectly lovely!" she gasped. "Do you see that little green knoll just where the pine-trees stop, where the wild apple-blossom has fallen?" asked Rory with excitement. "Yes." "Well, that's where They are; it's where we find the rings, you know, and once Pan found nine hazel leaves in a sort of circle."*

*"What a darling place; and if there are a Them, just the place for them," cried Jill. "Now let's go and lay the green dress on the knoll as a peace-offering and then go down there and pick millions and millions of bluebells."* [18]

*Jill never smiled as she made this speech, in fact she looked so solemn that Rory hugged herself and Satan [a black Persian cat] with joy; for to be in a wood just after dawn with a girl who made an offering to the fairies thrilled her imagination, as she really believed in the Little People as firmly as did her old nurse, and to her every tree and flower in the Glen was haunted by the fairy folk.* [19]

*In the meantime, Jill had left the house by the garden door just as the hall clock struck twelve, and made for the enchanted island with a courage that really amazed herself. Under the pine-trees the bracken fronds were uncurling their tiny green goblin fists, and the pale primroses gleamed like fallen stars. Jill picked a handful of them and twisted them in her dark hair, and danced in the pool of moonlight like some wild wood-nymph...* [20]

## Pagan Gods and Goddesses

A fellow writer of children's books, Mabel Esther Allan, comments about Katherine Oldmeadow: ... *as far as I can remember, there isn't a word about religion in any of the books.* [21] This is certainly largely true of the Christian religion, as Ian Stevenson comments:

I spent seven years at boarding school and you couldn't ignore religion - morning and evening prayers, to church twice on Sundays. Yet KLO never seems to mention religion at her girls' boarding schools. There's talk and dressing up to do with mythological gods and goddesses - but no God with a capital G. [22]

On looking through her books, I verified these comments. Divinity is represented almost exclusively by reference to Pagan gods and goddesses. As with Dorothy's diaries, there is hardly a mention of the Christian God, and no mention at all of Jesus, in any of Katherine Oldmeadow's books, but there is a profusion of classical and other pagan deities. This is a very popular theme, occurring several times in different stories, but again particularly in *Princess Charming*.

*"It's lucky we had classical dancing this term,"* said Nancy, *"it will be jolly to have the nymphs barefoot, and those green Greek dresses will just do". ... "We must have twelve nymphs,"* said Barbara ...[23]

*... in the middle of the door there swung an old copper knocker - the head of Pan, the woodland god, holding a round copper ring between his grinning lips.*[24]

*"Let us have Greek statuary in the woods. There won't be a thing to learn, and we'll only have to get the dresses and practise the posing." ... "I thought we would make a little setting for the most well-known Grecian deities in the gardens and woods"*[25]

*"I'll be Pan,"* announced Jill with determination. *"I don't care if he is a boy. I simply love him, and I'm like him, too, because I adore wandering over mountains and rocks and woods and having people dance round me and teasing them." ... There in a little fern-grove, on the grassy knoll before a tall beech-tree, sat Jill, or rather Pan, for her small mischievous face against the background of greenery, her dark silky hair wreathed with leaves, and her expression of almost fiendish merriment was the very Pan of one's imagination. She was half-draped in a goat-skin, and in her brown, slender fingers she held a flute of reeds.*[26]

## May Day Festivities

The Christian festivals of Easter and Christmas are hardly mentioned, but there is one festival which dominates the books, and it is one which present-day pagans would equally emphasise - May Day. The thing I noted in the stories is that these festivities are not imposed from above - the girls themselves have created them. And, in so doing, have included many specifically pagan themes. The descriptions of the May Day celebrations, particularly in *Princess Anne*, could well be those of the preparations for and enactment of any modern pagan ritual.

In Katherine Oldmeadow's first book, *Madcap Judy*, are some very colourful descriptions of May Day celebrations:

*A great, spreading, pink thorn-tree grew there, which would make a flowery and fragrant canopy for a May Queen. ...The evening before the birthday was spent in the woods, and the girls returned laden with wild flowers, and great branches of pink and white May ...*[27]

*Bettine, dressed as a wood-nymph, all in green, danced in with a crown of golden flowers, which she placed on the May Queen's head. Then very soft music sounded, and twelve nymphs in silver and green came running from the pine-wood in the distance, garlanded with flowers, six of them bearing great branches of white May, and six carrying Spring flowers of blue and gold.*[28]

And *Princess Anne* is largely centred on May Day:

*At five o'clock the next morning Anne was awake, and because she liked doing pretty things as well as seeing and hearing them, she decided she would get up and wash her face in May dew, and pick a posy for the Queen of the May ... Last May Day, father had been with her, and she had made him wash his face in May dew, and afterwards they had sat on a rocky tor on Dartmoor, and father had told her about all the ancient rites of May.*[29]

*"If we don't laugh on May Day, and make others laugh, and dance the winter out and the summer in, we shall all cry*

*before the year's out." "Who said so?" demanded Elma. "Father did - he knew such lots of things about old May Day; he knew what all the old Morris dances meant, too, and heaps of things."* [30]

*...a hollow, suitable for disrobing, appeared magically before them, and when they fluttered up from it again in their white skirts it was as though twenty bright little butterflies had awakened from their winter sleep. It was fun building a cairn of stones over their school frocks, and fun loosening hair from ribbons and clasps and to let it blow wildly in the wind; never could any one remember such a gay May Day as this.* [31]

*They joined hands and danced round the first oak tree they saw, because Anne Golden said it was a rite of May to dance round a tree - the most wonderful thing in Nature - clapping your hands with joy that it is green again.* [32]

*It was decided that the Queen should be enthroned beneath a canopy of willow branches held by four of her maidens. ... Thirteen maidens stood in a semi-circle round the canopy, bearing hazel staves entwined with flowers and greenery...* [33]

And in *The Fortunes of Billy* [34] there were twins, April and May, one born right at the end of April, the other right at the beginning of May, very symbolic of the pagan themes of fertility and new life.

## "The Folklore of Herbs"

In contrast to Katherine Oldmeadow's other books, one appeared in 1946 which, when I saw it on a list of her published works, immediately caught my eye. It was her only non-fiction work and was not specifically for children, which was probably a welcome change for her because, commenting about children's books, she wrote to fellow author, Mabel Esther Allan: *It is a great refresher to get away from them occasionally and write for the adult mind.* [35] It brings together two subjects which are of great interest to present-day witches: it was entitled *The Folklore of Herbs.* [36]

Katherine had clearly been interested in herbs since before her first book was published in 1919:

*The walls round this charming place were so old and broken that seeds blown by the wind from the garden herbs had rested in their big holes and crannies, and great bushes of golden pansy, lavender, and thyme, grew high up amongst the stonecrops and gilly-flowers, in all their scented loveliness. Blue borage, and sage, sweet basil, mint, rue, penny-royal, and parsley, sweet rosemary, chervil and lemon thyme, fennel and dill, camomile and pot marjoram, all grew within these sunny walls, and every morning Jean, gathered great trays of them, dried them in the sunshine - for Madame was a famous herbalist, who cured all their aches and pains with her wonderful tisanes and cordials.* [37]

That the one non-fiction book that Katherine Oldmeadow wrote was devoted to the folklore of herbs is an indication of her interest in these topics. In it, there are, perhaps significantly, frequent references to the pagan aspects of herbs.

*The pagans believed that the lovely tall Mullein, that grows by the wayside like a fairy lamp post, was the plant Circe used for her sorceries...* [38]

*Only a few days ago a gypsy woman came to the house and told us she had been in the forest picking blanket leaf to make cough mixture; and, following Sir Walter Scott's excellent custom of always rewarding the person who told him a new word, we gave her a shilling for this new name for mullein. In spite of its holy uses and healing virtues, this plant was always strangely looked upon as one of the witches' herbs and was under the dominion of Saturn.*[39]

She also suggests planting a garden with solar herbs, and including a sundial "to represent the Deity of the garden"[40].

Throughout the book there are several references which seem to indicate an awareness of a pre-Christian culture which used herbs magically, and Katherine Oldmeadow leaves strong hints that she favoured the older pagan approach.

*The ancient Greeks and Romans worshipped flowers and herbs because of their beauty as well as their healing virtues. They dedicated them to their gods, decorated their altars and crowned their priests with them and wore wreaths themselves on gala occasions.*[41]

The virtues of herbs were known to the ancients and books on them were written in England in pre-Christian days, but mixed up with all the knowledge of medicine these contained there was a vast amount of superstitious beliefs.

*Some of these linger in remote country districts to this day.*

*In Christian times [a very odd phrase to use?] the monks re-wrote the old herbals. They left out the heathen rites and ceremonies connected with the picking of plants and substituted prayers and psalms.*[42]

Katherine Oldmeadow seems to be suggesting here that there were earlier more pagan texts, which is an awareness that I imagine was fairly rare in her time, though it has become common knowledge since.

She made other significant references to herbal practitioners:

*They taught the people that herbs were God's gift, given to them for their health and well-being, and that while gathering them it would be holy to say a few paternosters, a psalm or the salutation:*

*"Hail thou holy herb*
*Growing in the ground"*

*In spite of the efforts of the monks, however, it took centuries to put an end to pagan rites and stamp out certain superstitions.* [43]

*She would, of course, be superstitious, with a firm belief in charms, pagan rites and ceremonies connected with the stars. These she would practise while gathering her physic herbs, and it is probable that she would supplement them by muttering a few little monkish prayers.* [44]

*We have heard how, for centuries, the gypsies gathered healing herbs and administered them, and yet remained ignorant of their proper names, calling them by their shapes or their healing virtues. Also how in pagan days there were stories about plants dedicated to the gods. ... We have mentioned, too, the heathen rites and ceremonies attached to the picking of plants, and how the monks, with the object of making the people forget these heathen customs, dedicated flowers to the saints and taught special little prayers to be said at their gathering.* [45]

*William Coles [in the 17th century] flouted the ancient belief that celestial bodies had anything at all to do with plants, taking as his argument that plants were in existence before planets; or, to put it in his own quaint words: "Herbes are more ancient than the Sunne, or Moone, or Starres, they being created on the 'fourth' day, whereas plants were the 'third'." Thus, with the scriptures as his authority, did this old herbalist light a candle in the dark age of ignorance.* [46]

I do not take this as indicating a sceptical position about astrological influence: it seems to me fairly obvious that she was writing ironically!

## Divination

There is a strong awareness in Katherine Oldmeadow's books of the world underlying physical reality and various methods of divination, such as witch balls and scrying mirrors, dream books and dowsing, as well as a belief in numerology.

She refers to the witch mirror, used for scrying ('far-seeing') in the same way as a crystal ball:

*"Surely you've heard of witchs' mirrors and crystal balls that you can gaze into and see the future? And every one knows Queen Elizabeth kept a pet astrologer or magician to look into a mirror for her. Didn't your aunt say yours might have belonged to a queen? As a matter of fact I believe it belonged to Queen Elizabeth." "But who can see the future in it now?" "I can." Louise spoke solemnly, and a cold shiver crept down Elizabeth's spine. "And I can see the past, and the present, too."*

*"Of course most people wouldn't see anything in your mirror but their own reflections," went on Louise, "but I'm 'fey' - always have been - and if I like to give my mind to it I can see anything - in the right sort of glass."*

*Elizabeth had heard of Queen Elizabeth's superstitious dabblings in astrology, and of her belief in reading the future in crystal balls, and in a flash she remembered her first visit to the House with the Red Door, when her aunt had told her to go and examine the many curious things on her table. She had taken up a worn leather case which contained a cracked glass, and Aunt Mary had smiled and said, "That was called a Witch's Mirror in the seventeenth century;" but to hear that there were people in the world now who could see the future in mirrors startled her but thrilled her too.* [47]

An extended part of *Princess Candida* [48] is about the Delphic Oracle and the schoolgirls' imitation of it, and there are divinatory techniques in several of the books:

*Then she played her favourite game of shutting her eyes and putting her finger on the page, just to see if the words fitted the moment.* [49]

*"I put all the school prospectuses on the floor in a ring, and then pointed Peter Moone's cutlass at them with my eyes shut. It stopped at King's Corner."* [50]

*Princess Elizabeth* includes much on numerology:

*"I'm silly, I know - but what is numerology?" "It's a sort of cult" (Elizabeth was no wiser.) "and a tremendously ancient one - I believe the Egyptians believed in it. By studying certain numbers you can find out in which element you were born - Fire, Air or Water, and from that you can find out which days and months are particularly lucky to you."* [51]

The system of numerology put forward was based on their names, with each letter of the alphabet being allocated a number from one to nine.

The word 'cult' is used again in a further explanation:

*"I've told you we've got a cult - numerology - and this cult teaches us that we are the children of Fire, and that is the element which must rule our lives" - Elizabeth shuddered - "Fire is our emblem, that's why we wear red, and because red is the colour of Liberty too, 'Liberty' is our watchword...The Red Circle works for Liberty..."*

*"How many people belong to the Red Circle?" asked Elizabeth timidly. "Only three so far, because every member must belong to Fire, and the queer thing is that not one other girl in our form does...Think it over for two days - your lucky number, you know - and then let us know if you'll join..."* [52]

## Secret Societies

This leads on neatly to the subject of secret societies, which, with suggestive names and initials, are a common theme. Katherine Oldmeadow was not alone in introducing secret societies into her school stories: they were one of the staple elements in such books. But there is, perhaps, a particular emphasis in her writings including some familiar characteristics. The names of the societies include the Secret Seven [*Madcap Judy*], also known as the S.S.S.S.; the Black Brotherhood [*The Pimpernel Patrol*]; the Society of School Savages (S.S.S.) and the Bad Brownies Brigade (B.B.B.) [*The Fortunes of Billy*]; the Red Circle [*Princess Elizabeth*] and the Boys' Brigade (B.B.) [*The Fortunes of Jacky*]. Note the preponderance of two initials, Bs and Ss, which even extends to the initials of some of the main characters, such as Bill Briggs, the hero of *The Fortunes of Jacky* [53], and Susan Silvertrees, the heroine of *When George III was King* [54]. It is interesting that present-day witches use both these initials as abbreviations, B.B. meaning "Blessed Be" and S.S. being symbolic of the Kiss and the Scourge.

There are also initiation ceremonies which include much archaic language, so, for example, we get:

*"Behold!" said Judy, "if thou art really true, and wish to join the Secret Seven (it simply can't be Eight, or everything's spoilt), take this deadly instrument and plunge it into thine arm, and with the blood that flows, write thy initials on this brave scroll."* [55]

*"Tis well," cried Judy; "truly thou art a sport," and as she waved her hand the Secret Seven clapped softly. "If you prove true during the next seven suns, thou shalt receive the badge of the S.S.S.S., and also we will initiate thee into the signs, and our secret language, and then thou shalt be an active member."*

*She waved her hand again. "Ye of the Secret Seven, salute our new Sister!"* [56]

"The Bravery Test, O Monica Eunice Langford, is to prove to the sisterhood that thou hast spunk, for without it never canst thou bear a part in their great schemes ... Dost know the little house at the end of the shrubbery ...?" [57]

*... Sisters must swear never to divulge the Secrets of the Society.* [58]

There are various ritual actions undertaken:

*The Seven rising, marched solemnly round Jean's bed seven times ...* [59]

*...Judy solemnly made the sign of an 'S' in the air.* [60]

*"The Pass Sign is "xxxxxxx" on the back of thy right hand. ... Beloved Sister, we greet thee as one of us. 'S.S.S.S.' ...the Pass Sign was seven kisses on the back of her right hand."* [61]

*At this speech, the S.S.S. made mysterious signs - which were maddening to the uninitiated.* [62]

## Ritual Elements

Ritual elements, such as dancing barefoot, and the use of candles, wands and knives are referred to frequently. As Ian Stevenson comments: *KLO clearly liked to be close to nature and I am sure she felt closest when she went barefooted. In different books, she has girl characters who do this. I think one of the attractions of gypsies to KLO was that they lived close to nature, with the children going shoeless.* [63] To give just a few examples:

*They disappeared into the glades of the Forest, where Diana, immediately taking off her shoes, hung them round her neck.*

*It was delicious to race on the springy turf ...* [64]

*Elizabeth longed to take off her thick shoes and stockings and walk in the long grass barefoot...* [65]

*"...our fingers are ten magic wands given to us by the fairies" ...she liked the idea of the magic wand so much that she thought she would try her power in using one ...* [66]

*...they provided themselves with fresh birch rods from the woods with such delight that Dorothy wondered if she had been wise in advising a St. Nicholas revel.* [67]

*The news that Billy was tattooed all over like a person in a show thrilled the small girls immensely, and the further news that she kept a sort of curved dagger over the head of her bed, and had a chest full of the sort of things one finds on desert islands, and a ghost uncle who had sent her to King's Corner, was even more thrilling.* [68]

*"Let's have the Twelve Dancing Princesses. There are twelve princes, twelve princesses, the king, the soldier, that's twenty-six, and we could put in a queen and some waiting-maids."* [69]

*To the horror of the little girls, the new pupil at Miss Lamb's kicked off her bedroom slippers and began to dance elfishly in and out of the lighted candles. She whirled round like some scarlet-clad witch, and her shadow on the wall as she held out her arms bore a terrifying resemblance to a great bat. The more they begged her to stop the more she whirled round, and the clock had struck one before she tossed all the pillows by the door at the heads of their owners, put out the candles with her toe, and condescended to return to her own bed, leaving the wreck of the feast upon the floor.* [70]

## Local Tradition

The death of William Rufus and the prevention of threatened invasion are prominent themes in Katherine Oldmeadow's books as well as being important themes in the history of witchcraft in the area, as recounted by Margaret Murray and Gerald Gardner, though it should be noted that *Madcap Judy* predates *The Witch Cult in Western Europe* by two years. It is, I think, significant that Katherine Oldmeadow chose to emphasise just these events - the death of Rufus, the Spanish Armada, and the threatened Napoleonic invasion.

*"I have already told you that Canterton Glen is only the traditional spot of William's death, and the Rufus Stone is but a monument to commemorate the event. Probably the fatal arrow which caused his death found its mark miles away from the place we intend to visit. It is the event itself that I wish to impress upon you. That the King rode in the Forest is certain, that an arrow caused his death is also certain. The immediate events after his death, his character, etc., we will speak about tomorrow, while we walk through the district where he probably rode that fatal morning in pursuit of the chase."* [71]

*"Joan, do you consider that the king's death in the Forest was the result of accident, conspiracy, or murder by his attendant knight, Sir Walter Tyrrell?"* [72]

There is also a whole scene involving the re-enacting of the death of Rufus in *Princess Charming*. [73]

Whilst Katherine Oldmeadow frequently uses historical themes, or brings history into her stories, the threat of invasion by enemy troops is a prominent theme. *The Three Mary Anns* [74] is partly focused on the last invasion of the British mainland in 1797, in Pembrokeshire. *The Fortunes of Billy* has a scene about the Spanish Armada, and *When George III was King* has as its central theme the possibility of imminent invasion by Napoleon.

This interest is perhaps of particular note in view of Gardner's statement that the ancestors of the witches that he met carried out rituals to help prevent any invasion by Napoleonic forces and, at an earlier date, to defeat the Spanish Armada.

## Witchcraft

I felt that Katherine Oldmeadow's mentions of witchcraft might be particularly interesting and revealing, and so they proved to be.

In her earlier books most of the mentions are negative, describing witchcraft in terms of something to be feared, for example:

*"If we find Miss Miranda is a witch, we must tell the vicar, and he will have her ducked as an example to the other witches ..."* [75]

*It was a warm, misty night. "Just the night for witches," Judy said, which gave Jean another shiver.* [76]

*... she hated the gipsy woman with the gray beard, she was so like a witch.* [77]

*...she hated going to bed alone, with a witch living under the staircase!* [78]

*"She's a witch, you know. If you poked your nose through that door which leads into her part of the house, she'll cast an awful spell on you."* [79]

Whenever witches are mentioned in the earlier books, they are referred to in such terms.

However, a change seems to occur in about 1925-1926. After that time, witchcraft is shown in a more positive light. This can be seen with references to ash trees. In 1925, she was writing: *They crossed their thumbs as they fled past the stunted ash tree near the stone wall, because Juanita said a witch lived in every ash tree.*[80]

By the following year there is a very much more positive attitude to witches and witchcraft. In one story, 'The Witch of Whitestones', Billy, a girl who pretends to be a witch, says that "ash trees are fearfully witchy, you know"[81] and holds "... a long conversation with the ash-trees"[82]. This was a long time before most people had ever heard of "talking to trees"!

The early writings refer to witch balls as keeping witches away:

*"We used to have splendiferous times, too," said Jean Macdonald. "Dad's got a witch's ball." "A witch's ball, what's that?" asked Bobby. "The rummiest thing. It's all colours, and you hang it up outside over the doorway on All Hallows' Eve, and it keeps away the witches."*[83]

However, this changes with her later writings:

*"Oh, look! There's a witch's ball!" She pointed to a large, silver ball. The words on the card attached to it were, "Genuine crystal Ball. Will keep off the Evil Eye."*[84]

*...very likely would hang among them a witch's glass ball, a gaudy thing with coloured stripes that must never be dusted and was considered marvellous for keeping off the evil eye.*[85]

These are positive statements about witch balls, making it clear that those who used them (who must have been witches because they were witch balls) were afforded protection against the "evil eye".

Katherine Oldmeadow also writes other interesting positive things about witches in *The Folklore of Herbs*, which seem to demonstrate a familiarity with witchcraft. She was certainly sufficiently aware by 1926 to know that there were witches who healed. She calls them "white witches", and there are extended passages in The Folklore of Herbs where Katherine Oldmeadow makes a clear distinction between "white" and "black" witches, after which she makes a very interesting statement:

*The white witch of today still holds queer beliefs about mixing creatures with her simple medicines, and only a short time ago a gypsy woman advised the author to take "a strong cup of snail tea" for a bad cough.* [86]

This is a very clear statement which implies that witches still existed when she was writing and that she knew at least one of them sufficiently well to know what they believed.

She states that "witches always had herb gardens", a very definite statement, perhaps implying that she knew some that did.

Her continuing distinction between "white" and "black" witches clearly demonstrates that she was aware that there are witches who do not do harm (presumably because she had personal knowledge of them) and wanted to distinguish them from the "other kind". This distinction is totally absent from her pre-1926 books, which refer to witchcraft in purely negative terms.

This down-to-earth attitude to witchcraft appears to be firmly established by the time *When George III was King* was published in 1934 [87]. When one of the heroines of the story, which is set at the time of the threatened Napoleonic invasion, was asked what she would like to be, she replied that she wanted to be a travel writer, but that because she was a girl, she couldn't, and she would have to stay at home:

"But I shan't be only a housewife," continued Charlotte. "I shall be a witch too."

"A witch! Oh, Charlotte, but witches are wicked!" cried Susan in distress.

"Not a white witch ... They are wise old women and know all about herbs that heal. I shall learn Latin, and study plants and herbs, and grow them in the garden and make them into medicines and ointments for Father's patients. I shall be a wise young woman ..."[88]

... "You can't be a white witch and a wise woman unless you understand all about herbs ..."[89]

What caused Katherine Oldmeadow's sudden change of approach to witchcraft? Could it be that she met someone in about 1925 who caused her to change her opinions? Someone who healed people through the use of herbs? Someone who revealed to Katherine that she was a witch?

I think that this is highly likely, and in the next chapter I suggest the identity of this individual.

## Conclusions

What are we to make of Katherine Oldmeadow's writings? Clearly, because of their emphasis and repeated occurrence, there is much in her works of fiction which echo her own personal feelings - her sympathy with the landscape, with pagan deities and traditions, particularly seasonal festivals, and an awareness of a variety of divinatory techniques. Secret societies with specific practices are also prominent.

Professor Ronald Hutton has urged a note of caution and stressed that *"Oldmeadow was not that unusual in her tastes and attitudes"*. He asks:

*I wonder if you underestimate the quantity of classically-based paganism and nature-worship which infused lettered English culture in general by the early twentieth century. As Oldmeadow herself says, references to classical deities, with little or no Christian imagery, are scattered throughout Elizabethan verse, as through that of lyrical poets ever since, and the work of Chaucer long before. May is the main festival mentioned in the same poetry, and in Chaucer, rather than Easter or Christmas, and also (since the late Victorian revival of Merry England) the main one actually celebrated within girls' schools ... If you work through Edmund Spenser's* The Faerie Queene, *you will find a long story by a dour evangelical Elizabethan Protestant which is stuffed with pagan deities. On face value, and using the same arguments as yourself, one could make an excellent case for C.S. Lewis's* Narnia *stories as proof that the author was part of a secret pagan cult devoted to a dying and returning god - not Jesus, of course, because the Trinity and Virgin are never ever mentioned, nor any references to Biblican episodes, but they are full of figures from fairy lore and classical paganism. Does not Pomona herself appear to bless the orchards in* Prince Caspian? *Likewise the pagan roots of most of the imagery and plot-lines in* The Lord of the Rings *is patent, and only good knowledge of the personal lives of Lewis and Tolkien makes clear their fervent Christianity."*[90]

I am sure that Professor Hutton is right in that such topics were common amongst a certain type of writer of the early 20th Century. Nevertheless, I still consider that it is most interesting that a near neighbour and close friend of someone who has been repeatedly identified as being a witch (Dorothy Clutterbuck) should have written a book combining two topics of particular interest to modern witches (folklore and herbs) and moreover have written positively about witchcraft and many of the themes with which that craft is associated.

It is clear to me that, certainly after 1925, Katherine Oldmeadow knew certain people who called themselves witches and that they were interested in the cultivation and preparation of herbal remedies. When taken together with an analysis of Dorothy's 'diaries', such as provided in my *Wiccan Roots*, we have two individuals living in close proximity, both of whom seemed to have exactly the beliefs and interests that one might expect from those who would be sympathetic to and nurturing of a pre-existing tradition of witchcraft.

# Chapter 3

# Mother Sabine - Matriarch of the Coven?

I was looking through the wealth of papers and books formerly owned by Doreen Valiente when something struck me in her copy of *Gerald Gardner Witch*. It was just a little annotation on page 166 where Gardner is talking about the coven which his friends claimed to have discovered. He says: "I found that Old Dorothy and some like her, plus a number of New Forest people, had kept the light shining".

After the phrase "New Forest people" Doreen had put an asterisk and, at the bottom of the page she had written "* Mother Sabine".

This was an exciting moment for me: it seemed on the surface that I had found the name of another member of the New Forest coven. I mentioned this in *Wiccan Roots*, adding "Although there is little to go on, apart from the name, I am trying to find out what I can about her."

Now, Sabine can be a personal name or a surname. I started with the latter and, enlisting Ian Stevenson's help, found that in the 1939 Kelly's Directory for the Bournemouth area, there were only three Sabines listed, one of which was in Avenue Road, Walkford, the same road where Edith Woodford-Grimes lived from 1940 to 1975.

This sounded a hopeful lead, and so I started to find out what I could about the married couple, Thomas George Alford Broadfield Sabine and his wife Rosamund Isabella Charlotte Sabine.

## Rosamund

I found that Rosamund was born on 12th October 1864 at Launders, Crowan, Cornwall, to Elizabeth, the wife of Henry Carnsew, a copper miner. I cannot be absolutely certain that this baby girl born in Cornwall was Rosamund, for there is no personal name given on the birth certificate. Her names are, however, I think, significant and she may have chosen them herself, particularly her first name, Rosamund, which means 'Rose of the World'. Queen Isabella (b. 1830) and Empress Charlotte (Carlotta) (b. 1840) were both recipients of the rarely awarded Papal Order of the Golden Rose, which is presented by the Pope as an award for devotion to the Roman Catholic Church.

There is no mention of the family in the 1881 Census and I think it likely that they followed Henry abroad to some exotic part of the world where he may have "made his fortune" in mining. Certainly by the time of Rosamund's marriage in 1911 Henry is described as being "of independent means".

I then found her name in another context. I was looking through R.A. Gilbert's *The Golden Dawn Companion*[1] where are to be found lists of members of the Golden Dawn and its various offshoots, and there she was: an exciting moment. On 1st May 1905 a Miss Rosamund Carnsew applied to be a member of the Order of the M[orgen] R[othe], also known as the Independent and Rectified Order R.R. et A.C. (Rosae Rubae et Aureae Crucis - the Red Rose and the Cross of Gold) or the Independent and Rectified Rite of the Golden Dawn.

**BENEDICTUS QUI VENIT IN NOMINE DOMINI**

## Order of the
## M∴ R∴

**FORM OF APPLICATION FOR CANDIDATES**

To the Wardens of the Order

I, *Rosamund Carnsew*,

being of the full age of 21 years, and having complete liberty of action, do hereby solemnly and sincerely affirm:—

   I. That there is an Eternal God.

  II. That man may attain or receive Everlasting Life.

 III. That I desire the Knowledge of Divine Things, and Union with God.

 IV. That I desire of my own free will to be received into the Secret Order of the M∴ R∴

  V. That I accept all the obligations which it may impose upon me, unless incompatible with my civil, moral, or religious duties.

In witness whereof I hereto append my name, address and civil qualifications, with the Sacramental Name by which I desire to be known if admitted into the Order.

*Mrs T. Carnsew*
*Bungalow, Sutton*
*Pulborough, Sussex*
"*Vacuna*"

Date *1 May 1905*

9. *Rosamund Carnsew's application form for membership of the Order of the Morgen Rothe (courtesy of R. A. Gilbert)*

This was a breakthrough. It showed to my own satisfaction that Rosamund was indeed 'Mother Sabine' for it indicated what was a relatively rare interest in esoteric, occult and magical matters.

## The Golden Dawn

To put this in its context, we must start with what is probably one of the most famous and influential magical orders of all time - The Golden Dawn. It certainly seems to have played a fundamental part in the history of the Gardnerian Craft.

The Hermetic Order of the Golden Dawn, to give its full name, was founded in 1887. The story of its foundation is that Rev. A.F.A. Woodford, a member of the Societas Rosicruciana in Anglia (S.R.I.A.), a masonic Rosicrucian society, found some old documents which gave details of rituals which seemed to be Rosicrucian in character and to originate in Germany. He gave these to Dr. Wynn Westcott, who then approached two other members of the S.R.I.A., Dr. W.R. Woodman and Samuel Liddell Mathers. They managed to contact a German woman named Anna Sprengel who authorised them to form an Order in England to be known as the Golden Dawn.

It is now generally considered that Mathers and Woodman were taken in by the documents, which were likely forgeries, and that Anna Sprengel never existed. However, the Golden Dawn philosophy and practices are substantially rooted in what has been called the Western Mystery Tradition as opposed to the Eastern traditions which were in large part the inspiration for Mme. Blavatsky's Theosophy.

Most modern magical orders owe something, and probably a great deal, to the Golden Dawn, for example its subdivision into ten degrees. The name "Golden Dawn" strictly related only to the Outer Order made up of the lower degrees. The higher degrees constituted the Inner Order of the Rosae

Rubae at Aureae Crucis.

As well as London and Paris, the Order had temples in Weston-super-Mare, Bradford and Edinburgh and included amongst its membership such notables as W.B. Yeats, Arthur Machen, J.W. Brodie-Innes, Aleister Crowley, A.E. Waite and Annie Horniman.

## The Rectified Rite

In 1900, the Golden Dawn split over Mathers' admission that the 'Anna Sprengel' letters had been forged by Westcott. This was reinforced after 1903, when there was a schism between those who favoured the focus being on magical working and those for whom mysticism was most important. Of course, these need not, and indeed should not, be seen as mutually exclusive, but it was very much a question of emphasis, together with the interpersonal difficulties which beset most organisations at one time or another.

So those who favoured continuing the magical tradition left the Order and in 1903 Felkin established the Stella Matutina and Brodie-Innes the Alpha et Omega.

The London Isis/Urania temple of the Golden Dawn was taken over by the mystically inclined Arthur Edward Waite (1857-1942). He had originally been a Roman Catholic, but started to explore the occult, joining the Golden Dawn in 1891. He eventually became dissatisfied with the magical aspects and encouraged members towards a more mystical approach. In 1901, the Order changed its name to the Hermetic Society of the Morgen Rothe and in 1904 constituted the Rectified Rite, the full title of which was 'The Holy Order of the G[olden] D[awn] under the obedience of the Independent and Rectified Rite'. However, it began to be greatly affected by internal feuds and in 1914 Waite closed it down.

The following year, Waite formed the Fellowship of the Rosy Cross, which seems to have been intended as a replacement for the Rectified Rite and which introduced solstice celebrations. It was based on the Golden Dawn teachings and rituals, but was more Christian in tone, emphasising (as might be expected) Rosicrucian ideas. As McIntosh writes:

*Waite's ceremony has a much more prayerful tone, with the emphasis on the seeking of spiritual attainment rather than secret knowledge. ... In Waite's order, the formerly "Hermetic" Golden Dawn has become totally "Rosicrucianized", that is to say, everything is done by the participants in a spirit of reverence toward the Godhead rather than identity with it.* [2]

Waite also formed an inner order, the Ordo Sanctissimae Rosae et Aureae Crucis, which drew its members from the Fellowship of the Rosy Cross, which continued until his death in 1942.

I have found no further record of Rosamund's involvement in the Rectified Rite, how long she was a member, or even whether she was accepted into membership. However, the Rite was not really the sort of thing that a complete beginner would wish to join or even know about, which suggests that she may have had some previous involvement in Golden Dawn type activity.

Gareth Medway [3] has drawn my attention to an article in *The Occult Review* Vol 52 August 1930 by one R. Sabine, entitled "Rose of the World" about the Golden Dawn lamen. He commented to me that such an article at that date "must be by an initiate, so she must have gained admission to some branch of the Golden Dawn". R.A. Gilbert [4] states: "... she clearly was familiar with the Golden Dawn form which suggests that she had entered one branch of the original Order; probably Waite's, but possibly one of the others". I have already pointed out that the name Rosamund means "Rose of the World", and leads me to think that she may have chosen her first name following her interest in Golden Dawn activities.

*The Occult Review* was a well-respected journal in its day and to have an article published in it shows a certain degree of confidence in one's own knowledge and also confidence on the part of the editor. Of course, this is what one would expect from someone who had been involved in occult matters for at least the previous 25 years.

## Marriage

At the time of her original application to be a member of the Rectified Rite, Rosamund was living at The Bungalow, in the village of Sutton, near Pulborough, Sussex. She probably lived there for six or seven years from 1903 to 1909/10.

On 22nd May 1911 she married Thomas George Alford Broadfield Sabine. He seems to have been known as George, as he is referred to in both Kelly's Directory and the Army List as "George A. Sabine".

He had been born, probably in Ireland, in 1871 and was educated at Trinity College, Dublin. In 1895, he was commissioned as a 2nd Lieutenant into the 3rd (Reserve) Battalion Inniskilling Fusiliers. He was promoted to Lieutenant in 1897 and to Captain in 1899. By the time of his marriage he had retired from the Army and was living at Burton Common, Barlavington, the next village to Sutton. This had been a centre for the Catholic faith in Sussex since the Reformation [5]. There was a sanatorium for members of the Society of Jesus there, but it is not clear whether George was a member of staff or an inmate. He did retire from the Army at the relatively early age of 39 and may have been going through some sort of crisis in his life.

*10. The Bungalow, Sutton, Sussex - Rosamund Carnsew's home from 1903 to 1910*

He was called up again to serve in the Great War with The Duke of Edinburgh's (Wiltshire Regiment). His service in the War probably did little to help his health and by 1928 he is reported as having been charged with obtaining money by means of worthless cheques. A medical report, produced in his defence in court, indicated that George "suffered from nervous instability, malaria, sunstroke, and was abnormally sensitive to alcohol." [6] Mention of malaria and sunstroke suggests that he may have spent some time in the tropics, possibly in Africa.

The marriage took place at the Catholic Church of Saints Anthony and George at Burton Park, by which time Rosamund was living at 84 Lexham Gardens, Kensington, a prestigious address.

Whilst they were married in a Catholic church, the one clue we have suggests that by the 1940s they may have been unorthodox members of the Church, to say the least. Indeed, George's education at Trinity College, Dublin suggests strongly that he had Protestant roots. In their wills they both requested that their bodies be cremated and, in addition, George requested that his ashes be scattered in a Garden of Remembrance. Now, the Catholic Church placed an official ban on cremation in 1886, which was not lifted until 1963. Between those dates the practice was strictly forbidden. Interestingly, the objection seemed to be, at least in part, that it was associated with what were seen as anti-Catholic organisations, particularly Freemasonry. The scattering of ashes was particularly seen as being undesirable.

There is so much we still do not know, but I suspect that Rosamund knew George as early as 1905. On their application form for the Rectified Rite, everyone had to give a Sacramental Name by which they would be known. Rosamund gave her Sacramental Name as 'Vacuna', who was a Roman Sabine Goddess. The Sabines were the ancient people of what is now central Italy and their religious practices influenced many Roman customs. Ovid and Horace describe Vacuna as a very early water goddess, whose cult was celebrated near Lake Cutilia, in Italy. She became a goddess of the waters and the forests and a goddess of victory. There was a temple dedicated to her near the present village of Vacone, whose inhabitants still celebrate her festival with a feast.

As well as hinting at the name Sabine, the name is interesting in another sense. Most of the applicants to the Rectified Rite gave as their Sacramental Name a Latin motto of some sort. Rosamund was the only one of the 80 or so applicants to give the name of a goddess. Further, it may be significant that

Rosamund was also the only one to have submitted the form on 1st May, which is the major pagan festival of Beltane.

## Avenue Road

In 1923 or 1924, the Sabines moved into a house near Chewton Glen Farm, Walkford, not far from Highcliffe. They named the house 'Whinchat'. It seems to have been one of the first houses in what was to become Avenue Road, Walkford, the very road which would later be home to Edith Woodford-Grimes. The house was referred to as No. 1 Avenue Road. It has now been demolished and a bungalow, which retains the name, built in its place.

The Whinchat (*Saxicola rubetra*) is a migratory small, short-tailed bird, common on open farmland, but not particularly special or striking in any way. However, it has an interesting name. Ian Stevenson, with his crossword-solver's mind, pointed out to me that it includes the word 'witch'. Not only this, but I realised that if you take alternate letters thus - W<u>h</u>i<u>n</u>c<u>h</u>a<u>t</u> - you get the word 'Wica', which is what, according to Gardner, the witches called themselves. I see the same sort of mind behind the choice of name as chose 'Vacuna' as Rosamund's 'Sacramental name' - a subtle joke for those 'in the know', a play on words which the Sabines seemed to enjoy.

George almost certainly knew Gardner during the War, and Dorothy Fordham as well. He held a major position (P.R.I.) in the Highcliffe Local Defence Volunteers, the forerunners of the Home Guard, of which Gardner was also a member. John Yeowell tells me that P.R.I. "stood for President of the Regimental Institute, which is not as grand as it sounds. When I was in the Army sixty-odd years ago the P.R.I. was chairman of the canteen committee".[7] Dorothy had provided the Friar's Rest, also known as the Garden House, in the grounds of one of her homes, Latimers, for the use of the troops for recreation and refreshment. George wrote a letter

*11. The garden of "Whinchat" at the junction of Avenue Road and Chewton Farm Road, Walkford - Rosamund and George Sabine's home from 1924 to 1948*

to the *Christchurch Times* informing members of the Local Defence Volunteers that the Garden House was available for them to use also.[8]

### Herbs

Gardner must have mentioned 'Mother Sabine' to Doreen Valiente, but he also refers to her in a letter to Cecil Williamson, written in December 1953:

*Old Mother Sabine died recently & Ive got her very nice little cabinet of little draws & lots of little Boxes & things etc. but the Herbs have mostly mouldered away. It smells wonderful though, & theres an Old Culpepper with 1684 Original binding.*[9]

Now, Rosamund died in May 1948, over five years before Gardner is writing "Old Mother Sabine died recently". Could Gardner have described someone as having died "recently" when he meant five years ago? Although Gareth Medway thinks this to be in character for Gardner[10], could I have wrongly identified Rosamund? I don't think so because of the close pointers to her to which I have referred above. Sabine is an unusual surname. In 1939 there were only three families of that name in the whole of the Bournemouth area. The fact that one of them not only lived in Highcliffe but in the very road where Edith Woodford-Grimes lived seemed too much of a coincidence, as did finding her name as an applicant to the Rectified Rite.

There could be another explanation for Gardner's comments. Gardner had moved away from Highcliffe in 1945, over eight years previously, and I strongly suspect that the only contact which he had maintained in the area was Edith Woodford-Grimes. It is likely that any local news was filtered through her.

George survived Rosamund by over two years until he died in December 1950. At the time he was living in a nursing home and I imagine that 'Whinchat' was probably sold shortly after Rosamund died. If, as I suspect, George and Rosamund were both involved in the Craft, then it is more than likely that he would have passed on any of Rosamund's artifacts, her magical tools, her herb cabinet and books, to someone in the Craft who would appreciate them. Edith is the obvious choice, as she is the only one we know of and she was living in the same road. If the sword which I write about in Chapter 4, belonged to Rosamund, this timing would fit in with its first loan to the Druids by Gardner.

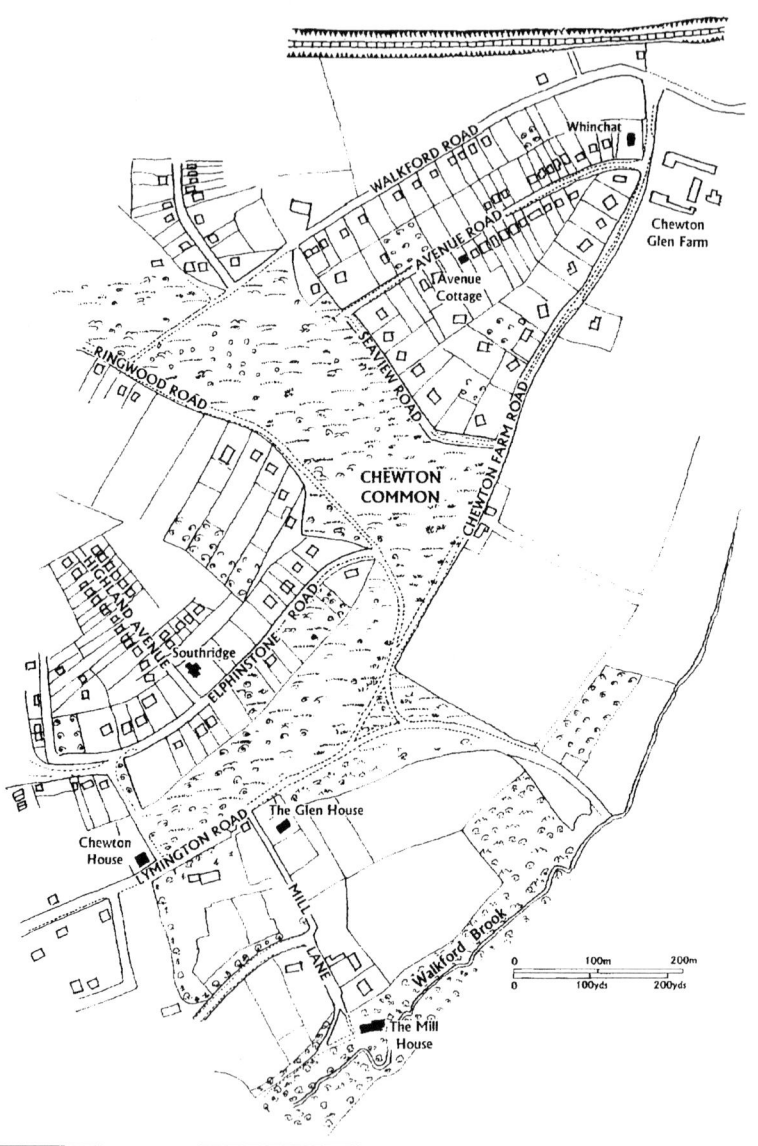

12. *Highcliffe, Walkford and Chewton Common in 1939 (based upon the 25-inch Ordnance Survey map)*

After the debacle with the Southern Coven artifacts (see Chapter 16), it is highly likely that Edith would only have passed on the cabinet to Gerald after he had told her that he wanted to take over the museum from Williamson, probably in September 1953.

The date of Rosamund's death may or may not have been mentioned. In any event, Gardner seemed convinced that it was 'recently' in late 1953, so Edith may just have withheld that information from him.

## *Connections*

I have not yet established any definite connection between them, but I would be most surprised if Katherine Oldmeadow and Rosamund Sabine did not know each other. They lived only half a mile apart on the edge of Chewton Common for 24 years. They both had a great interest in herbs; in Rosamund's case possessing a 1684 edition of 'Culpeper' and a cabinet with drawers for keeping herbs; in Katherine's case, having a book about herbs published. Is it not highly likely that they would have met whilst walking on the Common or in Chewton Glen and the conversation getting around to their common interest in herbs? They would then have found that they had other interests as well - pagan gods and goddesses, fairies and possibly divination.

Could it have been friendship with Rosamund that resulted in Katherine's attitude to witchcraft, at least as expressed in her books, changing suddenly in the 1925/26 period, as if she had met someone whose knowledge had caused her to change her mind?

One other point struck me. Whilst Rosamund had never been a member of Waite's Fellowship of the Rosy Cross [11], she was likely to have been familiar with Rosicrucian concepts and it is quite reasonable to speculate that she could have become involved in the Crotona Fellowship after it moved its centre of operations to Somerford in 1935. Her name does not appear as a cast member in any of their theatrical performances, but this does not mean that, at the age of 71, she was not involved in some other capacity. Indeed, she may well have known Catherine Chalk, who donated land for the Crotona Fellowship's Ashrama and who was exactly the same age. I have also received confirmation that Catherine Chalk was a Co-Mason.[12]

If Rosamund had been a member of the Crotona Fellowship it might give a solution to the problem of how the witches that Gardner met (Edith Woodford-Grimes and the Mason family) made contact with the "old coven" which was apparently already in existence.

# Chapter 4

# Druidry, Aunt Agatha and the Sword of Nuada

Gardner was never the sort of person to limit himself to one particular philosophical path. His mercurial personality was such that he was open to inspiration from a variety of sources. And certainly witchcraft, which seemed to Gardner to be practised by only a few elderly individuals in the Highcliffe area, was not enough on its own to hold his interest when he was away from the area. Following his initiation, he continued his long-held interests in anthropology, archaeology and folklore and sought out books, groups and individuals who were concerned with subjects which threw a light on witchcraft, such as magic, unorthodox religious movements, spiritualism and psychic research.

One path that has parallels with witchcraft is Druidry. Gardner had undoubtedly read about the ancient Druids and their modern revival and this attracted his attention. From what Gardner had heard about them they had a similar philosophy to the witches but with more of the grand ritual that he so liked.

Whilst it is uncertain when Gardner became involved, he had ample opportunity to meet Druids. The first definite date we have for Gardner's involvement is December 1946, but as early as 1938 at the Crotona Fellowship gatherings in Christchurch, he had met Irene Lyon Clark, who was a prominent member of the Ancient Druid Order. By 1943,

Gardner was certainly friendly with Mary Dowding, who later became a member of the Order of Bards, Ovates and Druids (OBOD).

### The Ancient Druid Order

What is Druidry, and what influence did it have on Gardner? One might say that modern druidry is a re-creation of the ancient Celtic mystery tradition of poetic inspiration, divination and sacred mythology. What has been called the Druidic Revival began in the late 17th and early 18th Centuries, when groves (small groups and individuals) began to arise spontaneously.

Several different Druidic traditions developed. For example, the Ancient and Archaeological Order of Druids (often simply referred to as the Ancient Order of Druids) had been formed in 1874, but membership was restricted to Freemasons.

The Order that Gardner became involved with was the Ancient Druid Order, otherwise known as An Druidh Uileach Braithreachas, the British Circle of the Universal Bond, or simply The Druid Order. The Order started to claim in the 1950s that it originated in 1717 and produced a list of "Chosen Chiefs" which included such notables as William Stukeley and William Blake.

Gareth Medway, from whom much of the information in this chapter comes, has carried out considerable research into the individuals concerned and is convinced that the Order actually only started in 1906 when John Barry O'Callaghan became Chief. His reasons for deducing this are as follows:

*The first nine of these men, up until Gerald Massey, were all distinguished enough to gain an entry in the Dictionary of National Biography. No subsequent Chief has been thought worthy of inclusion. However, in no case does the DNB entry mention the Ancient Druid Order, still less that the person concerned was its Chief.* [1]

*He also points out that Massey did not die until October 1907 and states that: We may suspect that this glitch represents the join between the fictional list (of distinguished men) and the real list (of undistinguished men) and that the Ancient Druid Order was founded in 1906.* [2]

Medway suspects that one of the motivating factors in the formation of the Ancient Druid Order was that some members left the existing Ancient Order of Druids in protest at the offering of membership in 1905 to Sir Edward Antrobus, the owner of Stonehenge who had fenced it off the previous year and started to charge admission. These disaffected members got together and founded the Ancient Druid Order.

The first Chosen Chief whom Gardner would have known was George Watson MacGregor-Reid, who was Chosen Chief from 1909 until 1946. He was a naturopath by profession and was Editor of *The Nature Cure* journal. He travelled in India and elsewhere and incorporated Hindu and Buddhist concepts into Druid rituals, translated into a Western form.

The alternative title of The Universal Bond was introduced by Reid as a reflection of his strong universalist beliefs, which emphasise the similarities between world religions, the recognition of value in all religions and denial of the doctrine that one had to choose between them. Ever since knowledge of Eastern religions had been brought to the West in the early 19th Century there had been a growing recognition of this, culminating in the formation of the Theosophical Society in 1875. As Ithell Colquhoun writes:

*Perhaps more ardently than the Theosophical Society itself, the Universal Bond desired the union of East and West: a Druidism stretching from the Celtic Fringe to Persia, India and beyond.* [3]

81

This approach is undoubtedly one about which Gardner would have been enthusiastic, in view of his experiences in the East and his contacts with Buddhism and various native traditions.

## Links with the Golden Dawn

In fact, the universalist tradition was only one of several strands from which the Ancient Druid Order was woven. An important influence was that of the Order of the Golden Dawn. MacGregor-Reid knew many of the Order's members, according to Ithell Colquhoun [4], including Samuel L. MacGregor Mathers, J.W. Brodie Innes, Aleister Crowley, G.C. Jones, Charles Rosher and William Sharp ('Fiona McLeod'), many of whom used to gather in an early version of what today many would call a "pub moot" in a tavern near the British Museum.

When Colquhoun first made contact with the Ancient Druid Order in the early 1950s, she noted that its structure was threefold "in the Golden Dawn tradition", but that it had applied Celtic names to the degrees. She also pointed out that *The Pendragon*, the journal of the Order:

*...was in the habit of publishing characteristically Golden Dawn material - elementary Qabalah, esoteric Astrology and Taro - having little to do with the Druidry of the Celts.* [5]

Following up these similarities, Colquhoun was given a remarkable suggestion:

*Mystified by certain resemblances in structure and wording between the Druid-rituals and those of the Hermetic Order of the Golden Dawn, I once asked Dr. Robert A. F. MacGregor Reid ... what connection there was between the two fraternities. He replied: 'Doesn't it occur to you that the Druid Order is the survivor of the Golden Dawn?'* [6]

*She also noted that: ...the colours of the regalia used in An Druidh Uileach Braithreachas's Ovate Og ceremony are those prescribed for Officers in Waite's Fellowship of the Rosy Cross ...*[7]

Gareth Medway has studied the connections between the Ancient Druid Order and the Golden Dawn in some detail. In particular he has drawn attention to the fact that from 1900 onwards various individuals and groups started to break away from the Golden Dawn and that this would tie in well with the likely foundation date of 1906 for the Ancient Druid Order. He also writes:

*On 25 June 1929 The Times briefly stated: "The Berashith Lodge of Druids conducted the service of the Golden Dawn at Stonehenge on Sunday" (i.e. the 24th.) The reference to "Berashith" and "Golden Dawn" make it clear that the Order owed something to the Hermetic Order of the Golden Dawn. So does their headed paper, seen in a letter from their Secretary in 1923 ... in which the Golden Dawn Rose Cross can be made out.*[8]

There was an inner magical group within the Ancient Druid Order known as the Nuada Temple, named after the Celtic god of the moon and of death. It was probably founded in 1907 by Charles Rosher, a member of the Ancient Druid Order, who was a friend of Aleister Crowley. It seems to have worked along Golden Dawn lines and, according to Ithel Colquhoun, was also influenced by A.E. Waite. Not much is known about the Nuada Temple, but its existence emphasises the links between the Ancient Druid Order and the Golden Dawn.

There is also the matter of the Sword of Nuada, which I refer to later in this chapter and which links directly to Gerald Gardner.

*13. Letterhead of the Church of the Universal Bond (An Druidh Uileach Braithreachas) showing the rose cross*

### The 1946 Split

As we have seen, George Watson MacGregor-Reid was a Universalist. Indeed, he was one of the first to use that term. Ross Nichols writes:

*In his later life MacGregor-Reid's universalism took an unfortunate form; he tried to make Druidry into a religion, which in modern times it has never been, and he discovered and adopted a certain Universalist Church, announcing that it and Druidry were in effect united - they were aspects of the same thing.*[9]

Many of those Druids who were Christians or of other religions took exception to this, and when MacGregor-Reid died in 1946 he indicated his successor as one Arthur Peacock. Medway writes that Peacock:

*... was a minister of the Universalist Church, but uninterested in Druidry, which he did not even mention in his account of the life of MacGregor-Reid. It is easy to see why this would have led the Druids to split away from the Church, which until then had been the Outer Movement of the Order.*[10]

This provided an opportunity for members to show their concerns about the direction in which the Order was going, and the movement split. MacGregor-Reid's son, Robert, was persuaded to put himself forward and he was installed as Chosen Chief at the Winter Solstice 1946.

There were 17 members present at that meeting, which was held at Leamington Spa, one of whom was Gerald Gardner. The Instrument of Appointment is signed by A.J. Steer, who is described as "Leader and Scribe of the Mother Lodge and of the Council of the Bond". Gareth Medway tells me that this was Miss Allan Steer, who ran a hairdressing salon in that town.[11]

Whether Gardner was formally on the Council I do not know. I suspect that the meeting was open to all members and that all those present signed. As well as Gardner, these included R.J. Innis, W. Bromley, Ivy Arthur, H. Chellew, J.C. Duncan, Pat Soul, Marie Soul, Lyon Clarke, C. Trelawny, William Evans, C.D. Boltwood, John Clee, R. Millard and H. Neil. Also present was Anne MacGregor Reid, who is described as "the oldest living member of the Mother Lodge GAIRDEACHAS". She was probably George Watson MacGregor Reid's sister or daughter-in-law.[12]

## Irene Lyon Clark

Two names in that list struck me immediately I saw them as having a link with Gardner in ways other than Druidry.

Irene Margaret Lyon Clark (1899-1947) could well have been the first member of the Ancient Druid Order that Gardner met, for she had been an active member of the Crotona Fellowship, performing in several of their plays and designing and making most of their costumes. She had been born Irene Margaret Guy on 28th November 1899, at Walsingham in Norfolk, the daughter of the schoolmaster, William Guy.

Until she moved into a bungalow which was built for her near the Rosicrucian Theatre at Somerford, she had lived at Ballard Lodge, New Milton, possibly in association with the school at Great Ballard. During her time with the Rosicrucians she wrote a series of articles for the local paper, the *Christchurch Times*, on "Literary Links with Christchurch". [13]

Less than a year after the Winter Solstice 1946 meeting, however, she died in Ipswich in December 1947 at the comparatively young age of 48. Gareth Medway has pointed out that the 1951 issue of the Druid magazine *The Double Circle* was dedicated "to the memory of our esteemed companion Irene Margaret Lyon Clarke [sic]". [14]

## Charles Dennis Boltwood

C.D. Boltwood (1889-1985) was another of the signatories at the Winter Solstice 1946 meeting. His Druid name was "Wayland". He had also been consecrated a Bishop in the Ancient British Church and it is thus highly likely that Gardner would have got to know him through his friendship with J.S.M. Ward, any time from 1936 onwards (see Chapter 6).

As well as being involved in the Ancient Druid Order and the Ancient British Church, Boltwood was the author of several books, published between 1937 and 1941, which he claimed were channelled from the author Charles Kingsley. He later became Primate of the International Free Protestant Episcopal Church from 1954 to 1979.

## W. G. Hooper

Ithel Colquhoun, in her *The Sword of Wisdom*,[15] includes a list of members of the Ancient Druid Order, probably derived, according to Medway, from the Druid magazine, *Pendragon*, published in the 1950s. This includes one William George Hooper, whose Order name was "Andrew".

Someone with this name was living in Nottingham in the early 1900s and had published a book entitled *Aether and Gravitation*, which, according to Medway, was "ostensibly devoted to scientific problems of the time, but with a definite mystical touch".

Later in his life, Hooper became a vegetarian and a Wesleyan lay preacher and was involved in spiritual healing. Following an "angelic message" in 1916 which mentioned the "Eternal Order of Melchizedek", Hooper was led to Los Angeles where he became convinced that he had been a worker in the Temple of Atlantis in a previous lifetime.

Hooper returned to England in 1921 and started the Cranemoor Guest House at Highcliffe. This was the house immediately to the north of Latimers in Station Road (later Hinton Wood Avenue). He later expanded it to become "The Cranemoor Divine Science College and International Fellowship Centre".

Medway further states:

*The same building also functioned as "The Home School" for boys from 10 to 17, whose principal was their [i.e. Hooper and his wife Florence] son in law, Frank Pettipher. Grace Pettipher [Hooper's daughter] did "Vibraclair readings". ... Hooper published a magazine, The Pathway of the New Age, which had contributors from all over the world ... He also published several more books and pamphlets, including The Pathway of the Gods, 1926, and The Ministry of Angels, 1935.*[16]

Although he was still at Cranemoor in 1935, by 1941 Hooper was living at The Retreat, 2 Queen's Park, West Drive, Bournemouth. However, the boys' school, which may latterly have been called "Luckham's School", continued at Cranemoor until the late 1940s, although during the war the house was used by the Fire Service.

The implication of all this is that for a year at least (1934-1935) and possibly for several years, Dorothy Fordham was the next door neighbour to Hooper. Interestingly, there was another W.G. Hooper in the area, a pioneer photographer who produced picture postcards from the village of Wick, near Christchurch.

## Stonehenge

Gardner seemed to relish the midsummer rituals at Stonehenge after they had been started up again in 1946 after the war. He probably attended them each year, and we certainly know of three which he went to. A booklet published in 1951, which is described as a Festival Souvenir Brochure and had the alternative titles *Stonehenge and the Druids* and *The Double Circle* contains a description of the midsummer ritual which took place at Stonehenge that year, for some reason some time after the solstice, on the weekend of 9th-10th July. (This was five days after the New Moon, so perhaps it was felt important for the ritual to be held on a waxing moon.) The booklet states:

*The Noon Ceremony saw the arrival of the delegates from the Isle of Man led by Dr. C. [sic] B. Gardner, carrying the ancient sword and oak leaf crown which he had constructed himself; he was in Scottish attire.*

The oakleaf crown (or wreath) is mentioned in Ross Nichols' description of the 1946 ritual, so it had obviously become traditional (as it still is in midsummer celebrations for many

Wiccan and pagan groups today).

The sword which Gardner brought was apparently of a size which fitted exactly into a cleft in the Heel Stone, from which it was pulled out as part of the Noon ceremony. This obviously made Gardner feel an important part of the whole process, not that he was only invited because of his sword!

## The Sword of Nuada

In 1959, the American writer, Daniel Mannix visited Gardner in his museum on the Isle of Man. In a subsequent article he wrote that Gardner had told him about a "very fine ritual sword" which they had lent to the Druid Order "for their annual midsummer ceremony at Stonehenge because it fits exactly into the cleft of the Hele Stone". [17]

The Museum Guide published the previous year, in 1958, and written by Doreen Valiente at Gardner's direction says of the former owner of some objects in a display case:

*She had a very fine ritual sword, which for many years was lent to the Druid Order which holds the annual Midsummer ceremony at Stonehenge, because it fitted exactly into the cleft in the Hele Stone.* [18]

In late April 1951, Gardner wrote in a letter to Cecil Williamson:

*The Druids wrote as they [want] me to come to Stonehenge this Midsummer + they hinted they could borrow the Sword and Bugle again. I wrote telling them of the Museum, saying the sword was a Witch sword, but I thought the museum would lend it for the occasion. Had no answer so far. I expect it gave them a scare. I know its the only one that exactly fits the hole in the stone + it has a sheath, + they must have a sheath for the ceremony.*

We know from the extract from *The Double Circle* which I quoted above that Gardner did indeed lend the sword again in 1951, and in fact took it himself. The quotations sound very much as if lending the sword had, contrary to the impression given in the museum guide, not been a regular event and that perhaps it had only been lent for the first time the previous year, at any rate by Gardner. Doreen Valiente's phrase "for many years" in the 1958 guidebook may have merely indicated the nine or ten years since Gardner had started lending it, or it could merely be that the tradition had been established by the time she first met Gardner in 1952, and she had assumed that it had dated back significantly further.

We will examine the various possibilities for the identity of the previous owner of the sword in due course, but it is of interest as a definite link between Gardner and the Ancient Druid Order.

The sword is still in existence. It is in the possession of a North London coven that is the direct descendant and continuation of Gardner's original coven at Bricket Wood and who used to meet in the so-called witch's cottage there prior to 1963. It appears to be the same sword as that illustrated in the lower plate facing page 96 of the original hardback edition of Gardner's *Witchcraft Today* and in Plate 15 of Tanya Luhrmann's *Persuasions of a Witch's Craft*[19]. The design on the hilt of this sword is identical to that illustrated in Plate XIV of Mathers' *Key of Solomon* (see Illustration 34)[20]. This coven knows little about the sword, apart from the legend that it was Dafo's, which seems to me to be an indication that it was in all likelihood passed on to Gardner by Dafo but I suspect that it was not originally owned by her. All that was known for certain was that it has been in the possession of the coven since Gerald Gardner was a member.

I have had the privilege of looking at and handling the sword in the company of other Wiccan historians, psychic sensitives and a sword expert and, whilst there are still many mysteries associated with it, there is something at least which can be said about it.

The blade is some 32.5 inches long by 1.25 inches wide, though it appears to have been shortened at some stage. It may originally have been made for an army officer in the 19th century. There is some relatively crude lettering deeply scratched into it on each side near the hilt. It has been suggested that these letters are Cyrillic. Certainly there are some which are the same as in the Cyrillic alphabet, but there are also some in the Latin alphabet and some which are neither. This suggests that they were inscribed by someone who had limited literacy, but was familiar with both the Cyrillic and Latin alphabets, perhaps someone with dyslexia. I note the presence of IHRE, which means 'there' in German, but apart from that, no interpretation has been suggested. It seems to have been put there either by the maker when the sword was new, or more likely by its first owner.

There is evidence that attempts have been made to erase this lettering. The abrasion marks indicate that this was done with the aid of a rotary wire brush, which would date it to the 20th Century. This has been done to such an extent that the blade has actually been made thinner next to the hilt. Despite these attempts, the lettering is still mostly very clear, which demonstrates the depth to which it was originally engraved. Further down the blade are scratched, in Hebrew, on one side, Jehovah Adonai Ehieh Jaye, and, on the other side, Elohim Gibor.

The hilt is probably of horn, decorated with a scale pattern, possibly French. The guard and pommel appear to have been added to the original sword, being based on the illustration which appears in Mathers' *The Key of Solomon the King* first published in 1888. It appears to be made of brass and consists of two back-to-back crescents approx. 8 inches in extent, with

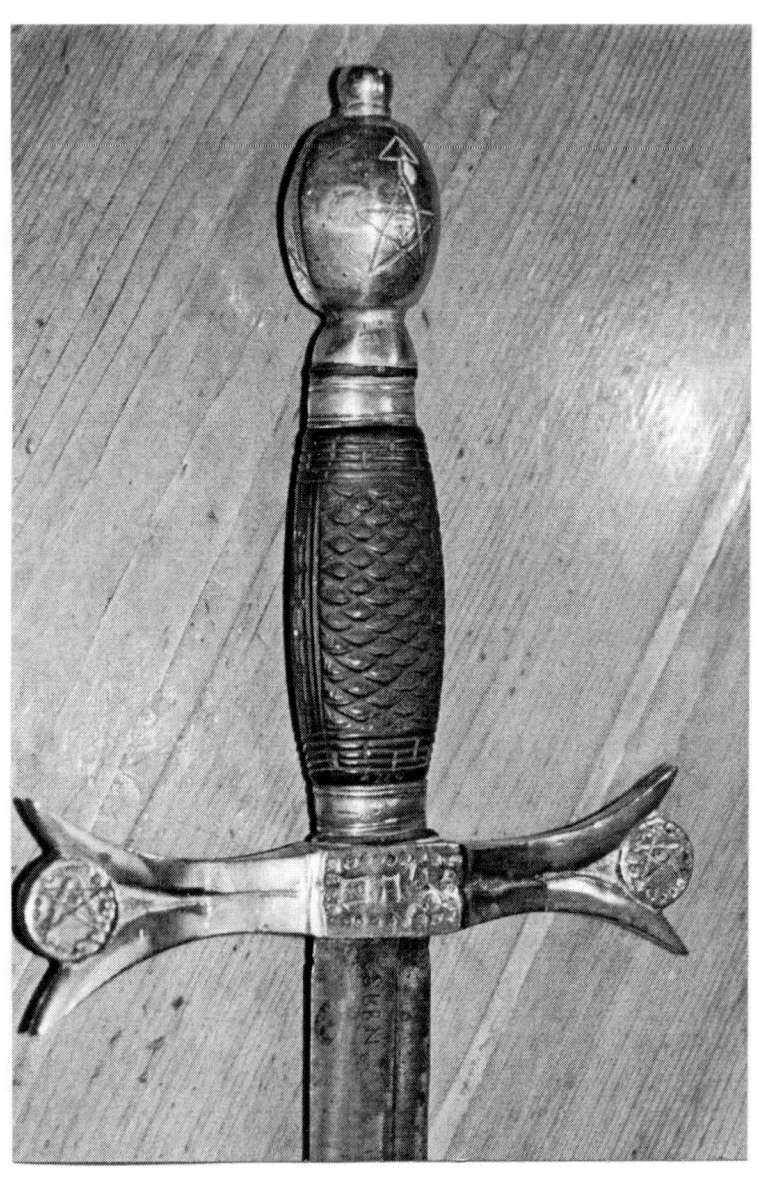

14. 'The Sword of Nuada' showing the stages of its adaptation to Golden Dawn and Wiccan ritual

a flattened section (see Illustration 14) nearest the blade with Hebrew inscriptions (Elohim and Gibor) on either side. Between the horns of the crescents are two discs with pentagrams inscribed on both sides, which have been seen by some to be suggestive of the pentacles in the suit of that name in the Tarot pack.

The brass pommel is again similar to the illustration in *The Key of Solomon* and appears to have been added to the sword at the same time as the guard. It has 'Michael' in Hebrew at the end, together with a socket which may have once held a jewel. There is a pentagram inscribed on one side and a 'third degree symbol' on the other, which I am told is identical to the symbol on the cover of Gardner's 'Ye Bok of Ye Art Magical' (see Chapter 12).

The scabbard is rather longer than the sword itself and some consider that it must have belonged to a different sword, although this need not necessarily be the case if indeed the sword had been shortened at some time in its life. In any case, as a collector of weapons, Gardner would probably have had no difficulty in finding one that would be appropriate, and it is interesting that the Druid ritual at the Heel Stone involved scabbard as well as sword.

A Wiccan High Priestess of my acquaintance who is psychic and who examined the sword got the same feelings from it as she had from tools used in Ceremonial Magic. She described this to me as very intense as opposed to the tools used by most of the witches that she knew which she describes as having "a subtler feeling that makes them seem so much an extension of the person they belong to". She also remembers that it "seemed to have two distinct auras that didn't quite match - the pommel, hilt, and guard had a silvery aura, but below that - the aura around the blade was mostly golden with flecks of blue". This is consistent with the suggested history of the sword.

It seems clear that the sword has had three stages of development. The blade is the oldest, probably from a 19th Century officer's sword, which has been remade with a new hilt and pommel, based on the design in *The Key of Solomon*. Subsequently, the symbol of the Wiccan third degree had been cut into the pommel.

The design based on the *Key of Solomon* suggests that the sword was re-made by or for someone who was involved in ceremonial magic or with a magical order such as the Golden Dawn, probably, in view of the method used to grind the blade, in the early 20th Century. As Gareth Medway says:

*"... this sword was certainly made in accordance with the instructions in the Mathers version of the Key: Mathers included a cross piece with two crescent moon shapes, which is not in any of the manuscripts he used, and was presumably his own innovation; so the sword cannot therefore have been made earlier than 1888."*

He suggests that the sword was originally intended for the Druid Order, and only used in the Craft at a later date. He states:

*Since it was used by the Druid Order, I would guess it was originally made by a member of the Nuada Temple, the inner circle of the Druid Order, who were greatly influenced by Mathers, which places it after 1908. In any case, the "working tools" of Wicca are for the most part the same as those used in the Key of Solomon. It is evident that somebody took up ceremonial magic and had a set of Solomonic magic weapons made, and then later adapted them for use in Witchcraft.*[21]

There is support for this statement in *The Meaning of Witchcraft*, where Gardner gets very close to confirming the connection when he writes about the Sword of Nuada being one of the four magical talismans which the Tuatha de

Danaan brought to Ireland with them. He continues:

*"... the Sword of Nuada, "from whose stroke no one ever escaped or recovered", is none other than the sword of the Old God of Death Himself, which is yet borne symbolically by His representative in the rites of witchcraft."* [22]

Indeed, I suspect that 'The Sword of Nuada' was actually the name of the sword I have been describing. If this is so, then it seems more than likely that its owner had been involved with the Nuada Temple.

## *"Aunt Agatha"*

We know that, latterly, until 1963, Gardner had the sword until he passed it on to its present guardians. It is uncertain whether it was regularly, or indeed ever, exhibited in the museum, or whether Gardner felt that it was so valuable, or he used it so frequently, that he kept it in his own house.

Certainly the use of a phrase like "She had a very fine ritual sword ..." in the 1958 museum guide suggests that it wasn't on display, otherwise the guide book would refer to it directly as an exhibit, such as "Prominent in this display is a sword which..." or "One exhibit is a ..."

There seems to be a consensus that the sword belonged to a witch who died. We must be somewhat cautious about the museum guide entry since Doreen Valiente reveals in her notebooks that she wrote the guidebook under Gardner's direction, and some misinterpretation may have entered the text.

We can distinguish between the two separate descriptions. The full guidebook entry reads as follows:

*A large number of objects belonging to a witch who died in 1951, lent by her relatives, who wish to remain anonymous. These are mostly things which had been used in the family for generations. Most of them are for making herbal cures. The herbs required to make charms or medicines had to be cut at the time when the moon or the planets were in the particular part of the Zodiac "under the right astrological aspects", as a practitioner of the art would say; and the curved sickle or "boleen" was used for this purpose. She had a very fine ritual sword, which for many years was lent to the Druid Order which holds the annual Midsummer ceremony at Stonehenge, because it fitted exactly into the cleft in the Hele Stone.*[23]

It has been assumed that the mention in the guidebook text of "a witch who died in 1951" referred to "Old Dorothy", who died in that year. And, although Doreen Valiente famously used that phrase to find Dorothy's date of death, we must go back to the original caption accompanying the display case, which actually said something rather different. In 1959 Mannix noted it down as follows:

*"As a tribute to Aunt Agatha, one of our most outstanding witches, this collection of paraphernalia which she used is affectionately dedicated. Presented by her family in loving memory, 1951".*[24]

Now, this is very interesting because it was likely to have been written by Gardner himself rather than Doreen Valiente, and it differs from the entry in the museum guide in several ways. Note, for example, that it gives the former owner a name, albeit a pseudonym, whereas the guide does not. It may be that, on searching round for a pseudonym, Gardner picked on the character of "Aunt Agatha", who appears in P.G. Wodehouse's *The Inimitable Jeeves* (1923), a formidable figure with which Gardner was doubtless familiar. Patricia Crowther mentioned to me that, when she first met Gardner, he used to refer rather mysteriously to "Aunt Agatha".

Also, "Aunt Agatha" is described as "one of our most outstanding witches" whereas the guide merely calls her a witch. The use of the word "our" and her description as "outstanding" both suggest that she was someone known to the caption-writer (almost certainly Gardner) well enough to be able to use those terms.

Perhaps one of the most significant differences is that there is no mention of her year of death in the caption, merely a date, which, from the context, seems to be the year when the collection was presented to the museum. Now, it would be reasonable to suppose that Doreen Valiente could have misinterpreted the existing caption when writing the guidebook and assumed that the date given was the date of death rather than the date of acquisition. If this is so, then the guidebook description would certainly fit Rosamund Sabine. We know that she was very interested in herbs and more than likely would possess the various items for making herbal remedies. Also, unlike Dorothy, she had a surviving relative (her husband, George) to donate the items displayed.

It seems to me that Gardner first took the sword to the Ancient Druid Order's Midsummer ritual at Stonehenge in 1950, that it had been given to him by the relatives of a witch who had died and that this witch was someone who had been a member of the Golden Dawn or an associated body such as the Nuada Temple of the Ancient Druid Order.

The most likely candidate is Rosamund Sabine. As I mentioned in Chapter 3, she was clearly involved in Golden Dawn type activities and she could well have had a sword constructed of the type we have seen. With George's military connections, he could well have acquired the blade as described. Also, she died in May 1948 and it seems feasible that George may have given it, along with the rest of the collection, subject to an anonymity requirement, to Edith Woodford-Grimes, who passed it on to Gardner in time for him to lend it to the Ancient Druid Order for the first time in Midsummer 1950.

There is some confusion, perhaps deliberate, over the identity of the older members of the coven into which Gardner was initiated and I think it is quite significant that *Gerald Gardner Witch* says regarding the publication of *High Magic's Aid*: The embargo was not lifted - and then only partially - until Dorothy died.[25]

Now, I suspect that Gardner was, in 1959, still somewhat circumspect in what he told his biographer, Idries Shah, and we know he was quite capable of giving a deliberately misleading impression whilst keeping to the literal truth. It is therefore quite conceivable, and certainly chronologically far more likely that it was not Dorothy's death (in 1951) that triggered the permission to publish *High Magic's Aid* (published in 1949) but that of Rosamund ('Mother Sabine'), who was, I believe, the real 'matriarch' of the coven until her death in 1948.

I say this for several reasons. As I have already mentioned, Rosamund's involvement in the Golden Dawn has identified her as being the most likely original owner of the sword. She was of a generation older than Gardner, the sort of person to whom the epithet "Aunt Agatha" could well be applied. And I have argued in *Wiccan Roots* that whilst Gardner's initiation was very likely to have been at Mill House, the written account suggests very strongly that Dorothy was not actually present. There would have to be somebody there of sufficient authority to oversee the ritual - Rosamund Sabine seems to be the only one that would fit.

In *Witchcraft Today* there is a very interesting passage which reads:

*Now the god is represented by the high priest (if there is one) and it is he who was called the Devil in the old days. I was very curious about him and asked at once when I was 'inside', by which they mean a member of the cult: 'Who and what is called the Devil?' Though members of the cult never use and, indeed, dislike the term, they knew what I meant and said: 'You know him, the leader. He is the high priest, the high priestess's husband.'*[26]

Now, Gardner says that he was initiated 'a few days after the war had started', i.e. in September 1939, and we can imagine that he would have asked the above question almost immediately. Their answer gives a clue - the high priestess had a husband, and this narrows down who the high priestess might have been. Dorothy's husband, Rupert, had died in May 1939 before Gardner was initiated. Edith Woodford-Grimes was separated from her husband. Katherine and Anne Oldmeadow were unmarried, as were Ernie and Susie Mason. Their mother, Rosetta, had been widowed back in 1938.

There is one, and only one, married couple whom I have identified as possibly having been members of a local coven, and they were Rosamund and George Sabine.

This might also be the place to mention another matter that points to the Sabines' involvement and that is the intriguing matter of the first and last house. Gardner writes in *Witchcraft Today*:

*They ... tell me that in most villages the witches arranged that the first and last house was occupied by a member of the cult, and any strange witch, travelling or 'on the run', could go where she would be sure of help and protection.*[27]

Now, realistically, even in a period with little new housing development on the outskirts of villages, this would have been very difficult to arrange, and certainly not something to rely on in a time of persecution.

So, where did this idea originate? It seems to me to fit in very well with what we know of the Sabines' sense of humour. If we look at the map of Highcliffe (see Illustration 12), we can see that Dorothy, the Oldmeadows and the Sabines all lived in what could be considered 'the last (or first) house in the village'.

At some point, someone noticed this and made a joke of it, perhaps fooling Gardner into taking it seriously, or perhaps he was in on it or even originated the joke himself. It certainly confirms for me Gardner's comment, which is on the same page of *Witchcraft Today*, that "Witches are good leg-pullers"!

# Chapter 5

# Gymnosophists And Dionysians

Gardner became an enthusiastic naturist (nudist) in the latter part of his life and many have seen the Gardnerian practice of performing rituals skyclad (naked) as springing direct from this enthusiasm. However, as I hope to show in this chapter, there were others associated with the early years of the modern Craft who were also naturists and whose influence may have been substantial. Certainly Gardner's interest in naturism and the healing power of sunshine dates back to his time in Malaya when he was cured of synovitis in his knee by its application.

Although there was a 'Fellowship of the Naked Trust' established in India in 1891, it had little influence, and it is in Germany at the turn of the 20th Century that anything like modern naturism first appears. It was referred to at first as Gymnosophy, which is Greek for 'the wisdom, or philosophy, of nakedness', gymnastics being so called because it used to be carried out naked.

Harold Clare Booth (1875-1943) was in many respects the 'founding father' of English naturism. Born in Ripon, Yorkshire, he seems to have spent at least some of his formative years in Liverpool. He became a civil servant and, in about 1913, he read about the naturist movement which had been established in Germany. By 1914 he had had articles published in the magazine Physical Culture. And when the war finished he visited some of the naturist pioneers in Germany.

Inspired by these examples, Booth founded the English Gymnosophical Society in late 1922 with Mark Harold Sorensen (1887-1974) and Rex Wellbye (1873-1963). It had meetings at the Minerva Cafe, 144 High Holborn, London, the headquarters of the Women's Freedom League. They soon started to look for land and premises where they could practise their nudity in seclusion.

## The Moonella Group

The opportunity came in 1923 when a member inherited a house and land near Wickford in Essex. She made it available to what had by then become known as the New Gymnosophy Society. The identity of this lady has never been revealed, but the group became known by her own special or 'gymnic' name of Moonella, and Cinder [1] puts forward evidence to support the claim that she was the prolific author, Ursula Bloom (1893-1984), who had written articles for naturist magazines.

The site became known as 'The Camp', and Wellbye, writing as 'Ancton Tuqvor', tells what happened next:

*In the middle of 1924 the now enlarged circle of mutually congenial people, armed with a new invitation from Wickford, started weekly meetings on the old ground. Some solid fencing was now put up and the site made suitable for games without risk of observation. A dozen to 15 persons formed the nucleus, increasing, later, to perhaps 25 or more, a very fair proportion being women. The gatherings went on well into the summer of 1925, with only a small break for winter ...* [2]

The original members, known as the "Old Pack", included Fflang (Harold Clare Booth), Zex (Rex Wellbye), Chong (Harold Sorensen), Thweng (Roland Berrill), Lorelli (Helen

Sorensen), Gart (probably Harry 'Dion' Byngham) and Tob. There were very definite rules:

*Every person who comes to the Terrain chooses for himself a new and strange name. Male names are of one syllable and begin and end with a consonant other than a liquid. Female names are of two or more syllables each of which must begin and end with an open vowel sound or with one of the four liquid consonants L M N and R.*

*The definite article and an adjective "Gracious" in the case of a woman and "Noble" in the case of a man are placed before the name when the bearer is referred to in the third person.*

*Postal communications begin - "To The Noble Blank - Greeting" and conclude with a wish expressed without verb or subject, e.g. "Blue Sky" and the signature quite simply.*

*The ordinary handshake is offered in greeting on the Terrain, the left foot being placed well in front of the right, as on a chalk line, knees slightly bent and heels raised, the left hand being disposed behind the back in the same plane, palm to the right.*

*The utmost secrecy must be observed by all as to the place where the Terrain is situated and as to the true names of members and visitors.*

*.... The wearing of sandals and head bands of brilliant colours is encouraged, but in these matters the newcomer should look to Hellas rather than to the Orient for inspiration. The Old Pack are inclined to frown upon the wearing of jewelry.*

*Care should be taken to avoid complimenting visitors and members upon their beauty.*

*Members should not leave the Terrain without signing their names in the Visitor's Book with the special ink provided.*[3]

This gives us quite a few insights into the ethos of the group. First of all, it is highly prescriptive, with "The Old Pack" determining even small details of behaviour. There is clearly some doctrine underlying much of this, the origins of which are somewhat obscure, such as the avoidance of compliments on beauty and the leaning towards Greek rather than Eastern inspiration. Some seem to echo rather juvenile "secret societies" such as the special ink and secret handshake. Others seem to show a definite awareness of elements which would later appear in the Gardnerian Craft, such as the taking on of a special name, the importance of the intoning of sound, the need for secrecy about membership, visitors and places, and, of course, the nudity.

In 1925, the members had to stop meeting at Wickford. Houses were being built on adjacent land and Moonella needed to dispose of the property for financial reasons. They had to find somewhere new.

### Fouracres

Members began searching at once for an alternative site at a price they could afford, but it was to be 18 months before they found anywhere. A member living locally heard that some woodland at Lower Lyes and Blackboy Wood near the village of Bricket Wood in Hertfordshire was being sold off in lots. A timber company had bought it ten years previously and had denuded the land of all commercially marketable trees, leaving scrubland.

Members of the group looked at the land in January 1927 and it seemed suitable. But could they raise the money? The results of an appeal to members of the New Gymnosophy Society for funds were disappointing, raising only about £50. Then, in April, a reply was received from a member living in

Derbyshire. He wished to remain anonymous, but called himself 'The Major', being a retired major of militia, a local squire and considerable property owner. He offered to put up the money (£300) to buy the land and then lease it back to four of the society's members. This would be at an annual rent of £16.10s, plus an initial payment of £25 each. He described the offer himself as being "6% philanthropy".

Shortly afterwards, again with financial help from 'The Major', Wellbye bought several acres of adjoining woodland which was on sale for housing development. He did it partly to preserve the privacy of the site because it was on the facing slope of a little valley. To have had houses built there would seriously compromise the extent to which the site could continue its naturist activities without overlooking. This land would later form the basis for 'Five Acres'.

The club opened on 16th May 1927 and was "the first genuine English nudist club site" [4]. It was initially called 'The Camp', in remembrance of the site at Wickford.

In the early days of naturism, there was a lot of caution and, following legal advice, the site operated so that the four lessees were "hosts" and the other members were "guests". There were no membership fees, only donations. This early caution was relaxed in 1931, when it formally became a club, levying subscriptions and changing its name to 'Fouracres Club'.

Fouracres developed a very distinctive ethos, partly because it was a continuation of the old Moonella group. Cottie Burland confirms this:

*The little group at Four Acres flourished in their wild patch of woodland. They happened to be a companionable crowd of people who did not want to tame the woods and fields. They camped, built a very pleasant club house with a lawn in front* of it, and talked philosophy a great deal. The membership was never up to fifty, but there was a quality about the club which made it a centre of opinion. It did not advertise its ideas, but its members were people who were nudists by conviction. Their conversation spread the idea widely.[5]

In June 1930, nude sunbathers on private land at the Welsh Harp reservoir in North-west London were attacked by an angry mob. This generated a lot of publicity and comment. The author, Evelyn Waugh, wrote:

*The people who made such a fuss at the Welsh Harp simply detest the spectacle of bodies of any kind, beautiful or ugly. But do they cherish their over-delicate sensibility and avoid places where they are liable to be shocked? No. These astonishing people assemble in a large crowd at the one place where they know they will see the very thing which displeases them.*[6]

Nevertheless, this provided an impetus for wanting the protection that the naturist clubs offered, as Wellbye, writing as 'Ancton Tuqvor', recounts:

*Among them ... was a West End doctor. He looked round for something more secure, discovered Fouracres, joined with his charming wife, and soon brought in doctor friends and their wives, until before long the Club had no less than 11 members of the medical profession, including two women.*[7]

To return to Gerald Gardner. He arrived back in England following his retirement in April 1936. His wife, Donna, who had preceded him, had taken a flat in Charing Cross Road. After much of a lifetime spent in the tropics, the English climate didn't suit him. He quickly caught a persistent cold and went to visit a doctor, as Bracelin recalls:

*The doctor said, "I could suggest something that would cure you, but I expect you will refuse to do it". It was a visit to a nudist club. "I'll die there", said Gardner, but the doctor was adamant that it would help him. He was thus introduced to a club in Finchley.*[8]

This was the Lotus League at 92 Friern Park, Finchley, which consisted of a large house with many indoor facilities and a secluded garden. There was dormitory accommodation and meals could be provided. But Gardner was an outdoor person, extolling the virtues of sunbathing, and he must soon have heard of the naturist clubs at Bricket Wood, fewer facilities but more nature.

It was rather unusual at that time for a doctor to be recommending naturism and it seems possible that he was a naturist himself. If so, he may have been one of the 11 medical practitioners who were members of Fouracres. It would also make it more likely that Gardner, as well as being a member of the Lotus League, would join Fouracres as well. The distinctive Fouracres philosophy could well be the origin of Bracelin's statement about Gardner:

*...he felt that he met people in this way whom he did not know existed in England; interesting people, prepared to talk, argue and discuss. Many had a faint occult interest; fortune-telling, palmistry, astrology, vague spiritualism.*[9]

Publicity material produced by Fouracres suggests that activities included "periodical gatherings for folk-dancing, communal suppers and discussions." The emphasis certainly seemed to be on the intellectual side, as Iseult Weston remembers that the swimming pool was really just a muddy hole in the ground and that, unless you were first in, it got very muddy. To climb out you had to use a rope ladder. A member's impression of the club at the time Gardner may have joined it is revealing:

*On entering some acres of copsewood one is at once transported to another world. A carpet of blue at one's feet, screened by the surrounding bushes, which, one knows, will keep their healthy green throughout the summer months. After traversing a winding path we come upon a clearing turfed with soft grass, with a pavilion in the background. This strikes us as a lush enough haven in which to idle away many hours; but every member is encouraged to do his or her share of work, of which there is enough and plenty for both young and old. Pick and shovel, axe and saw, all come into their own, and throughout the year the work varies and progresses. ... Pleasantly tired we turn towards the pavilion and tea, looking forward to the delightful slack time that usually follows. Sitting round the lawn in groups, many are the interesting discussions that can arise from quite a casual remark, and sometimes startling is the contrast of opinions revealed, which open up new fields for the thoughtful.* [10]

An advertisement for the club, dating from this period, states:

*It seeks to be the gathering place of people possessing, besides sociable and genial dispositions, moderately cultivated minds, or at any rate serious interests, people of some character and independence of outlook, who will converse freely and interestingly, and work and play together the more congenially by reason of the basis of their association being wider than nudism alone.* [11]

The club stayed open all year, as opposed to some which closed in the winter. It had something of a reputation for exclusivity, as a report in 1937 concludes:

*That spirit of communal activity and friendliness is the most delightful feature of Fouracres; natural as it was in the early days of the club as a private group of friends, its persistence into our larger growth is mainly due to the fact that the club is not run for profit; membership is limited and prospective members are welcomed, not for their subscriptions, but for their ability to fit into the Fouracres atmosphere. Yet in spite of, or perhaps because of, our reputation for "exclusiveness", applications continue to arrive, and we are glad to make room for newcomers.* [12]

The Club's circular, sent to enquirers, used to state that "an atmosphere of intimacy has been maintained ... by keeping membership limited and selective" and a Report in 1939 defined the character of the Club as being "an intimate atmosphere among a company of interesting people". There were suggestions that the selection basis for members was largely class-based, a criticism which was vigorously denied by the Committee.

Membership of naturist clubs tended to be rather secretive. People frequently did not want it to be generally known that they were naturists. So, such things as membership lists, if they ever existed, were kept under lock and key and it is doubtful whether they have survived. Some, however, did not object to being known as naturists, and we can put together some sort of preliminary list of those whom Gardner may well have met and got to know whilst sitting and philosophising at Fouracres.

Along with Harold Sorensen and Harold Booth, Reginald (Rex) Wellbye (1873-1963) was a leading light in the Moonella Group, where he was known as 'Zex', and later in Fouracres. He certainly seems to have embodied the distinctive 'Fouracres spirit' in combining an intellectual approach with the outdoor life.

He was a pioneer member of the Sociological Society, along with Sybella Branford and Geoffrey Davies, at a time when sociology was in its infancy. He also wrote a series of guides for those touring by motor or cycle, from 1912 onwards, including *Wellbye's Roadfaring Guides*, which I remember from my youth. An indication of his character and approach is given in the text on the cover of one of his guides:

*Reginald Wellbye, the inventor of these guides, has spent his lifetime in compiling the essential information required by the traveller, more particularly the cycling and walking traveller, though he caters also for the motorist who is not afraid to leave the main road. He is quite prepared to label a famous sight as dull, but, more exciting, he introduces the tourist to many lovely and unknown roads, by-ways, plains, valleys, hills and historical monuments. He has personally covered every inch of the ground.* [13]

Cottie Arthur Burland (born 1905) is a name which crops up frequently in connection with Gardner, and they knew each other well. Lois Bourne confirms that he was "... a very old friend of Gerald's, a prodigious author of magic and mysticism and, until his retirement, a popular member of staff at the British Museum." [14] Gardner also refers to Burland in a letter to Cecil Williamson written in December 1953.

Like Gardner's friend, James Laver, Burland was a curator at the British Museum. He was in the Department of Ethnography until his retirement in the early 1960s.

When the Abbey Art Centre (see Chapter 6) opened in 1947, Burland was appointed as Honorary Curator, i.e. not a paid job. He contributed a section in the introductory leaflet to the museum in 1963, so his association with it seems to have been a long one.

He wrote over 40 books, on anthropological and cultural themes, particularly on pre-Columbian America, including ancient Mexico, the Aztecs and Incas. He also wrote on Ancient Greece, Egypt and China. He was an acknowledged expert on Primitive Art. His books also reflect an interest in what we might call pagan themes, with titles including *Echoes of Magic: a study of seasonal festivals throughout the ages; Beyond Science: a journey into the Supernatural; Myths of Life and Death; The Arts of the Alchemists; The Magical Arts: a short history* and *Secrets of the Occult*.

He was a member of the Fellowship of Isis and helped Adam McLean to establish *The Hermetic Journal*, contributing articles to it. He was also a naturist, writing an article in 1963 which looks as if it was destined for a naturist magazine, perhaps *Health and Efficiency*. It was entitled "Time will Tell" and it is about the history of naturism, with particular emphasis on Fouracres and Five Acres. The way he wrote about them suggests strongly to me that he had been a member of both, as my quotation on page 105-106 from the article indicates.

## Harry 'Dion' Byngham

There is one individual whom it is highly likely that Gardner met at Fouracres some time during the crucial years between 1936 and 1940 and who had a substantial influence on him.

Harry Byngham, a journalist from Catford in S.E. London was a member of the London Healthy Life Society and the Eutrophia Society. He started writing articles advocating naturism as early as July 1921 when his article 'A Tirade' (against clothes) appeared in Edgar Saxon's magazine *The Healthy Life*. This was followed in 1922 with 'Dithyrambos', on Greek mysticism and phallic worship.

Vitalism became a key life principle for Byngham. It had its roots in the philosophies of Plato and Aristotle, acknowledging that all living things possess a vital force which is non-physical and which cannot be studied by orthodox scientific method.

Henri Bergson (1859-1941), the French philosopher, was one of its chief exponents. His book, *Creative Evolution* (1907) postulated that the vital force was pure energy and lay behind all organic evolution and creative action.

Taking his key from Bergson's principle of the *'élan vital'*,

Byngham adopted the pseudonym of 'Elan Vitalgart', which he seems to have first used in a letter to *Health and Efficiency* in July 1922.

Other influences on Byngham were Ruskin's romanticism and anti-modernism; Richard Jefferies' mystical nature-worshipping; and the 'simple life' and pagan beliefs of Walt Whitman and Edward Carpenter, who knew about the Fellowship of the Naked Trust through correspondence with Charles Edward Gordon Crawford. Perhaps the greatest influence, however, was Nietzche, the German philosopher, who had also criticised modern civilisation and contrasted it with a life-affirming philosophy which he called 'Dionysianism', after the Greek god Dionysos, son of Zeus, who, with his followers, lived a life of savage wildness in the mountains of Macedonia. This was underlined by the work of Jane Harrison, who postulated that Dionysos was the Greek personification of Bergson's *'élan vital'*.

Byngham was inspired by the 'Dionysian Spirit' which he saw as being uninhibited and full of joy, energy and passion, attuning to the animal side of our nature. He wanted a new society in opposition to repressive forces such as Christianity. He also started to call himself 'Dion' Byngham in honour of the Dionysian ideal.

By 1923, Byngham, who was Secretary of the London Healthy Life Society, was organising a "Spring Dionysian Festival". He probably came in contact with the fledgling naturist movement through *The Healthy Life* magazine. His letter to *Health and Efficiency* in July 1922 was entitled 'Nude Life Culture'. It called for the formation of naturist groups. As a result, he and Booth formed what was the first British naturist organisation - The English Gymnosophist Society, which 'went public' in August 1923. It was from the members of this society that the 'Moonella Group', which I refer to above, emerged in Spring 1924.

It is likely that Byngham had been a member of Fouracres and, before that, of the Moonella Group. I cannot be certain of this because members' real names were never used. However, one of the male members used the name 'Gart', of whom Cinder says:

*The sometimes-present-sometimes-absent Gart has not been identified, but I believe him to have been either H. Dion Byngham or Wallace Arter of "Gorewell", Chilham, near Canterbury* [15]

That Gart was Byngham is highly likely, particularly as he was one of the founder members of the English Gymnosophist Society, and it would be most surprising, knowing his character and his great friendship with Booth, if he had not become involved with the Moonella Group when it was being proposed. Also, his nature seemed to be such that he was highly likely to be "Sometimes-present-sometimes-absent". The greeting 'Blue Sky' was common in both the Moonella Group and the Order of Woodcraft Chivalry, of which Byngham was an active member, the most likely explanation being that he transplanted it from one to the other. One might also see his Dionysian influence behind the leaning towards Greek rather than Eastern inspiration.

## The Order of Woodcraft Chivalry

In 1922, Byngham also joined another organisation which he felt was sympathetic to his Dionysian leanings - the Order of Woodcraft Chivalry, which had been founded in 1916 by Ernest Westlake and his son Aubrey. They were becoming disillusioned with the Boy Scout movement, with which they had been involved, for several reasons, including the militaristic side of Scouting. They had been inspired by the writings of Ernest Thompson Seton (1860-1946), a Canadian naturalist who taught a form of 'woodcraft' based on native American practices.

15. Harry 'Dion' Byngham at an Order of Woodcraft Chivalry ritual

There was certainly a mystical and overtly pagan side to Seton's Woodcraft. Adults were admitted into what were called Red Lodges, which had three degrees of initiation [16]. Within a ritually cast circle, which had four lamps to mark the quarters, they celebrated a Red God, which has been described as "the spirit wind chasing across the plains ... the thunder of buffalo, the fire of the Council Fire, the power that inspired and made possible all else in the world". [17]

Paganism had existed within the Order of Woodcraft Chivalry long before Byngham became involved, but it was usually seen as complementing Christianity rather than replacing it. As Ernest Westlake pointed out: "One must be a good pagan before one can be a good Christian". But Byngham wanted to go forward to what he called the post-Christian age.

With Seton as an inspiration, it is perhaps not surprising that naturism, or 'Gymnosophy' as it was still being called, found fertile ground within the Order, not just because of its 'back to nature' stance but also because it seemed to fit in with the controversial philosophy of recapitulation - the need to relive human evolution in the present life.

Another strand that found fertile soil was Byngham's Dionysianism. His journalistic skills very quickly propelled him into the position of editor of the Order's new journal, *Pine Cone*, the first issue of which came out in July 1923. Inevitably, he used it as a vehicle to put forward his Dionysianism and to shift the inspirational emphasis of the Order from the Native American to the Greek:

*... Life, this young virile Becoming force, was imaged by those inimitable godmakers the early Greeks as Dionysos, a wild-souled and supple-bodied youth who carried a wand or thyrsos as the symbol of his will, love and power ... the central experience aimed at and attained in the Dionysiac ... religion and ritual was ecstasy.* [18]

The second issue of *Pine Cone* had a picture of a nude Dionysos on its cover and on the inside cover of the fourth issue there was a photograph of two figures - a nude Byngham and his partially clothed girlfriend, Mary Parkins, dancing the 'Dawn Dance of Spring'. That issue also contained a piece of drama written by Byngham's friend, the poet and mystic, Victor Neuburg, who shared Byngham's enthusiasm for Dionysianism as well as for the occult and magic. It is possible that Neuburg introduced Byngham to the occultist, Aleister Crowley.

Within the Order, Byngham found some support for his naturist and Dionysian principles. He was certainly confident enough at the 1924 Folkmoot to advocate mixed nude bathing at Sandy Balls and, in 1926, suggested that there was a place for nakedness in ritual:

*Perhaps the nearer we approach to the god-life or life-god of the universe, the more we shall strip both spiritually and physically. In complete union with that god-life, we shall, perhaps, in the ultimate reaches of creative evolution, strip off the garment of the flesh and become naked spirit. Therefore, the religious life of the Order might ... tend to become more naked in its expression, not, however, as it becomes more infantile, but as it becomes more 'grown up' or fully grown.* [19]

By 1928 he was expressing himself in ways which the more conservative members of the Order could not accept:

*Let us become ... a leaping and dancing movement of Modern Bacchae through the land ... Symbolically, the Order ... should be proud to regard itself as the erect Penis of the social organism (nation or civilisation) of which it is a part. The phallic organ and function (Thyrsos or Dionysos) essentially symbolizes a Bacchic Movement committed to creation of the Future.* [20]

*Byngham also advocated Dionysian chants and pagan drama and ritual within the Order. To further this he drew up a detailed ritual entitled 'Invocation of Dionysos'.* [21]

There was, inevitably, a backlash amongst the more conservative and Christian members of the Order, who saw this as unbridled paganism (which, of course, it was!). As Edgell says: "Here was a man who not only talked about a pagan code, but actually attempted to live it".

An example occurred towards the end of 1925. Byngham and his girl friend, Molly Crick, danced naked in a field on the South Downs "in honour of the sun god". Edgell reminds us that "at that time it was still possible to be placed in a mental hospital for going naked in a public place".[22] It is unclear whether there were any witnesses. Edgell[23] says "he took care it was done when no one was about", yet he also says that "representatives from the press, invited especially for the occasion, looked on". At any event, these activities were reported in two daily papers and, as a result, Byngham was suspended from his post of Grand Herald with the Order. Eventually, in 1924, Byngham was replaced as editor of Pine Cone with an editorial board.

There are some remarkable similarities between the format for meetings of the Order of Woodcraft Chivalry, apparently based on what was known of Native American spiritual practices, and those later to become common in Wiccan circles, as well as occurring in the same sequence, as Aidan Kelly[24] points out:

- consecrating a circle;
- invoking the spirits of the four directions;
- invoking the Great Spirit;
- dancing around the circle, with drumming;
- sharing a small feast;
- thanking and dismissing the spirits;
- opening up the circle

Steve Wilson[25] states this more dramatically. He claims to have proved: ... *that there was, in the New Forest, a group working the 4 quarters, stark naked, and invoking a horned god and moon goddess using Crowley's Hymn to Pan by 1923* ...

This was only ever a minority within the Order, and a controversial one at that. Byngham undoubtedly gained something during his time with the Order of Woodcraft Chivalry and one can well imagine him introducing similar rituals to other groups he was associated with, such as the Moonella Group and Fouracres, and discussing these at great length with Gardner and others. But in 1931 he left the Order and moved to a community in Sussex, known as The Sanctuary.

## The Sanctuary

The Sanctuary was a self-sufficient idealistic community founded by Vera Pragnell in 1922 on 50 acres of land at Heath Common, between Washington and Storrington in Sussex, just a mile or two from the scarp slope of the South Downs.[26]

Vera was a Christian, but of a rather unorthodox kind, being in addition a socialist and mystic, not easily adhering to conventional morality. She was inspired by such characters as Rev. W.E. Orchard and the utopian writer Edward Carpenter. She used her inheritance from her father, textiles magnate Sir George Pragnell, to buy land and create what has been described as a free association of individuals, each being given a half-acre plot to cultivate and build their own home (usually a hut or caravan).

*16. The Sanctuary in about 1930*

There were no rules and a variety of different individuals, including communists and anarchists, were welcomed. No questions were asked of potential settlers - they certainly didn't have to prove they were 'deserving'. It has been described as 'Arcadian Anarchy'. The high point of the community was probably the summer of 1927, by which time there was a theatre/chapel in a converted barn, general stores, a school in an old bus, and much communal activity including folk-dancing.

Marriage was not a big issue for Vera. But it was for the popular press of the day, who seized on the freedom of the community, with headlines about "free love" and "settlers frolicking naked". These attacks seemed to affect Vera adversely, and the community gradually faded away, becoming eventually just another expensive housing estate.

*17. One of the Sanctuary's wooden bungalows*

Whether Byngham was the origin of the "settlers frolicking naked" story, I have so far been unable to discover, but he was welcomed into the community. He was certainly still advocating pagan ideas as late as 1934, when he was living at The Sanctuary. He appeared nude in a photograph which illustrated the September issue of *The Healthy Life*, performing the "Nature Dance Prayer to Pan". He also wrote for that journal on sun worship, magic and Aleister Crowley. And he was still living there in 1935 when, in his application to join the Folk Lore Society, he gave his address as Lark's Nest, Hampers Lane, Storrington.

Fellow naturist, Harold Clare Booth also owned property in Storrington and Washington, including Rosebay, Hampers Lane and Glenwood and Wee Croft, George Lane, all of which were within the area of The Sanctuary. The implication of this is that, whilst The Sanctuary was neither pagan nor naturist in its philosophy it was tolerant of people who were, and it would appear that both Byngham and Booth lived there at least part of the time, whilst still keeping their contacts at Fouracres.

There is also a persistent rumour of a witch coven in existence in the area since at least the 1940s, which was supposed to meet in the vicinity of Chanctonbury Ring, a prominent beech clump on the top of the Downs. Gareth Medway has informed me that "... Steve Wilson was told that ... Byngham ... was one of the founders of the Chanctonbury Ring coven in about 1940". [27]

## Victor Neuburg

One significant individual whose name has been linked to such a coven and who was a close friend of Byngham was Victor Neuburg (1883-1940), the poet, mystic and anarchist. I do not know when they first met, but Neuburg had published his volume of Dionysian poetry, *The Triumph of Pan* [28], as far back as 1910, so it is likely that Byngham would have gone out of his way to make contact with a fellow Dionysian, probably in the early 1920s. Indeed, it may have been Neuburg that first inspired Byngham to start thinking of himself as a Dionysian.

Neuburg's first literary contributions were to *The Freethinker* between 1903 and about 1908. One article, in 1907, is entitled "Paganism and the Sense of Song". At Cambridge University, he came under the influence of Aleister Crowley for about ten years, working rites with him and helping him to bring out *The Equinox* journal. The relationship turned sour and it is said that Crowley put a curse on Neuburg. Meanwhile, Neuburg brought out volumes of poetry, including *A Green Garland* in 1908 [29] and *The Triumph of Pan*, mentioned above.

Free of the influence of Crowley, Neuburg moved to Steyning in Sussex in 1919 and, with the help of his friend, Hayter Preston, founded the Vine Press. In 1921, the Press brought out another volume of his poems, *Songs of the Groves* [30], which contains much explicit pagan imagery. *Larkspur*, published in 1922, was similar. Following a printing request, Neuburg got to know Vera Pragnell well and spent much time at The Sanctuary, only five miles from Steyning. In 1928, the Vine Press published her *The Story of The Sanctuary* [31]. In the 1930s, Neuburg was editor of Poets' Corner in the *Sunday Referee* and later of *Comment* magazine. Associated with this were the Zoists, a circle of poets, one of whom was Dylan Thomas, whose poetry Neuburg helped to get published for the first time.

Neuburg died in London on 31 May 1940 of tubercular pneumonia. The date made me wonder whether he had been one of those who had performed the ritual with Gardner in the New Forest to stop the threatened invasion: several are supposed to have died shortly afterwards, and pneumonia is specifically mentioned. However, it seems unlikely that

Neuburg would have been well enough to make the trip to Hampshire, particularly as he was said to have been very weak and could not even shave. Moreover, his wife, Runia, would almost certainly not have allowed it. He may however have taken part psychically in some way, which might have hastened his death.

There are some who considered that Neuburg belonged to the kingdom of faery. Vera Pragnell's husband, Dennis Earle, put it this way: "He was a spirit riding on a cloud. He wasn't human. He was a pixie".

The friendship between Byngham and Neuburg was probably fairly close. Neuburg frequently contributed to *Pine Cone*, one verse from his poem, 'Night Song of Bacchus' appearing on the cover of each issue. And as Edgell says: "Both Neuburg and Byngham shared an interest in poetry as well as in the occult and magic."[32]

## Gardner and Byngham

One can see immediately the attraction that Byngham's Dionysian ideals would have for Gardner and, knowing the philosophy underlying Fouracres, there would probably have been ample opportunity for the two to have met and had long discussions in the 1936-40 period. Byngham's influence on Gardner would probably be because of the way he brought the religious pagan element into naturism. If I am right and they had deep philosophical discussions sitting on the lawn outside the pavilion at Fouracres, then I suspect that Gardner would have been much taken with Byngham's Dionysianism, with the energy associated with vitalism and the underlying principles of the Order of Woodcraft Chivalry, which they would undoubtedly have talked about.

There are at least five strands of Byngham's Dionysianism which would have enthused Gardner.

Firstly, Gardner would have been knowledgeable enough about classical mythology to know that the horned god and the moon goddess were a part of it. He had always been one for whom the feminine aspect of divinity was important and who would thus be attracted by any representation of this.

Also, Byngham's recognition of the '*élan vital*', or life force, would have been attractive to Gardner who, again, would have been knowledgeable enough to have seen the connection with the tantric practices of the East and the use of sexual energies, together with his linking of Greek mysticism with phallic worship. The witches that Gardner met were certainly well aware of the use of this power.

The nude seasonal rituals which Byngham seems to have practised, including the Nature Prayer Dance of Pan, would have attracted Gardner because of the combination of nudity with religious expression, something which he was able to find classical references for.

Sun worship in a literal rather than symbolic sense would have been something Gardner could relate to, in view of his experiences out East, and his probable yearning for the sun that his return to England would have been likely to have engendered.

Gardner was well aware of magical practices from his contacts with the native peoples of Borneo and Malaya. Byngham's interest, particularly following his meeting with, or discovering the works of, Aleister Crowley, would, I am sure, have enabled the two to talk at length on the subject.

Byngham had probably met Crowley, and was certainly familiar with his writing, as early as 1927, for he writes in a letter to Crowley dated 14 June 1947: "I was still, I found, word-perfect with Dionysus, memorised 20 years ago."[33] This was a reference to a gift of a book of Crowley's poetry.

Byngham was undoubtedly the chief advocate of a combined naturism and paganism in the 1920s and 30s and thus his contact with Gardner, possibly as early as 1936, could be significant in the development of Wiccan practice following Gardner's initiation.

I have found no convincing evidence that Gardner was ever directly involved with the Order of Woodcraft Chivalry, as has sometimes been stated, though Byngham would undoubtedly have talked to him about its ideas and activities.

It is also interesting to note that Byngham contributed an article to *The Occult Observer* in 1950 [34], which seems to indicate that he was in touch with at least some of the people informally associated with that publication and with the Atlantis Bookshop, including Ross Nichols and Cottie Burland. And Doreen Valiente seems to have been in contact with Byngham in the early 1970s - he was one of about 30 people on her Christmas Card list for 1971!

## Spielplatz

According to Rex Wellbye, Fouracres ceased operations in 1940, at which time he purchased the land from 'The Major'. Iseult Weston, however, says that it kept open throughout the war. Perhaps people did continue to go and use the facilities but on a less formal basis.

I have referred in Chapter 1 to Gardner's move to Highcliffe, in Hampshire, in 1938, and that this may have been because, through his contacts at the Lotus League and Fouracres, he knew members of the New Forest Club, possibly friends of Byngham or even Byngham himself. However, as was his wont, Gardner kept on his house in London for at least another year. And he was certainly a regular visitor to a naturist club at Bricket Wood that did stay open throughout the war - Spielplatz.

Whether it be ice-cream sellers on a beach or second-hand bookshops in the small Welsh border town of Hay-on-Wye, it seems to be a law of economic geography that similar enterprises tend to cluster together to their mutual benefit. It has certainly been so with naturist clubs. Following the establishment of 'The Camp' in Bricket Wood in 1927, there are now four clubs within a two-mile radius. In fact, the area became known humorously as "The Hertfordshire Nuderies".

One of the earliest, Spielplatz, had been founded in 1930 by Charles Macaskie (1885-1967) and his wife, Dorothy (1899-1968). They had responded to an advertisement placed in the "Personal Ads" column of a London newspaper, which read: "Professional gentlemen practising Gymnosophy (nude sunbathing) and Exercise Regime would welcome any likeminded folk to join them for a few quiet, relaxing hours at the weekend." They were subsequently invited up to The Camp, where they met Rex Wellbye and four or five other naturists: they became regular visitors.

Later that same year, they decided, on something of an impulse, to bid for 12 acres of woodland, known as Cowley's Wood, which was being auctioned, in order to establish their own naturist community. Appropriately in some ways, it was originally part of a monastery garden, and some have called it a 'Green Monastery'. Their bid was successful and they decided to call the place Spielplatz. It differed from other clubs in that they ran it themselves rather than having a members' committee. Also it was unusual in that some members lived there all the year.

Iseult Weston, who has written a history of Spielplatz [35], is Dorothy and Charles' daughter, and she still lives there. She remembers Gerald Gardner being a regular visitor to Spielplatz during the war, though he didn't have a hut: he seems to have been a "day visitor". She describes him as an "old windbag" and "always ready to expound upon his views on the subject in question"[36]. Philip Carr-Gomm writes:

*On talking to Iseult to try to pinpoint the exact years she remembers Gardner visiting Spielplatz, she is sure he visited throughout the war years, and can remember distinctly him being present on a memorable day in 1943 when the clubhouse caught fire ... She remembers Gardner standing in front of the blaze with his friend (and fellow Druid who later joined OBOD) Mary Dowding.*[37]

According to Iseult Weston, Mary Dowding was in her late twenties at the time. She had a caravan at Spielplatz, later moving to Five Acres. She remembers her visiting Spielplatz a few years ago, when she seemed to be in her 80s. Neither Philip Carr-Gomm nor I have yet been able to find anything very much about Mary Dowding, but the fact that she was a Druid suggests that Gardner may have become involved with Druidry at least as early as 1943.

We don't know for certain when Gardner started visiting Spielplatz, but as Wellbye claimed that Fouracres closed down in 1940, I would guess that it would probably be some time after that, which ties in with Iseult's estimate. The fact that Gardner was a regular visitor to Spielplatz throughout the war years rather confirms my impression that he was never happy staying in one place. Even during the height of the war, when citizens were being pointedly asked in propaganda posters "Is your journey really necessary?", Gardner seemed to have been travelling between Highcliffe and London on a fairly regular basis, or he may have had a flat somewhere in the London area (see Chapter 11).

## Ross Nichols

One of the people that Gardner met at Spielplatz was Ross Nichols (1902-1975). He is known today as the founder of the Order of Bards, Ovates and Druids (OBOD), and it now seems likely that it was Gardner who introduced him to Druidry.[38]

Born in Norfolk, Nichols' attitude to life was in part formed by his experience of family and boarding school and living through the First World War. This encouraged an unorthodox approach, always challenging the status quo, expressed from a young age through poetry.

He read History at St. John's College, Cambridge, from 1921 to 1924. As a socialist and pacifist, he was rather out of step with the conservative atmosphere of the place, but his inspirations included the philosopher, Bertrand Russell, and the poet, T.S. Eliot.

A major influence on Nichols was John Hargrave (1894-1982). He had been involved with the Scout movement but, like the Westlakes, found it too militaristic and with too close connections with the Church. As with them, he was inspired by the example of Ernest Thompson Seton. In 1913, Hargrave had published a manual entitled *Lonecraft*, which led on to the formation, in 1920, of the Kibbo Kift Kindred, which combined elements from the Scout movement with Seton's Woodcraft, but also had a spiritual dimension with an acceptance of karma and what Philip Carr-Gomm describes as "the universal religion of the great spirit".

Hargrave was also one of the instigators of the Social Credit Movement, which advocated the adoption of the ideas of C.H. Douglas for reform of the monetary system.

While at Cambridge, Nichols developed an interest in mysticism and mythology. He was much influenced by Sir James Frazer, who had been at Cambridge and whose *The Golden Bough* had appeared in 12 volumes between 1890 and 1917. Nichols went into teaching for a living, but continued to write poetry, much of which was published.

*18. Ross Nichols outside his hut at Spielplatz*

We do not know where Nichols derived his impulse to naturism, but certainly by the mid 1930s he had joined Spielplatz and had his own wooden chalet, about 10ft x 8ft in size, which was located on a particularly secluded plot (Plot 53) in the woods, with its own track leading to it [see Illustration 18]. According to Iseult Weston, he spent weekends and several weeks each summer at Spielplatz, including the war years.

Philip Carr-Gomm notes Iseult Weston as saying that she held Nichols' chalet in awe. She told him:

*It was a simple wooden hut, like a garden shed, which I remember him assembling himself. But on the floor he had painted what looked like a magic circle, which most of the time was covered with a rag rug. On the walls and door he had drawn symbols with different coloured chalk.*[39]

Iseult described the floor symbol to me more specifically as a pentagram, the full width of the floor. And the drawings on the walls and door turned out to be something more permanent than chalk, for she told me that years later, she and her husband moved into a house and she recognised Nichols' hut in use as a shed and the symbols were still there.

By 1941, Ross was praising naturism in his *'Dionysiac Song'*[40]. Its title certainly suggests that he could have known Byngham, as both were frequenting naturist clubs in Bricket Wood in the 1930s. Certainly in 1950, when Nichols was Assistant Editor of *The Occult Observer* it published an article by Byngham.

It is even more likely that Ross Nichols and Gerald Gardner would have known each other at Spielplatz, probably spending many hours in deep philosophical discussion on topics such as mythology, folklore, witchcraft and Druidry. Although they were of different political persuasions, the fertility of ideas during these sessions would have been of benefit to both men and would later have fruitful outcomes in several different directions.

Philip Carr-Gomm has described Spielplatz as "an idyllic environment where alternative thinkers could meet in a natural setting". He concludes:

*It is ... likely that the two seminal forces in the revival of Western Paganism in the twentieth century met, swam and talked together skyclad in the woods and on the lawns of a Hertfordshire naturist resort, whilst not far away the German and allied forces battled against each other grimly for year after year.* [41]

Ross Nichols remained a regular visitor to Spielplatz until the end of the war, when he bought a small plot of woodland near Hambleden in South Buckinghamshire, near the Oxfordshire border, where he erected a small wooden hut. The woodland was private enough for him to continue practising naturism as well as painting and writing. He also had a hut at Five Acres for many years, following Gardner's involvement with the club.

It seems that he retained his links with the Wiccan community because, probably arranged via the writer Justine Glass (Enid Corrall) his hut was to be the scene of the handfasting ceremony presided over by Robert Cochrane (Roy Bowers) recounted in Doreen Valiente's book *The Rebirth of Witchcraft* [42].

## Dion Fortune

Violet M. Firth (1890-1946), better known under her pen-name of Dion Fortune, was one of the most influential occult writers of the 20th Century, particularly through her series of novels which are considered by many to be some of the finest ever published.

There is an intriguing possibility that she may have visited naturist clubs in Bricket Wood or even have had a chalet there. Gareth Knight (Basil Wilby) refers to some land which had been acquired by Dion Fortune's Society of the Inner Light in 1948 which "was situated at ... Brickett's [sic] Wood, that had been part of a naturist colony and which was now used only as an occasional country retreat for residents of the London headquarters." [43]

Dion Fortune's biographer, Alan Richardson, has confirmed to Philip Carr-Gomm that the Fraternity of the Inner Light owned a small chalet (probably on the Fouracres/Five Acres site) which they called 'Avalon'. He wrote: "Sometimes, when the Inner Lighters talked guardedly about visiting Avalon for the weekend, they were actually talking about the nudist camp. They sometimes qualified it by saying 'Avalon - the wooded place'". [44]

Dion Fortune died in 1946 and, whilst Knight refers to the land not having been acquired until 1948, Richardson told Carr-Gomm that "... during DF's lifetime they bought the chalet at The Camp. Whether DF went there earlier or not - or even if she went at all but merely encouraged, I really couldn't say". [45] 'The Camp' was, as we have seen, the original name for what became Fouracres/Five Acres.

So, Dion Fortune may or may not have visited Fouracres on a regular or occasional basis: we cannot at this stage be sure. However, we can speculate that she would have used her time at Fouracres as a form of retreat, probably only using a 'gymnic' name, so that Gardner, for example, may not have known who she was, even though they may have had long discussions together.

Whilst the evidence seems to point to Fouracres/Five Acres as the location of 'Avalon', there was a chalet at Spielplatz named 'Avalon' which is currently occupied by Iseult Weston.

**131**

I now think that this is purely a coincidence and that 'Avalon' may have been a popular name amongst naturists of the time.

So did Gerald Gardner meet Dion Fortune? Whether they met physically or not, there are some remarkable parallels between Dion Fortune's writing and the emerging modern witchcraft, as Chas Clifton and Ronald Hutton have pointed out. Clifton summarises her approach as being "an earth-based Western tradition of esoteric, magical religion, which exalted the feminine principle", and perhaps one of the most striking features of her novels is the prominence which she gives to the feminine aspect of divinity.

Another powerful parallel is in the technique which, in Gardnerian witchcraft, is called "Drawing Down the Moon" where the Goddess is invoked by a priest into the body of the priestess. Clifton reminds us that this is precisely what happens in *The Sea Priestess* (1938):

*... In this sacrament the woman must take her ancient place as priestess of the rite, calling down lightning from heaven; the initiator, not the initiated ... She had to become the priestess of the Goddess, and I [Wilfred Maxwell], the kneeling worshipper, had to receive the sacrament at her hands ... When the body of a woman is made an altar for the worship of the Goddess who is all beauty and magnetic life ... then the Goddess enters the temple ...* [46]

Clifton comments:

*This is not just Fortune's description of the magical side of marriage, but a virtual schematic of the Drawing Down the Moon ceremony and its concluding Great Rite ...* [47]

If Dion Fortune did visit naturist clubs, then the nudity that features in her novels, particularly the later ones such as *Moon Magic* (mainly written 1940) becomes less surprising. As Ronald Hutton states:

Dion Fortune had directed that magicians should be nude under their robes, 'as nothing mundane is worn in magic', and in her writings portrayed powerfully how this custom could increase greatly the creative sexual tension between her female and male protagonists.[48]

Clifton concludes by observing: ... *it is difficult not to see Dion Fortune as a previously unadmitted but significant influence on the development of Gardnerian Witchcraft.* This is particularly so if, as now seems at least possible, she and Gardner actually met on more than one occasion.

It is tempting to speculate as to whether Dion Fortune, Gerald Gardner and Ross Nichols ever sat around discussing the Goddess, the role of Pan and the Dionysian energy in a new pagan approach to religion and the land. Or even performed skyclad rituals based on those principles. They would certainly have had much in common and the three-way interchange of ideas could have been most fruitful in the philosophical development of each of them, though Philip Carr-Gomm says that Ross Nichols never mentioned having met her. Though if she only used her 'gymnic' name perhaps he met her without realising!

And then there is the coincidental matter of the two Dions in our story. It is well known that Violet Firth took on the name 'Dion Fortune' as an adaptation of the Firth family motto - '*Deo non Fortuna*'. Yet it is a pleasing coincidence that two of the undoubted influences on Gardner both took on the name 'Dion' and one wonders whether there was any contact between the two. Was Violet aware of Byngham and his Dionysian ideas, perhaps from fellow naturists? Both Violet and Byngham may have frequented naturist clubs in the Bricket Wood area at roughly the same time - the late 1930s. Both were involved with magical practice, and the energies which are made manifest in, for example, Fortune's *The Goat-Foot God* (1936)[48] are ones which Byngham would have been totally in tune with.

There is clearly more to be unravelled, but already it can be seen that the net that was being woven out of the strands of naturism, woodcraft, Dionysianism and occultism was not just lively and strong, but contained links to the Gardnerian Craft that need further investigation.

Gardner's association with naturism in Bricket Wood continued after the war, particularly at Five Acres, but first we must look at another acquaintance who had a big influence on him - J.S.M. Ward.

# Chapter 6

# The Abbey Folk Park And The Ancient British Church

## J.S.M. Ward

John Sebastian Marlow Ward [1885-1949] was one of those strange characters whose lives intertwined with Gardner's for a while and who influenced him greatly. He was born in British Honduras on 22nd December 1885, the son of an Anglican clergyman, Herbert Marlow Ward.[1] The family returned to England in 1888 and Ward was educated at Collet Court, Merchant Taylors and Charterhouse. He was a graduate in History from Trinity Hall College, Cambridge. He had travelled extensively in the Far East, became the head of a Church of England school in Burma, and was subsequently Principal Officer of Customs in Lower Burma. During that time, Ward had acquired considerable knowledge of Chinese secret societies and was the co-author of a book which was a standard reference work for many years[2]. In fact, Ward had over 30 books published on such subjects as mediaeval history and Oriental theology. He returned to England from the Far East in 1918 and was appointed Director of Intelligence for the Federation of British Industries. He was also a Freemason, and according to Tillett[3], "one of the best-known authorities on Freemasonry in England", having written several books on the subject, including *Freemasonry and the Ancient Gods*[4] and *Who was Hiram Abiff?*[5].

It is tempting to speculate as to whether Gardner met Ward in the Far East. But there is no evidence for this: Ward had returned to England five years before Gardner became a Customs Officer, and Gardner never claimed it.

His brother, Reginald Lucien Ward, was killed in the First World War, and this seems to have started an interest in Spiritualism and led to his book *Gone West: three narratives of after-death experiences communicated through the mediumship of J.S.M. Ward* published in 1917 [6], followed by *A Subaltern in Spirit Land*, which had a preface by Arthur Conan Doyle, in 1920. [7]

His first wife having died, Ward married a headmistress, Jessica Page, in April 1927. The following year something very interesting happened, as Bracelin describes:

*Eventually he and his wife began to have visions. In these mystical experiences, they were warned that the end of an age was approaching, and that the civilisation of the West was doomed. To prepare people for the Second coming of Christ, in accordance with their revelations, they gave lectures.* [8]

In early 1929, under the guidance of the 'Angelic Guardian' of this work, they founded the Confraternity of the Kingdom of the Wise, and a book was published that year entitled *The Kingdom of the Wise - Life's Problems* [9], which detailed their beliefs. Jessica Page became the Reverend Mother and the community changed its name to the Confraternity of Christ the King.

By 1930, they had bought property at 89 Park Road, New Barnet and had established an Abbey there. This was a rambling old Georgian manor house known as Hadley Hall, in five acres of its own grounds. Initially, it was a lay Order, under the auspices of the Anglican Bishop of St. Albans, and had been dedicated by him on 14th February 1931. To start with, a local clergyman came in on a regular basis to celebrate

Communion. The community was, however, somewhat unorthodox, with a number of men and women, including unmarried couples, who had taken religious vows. According to Bracelin:

*This sect required that all possessions be handed over to the Order, names were changed and the community did all their own work, even making their own shoes.*[10]

Gardner mentions a revealing aspect:

*In the Abbey Church at New Barnet, on the right side of the altar, is a large picture of Christ, and on the left is a large picture of the (feminine) Holy Ghost, shown as a woman in white, the White Goddess. The priests of this church told me some years ago that Christ was born of the Father, conceived by the Holy Ghost, and that only a woman could conceive. They had a number of proofs of this being a very ancient doctrine.*[11]

The ceremonies were colourful and seemed to lean towards the Greek tradition. This was obviously all too much for the new local vicar, who persuaded the Bishop to withdraw Church of England support and approval. Ward writes that, following its foundation in 1930:

*... for five years it had struggled to remain in communion with the Anglican Church. But towards the end of 1934 the Bishop of St. Albans broke the one slender link which connected the Abbey with the Anglican Church by refusing to renew the licence for a Chaplain, on the grounds that the Rev. Father Superior* [Ward himself] *had no authority to Minister the Word and yet had done so by Opening the Abbey Church to outsiders.*[12]

Ward was undaunted by this, and the fact that the Bishop's actions, which were seen by Ward as an "attack on the work of the Abbey", were based on the question of "authority" led

Ward to "study carefully the whole question of the validity of Anglican Orders and therefore the right of an Anglican Bishop to make such a claim". These investigations led Ward to the conclusion that:

> ... in the ecclesiastical sense the Anglican Church has no valid Orders, and therefore no Priests and no Bishops, and that the gentleman who calls himself a Bishop is only a layman given the name of a Bishop by Act of Parliament, and appointed by the State like any other State Official. [13]

During these investigations Ward had made contact with those who felt the same, as a result of which, he wrote: "At length the Abbey of Christ the King sought union with a branch of the Church which unquestionably had valid Orders, and ultimately, in October 1935, the Abbey joined the Orthodox Catholic Church." This had been established in 1929 under the leadership of John Churchill Sibley. Ward was re-baptised and confirmed by Sibley, admitted to the Minor Orders, ordained Deacon and Priest, Consecrated as a Bishop and had conferred on him the office of Chancellor of the Province, all within a few days! Following Sibley's death three years later, Ward was elected Archbishop of the Orthodox Catholic Church on 19th December 1938.

## The Old Catholic Movement

The Orthodox Catholic Church was just one of a variety of separate churches all of which were under the umbrella of what might be called the Old Catholic movement. They had names like The Gnostic Catholic Church, The Ancient Orthodox Catholic Church, The Catholicate of the West, The Independent Catholic Church, The Catholic Apostolic Church, The British Orthodox Catholic Church, The Old Catholic Orthodox Church, The Western Orthodox Catholic Church, The Holy Orthodox Catholic Church of Great Britain and Ireland, The Ancient British Church, The Liberal Catholic

Church and The Ancient Universal (Orthodox Catholic) Church. And these are just a few of them! Perm any combination of Orthodox, Catholic, Ancient, Apostolic, Holy, Independent, British and Western to make up your own name! In fact, some of these were alternative names for the same organisation, though there were still quite a lot of them.

It all started in the 18th Century when the Pope suspended the Bishop of Utrecht for supporting the views of Bishop Jansenius, which were contrary to the opinions of certain Roman theologians of the day. The rift resulted in the formation of the Old Roman Catholic Church of Holland, which believed that it embodied the true Catholic tradition as against the Roman church which had introduced innovations of doctrine and discipline. Such a movement was

19. *A consecration in the Catholic Apostolic Church. The figure in the centre of the front row is W. B. Crow*

strengthened by reactions to the dogma of Papal Infallibility, which was introduced following the first Vatican Council in 1870. The Old Catholic movement admitted only Jesus Christ as the infallible Head of the Church.

According to Morgan Davis [14], other characteristics of the Old Catholic movement were that services were held in the vernacular rather than in Latin, there was no fasting or confession, there were fewer compulsory feast days and the sacraments of Eucharist and Baptism were elevated above the others.

In time, various different churches grew up within the Old Catholic movement, each with their own distinctive lines of Apostolic Succession derived from a variety of different traditions dating back to the Patriarchs of Antioch, the Armenian Church and other historical lines, such as the Syrian-Malabar, Chaldean-Uniate and Syro-Chaldean. There seems to have been something of an obsession with Apostolic Succession among these men (no women are ever mentioned!), with the same names cropping up time and time again. There seem to be dozens of different lines of succession and they seem to have spent quite a substantial proportion of their time consecrating each other to the Sacred Episcopate of the dozens of churches that are also involved, often taking as their titles places of historic significance in Britain, such as Iona, Selsey and Caerleon. Compared to this, the discussions amongst Wiccans about coven lines and how any individual can trace their initiation back to Gerald Gardner seem relatively straightforward! I leave it to others to study this whole movement in the depth which it deserves and will limit my own enquiry to the extent to which Gardner was involved.

## The Ancient British Church

In the list of books formerly in Gardner's Library [15] is reference to a diploma dated 29th August 1946 ordaining

Gardner "to the Holy Office of Priest of the Ancient British Church". It is signed by Dorian, Bishop of Caerleon and witnessed by W. Ohly and M.S. Sauders.

Tillett, who had been investigating Ward, seems to confirm this when he writes:

*...amongst the signatures on one document from 1946 was that of one "Gerald Brosseau Gardner, Priest, Ancient British Church". Gardner was a regular visitor to the Abbey, and frequently appeared wearing a clerical collar...* [16]

What was all this about? Why was Gardner, who was supposed to have been initiated as a witch in 1939, becoming ordained as a priest? And what was the Ancient British Church?

To try to answer this, we must imagine Gardner's situation in the immediate post-War period. He had just moved back to London and, for the first time for several years, was not in day-to-day contact with Edith. He was the sort of person who always wanted to explore new things and in Chapter 8 we will see the various societies which he joined. He would undoubtedly have re-established his pre-war friendship with Ward and, very easily, been drawn into the various activities Ward was involved with, most obviously the museum and exhibits, but also his other interests such as freemasonry and folklore. Ward would undoubtedly have talked to Gardner about the Old Catholic movement and the various churches of which he was a member. As we have seen, in their desire for valid and unchallengeable Apostolic Succession, they became inextricably intertwined, with the same individuals being ordained in some cases into several different Old Catholic churches.

Probably initially because of its name, Gardner was attracted to the Ancient British Church. This was founded (or "erected") in 1874 at Marholm, in the Soke of Peterborough,

Northamptonshire, by the Right Reverend Jules Ferrette (Mar Julius, Bishop of Iona), in communion with the Apostolic Throne of Antioch. Successive Patriarchs of the Church were:

> Richard William Morgan (Mar Pelagius I) (1815-1889)
> Charles Isaac Stevens (Mar Theophilus I) (1835-1917)
> Leon Chechemian (Mar Leon) (1848-1920)
> Andrew Charles Albert McLagen (Mar Andries I)
> (1851-1928)

The last Patriarch was Herbert James Monzani Heard (Mar Jacobus II) (1866-1947). Also known as the Bishop of Selsey, he was Chancellor of the International Orthodox Catholic University, but it must be remembered that this was a period of grand-sounding titles, not just for churches, but for academic and other bodies as well, many of which may have had very little practical support.

By a Deed of Declaration dated 23rd March 1944, The Ancient British Church, The Independent Catholic Church, The British Orthodox Catholic Church and The Old Catholic Orthodox Church were all united into The Catholicate of the West. Now this is strange, since Gardner seems to have been ordained into the Ancient British Church in 1946, over two years after it ceased to exist!

I think what probably happened is that Dorian, Bishop of Caerleon, had an affection for the Ancient British Church and continued using the name. It certainly seemed particularly willing to accommodate those from a wide range of religious backgrounds within its fold. For example, he seems to have established the Fellowship of the Holy Grail, of which he was the Prior. It was stated to function "within the jurisdiction of the restored Ancient British Church" and not in any way subject to the authority of the Church of England, the Roman Catholic Church or any other Christian Communion.

One of the purposes of the Fellowship is described as the "unity around the Holy Chalice of all, irrespective of religious attachments, or differences of philosophic or doctrinal interpretation". This is emphasised by the requirements for Associate Membership:

*It matters not ... whether you be a Roman Catholic, Freemason, Anglo-Catholic, Protestant, Orthodox, Nonconformist, Trinitarian, Unitarian, Jew, Literalist, Rationalist, or whether you are a member of a non-christian religion; provided that you can conscientiously declare that you acknowledge THE ONE TRUE GOD, and are prepared to share the common Chalice of holy brotherhood you may, at least, become an Associate of the Fellowship of the Holy Grail.* [17]

Much is made, however, of ordination:

*The Royal Priesthood (Keeper of the Temple) is inherent in every soul, and is not necessarily the prerogative of a specially privileged professional class of persons. ... application may be made by Members (not by Associates) of the Fellowship of the Holy Grail ... for appropriate Ordination for the exercise of the religious offices or services in their respective private oratories or public chapels.*

It is further stated that, as well as Associates, the Fellowship is composed of:

*Members, being those who, by making the Caerleon Declaration, voluntarily enter into full communion with the restored Ancient British Church. Each member has the privilege of recognition, under Charter of the Bishop of Caerleon, of his, or her, individual (a) cell for study, (b) private oratory, (c) (in the case of those ordained) chapel for public devotions.*

Gardner must clearly have accepted this in order to be ordained. Indeed, I think that mention of a chapel for public devotions made Gardner think about using the Witch's Cottage that he had acquired from Ward (see Chapter 7) in that way. Whether any meetings or services of the Ancient British Church were actually held there is another matter.

There seems to be an inconsistency between Tillett's statement that Gardner was a regular visitor to the Abbey wearing a dog-collar with the fact that whereas the Abbey probably closed in late 1945, Gardner's ordination was not until summer 1946. Perhaps, in common with the ethos of the whole movement, Gardner was ordained into more than one such church. Certainly Tillett reports that when Gardner visited Ward in Cyprus in 1949:

*Ward* [sic - he obviously actually means Gardner] *was ordained to the Priesthood by Bishop Colin Mackenzie Chamberlain, whom Ward had consecrated; the precise reasons for his ordination were not made clear, but it took place at the direction of the Reverend Mother, much of whose authority derived from visions and revelations she claimed to receive from the Holy Spirit. Gardner was never actively involved in the work of the Orthodox Catholic Church or the Confraternity of the Kingdom of Christ, and made no mention of his Priestly status in his published works.*[18]

At what stage, and how, Gardner got to know Ward we do not know. With his interest in museums (see Chapter 14), particularly of the progressive sort represented by the Folk Park, and his presence in London following his retirement in 1936, Gardner could well have heard about the Folk Park and decided to pay it a visit. Then again, with his interest in Freemasonry he may also have read some of Ward's books, particularly *Freemasonry and the Ancient Gods* [19].

Gardner had certainly met Ward by early 1939, as he mentions him as having examined a collection of witchcraft relics in Gardner's possession in an article which appeared in Folk-Lore later that year [20].

Why was Gardner ordained? I think he probably looked upon it as rather a status symbol, perhaps compensating for his lack of academic qualifications. Indeed, expanding on Tillett's statement above, I have no evidence that Gardner took an active part in any of these churches.

## The Abbey Folk Park

Ward's most lasting legacy was undoubtedly the Abbey Folk Park. The idea of a folk park had long been discussed in museum circles, but following a decision by The Chapter of the Abbey of Christ the King to make this its educational work, progress was rapid. Eveline Marlowe has defined it as follows:

*A Folk Park is a kind of open air museum which sets out to show the evolution of the everyday life of the folk or people of a country. In the grounds are erected old buildings or replicas of old buildings, which are then furnished appropriately.* [21]

This is all very familiar to us and there is now a multitude of excellent examples to visit. But it was all very new in the early 1930s. There were examples in Scandinavia and America, but, when the Abbey Folk Park opened on 28th June 1934, it was reputed to be the first in the whole of the British Empire.

Ward was very much a pioneer in the rescue and subsequent conservation of historic buildings of all types. Whenever he heard about an old building which was about to be demolished, several members of the community would rush over, dismantle the building carefully, numbering all the

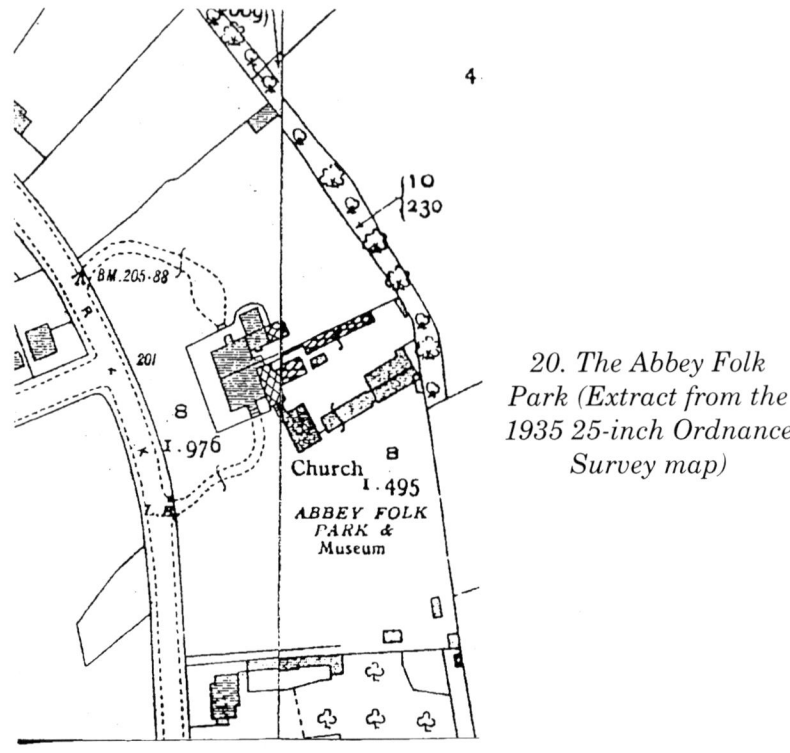

20. The Abbey Folk Park (Extract from the 1935 25-inch Ordnance Survey map)

pieces, and then re-erect it in the grounds of the Abbey. The same with furniture and other antiques, on which Ward was an expert. He attended auctions all over England, often obtaining pieces for a lot less than their true value.

When fully operational, the Folk Park consisted of a range of buildings and displays from prehistoric to Victorian times, all furnished to provide a realistic idea of what life was like in the period concerned. We are so familiar with this approach, adopted by virtually every present-day museum, that it is difficult to appreciate the impact which the Abbey Folk Park had in its day. It attracted crowds of visitors, including coachloads of school parties, Prime Ministers (unspecified) and even the present Queen as a young girl. Gandhi also paid a visit, and Eveline Marlowe (who was probably Ward's daughter, Blanche Evelyn Marlow Ward) recalls that he "pointed out that a bronze statue of Buddha labelled as being made in Benares in the eighteenth century, was, in fact, a product of Birmingham, and less than ten years old!"[22] Ward apparently had assistance from Queen Mary of Teck in building up the collection.[23]

He had constructed the likeness of a prehistoric village, with examples of a Magdalenian Hunting Lodge, a Neolithic Pit-dwelling, a Lake Dwelling and Bronze Age and Iron Age huts. Doubtless much speculation was involved, but for the time, and on a limited budget, it was undoubtedly an amazing achievement.

The most prominent building on the site was The Abbey Church which was used for several years as the chapel for the Abbey. It was originally a 13th Century tithe barn from Birchington in Kent. Ward gives an account of its reconstruction:

*We ... purchased it, took it down timber by timber, numbered each piece, brought it to New Barnet, and then re-erected it here. And what tremendous timbers some of them were. The pillars were 14 feet high and weighed 7 or 8 cwt., while some of the cross pieces are 20 feet long and weight half a ton. It has made a beautiful aisled church, and into it we have fitted all kinds of Ecclesiastical treasures.*[24]

Other buildings and displays included a 16th Century Armourer's Shop, an Elizabethan bedroom, a 17th Century Pottery Shop, an Apothecary's, a Jacobean dining room, an 18th Century weaver's shop, a Victorian jeweller's, a Carriage Shed and Harness Shop, and a wheelwright's shop and smithy.

By 1936[25] there was also a 16th Century witch's cottage, which is so important to our story that it is worthy of a

*21. The former Abbey Church at the Abbey Folk Park*

chapter to itself (see Chapter 7). Ward had furnished it appropriately. He says of it:

*A most interesting building this, of half-timber work, thatched with reeds and with a central hearth and a louvre instead of a chimney. It is furnished with the pottery and furniture of the period and all the appurtenances of a witch, including blasting rods, magic staff, dowsing rod, and the like.*[26]

Arthur Mee adds the further bizarre details that it had: "... a stuffed crocodile and other monsters hanging from the beams, and, of course, the witch's broom."[27] In another article, Ward adds:

22. J. S. M. Ward in the Witch's cottage at the Abbey Folk Park

> ... all the furniture is of the sixteenth century. Hanging from walls and roof are weird emblems and the grim implements of her trade: a stuffed crocodile, a human skull on a shelf, the magic staff, blasting rods, the sword of exorcism and the Magic Circle on the floor.[28]

Eveline Marlowe gives a vivid picture of the Folk Park in operation:

> The grounds were beautifully laid out by a twentieth century Capability Brown, and there was an Elizabethan herb garden modelled on the one at Hampton Court, in which grew every herb mentioned by Shakespeare. ... There was also a coppice of dwarf conifers in which the children, who were admitted for

*the modest sum of ninepence on two days a week, loved to play. ... Fr. Ward himself, who had a cherished ambition to be a curator in a museum or a guide in the Tower of London, loved to conduct parties of visitors (these numbered thousands in the first year of its existence alone) round the park delivering lively and enjoyable lectures to parties of eager and excited schoolchildren who arrived daily by coachloads from all over London.*[29]

She tells of the occasion on which a carving of Kali was stolen: Three months later the image was returned mysteriously through the mail together with a note saying: "Take this accursed thing back. I've had nothing but bad luck since I pinched it!"[30]

The Park was very popular, as C.A. Gentle recalls: *"It was not by any means unusual to see quite a crowd waiting to enter the grounds and museum. The entrance gates were kept closed by chain and lock, and opened only at stated times for visitors."*[31]

## Closure of the Abbey Folk Park

The Folk Park had stayed open throughout the war, although the number of members of the community gradually diminished. In early 1945, however, Ward was in trouble. He was being sued by an irate father, Stanley Lough, who claimed that Ward and his wife had enticed his 16-year-old daughter, Dorothy, away from her family to live in the Abbey.

The court case took place over a period of 11 days in May 1945[32]. C.A. Gentle[33] remembers that Ward attended court every day wearing scarlet robes, accompanied by his wife in white. Although it seems clear from the evidence that Dorothy was acting of her own free will, the judge found against Ward, awarding Mr. Lough £500 damages and granting an injunction restraining the defendants from continuing to harbour Dorothy Lough.

In his judgement, Mr. Justice Cassels did say that: *He realized that such an award was probably a mere formality, because the defendants had put it out of their power to possess so sordid a thing as money.* [34] However, Keith Chisholm informs me that: *Ward was, by design, a bankrupt when judgement was delivered against him in court and was hence unable to personally pay the £500 ordered - although it may subsequently have been paid by the Trustees of the Confraternity.* [35]

The only way that these damages, plus costs, could be paid was to put the Abbey and contents up for sale, the liabilities being discharged in September 1945 [36].

In fact, it seems quite likely that Gardner would have at least contemplated acquiring the whole of the Folk Park as he almost certainly by this time had the idea of running a museum himself, partly inspired by the example of Ward and partly by his long-standing passion for collecting artifacts. However, his interests seem to have been more specifically witchcraft and magical practice and so he limited himself to the Witch's Cottage, which he had probably coveted for some years.

Ward pondered on the possibility of moving to Canada, but this proved impracticable without adequate resources. Gardner suggested that the plot of land that he had bought in Cyprus in 1939 might be suitable and he made a deal with Ward whereby Gardner acquired the Witch's Cottage in exchange for the land in Cyprus. Ward liked this suggestion. He was in sympathy with the beliefs and rituals of the Greek Orthodox Church, which was the predominant Church in Cyprus.

## Cyprus and Australia

As it turned out, Gardner's land was unsuitable for agriculture, so Ward and his community sold it and bought a small farm nearby. Ward died on 2nd July 1949, but his wife carried on as leader of the community. Gardner visited Cyprus that same year and went to see how they were getting on. They were managing, and were on good terms with the local people, but the political situation was having an impact, particularly the EOKA guerrillas. It was during this visit that Gardner was again ordained to the Priesthood, as mentioned above.

In the end, things got too difficult in Cyprus, and the community travelled to Australia, via Egypt and Colombo, in Ceylon, reaching Australia in 1956 and finally settling, in 1966, in Caboolture in S.E. Queensland.

Keith Chisholm informs me that Dorothy Lough went with the community to Australia. She died in Brisbane on 23rd January 1963 and was buried under the assumed name of Lilian Knight, probably because she felt that living with the community was breaking the terms of the court injunction.

Some of the more easily portable museum items from the Folk Park had been retained by the community. They remained in storage and in 1978 they decided to have a go at establishing another museum. Building commenced in 1983 and, after raising almost $1 million, and with the help of several grants, the Abbey Museum of Art and Archaeology was finally opened in June 1986 by Sir Gordon Chalk [37]. It remains one of the finest private collections in Australia and has a particular educational emphasis.

## The Abbey Museum

Meanwhile, back in England, Ward had offered the old Folk Park premises and grounds to his friend William F.C. Ohly,

FRAI, sculptor and art connoisseur, to house his private collection: "His aim in founding the Museum and Art Centre in 1946, was to provide a stimulating and satisfying place of study for the artists from home and overseas he intended should live and work there." [38] A pottery was also constructed in the grounds, with an oil burning kiln to make modern wares for the home and overseas markets. The 13th Century Tithe Barn was Listed in 1947 as a building of architectural and historic interest. Ohly also established the influential Berkeley Galleries in London, which provided an outlet for his particular interest - primitive art - as well as for those working at the Abbey Art Centre, including such artists as the sculptor, Peter King (1928-1957), who worked with Henry Moore.

Ohly was one of the witnesses to Gardner's ordination as a Priest of the Ancient British Church in August 1946. I don't know exactly when Ohly took over the property, but it was probably by mid 1946. Certainly there were consecrations going on at least until September 1945 at the Abbey Church [39], if not until June 1946 [40], but these may well, in view of his interest, have continued after Ohly had taken over.

Pevsner makes a rather strange comment about the former Abbey Church in his *The Buildings of England - Hertfordshire* published in 1953: At the time of writing it served as a Nestorian church. It has recently been converted into a museum and art centre. [41] The Nestorian Church is another 'heretical' church, dating back to the 5th Century, but I suspect that Pevsner may have mistaken its denomination.

The Museum was opened on Thursday 27th March 1947 under the Directorship of William Ohly. It seemed to be very much ancillary to the Art Centre and was only open to the public on Saturday afternoons: certainly not sufficient to justify a full-time curator. However, Cottie A. Burland, FRAI is indicated as being the 'Hon. Curator', which suggests that he was personally involved and was doing this as a voluntary activity in addition to his main work in the British Museum. We have seen in Chapter 5 that Cottie Burland was very likely to have been a member of Fouracres and Five Acres and to have known Gardner before the war. Indeed, he could have been the one who introduced Gardner to Ward in the first place.

# Chapter 7

# The Witches' Cottage In The Woods

### Five Acres

Gardner came back to live in London some time in late 1944 or early 1945, although as he may have had two homes throughout most of the war his "movement back to London" may not be as clear as might be imagined. Certainly we have seen how he continued to visit Spielplatz fairly regularly throughout the war. He had been involved in activities there and in the vicinity through most of the war, though his occupation of 47 Ridgmount Gardens, a superior apartment in purpose-built "mansions" close to Tottenham Court Road, marked his and Donna's formal return to the capital. This was very conveniently located for the British Museum and a lot of the activities in which he was involved.

Meanwhile, when Fouracres closed in 1940, Wellbye had bought the site from 'The Major', together with adjoining land fronting onto Oakwood Road and Woodside Road. In respect of this, he wrote:

*I took this last on in the hope that people would be found willing to reside there, "respectable" in front, with back doors into club ground. Unfortunately such people never materialized, and I surrendered most of that strip of frontage. It was a pity as now I think the idea would work.*[1]

When the war ended, it is likely that Wellbye wanted to start

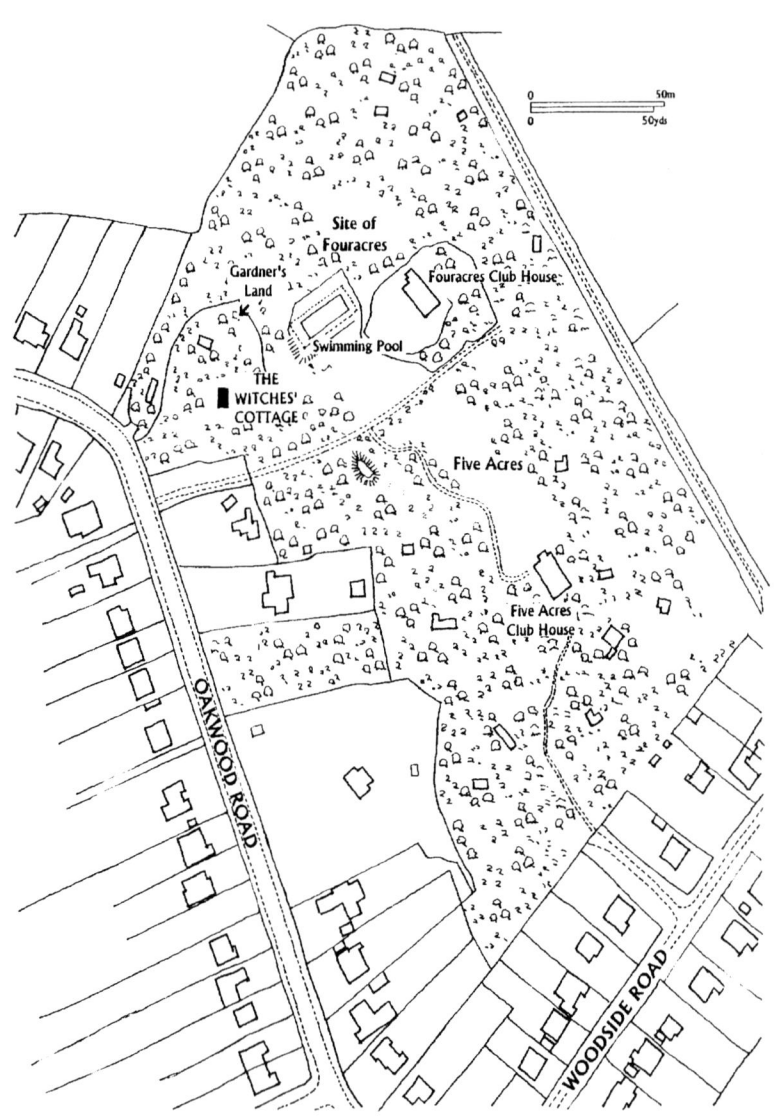

23. *Part of Bricket Wood in about 1950 showing the sites of Fouracres, Five Acres and the Witches' Cottage (based upon the 25-inch Ordnance Survey map)*

up a naturist club again on his land, and some time in 1945 he created the Woodside Close Property Company to manage this and his other land holdings.

The first person to set up on the site was Douglas Powell, who had had a hut at Spielplatz by the name of 'Sun Tan'. He had a group of friends who used to cater for themselves rather than use the communal facilities at Spielplatz, so were already rather 'semi-detached'.[2] Anyway, in April 1945, Powell and his group moved 'Sun Tan' onto Wellbye's land and established what they initially called "The Sun Tan Club". At some stage, probably in early 1946, this changed its name to Five Acres.

The Club seemed in its emphasis to be the spiritual successor of Fouracres, as a note published in Spring 1946 recounts: *... a special feature of Five Acres is its "cultural" side - in connection with which a programme of talks and discussions was adopted last season* [i.e. Summer 1945], *with such success that a further series is planned for this year.*[3] An advertisement of the time referred, more formally, to 'lectures' and also to dramatics.

Gardner had obviously involved himself in the Club fairly early on, certainly by early 1946, because there is a record of an Extraordinary General Meeting of the Company which was held on 28th July 1946 at which a Special Resolution was passed which would alter paragraph 12 of the Articles of Association to read:

*The following persons shall be Directors of the Company, viz: Gerald Bressau* [sic] *Gardner, and Reginald Wellbye. They shall be Permanent Directors of the Company, and each of them shall be entitled to hold such office so long as he shall live ...*

Gardner had financed Wellbye and received a 50% share in

the company in return. This is confirmed in a letter which Gardner wrote to Cecil Williamson in February 1951 in which he said: *I and a friend* [almost certainly Edith Woodford-Grimes] *hold half the debentures.*

Wellbye was obviously keen to use the extra money which Gardner brought in for developing the Club. I am guessing that, in exchange, Wellbye had agreed to sell Gardner a plot of woodland on which the Witch's Cottage could be relocated.

Certainly by Spring 1947 the Club was being referred to as having just been reorganised, presumably at least partly as the result of Gardner's financial involvement. The distinctive character of the Club was, however, still being emphasised:

*This club ... aims at breaking new ground, making nudity a cultural agency, and so appealing to many not ordinarily attracted, or apt to be bored by "just nudism". As a social, recreational and cultural club on a nudist basis, it has as its object the bringing together of thoughtful and well-informed people for play, conversation and such cultural activities (e.g. discussions, talks, dramatics, etc.) as can be most pleasantly associated with social nakedness.* [4]

Gardner's old friend, Ross Nichols, seems to have become a member of Five Acres in about 1947, perhaps in part because of its philosophy and Gardner's involvement. [5]

Gardner's relationship with Wellbye certainly seems to have taken a turn for the worst, for by early 1951, Gardner wrote to Williamson as follows:

*There is a row on at the Club where I took you that day, & one section say sell the damned place ...* [6]

Referring to Wellbye, he wrote: *The position is that the blighter who is giving me so much trouble is trying to wreck the Club and get it all in his own hands.* Later that month he wrote:

*I have told you of Rex Wellbye, my bad neighbour, he has been trying to get the Council to Dig Drains through my land to spoil it. ... If Wellbye wants the drains dug they should go through his own land which is the shortest way & would not spoil his land.* [7]

From Wellbye's point of view, the problems looked rather different:

*Our Sec. ... had to resign, and no successor has been appointed. ... We have very charming members — but they just do not want to be bothered to do any work or even sit on a committee. When we took over it was a proprietary club, and so far my efforts have failed to make it a members' club, the only result being to let in an unrepresentative clique. This might have worked for a time if the additions to the Board had displayed energy, but the lethargy has been colossal, and the slowness and reluctance to meet unbelievable ... One of the enlarged Board has resigned, another is so ill and old that he is sure to resign, too, a third will only attend a meeting if he happens to be on the spot, while the fourth, to whom they all look for action, is procrastinating and unbusinesslike — but wont let go! [This sounds like Gardner!] I have now taken steps to end the situation one way or the other, but the position will not become clear for a few weeks more.* [8]

It is clear from the date of this letter that the situation is the same one as that described by Gardner. Exactly how all this was resolved, I do not know, but Fred Lamond, who became a member of Gardner's coven in the late 1950s, gives this account of Gardner's involvement:

*... he had no interest in running the club itself, and appointed a salaried administrator to run the club on his behalf. This*

*man deliberately ran the club at a loss by setting unrealistically high requirements for membership, hoping thereby to persuade Gerald eventually to sell the club to him at a low price. But Gerald saw through the ploy, sacked the administrator and appointed his right-hand man in the coven, Jack Bracelin, in his place. This time he did not pay a salary, but told Jack he could live off the club's income.*[9]

Bracelin certainly put energy into the club and, according to Lois Bourne, not only built his own chalet in the club grounds but was always on the go with mechanical dumper and gumboots landscaping the grounds, planning and building a swimming pool, and so on.[10]

At a later date, Gardner and Bracelin started a company entitled 'Ancient Crafts Limited' to run the club following another reorganisation in 1957. Although there were, on paper, several shareholders, including Edith Woodford-Grimes, I think it fairly clear that most of the money came from Gardner.

## The Witches' Cottage

As soon as Gardner heard that Ward was having to sell the Folk Park, in the summer of 1945, he probably expressed interest in the Witch's Cottage, with the hope in the back of his mind that he could use it for witchcraft rituals. Ward was probably only too pleased to 'offload' it, or let it go to a 'good home', and so was delighted when Gardner offered his land in Cyprus in exchange.

But Gardner was then faced with the problem of dismantling the cottage, finding some land on which it could be re-erected, transporting it and then reconstructing it - a major undertaking. I imagine that Bricket Wood would have immediately sprung to his mind and that he would have asked Wellbye for some land to erect the cottage. I suspect that Wellbye wasn't very keen at first, but that he was persuaded by Gardner offering to 'buy in' to Five Acres on an equal basis with Wellbye, which is probably the origin of the rumour that Gardner bought some land in order to start a naturist club. Wellbye offered Gardner an area of fairly dense woodland approximately half an acre in extent, close to the entrance to the site on Oakwood Road, but whether this was a sale or lease I am not certain.

We don't know how long the cottage stayed in a dismantled state before being re-erected, but we do have an eyewitness account, which demonstrates that it had certainly been erected by early 1946. Gardner's American niece, Miriam ('Mimi') stayed with Gerald and Donna while she was attending school in London for a year in 1946. She told Morgan Davis: *He had a little Witch's Cottage set up, as a matter of fact, with the Greek Orthodox reform group (this is how Miriam identified Ward's group).* [11]

A vivid picture of Gardner at this period is provided by Mimi, who told Davis: *... my uncle ... was usually fully clothed in about fifty things of clothing because he was freezing to death!*
[12]

She also told him that she had met some of the group, which rather indicates that, when it was first erected, probably very early in 1946, it may have been used for meetings of the Ancient British Church, although it is possible that Gardner used the name as a relatively respectable cloak for witchcraft activity.

To those who are at all familiar with books, articles and television programmes on witchcraft over the last 40 years, it has taken on an almost iconic quality: the half-timbered cottage in the middle of the wood. Most of us have probably seen its image: it's what a witch's meeting place should be like. To quote Ronald Hutton:

24. *The Witches' Cottage (courtesy of Patricia Crowther)*

*Until the reality of the New Forest coven or of any earlier group is securely established, this spot in Hertfordshire is the best-documented place on earth to bear the name of the birthplace of modern pagan witchcraft.*[13]

The cottage has played an important role in the history of the modern witchcraft revival and, for that reason alone, is worthy of preservation.

It started life, probably in the 16th Century, and probably from somewhere in the vicinity of Ledbury in Herefordshire. In the early 1930s it was latterly in use as an apple store on a large farm. At some stage, it came under threat of demolition and Ward got to hear about it and acquired it for the Folk Park. According to Williamson (who had apparently spoken to some of the former workers at the Folk Park) "the building had arrived as dismantled baulks of numbered timbers which were dumped and lay around for many months before reassembly"[14]. Jennie Cobban describes the cottage:

*The witch's cottage (now only about 5m long) seems to be only the central section of what was originally a larger building, as what appear to be non-functional timbers extend horizontally into space at either end of the building. Dowel holes around the doorway also suggest that a porch may have been present at some period.*[15]

The cottage originally had wattle and daub infill panels of the traditional sort, and it seems likely that Ward replicated this when the cottage was re-erected at the Folk Park. The roof was thatched with reeds, but had a louvre rather than a chimney, above a central hearth. The interior had been altered at some stage to make one large room.

Certainly in Gardner's eyes (and, it must be said, those of many others), the land and the cottage were clearly meant for each other, and so he had the problem of dismantling the cottage, transporting it from East Barnet to Bricket Wood, and then re-erecting it. In doing so, the building was "modified" to some extent, partly on purpose and partly by accident. It is clear that the wattle-and-daub would have disintegrated when the building was dismantled, so, when replacing them, Gardner got the outside cement rendered and the interior whitewashed. Also the thatched roof was replaced with tiles, ostensibly in order to comply with the fire regulations.

The door, of solid oak, is reputed to be that of the old St. Albans jail, though at what stage that was acquired, and by whom, is not known. The windows were diagonally leaded lights, one large one in the gable-end elevation and several smaller ones along the walls. The timbers were painted black.

It is my guess that Gardner wanted to use the cottage for witchcraft rituals right from the start, but that at that time the only witches he knew were down in the New Forest area so, rather than leave it empty, he tried to get the Ancient British Church interested, although I suspect that few, if any, meetings were held there.

At the same time, the existence of the cottage probably provided an impetus to Gardner's desire to publicise the Craft and I suspect that he again tried to persuade Dafo and possibly the other witches in Highcliffe to allow him to write something.

This time he succeeded, as we shall see in Chapter 10, but it was to be another three years, in the summer of 1949, before *High Magic's Aid* would appear and generate a certain level of publicity which would attract members to a hoped-for coven.

In the meantime, Gardner probably used the cottage to sleep in when staying at Five Acres. Several more recent commentators, such as Patricia Crowther and Lois Bourne have mentioned the presence of a four-poster bed in the cottage, only used, in their experience, for the depositing of coats. Could this, however, have dated back to the time when Gardner might have used the cottage to stay overnight, even if only in the summer? In the 1945/46 period accommodation at Five Acres seemed to be limited to members' caravans and, rather than go to the expense of acquiring a caravan, I suspect that Gardner made use of what he had - the Witch's Cottage, as soon as it had been reassembled on his own land.

It has long been rumoured that Gardner registered the cottage as a place of worship under the name of the 'Ancient British Church'. This probably originates from an article by Peter Bishop which appeared in *The People* on 11th January 1959. He wrote:

*... they have had the effrontery to register their temple as a place of worship. I have seen the form sent to the local Registrar in St. Albans. It describes the cottage in Bricket Wood as "The Ancient British Church" and the "congregation" as "undenominational".*[16]

On the face of it this seems fairy specific and likely. The Registration would have been under the provisions of the Places of Worship Registration Act 1855. However, when I approached the local Superintendent Registrar's office, neither they nor the Office of National Statistics[17] had any record of such registration.

Perhaps the form was never sent. In any case, the relevant point here was Gardner's intention, which suggests that the cottage was first intended for use by the Ancient British Church, into which we know that Gardner had been ordained, unless it was merely that he liked the name, was no longer (if he ever had been) actively involved in the Church, and thought it a good "cover" for the witchcraft activity which was going on there, or that he hoped would be going on there in the near future. For Gardner, I think that after a while, the name "Ancient British Church" lost all its original associations and was merely another, slightly humorous, name for witchcraft.

The cottage was certainly later used for witchcraft rituals and Gardner made considerable efforts to create the right atmosphere in the cottage for these. In this he succeeded, as several who attended them testify. Lois Bourne, for example, says:

*The floor was covered by a black composition surface on which was outlined in white paint a double circle, the inner one of which was 9 feet diameter. Between the circles were cabbalistic signs, and in one quarter of the circle was a wooden chest used as an altar. ... the inside was painted white with magical symbols, pentacles, seals, etc. inscribed in black. There was no furniture apart from the bed and my memory is of a penetrating coldness and dampness as it was used only for magical rituals when, of course heaters were installed beforehand, otherwise it was empty and unused, and due to the lack of insulation it quickly cooled down.*[18]

Despite this, the atmosphere was overwhelming:

*The witch's cottage was to me a very special place. In a way it was sacred, since its walls were the repository of magical endeavours, healings and surging efforts to exceed the bounds of normal consciousness, to reach out into infinity and be touched by the wisdom of the gods. ... and on the night of the full moon at the stroke of midnight as we stumbled through the undergrowth by torchlight, laughing and joking, the cottage was magically transformed with the glow from flickering candles throwing strange shadows and wreathing incense curling to the ceiling in mystical shapes.*[19]

Patricia Crowther has very similar feelings: *There was a wonderful atmosphere in the cottage. It was like stepping back in time, and the aroma of incense seemed to permeate the very walls.*[20]

Whilst the coven which Gardner founded still meets, the cottage is no longer used as a witch meeting place. Since the coven carried out rituals there, the cottage has been moved because Gardner's site was sold off for housing development. The cottage is now a groundsman's store at Five Acres, no longer in the middle of a wood but near the swimming pool and surrounded by lawns and trees. There has been another change of roofing material - roofing felt. It looks in rather a poor state, with some modern timbers replacing the originals, though most remain intact. Jennie Cobban, writing in 1991, says:

*Nothing remains of the arcane decoration on the walls. ... A tiny part of the magic circle is still visible, but could not be viewed fully because of storage bags on the floor.*[21]

I saw the cottage for myself a few years ago. To see this building which has a very special place in Wiccan history was amazing, although it certainly had a rather neglected feel about it, even if the roof looked waterproof. It would be good if a fund could be set up to buy the cottage, dismantle it (for at least the fourth time!) and re-erect it on a site where it could be renovated and used again for Wiccan rituals. Such a venture would not be cheap but it would surely be worthwhile.

25. *The Witch's Cottage in 1999*

## Chapter 8

# Folk-Lore and Other Societies

### The Folk-Lore Society

Having returned in 1945 to the heart of occult and other activities in London, Gardner clearly participated fully, not just in the Five Acres Club but in a range of organisations most of which were associated, even if distantly, with witchcraft. One of these was the Folk-Lore Society, founded in 1878, which held regular meetings in London and produced the journal *Folk-Lore*. Folklore is defined by the Society as being "the everyday culture and cultural traditions of all social groups".

By this definition, Gardner became interested in folklore as soon as he went "out East" in 1900, getting to know the local peoples in Ceylon, Borneo and Malaya and learning from them about their customs and beliefs. His folklore interests were not limited to the East, however, for when he was back in England on leave in 1927 he applied for a reader's ticket at the British Museum to study Basque and Welsh folklore. [1]

His archaeological work in Johore led him to write articles for the journals of various learned societies and to his application for membership of those societies. I think Gardner rather liked the imagined prestige which he felt that membership of Royal societies gave, for he was elected a Fellow of the Royal Anthropological Institute in 1936 [2] And he certainly seems to have been associated with the Royal Asiatic Society as far back as 1933, when he had two articles (on gold coins found in the Johore River and on the Malay 'kris') published in the journal of their Malayan branch.[3 and 4] A major article by Gardner appeared in the Society's main Journal in 1937 entitled *'Ancient Beads from the Johore River as Evidence of an Early Link by Sea between Malaya and the Roman Empire'*.[5]

Gardner first attended a meeting of the Folk-Lore Society on Wednesday 15th March 1939, when the announcement of his name as a new member was made, the decision having been taken at the previous meeting. Gardner was proposed by Dr. W.L. Hildburgh, who had been a member since 1906.[6] Gardner's address is given as 23A Buckingham Palace Mansions, so it it clear that he kept on his London flat for some time after moving to Highcliffe in July 1938.

Although it was the first Folk-Lore Society meeting he had attended, Gardner was called upon (or offered) to exhibit and talk about his collection of witch relics. Gardner does not say how he acquired them, merely stating that: "Within recent years a box containing what appear to be witchcraft relics has come into my possession". One clue as to their origin is provided by a label on the back of the box, written, according to Gardner, about 1890 to 1900, stating that it was "given to me by my father Joseph Carter, of Home Farm, Hill Top, near Marlborough ... Signed S. Carter". It is possible that this is Sydney Carter, a member of the Society who seemed to know Gardner.[7]

The Society had regular monthly meetings until June 1940, when they ceased, presumably due to wartime conditions. However, Gardner did not attend any of the meetings between March 1939 and June 1940, presumably because his activities in the New Forest area kept him occupied and wartime restrictions meant that he could only come up to London on very special occasions. Meetings recommenced in 1945 and

Gardner attended frequently, except during his annual 'wintering abroad', until 1959.

The Folklore Society still possesses the attendance book in which members and visitors "signed in" at each meeting. This is interesting in that it reveals not only which meetings Gardner attended, but also the order in which people signed in, which gives an indication of who arrived with whom, and therefore possible friendships and acquaintances. On the basis of this, I think it likely that Elspeth Begg, Jacintha Buddicom, M.M. Banks, C. Ouless and Sydney Carter were particular friends of Gardner. However, he also clearly knew quite well several other influential members of the Society including Walter Hildburgh and Margaret Murray.

## "Art Magic and Talismans"

Gardner wrote on various topics for the *Folk-Lore* journal, including '*Hazel as a Weapon*'[8], but he gave only one lecture during the 20 years he was attending the Folk-Lore Society meetings. This was on Wednesday 19th June 1946 at 21 Bedford Square, London, when he spoke on "Art Magic and Talismans". We do not have a report of the meeting, but four years previously Gardner had an article on "*British Charms, Amulets and Talismans*" published in *Folk-Lore*[9] and I think I may have located his notes for the talk in part of the loose insert to 'Text A' (see Chapter 12).

Gardner started by remarking that, in his experience, they have been used quite commonly in the East, but those using them did not usually talk to Europeans about them. He defined them as "objects specially made or assumed naturally to possess certain powers to avert danger, to protect against disease, to guard against material influences and their accompanying dangers, supernatural influences for evil such as witchcraft and generally to bring luck to their owner".[10] This is interesting in that he refers to witchcraft in a negative sense, equating it with something evil. He was obviously at this stage not being open with his audience about being a witch himself and was prepared to make what is a disparaging statement about the Craft. Whether by 1946, when he gave his talk, he was able to be more open, I do not know.

The talismans used to illustrate the article are clearly based on illustrations in Barrett's *Magus* and appear later in substantially the same form in the endpapers to Gardner's *High Magic's Aid* in 1949 (see Chapter 10). How he came by them is interesting: one, "made for a Jupiter subject" he bought in Bournemouth and one was "borrowed from a shop in Christchurch". The following may well refer to one of Gardner's witch friends:

*I know of one belonging to a lady friend, it is some sort of crystal, cut into all sorts of queer irregular facets, it is of such a shape and size, that it could not possibly be worn. It was given to her by a friend who had it especially made for her at a place in London, where she understands, this work is a speciality. I presume each facet has its meaning. It is the odd or rare, certainly. I have not seen anything like it before and should very much welcome information as to the system on which the cutting of the facets is done, so as to apply to the individual owner. The same lady showed me a tiny gold hand, in the shape of the Horns of Power. It is probably of Italian origin, but as she told me that her father always carried it and firmly believed that it warded off all sorts of harm and brought him good luck, perhaps we may call it a British charm.*[11]

Only 15 people signed in for the talk, rather fewer than normal, but Gardner seems to have rounded up his friends and relatives, including Donna, who didn't usually attend, Donna's sister, Ida Rosedale and his American niece, Mimi, who at the time was at school in London and staying with the

Gardners. There was also Betty Lumsden Milne, who had edited *Keris and Other Malay Weapons* [12] for Gardner back in 1936 and whom Gardner was still obviously in contact with and living sufficiently near London to attend the meeting.

## The Folk-Lore Society Council

Gardner became a member of the Folk-Lore Society's Council in March 1946. (I never have to look that date up: it was the month I was born!). However, according to Caroline Oates, the Society's Librarian, he "attended few meetings [of the Council] and ... does not feature much in the Council's minute books". [13]

This is typical of Gardner and is repeated several times in his life, particularly in his dealings with Crowley (see Chapter 9): the enthusiastic taking on of status and imagined honours which, when it comes to work, responsibility and commitment, is plainly not sustained for very long.

Members of the Council soon became rather sceptical about Gardner, and particularly of his claimed academic degrees, as, incidentally, did members of other societies as well. John Yeowell writes:

*Gardner was a member of the then advisory council of the Royal Stuart Society during part of the time that I was principal secretary (ca late '50s - early '60s) ... When I asked Gardner about his doctorate he became visibly agitated. As I had no reason to doubt that it was genuine I persisted over several months, asking which university he had attended. At last he stormed out of the room when I asked him for what was to be the last time, muttering something about 'an American seat of learning' or words to that effect.* [14]

Frank Smyth [15] points out that, despite having been a member of the Society's Council for 18 years, its journal did not publish any obituary for Gardner. One reason was given by

Christina Hole, a former editor of the journal:

*Dr [sic] Gardner had a very curious personality. It did not inspire confidence - at least not in me, nor in a number of people interested in witchcraft and kindred matters. His theories were in themselves somewhat peculiar. I remember a meeting when the composition of the Council for the following year was discussed, and the question was raised as to whether his presence on our Council was really advantageous to the Society. Nothing was done about it, and his name was allowed to go forward as before, but the doubt was clearly felt and expressed.* [16]

If the Society was sometimes wary of Gardner, then he was also on occasions frustrated with the Society. In a letter to Gerald Yorke he wrote:

*I am on the Council of the Folk Lore Society, twice I've said at council meetings I've a couple of witches coming to tea tomorrow. Do some of you drop in casually & meet them, I cant be sure they'll tell you anything, but they may, & no one would come.* [17]

Even Margaret Murray comes in for criticism from Gardner: *... the Folklore Society, Dr. Hildburgh & the Rev. Proffessor James, are being very obstructive in London, & unfortunately Magret Murray, instead of being pleased that all her Theorys are proved Right, is most Damnably jealous that she didn't make the discovery.* [18] Later, she seems to have relented, as she did agree to write an Introduction to Gardner's *Witchcraft Today*.

## Walter Hildburgh

We have noted above that Dr. Walter Leo Hildburgh (1876-1955), MA, PhD proposed Gardner for membership of the Society. Whether they knew each other beforehand is not clear: it may be that Hildburgh was chosen to propose Gardner formally merely because he was a long-established member of the Society, or he may already have known Gardner as they had both been members of the Royal Anthropological Institute for several years previously.

Hildburgh was an anthropologist who donated a collection of Buddhist religious material to the American Museum of Natural History which is named in his honour. One of his specialisms was the iconography of Mediaeval English Alabaster Carvings, and he gave at least two lectures to the Folk-Lore Society on the subject. He was the third holder, in 1952, of the Society's Coote Lake Medal, which is awarded for outstanding research and scholarship.

Even if they had not met before 1939, they certainly seem to have become friends subsequently. Gardner seems to have made a special effort to attend the meetings where Hildburgh was speaking and they were also sufficiently close for Gardner to mention to him in 1951 that he was thinking of transferring his collection to Williamson's newly-established museum at Castletown (see Chapter 15).

## Elspeth Begg

Elspeth Begg frequently signed in next to Gardner, including the first meeting he ever attended, in March 1939, up until 1955. She lived in Bournemouth, probably Boscombe [19], and had first attended a meeting of the Society in January 1938, having become a member by November of that year. This coincidence of place and date suggests strongly to me that she may have known Gardner prior to that first meeting and that it may well have been she who introduced him, somewhat belatedly knowing his interests, to the Folk-Lore Society.

It is interesting that the only article that she wrote for the Society's journal is about witchcraft in Dorset. This relates to cases of witchcraft in the Woodlands and Verwood area in the late 19th Century told to her by a local farmer.[20] The article appeared in 1941 and raises the intriguing possibility that she may have been associated in some way with the group into which Gardner claimed initiation in 1939.

Gardner was still in touch with her as late as 1953, when they seemed to be bidding against each other at an auction: ... *I got a very fine Toad Stone Ring. Elspeth Begg was after it, but I beat her by a short head.*[21] Toad Stone is a precious stone supposed to have been formed inside the body of a toad and said to have magical properties.

## Jacintha Buddicom

Jacintha Buddicom was one of the 14 people who attended Gardner's talk in June 1946, when she signed in next to Gardner. She had attended meetings of the Folk-Lore Society back in 1938 and had become a member in 1945. She had also been a member of the O.T.O. (Ordo Templi Orientis) (see Chapter 9) and been friendly with Aleister Crowley.

She was born on 10th May 1901 in Plymouth and in her childhood (mostly spent in Shiplake-on-Thames in Oxfordshire) she was friends with Eric Blair, who became better known as the author, George Orwell. In her book *Eric and Us - A Remembrance of George Orwell*[22], there is a chapter entitled 'The Pagan', which is the title of a poem which Eric wrote for her in 1918. This was occasioned by an incident when she was at school in Oxford:

*I had got into the most frightful trouble in my first term at the Oxford High School. My parents were agnostics, ... at the same time they had recounted to me the legends of almost every possible mythology: with the result that I was a natural Pantheist, believing implicitly and impartially in all the gods.*

For the first three weeks of term we girls were sent each Sunday to the nearest church. The fourth Sunday, on being told that the crocodile was set for the same destination, I refused to join it.

'But you must go to Church', said the Housemistress.

'Why?' I asked.

'To worship God, of course.'

'But that's only the Christian God', I argued, 'and we've worshipped him three weeks running already. It's the turn for one of the others. Surely in a place the size of Oxford there must be a Temple of Astarte or somewhere we could go for a change?'

Angry as Miss Crosse was, thinking I was 'taking the Mickey' out of her, it was as nothing to her pained horror when she found I quite innocently meant it. ... I told this story to Eric that evening, which is why he called his poem The Pagan.[23]

Jacintha also wrote a poem in remembrance of a beautiful sunset, which starts:

> Circle as the dance
> Begins
> By the sun or Widdershins:
> Take your chance
> Till dance be done
> Widdershins or Way of Sun.[24]

We do not know whether it was just coincidence that Jacintha attended Gardner's talk, but she clearly had pagan sympathies and was a friend of Crowley's. She could well have conversed with Gardner after his talk and perhaps been instrumental in introducing the two the following year.

## Spiritualism

The reality of the survival of the individual following the death of the physical body had been accepted by Gardner ever since he read Florence Marryatt's *There is No Death* when a boy. His experiences with the native peoples of Borneo and Malaya certainly convinced him and, on his visits to England in 1927 and 1932, he made efforts to seek the guidance of a variety of mediums. Professor Ronald Hutton has said: "...my own suspicion is that the greatest invisible player in the story is spiritualism". [25] I am sure he is right and a study of the involvement of Gardner and other people in our story in spiritualism and with spiritualists would prove invaluable, but is a subject for further research.

Gardner had become a member of the Society for Psychical Research by May 1946. He seems particularly to have made the acquaintance of Dr. Alexander Cannon, writer on hypnotism and eastern mysticism, for he writes to Cecil Williamson in April 1951 that Cannon has a large house in Douglas in the Isle of Man where Williamson was living. Gardner's comments indicate that he was somewhat sceptical about Cannon's claims to carry out healing, make himself invisible and become immune to fire.

Another prominent member was Dr. E.J. Dingwall, who was also a naturist. He seems to have been acquainted with Gardner, for in a letter to Williamson, Gardner writes: *I met Dr Dingwell at the Soc for Phyecal Research meeting the other night ... [he] solemnly warned me against having anything to do with Witchcraft ...*[26]

Gardner obviously discussed witchcraft with various members of the Society, for in *Witchcraft Today* he implies that he put a suggestion of an experiment to a witch from a member of the Society for Psychical Research, about which the witch was rather scathing, saying that "...states of mind cannot be switched on or off at will to please the S.P.R." [27]

## Conclusion

As one might expect from his mercurial nature, Gardner joined various different organisations, flitting from one to the other as his interests fluctuated, never being fully committed to any of them. There are probably far more than I have indicated in this chapter, such as the Flying Saucer Society, to whom he gave a talk in 1955. I think it highly likely that Gardner was a member of several other organisations in the general area of his interests - archaeology, history, weapons, psychic studies.

And, of course, Gardner met individuals who had an effect on him in various ways. He undoubtedly welcomed contact with other people in furthering his interests, ideas and knowledge. Clues to the influences on Gardner in the crucial post-war period might be provided by looking at the people he was friendly with, their interests and activities, and this is a theme which runs throughout this book. Some of these people may well have been crucial in the development of Gardner's ideas, but more research is needed to determine how it all fits together.

The writings of one such individual were undoubtedly very influential on Gardner - his name was Aleister Crowley.

# Chapter 9

# Aleister Crowley and the O.T.O.

Gardner had probably been aware of the writings of Aleister Crowley long before they met in person. As Doreen Valiente found when Gardner let her read the rituals that he was using when she first met him in 1952, there was a lot of Crowley material included in them. We shall be looking at this in more detail in Chapter 13. In the meantime we shall examine Gardner's first meeting with Crowley in 1947, how it came about, and what emerged from it, for it is a significant step in our story.

Edward Alexander Crowley (1875-1947), who was born in Leamington Spa, was probably the most significant and certainly the most controversial ritual magician of the twentieth century. His parents belonged to the strict Plymouth Brethren sect but were reasonably wealthy, having made money from the brewing industry.

Crowley attended Cambridge University but failed to obtain a degree. He did, however, acquire there his life-long interest in magic and the occult. In 1904, whilst in Egypt, he received from an entity called Aiwass the text of a document entitled *"The Book of the Law"*, which presaged the start of what he called a 'New Aeon'. Crowley also joined the magical order, the Golden Dawn, founded in 1887. He had disagreements, however, with the leaders of that order and eventually joined the Ordo Templi Orientis (O.T.O.), of which he became the leader in 1922, remaining so for the rest of his life.

He wrote prolifically, much of it fine poetry and prose. He was, however, also a great leg-puller, with a purpose - to enable those seekers after truth to realise that the answers lay within themselves. He was a colourful character, undoubtedly treating some of his friends very badly, but as well as his magickal writing, he was an accomplished poet and mountaineer.

It was through his longstanding friend, Arnold Crowther (1909-1974) that Gardner had the opportunity to meet Crowley. Gardner had first met Arnold back in 1939 at a lecture on folklore given by the well-known author, Christina Hole. This was, incidentally, not a meeting of the Folk-Lore Society, but may well have introduced Gardner to it.

Arnold Crowther told Doreen Valiente that he came across Crowley in a rather unusual way, towards the end of the war, when working as a stage magician with ENSA.[1] Patricia Crowther tells me that her husband became interested in Crowley through reading his book on "Magick":

*At one of the army camps where he was performing, a soldier was unpacking a crate of old books which had been collected by a church organisation for the lads in the forces. Having seen Arnold performing his conjuring act the previous night, the soldier handed him a book. "This will be more useful to you than to us," he said. "You may find some new tricks in it."*[2]

Arnold expected it to contain something like card tricks, and so was rather puzzled by the title - *Magick in Theory and Practice* by the Master Therion - Aleister Crowley. It quickly became clear to Arnold on starting to read it that this was no manual about producing rabbits from hats or suchlike, but a treatise on ritual magic, which he read through, slowly, for it was hard going, but with growing interest. The volume was actually very rare, having been privately printed in Paris in

26. Aleister Crowley towards the end of his life, at Netherwood, Hastings (courtesy of Lucas Mellinger)

27. Netherwood, Crowley's last residence, in about 1905

1929 and available only to subscribers. Gardner later managed to acquire a copy of his own, however.

It was after the war, in April 1947, when Arnold was giving a private performance of his magic act, that a lady came up to him saying that she knew a magician with a similar name to his. It turned out that the lady knew Aleister Crowley and gave Arnold his address.

Crowley was living in Hastings at the time, in fact his last residence before he died. He had moved, on 17th January 1945 [3] to Netherwood, a large house in 3 $\frac{1}{2}$ acres of grounds, no. 379 on a road called The Ridge, a long road of mostly superior villas which, as its name implies, runs along a ridge

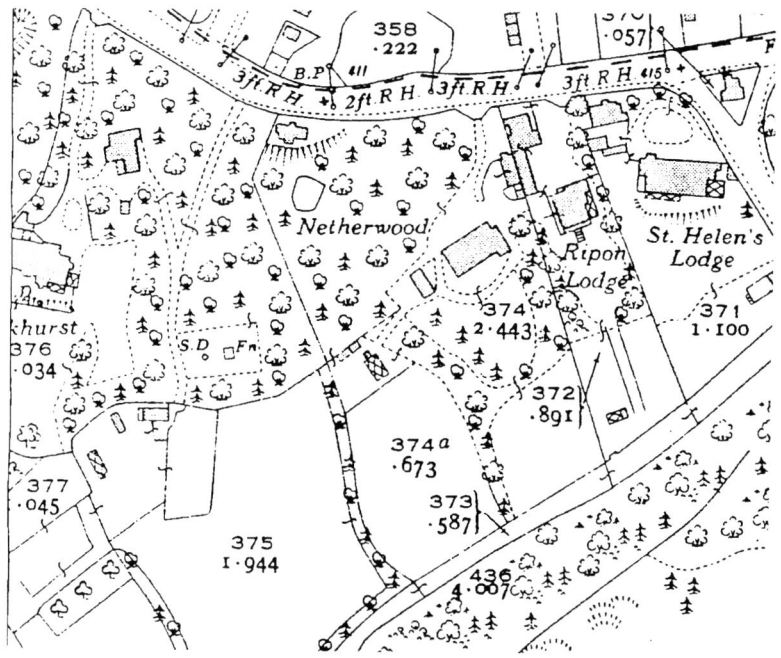

28. *Netherwood, Hastings (Extract from the 1937 25-inch Ordnance Survey map)*

which cuts across the northern part of the town. The house was surrounded by trees, approximately 2 1/2 miles from the town centre and 450 feet above sea level. The building, which was demolished in 1968, dated from the mid 19th Century and had been a boys' preparatory school in the early years of the 20th. It seems to have been run as a sort of residential home, the proprietor of which was Edmund C. Vernon Symonds, the brother of John Symonds, Crowley's biographer and literary executor.[4]

Arnold wrote to Crowley the following day and, about a week later, received a letter saying that he would be delighted to see him for tea at 4 p.m. the following Thursday. This turned out to be 1st May - Beltane - an auspicious and fruitful date for a first meeting. Did Crowley suggest it on purpose or was it just by "chance"? When Gardner heard that Arnold had arranged to see Crowley, he asked whether he could go along too. Arnold got in touch with Crowley again, who agreed: "Bring him along!"[5]

Whilst there is no reason to doubt the story that it was Arnold who arranged the visit, it is interesting to note that another acquaintance of Gardner, James Laver, who wrote the foreword to *Gerald Gardner Witch*, had visited Crowley only two to three weeks previously, at the end of March 1947 and one can well imagine Laver's account of his visit inspiring Gardner to ask Arnold whether he could go along with him to see Crowley. Indeed, it is possible that it was Laver who provided the key information about where Crowley was living. Laver was interested in naturism and it is possible that he had originally met Gardner before the war, at Fouracres, where his fellow museum curator, Cottie Burland, was a member. Further, Gareth Medway informs me that "James Laver is stated in a note made by [Ithell] Colquhoun in the 1960s to be a Wiccan."[6]

It is interesting to compare Gardner's account of his visit with Laver's, who writes:

*I went to Hastings (it was towards the end of March, 1947), took a cab about four miles into the country and was set down at a small Regency house, now a private hotel. Crowley was called and came downstairs to greet me. I was shocked by his appearance ... he seemed to have shrunk both in height and girth and he wore a little straggly beard ... His face was the colour of grey mud. His clothes, a tweed coat, a double-breasted waistcoat and voluminous plus-fours of different material seemed to hang loosely about him. He greeted me with great courtesy, explained that, as he was 'on a diet', he could not lunch with me, but I was to come up to his room afterwards.*

*After the meal I went up to Crowley's room, wondering if he had purposely chosen No. 13. I found him sitting on a divan bed with a little table before him. On another table was his luncheon - a boiled egg which he had not touched. He was drinking a glass of brandy and offered me some. It was excellent. He was in his shirt sleeves and the sleeves were marked with little spots of blood. A few books were on shelves and on the mantelpiece. Above was his self-portrait in the Chinese manner. Two of his water colours of the Himalayas were on other walls; also a reproduction of John's new portrait. On a chest of drawers stood a painted Egyptian stele and on the little table before him a pile of books, an empty tin to serve as an ashtray, a pipe, several bottles of medicine and a small box containing a hypodermic syringe.*

*He gave me a coffee and a cigarette. He himself smoked a pipe incessantly, only pausing to give himself an injection from time to time. ... Hardly pausing in his conversation he took up the syringe, dissolved a little scarlet pellet in the glass chamber, rolled back his sleeve and gave himself a piqure. The heroin injection seemed to give him new life. The muddy look in his face vanished, and the wonderful brown eyes glowed. From time to time he turned them upon me, and I began to understand the hypnotic fascination he must once have possessed.*[7]

As we shall see in Chapter 13, there is much of Crowley's work incorporated into the Gardnerian Book of Shadows. What is not so clear is when they were incorporated - before or after Gardner's visit to Crowley. It is, however, likely that Gardner was familiar with at least some of Crowley's works before they met, even though he probably had little knowledge of Crowley's life and his order, the O.T.O., beforehand. I think it is clear that Gardner's admiration for some of Crowley's writing both predated and provided a reason for their meeting.

Crowley was Head of the O.T.O. (Ordo Templi Orientis), an order which had been founded by the German occultist, Theodor Reuss in 1906. According to Sabazius $X^0$ and AMT $IX^0$:

It draws from the traditions of the Freemasonic, Rosicrucian and Illuminist movements of the 18th and 19th centuries, the crusading Knights Templars of the middle ages and early Christian Gnosticism and the Pagan Mystery Schools. Its symbolism contains a reunification of the hidden traditions of the East and the West.[8]

Crowley joined in 1912 and became Head of the Order in 1922.

Some have written of the connection between the O.T.O. and the Indian tradition of tantra. But according to Adrian Bott:

*The OTO didn't really contain anything resembling Tantra at all. That is a claim that is made for it, but it is baseless. Certainly under Crowley the significance of the female, which in Tantra is very great, is downplayed. This is because the OTO concerns itself with the religious veneration of the male creative force. The OTO was not originally about magic as such, and was not really about magic under Crowley either, except in the Eighth and Ninth degrees. The point was more the identification of the Masonic God - the Great Architect of the Universe - with the phallus. Even under Theodor Reuss ... this doctrine was found, though the symbology was much more Christian. ... In Crowley's eyes, women's energies could only re-arrange, they could never create. Creation was the province of men. Women could, at most, produce phantasms and mere bewitchments.*[9]

To divert from the story for a moment, it has been suggested at various times that Gardner actually knew Crowley before 1947. One piece of evidence is provided by Allen Greenfield, who states:

*My informant, Col. Lawrence, tells me that he has in his possession a cigarette case which once belonged to Aleister Crowley. Inside is a note in Crowley's hand that says simply: 'gift of GBG, 1936, A. Crowley'*[10]

Of course, Gardner was in the habit of giving cigarette cases - his first gift to his wife, Donna, was a silver cigarette case. But it was just the sort of thing which people gave each other in those days. However, I have another explanation for the note. Francis King[11] refers to a magical order, founded by one C. Russell, which seems to have taught a variation of the O.T.O. which advocated distinctive techniques of sexual magic. It was known as the G.B.G.[12], which stood for "Greater Brotherhood of God", and I think that this Order, which was in existence from 1931 to 1937, is a much more likely source for the cigarette case than Gardner who, from the evidence in Crowley's own diaries, did not meet him until 1947.

To return to the May Day visit, an extract from Crowley's diary for 1st May 1947 states the following:

*"Thurs 1 May: Miss Eva Collins, Dr. G.B. Gardner Ph D Singapore, Arnold Crowther prof. G. a Magician to tea. Dr. G. R. Arch."*[13]

This is the first mention of Gerald Gardner in Crowley's diaries. The "R. Arch" refers to Gardner's holding of the Royal Arch, a Masonic degree. The wording used also seems to imply strongly that this was the first time that Crowley had met Gardner because he is given a formal title and qualification, which one only does on the first occasion that one meets someone (leaving to one side for the moment the fact that Gardner almost certainly did not possess a PhD

187

Singapore, and probably not a Royal Arch either!). I think we can put Arnold Crowther's recollection of the year as 1946 down to simple lapse of memory.

Who Eva Collins was has never been satisfactorily explained. Whether she had anything to do with either Gerald or Arnold or whether she was someone who just happened to be visiting at the same time I do not know. The latter may be the case, as Patricia Crowther says that as far as she knows, Arnold and Gerald visited Crowley on their own. There was an "Eva C." in the list of O.T.O. members mentioned by Ithell Colquhoun[14]. Then again, she may have been a friend of Arnold's or Gerald's who for some reason they wanted to keep quiet about. One possibility is that she may have been Dafo. "Edith Grimes" does perhaps sound rather like "Eva Collins" to someone who was hard of hearing. But was Crowley going deaf towards the end of his life? At the moment, we must leave the identity of Eva Collins unresolved.

Patricia Crowther has relayed to me something of what Arnold told her had happened at that meeting. Crowley seemed to know a lot about witchcraft, but said that it was really a woman's cult and that it wasn't suitable for him, as the rites had to be conducted by a High Priestess and he wasn't the sort to be bossed around by women.

He talked a lot about magick and about how it could never be done under test conditions. The important thing was to really want to achieve a particular result. The trappings and paraphernalia of Ritual Magick would not of themselves achieve anything. Practical experience was far more important than reading about Magick. He said he had no idea that anyone was still interested in Magick, and he explained to them that he no longer needed magical tools as he could contact the masters direct.

Before they left, they joined Crowley in an adoration of the setting sun ritual. He then presented Arnold with a signed copy of his book of poems, *Olla*, which is still in Patricia Crowther's possession.[15]

Bracelin also recounts Gardner's impressions of Crowley, which accord with those of Laver:

*Once handsome, he was now reduced to a little, frail, gentle and archdeaconish figure, very bent. Could this be the Great Beast who had once boasted so many followers; who had thundered his way through life, determined to make his mark and leave a powerful organisation behind him? The fire was not quite all gone, however, even though he took heroin all the time.*[16]

Gardner also wrote about the meeting to John Symonds, Crowley's first biographer: *He was very interested in the witch cult, & had some idea of combining it w. the Order, but nothing came of it. He was fascinated with some snaps of the Witches Cottage.*[17] Gardner gave further details of the conversation to Cecil Williamson:

*By the way Alister Crowley was in the Cult, but left it in disgust, he could not stand a High Priestess having a superior Position & having to kneel to Her, & while he Highly approved of the Great Rite, he was very shocked at the nuedaty. Queer man, he approved of being nude in a dirty way, but highly disapproved of it in a clean & healthfull way. Also he disapproved of the use of the scurge to Release Power, for the practical reason if you teach a pupil the use of the Scurge, he can get a mate & do it on his own. If you have a highly paying pupil, if you teach them the Concentration & Meditation method, they go on paying you for years. But he didn't simple to pinch lots of the Witches Ritual & incorporate it in his works. he claimed that he Re Wrote the Ritual for them but I doubt this. He did re-write some Masonic Rituals, & made an awfull hash of them.*[18]

This also puts a new light on the oft-repeated passage in *Witchcraft Today* where Gardner states:

*The only man I can think of who could have invented the rites was the late Aleister Crowley. When I met him he was most interested to hear that I was a member, and said he had been inside when he was very young, but would not say whether he had rewritten anything or not. But the witch practices are entirely different in method from any kind of magic he wrote about, and he described very many kinds. There are indeed certain expressions and certain words used which smack of Crowley; possibly he borrowed things from the cult writings, or more likely someone may have borrowed expressions from him.*[19]

Rather than being duplicitous, I think that Gardner here is actually referring to the texts as they were presented to him, rather than the text as it was when he wrote *Witchcraft Today*, to which he freely admitted he had added much Crowley material. Note that in his 1951 letter, Gardner says that Crowley claimed to have re-written the rituals for the witches, but in *Witchcraft Today* (1954) he claims that Crowley would not say whether he re-wrote them or not. We will look into the truth of the matter in Chapter 13. Bracelin also records Gardner's recollection:

*At Oxford, Crowley said, he had been on the edge of witchcraft. Why had he not followed the way of the witches? Because he 'refused to be bossed around by any damned woman'.*[20]

Now, it must be remembered that this account by Gardner is from a period after he had distanced himself from Crowley and does not necessarily represent Gardner's feelings at the time they first met. (Incidentally, it should be pointed out that Crowley was at Cambridge rather than Oxford, but perhaps we may excuse this as a lapse of Gardner's memory in the intervening years.)

However, Thelemic scholar, Adrian Bott, remarks that:

*The idea that [Crowley] was offered membership of such and rejected it because 'he didn't want to be bossed around by any damn woman' is particularly ludicrous if one knows anything about what Crowley was actually like. He was quite happy to prostrate himself before the Female Principle and its representatives in the context of magic or religion. He considered himself to be the Beast upon whom the Great Whore rides - far from rejecting being bossed around by a 'damn woman' he positively dreamed of it.*[21]

In contrast, Gerald Yorke, who knew Crowley well, and was one of his literary executors, says that this comment was "in character".[22]

Perhaps Crowley, making the whole thing up to impress Gardner, had to give some reason why he left and on the spur of the moment mentioned that he didn't like being bossed around by women, even though in other spheres he did. The claim has certainly been disputed by Professor Ronald Hutton on the grounds that there is no mention of such involvement in Crowley's diaries, which were usually very revealing even of things which never appeared in his published writings.[23]

The most likely explanation is that Crowley pretended to Gardner that he had been involved, in order to retain the upper hand in their conversation and not to appear ignorant on the subject. He had previously told the same story to Louis Wilkinson[24] so it was fresh in his mind.

Doreen Valiente also took this view, for she writes: ... *I always took this with a grain of salt, thinking it probably just a piece of 'one-up-manship' on Crowley's part.*[25]

Gardner was obviously much taken with Crowley, as he visited him three further times in the next month. On Wednesday 7th May, less than a week after the first meeting, Gardner visited Crowley again. It seems on this occasion, Gardner must have asked about membership of Crowley's magical order, the O.T.O. and, I suspect, been accepted into it, because the entry in Crowley's diary is as follows:

*Wed 7 May: Dr. Gardner about 12. Tell him phone Wel 6709* [26]

The telephone number is that of Gerald Yorke, who at the time was living at 5 Montagu Square and who was able to supply Gardner with books. Crowley wrote to Yorke two days later asking him to send Gardner a copy of the *Equinox of the Gods*. This was a book published by Crowley and the O.T.O. in the 1930s. It includes a reproduction of *The Book of the Law*, and tells of how he received it. Clive Harper calls it: "... a handsome book, most copies being printed on japon and bound in cream buckram with gold blocking - and it sold for one guinea."[27] Crowley mentioned to Yorke that Gardner had already bought his own stock of four copies. This was presumably to distribute to others and this is confirmed by further correspondence.

It is probable that on this occasion, Crowley may have offered initiation to Gardner. Morgan Davis confirms this when he reports two (somewhat conflicting) accounts of the presentation by Crowley of a copy of *'The Book of the Law'* to Gardner. He mentions that "S.B.", an O.T.O. member, reported the inscription "To Fra Scire P.I. from ... Baphomet X[degree] O.T.O. on his affiliation". He also mentions a copy of *Liber Al* in the Toronto collection with the inscription "to Scire on the occasion of his Minerval" which is signed "Baphomet". He also states: *Karl Germer, who was the O.T.O. treasurer at that time, also made note that Gardner had paid the requisite dues and fees.*[28]

Gardner clearly wanted this, as did Crowley to have carried it out so quickly. Greenfield says:

*Crowley referred to Dr. Gardner and his OTO encampment in private correspondence almost to the time of his death, and spoke of it with optimism and enthusiasm. ... Crowley, and his immediate successor, Karl Germer, who also knew Dr. Gardner, likely set 'old Gerald' on what they intended to be a Thelemic path, aimed at re-establishing at least a basic OTO encampment in England.*[29]

I think that Crowley initially saw Gardner as a means of reviving the rather moribund state of the O.T.O. in Britain. Bill Heidrick says that "The Order was certainly not much in England in the 40s, probably less than a dozen members still in touch with Crowley and resident."[30] Doreen Valiente considered that it was "existing more on paper than in actuality".[31] As a result, Crowley may have rather "buttered Gardner up", flattering him by bestowing degrees within the O.T.O. which were the equivalents of what he already had.

## A Question of Degree

Clive Harper comments:

*I don't think Gardner understood the OTO degree system ... In High Magic's Aid he refers to himself as "4=7 OTO" which confuses A A (or GD) grades with OTO degrees.*[32]

Ben Fernee clarifies this:

*... in High Magic's Aid Gardner confuses his OTO degree with the A A grade of 4 = 7. He mentions ... that he has the rituals of the OTO up to Perfect Initiate a.k.a. Prince of Jerusalem or P.I. (the "I" and "J" being equivalent) which is an appendage to the 4th degree, the OTO equivalent of the Royal Arch.*[33]

One possibility is that, in accordance with his practice, Crowley bestowed on Gardner what he considered to be the equivalent of his Royal Arch Masonic degree. Morgan Davis says of the Prince of Jerusalem:

*"This degree is also described as "Companion of the Holy Royal Arch of Enoch". Since OTO ritual parallels Free Masonry, it seems likely that Crowley admitted Gardner to the IV[degree] under a process of affiliation, because Gardner had identified himself as a Royal Arch Mason."* [34]

There is some doubt about Gardner's Royal Arch status. Geoffrey Smith informs me [35] that masonic records show that Gardner was only an Entered Apprentice (1st Degree Mason) and not Royal Arch. However, Gardner may well have been a Co-Mason, though I am uncertain as to whether they have an equivalent degree.

Greenfield comments that Prince of Jerusalem (4th degree Perfect Initiate of the Order) normally takes years of training but also admits that Crowley "may have given Gardner an 'accelerated advancement' in his order".[36] Harper writes: *Gardner, as a Royal Arch mason, would have been treated by AC as being equivalent to IV degree OTO. In "*Magick Without Tears*", AC specifically refers to a lady Co-mason [Anne Mackay] joining OTO at the degree equivalent to her Co-masonic degree.*[37] This seems to be somewhat equivalent to the practice of academic and professional institutions, where a system of exemptions operates, particular qualifications exempting you from certain examinations.

By the time that Gardner's *High Magic's Aid* (1949) was going to the printers, it is likely that he had lost interest in being actively involved with the O.T.O. Crowley had died over a year previously and I suspect that Gardner put something on the title page that sounded impressive without worrying too much about its strict accuracy. Gerald Yorke, in an inscription in his own copy of *High Magic's Aid*, comments:

*Gardner was given a charter by A.C. to work Minerval and 1 to 3 degrees of O.T.O. He has not got the higher degrees, and at date of publication [July 1949] had not begun to work these degrees. He was never in the A.A. + is not entitled to call himself $4^0=7^0$* [38]

Gardner wrote back to Crowley on 14th June asking for a list of the Minerval fees, reminding him that he had paid 10 guineas up to the 7th degree.[39] Ben Fernee comments on this:

*Perhaps the reference to 7th degree in his letter to Crowley re dues is Gardners confusion, mixing 4th and P.I. with 4=7 A A with 7th OTO. ... He probably had the Minerval initiation with Crowley & Wilkinson ... and was read through the others which require 3 officers of the appropriate degree.*[40]

However, Geoffrey Smith informs me that 10 guineas was indeed the going rate at that time for the Seventh Degree.

According to Adrian Bott, this "reading through" would only take place "when there are not officers available to perform the ritual in full and only if the Candidate is affiliating across from Masonry or Co-Masonry". It would seem that Gardner met these criteria and that this was just what Crowley did in his case. This seems likely, as Doreen Valiente recalls, presumably having been told by Gardner:

*My impression, rightly or wrongly, is that at this time the O.T.O. existed mostly on paper only; and that "initiation" into it consisted of being given the papers to read.*[41]

She also says:

*I think at that time Crowley was rather desperate to find people to hand things on to. John Symonds describes how Crowley made him his literary executor upon quite short acquaintance.*[42]

**195**

Gardner's letter is signed "Scire", from the Latin for "to know", and this, together with the Charter already mentioned, seems to be his first known use of the name, which suggests that it may possibly have been a magical name bestowed on Gardner by Crowley at Gardner's visit on 7th May 1947. Bott states:

*Scire is one of the four Powers of the Sphinx - to know, to dare, to will and to keep silent. These are mentioned by their Latin names (scire, velle, audere, tacere) and made much of in the Second Degree of OTO; also in the Third.* [43]

This bestowing of degrees obviously worked with Gardner, and he began to see an important role for himself in the O.T.O. As was his nature, he could have sudden enthusiasms for things, and it certainly appeared to be true in this case. I think it fair to say that both Crowley and Gardner had something that the other needed at that time. Gardner was perhaps somewhat in awe of the 'great man' and certainly enjoyed the thought of being given an accelerated initiation and of being appointed what he imagined to be head of the O.T.O. in Europe. Crowley, in failing health, was gratified to find someone who seemed enthusiastic enough to take over the operation of the O.T.O. in Europe, which was on its last legs. But both overlooked the likelihood that Gardner's enthusiasm would come to nothing and that the seed would soon wither and die.

To understand the significance of this properly, it is important to realise their respective ages at the time of their meeting. Crowley was 71, in ill health and had just seven more months to live. Gardner was 62, in the twelfth year of his retirement and suffered, like Crowley, from asthma. He usually wintered abroad for the benefit of his health, and was shortly to have a severe bout of illness that necessitated his recuperation with his brother's family in America for several months. He was far from being a bright young spark ready to take over and revitalise a moribund O.T.O. but an ailing and ageing asthmatic who was set in his ways and, when it came to it, unwilling and unable to give the level of commitment that such a post demanded. Gardner was a bad choice, but Crowley was desperate.

## The Charter

For many years, Gardner displayed a Charter in his Museum of Magic and Witchcraft at Castletown on the Isle of Man. It purported to be from Crowley authorising Gardner to begin his own encampment of the O.T.O. The O.T.O. had various bodies of the order: Chapters were run from the Fifth Degree, Lodges from the Third and Encampments were run from the lower degrees. A Charter certainly exists. After the contents of the Museum were sold to Ripleys in 1973 (see Chapter 16), the Charter passed through various hands and was subsequently acquired by Dr. Allen H. Greenfield, DD in 1988. In his will he directs that it be turned over to the O.T.O. on his death. Its wording is as follows:

> *Do What thou wilt shall be the law.*
> *We Baphomet X Degree, Ordo Templi Orientis*
> *Sovereign Grand Master General of all English*
> *Speaking Countries of the Earth do hereby Authorise*
> *our beloved son Scire (Dr. G.B. Gardner) Prince*
> *of Jerusalem, to constitute a camp of the Ordo*
> *Templi Orientis, in the degree Minerval.*
> *Love is the law, Love under Will.*
> *Witness my hand and Seal*
>
> $+ \ Baphomet \ X^{0}$
> *seal        seal*

It is on parchment, written on the back of a land document and will from the County of Surrey for the year 1875 (incidentally, the year of Crowley's birth), and is fixed with four wax seals and ribbons which bear inscriptions and designs.

It is in Gardner's calligraphic hand - a similar style to that which he used for his Book of Shadows. This writing is very distinctive, particularly the thin stroke up towards the top right with which he finished many letters, showing that he must, unlike many witches, have been right-handed. Parts of it are written in red. Geoffrey Smith previously claimed that this was blood, but now informs me that this is not the case. The copy is certainly much less neatly written than Gardner's Book of Shadows, which indicates to my mind that he wrote it in a hurry.

With regard to the wording and layout of the Charter, the general style is unlike anything that Crowley ever wrote. Jerry Cornelius confirms this:

*Nowhere, in any archive world-wide, is the style of the likes of such a document found being used by Aleister Crowley. It's definitely NOT his style. He wrote or typed out everything and usually on regular paper ... at no time in his entire life did he allow others to write out 'the' authority he was granting.*[44]

The wording is also rather unusual. As Clive Harper says concerning the thelemic salutations:

*It is extremely unlikely that Crowley would have written 'Do what thou wilt shall be the law' and 'Love is the law, Love under will' rather than his customary 'Do what thou wilt shall be the whole of the Law' and 'Love is the law, love under will.*[45]

Cornelius is even more adamant. He says that Crowley:

*... would never have allowed, and I mean never allowed all the use of capitals in the Thelemic greetings. This is forbidden in Thelemic circles and something he would have reprimanded a student very severely for doing. To sign his name to such a document would have been blasphemous. Also, he would never,*

29. *The Charter on display at the Museum of Magic and Witchcraft (courtesy of Nicholas Culpeper)*

*never have signed his name to something which began 'Do what thou wilt shall be the Law'. The ultimate sin is misquoting Liber AL vel Legis.*[46]

In contrast, Greenfield says that the misquotation from The Book of the Law: "... *got by me for some months and probably got by Crowley when it was presented to him for signature ...*"⁴⁷

In addition, Cornelius points out that the term "Sovereign Grand Master General" is not one that was ever used in the O.T.O. and the authority to rule "all English speaking countries of the Earth" would also never have been appropriate because, as Outer Head of the O.T.O., Crowley would have ruled all countries regardless of language.

Adrian Bott also points out that Gardner is using a term from the Minerval initiation itself: 'I declare this Encampment open in the degree of Minerval, for the Quest of Peace and Wisdom'. He says that one did not have a Camp in Degree Minerval as a chartered body: "*It would have been far more likely for Gardner to have been chartered as Master of a Lodge or an Oasis with authority to initiate up to the Third Degree, if he had been chartered at all*". ⁴⁸

Harper goes on to say:

*... the term 'beloved son' is uncharacteristic of Crowley and the charters known to have been given by him in the 1940s tended to be handwritten on standard paper. Also in O.T.O. terms the degrees quoted are surprisingly humble. Prince of Jerusalem is only a side degree to $IV^0$ and Minerval is the introductory degree that precedes $I^0$.* ⁴⁹

Bott, whilst not disagreeing with this point, states that Prince of Jerusalem is not a side degree, but a sequel, and the completion of a series. ⁵⁰

There are gaps in O.... T.... O...., indicating to my mind that Gardner drew it up but did not really have any idea of what the initials stood for, leaving spaces to be filled in by Crowley when they next met. Clive Harper says that "... someone has filled in 'rdo empli rientis' after the letters OTO - the handwriting is intriguingly similar to Crowley's".[51]

But was the signature Crowley's? There seems to be a genuine difference of opinion about this. His sigil seems different - cruder than usual, and Harper confirms this when he says that "... the Baphometic cross and signature are very different from Crowley's usual style."[52], which he illustrates in his article. Yet Greenfield says "the signature and seals are certainly those of Crowley".[53] And Cornelius says that "real close examination, under a magnifying glass, convinces me that it is Crowley's signature."[54] Harper also said to me that Crowley had several distinct styles of writing, which seems to be the case.

Bill Heidrick gives a different view:

*I saw the charter on display back in San Francisco in the early 1970s, and was struck with the fact that Crowley clearly did not write or sign it ... it is not unlikely that Gardner prepared his surviving charter to replace a more informal document*

30. *A detail of the controversial signature on the Charter (courtesy os Nicholas Culpeper*

*actually signed by Crowley.*[55]

The seals are a further complication. Clive Harper has said that:

*For formal documents AC always used his Ankh-f-n-khonsu seal ring. I feel certain that AC would never refer to his "hand and seal" unless he used this seal ring.*[56]

But I know of no description of the seals on the Charter or whether they have the impression of Crowley's seal ring on them, but Greenfield confirms that they are Crowley's.

And what actually was the Charter supposed to be for? Greenfield makes this clear:

*...not only was this not a simple initiation certificate for the Minerval (probationary-lowest) degree, but, to the contrary, was a Charter for Gardner to begin his own encampment of the O.T.O., and to initiate members into the O.T.O.*[57]

Probably what happened is that at the request of Gardner, Crowley wrote out a charter on a normal piece of paper. Or, more likely, Crowley dictated the Charter to Gardner, who copied it down hurriedly, and possibly wrongly. In any case, this would not have been good enough for Gardner, so in the week before their next meeting he found the most impressive document that he could in a hurry, which turned out to be a 70-year old land record. He copied down Crowley's charter onto the document, making mistakes as he went along, and adding little bits that he thought sounded good.

Whether Crowley did sign and seal this unlikely document produced by Gardner, including filling in what "O.T.O." stood for, or whether he never actually saw that version of the Charter at all and that Gardner forged Crowley's signature, I don't know. I'm sure that Gardner wouldn't have thought of it as forgery. After all, Crowley had granted him authority - all he was doing was making a more impressive Charter than the one on ordinary paper that Crowley had signed. It wasn't intended to be a fake but a copy. Cornelius adds:

*Crowley was notorious for doing everything very similar. I don't doubt that he* [did] *scribble a quick note off giving Gardner some sort of authority ... However, Gardner's ego might have wanted something 'more' or maybe what he purchased didn't look impressive enough to flaunt (if stories are correct about money being exchanged). There is no way he could have known that this was all anyone ever got out of Crowley. In other words, Gardner might have felt cheated for the money he spent by getting a one-page handwritten document scribbled on a regular piece of paper. He may well have copied Crowley's signature from his 'real' document onto the parchment simply to impress people, possibly believing that this would have been his charter had it not been* [for] *Crowley's failing health. Of course it's not like anything AC had ever previously used.*[58]

On balance, I think the correct explanation is that Crowley did sign and seal the document, filling in the blanks left by Gardner, but that he was clearly in failing health which meant that not only did he not spot the errors of wording but that his signature and Baphometic cross were not as elaborate as usual.

Sutin confirms this when he states: This [the first meeting between Crowley and Gardner] was roughly six months before Crowley's death, and for most of that time, Crowley was in a state of severe decline.[59]

## Progress, or lack of it, on an Encampment

Gardner is mentioned two further times only (making four in total) in Crowley's diary:

*Wed 14 May: G.B.G.*
*Tues 27 May: Gardner here*

It is interesting that for the first of these entries, Crowley uses Gardner's initials - GBG. This probably amused Crowley because they are the same initials as those of the magical order, the Greater Brotherhood of God, which was mentioned earlier in this chapter. Anyway, these are the last entries that refer to Gardner, but there is only one further page of the diary, presumably because of Crowley's health (and, of course, he died in December the same year).

It was therefore possibly at their meeting on 14th May that Crowley added to and signed and sealed the Charter prepared by Gardner. At what was probably their last meeting, on 27th May, it seems likely that Crowley agreed to Gardner overseeing the Minerval degree, for a letter from Crowley to W.B. Crow, dated just three days later, on 30th May 1947, states:

*I suggest that you refer all your following in the London district to Dr Gardner so that he may put them properly through the Minerval degree, and some of them at least might help him to establish the camps for the higher degrees up to Perfect Initiate or Prince of Jerusalem.*[60]

Crowley had annotated the letter, stating "A Camp, very good, will be ready in a few weeks".

Gardner had obviously written to Crow informing him of what was going on, probably because Crowley had referred to him in their conversation, and Gardner realised that he already knew him, through his friendship with J.S.M. Ward.

Crowley then started to send any enquiries about the O.T.O. to Gardner. Copies of letters sent by Crowley to prospective candidates still exist. Indeed, Crowley wrote to Gardner on 10th June, probably setting out more details about the Minerval degree, and enclosing a list of people for Gardner to contact.

## Trip to America

It seems as if Gardner did very little to establish an Encampment following his meetings with Crowley. Davis[61] suggests that the two may have quarrelled, but the most likely reason lay in Gardner's health. In the summer of 1947 he was 63 years old and he became fairly ill. We do not know what was wrong with him but it may well have been a recurrence of his asthma (the so-called 'occultists' disease', from which Crowley also suffered). In any case, his doctor advised spending the winter abroad in a more congenial climate.

The war having ended, he turned his sights to America. His younger brother, Douglas, to whom he had been very close in his youth, was involved with the family timber industry on the Mississippi and had settled in Memphis, Tennessee with his wife Miriam and their daughter, Mimi. Mimi had stayed with Gerald and Donna in London the previous year.

So Gardner arranged a convalescent trip lasting for several months from late November 1947 until March 1948 (ironically, he was there in December 1947 when Crowley died). Gerald and Donna stayed with Douglas and Miriam in their small red-brick house at 282 Strathmore Circle, Memphis. Douglas was nearly blind and Gerald spent a lot of his time helping him with his everyday activities.[62]

Nevertheless, there were opportunities for travel, including a trip to New Orleans to study voodoo and a possible visit to California to meet Jack Parsons, who was running an O.T.O. chapter (the Agape Lodge) at the time Gardner was in Memphis. It was, indeed, to this chapter that Crowley's ashes were sent. Parsons had had published in 1946 *Liber 49 - The Book of Babalon* which forecast the revival of witchcraft in covens of 11, which was the Thelemic number of magic, rather than the traditional 13. He followed this up with *Magick, Gnosticism and the Witchcraft*. Gardner may well have been interested in meeting Parsons for this reason alone, although Jarving says:

*As for Parsons essays on witchcraft, dating from that same period, they bear no resemblance whatsoever to anything in ... "High Magic's Aid" or any other of his writings. Of course GBG coud've sparked off an interest in Parsons, without there being any similarities, but it seems as likely that Parsons may have been inspired by Leland's "Aradia", from the phrases he uses. If he had been in correspondence with GBG, or even in cohorts with him to raise Wicca, there would've been similarities somewhere. But there's none."*[63]

So at present it is rather uncertain whether Gardner actually met Parsons, or the extent to which they may have influenced each other.

However, he certainly met Germer, Crowley's successor. Gardner was intending to sail back to England from New York on 19th March 1948 and wrote to Germer arranging to visit him. Bracelin reports that the visit did in fact take place:

*In New York he met 'Saturnus', the enormous, hearty yet somehow seemingly humourless German who was, if anyone, Crowley's successor. He was interested to start a Crowley museum, and was looking for a house for it which he eventually found.*[64]

But, as Morgan Davis says:

*What actually happened between Gardner and Germer in New York is ultimately a mystery. ... Germer could have endorsed Gardner's claim and instructed him to continue his plans to start an encampment in England, but this encampment never materialized.*[65]

## Head of OTO in Europe?

The O.T.O. was in a moribund state in England when Crowley died, and it was generally acknowledged that Gardner, virtually by default, was head of the O.T.O. in Europe. Bracelin reports that : ...*Gardner found that many people seemed to regard him as Crowley's successor: though he was nothing of the sort.*[66]

Frieda Harris, in a post-script to a letter to Germer (Crowley's actual successor) dated 2nd January 1948 stated clearly that Gardner was the head of the OTO in Europe,[67] even though in a letter less than a month before to Frederick Mellinger, she was writing as a post-script: "Are you the head of the order here or was Gerald Gardner. I can't find him, I fancy he died?".[68] This was during the time Gardner was in America, which might explain why she failed to find him. Obviously in the intervening month someone had enlightened her about him, possibly Vernon Symonds, to whom Gardner had just written. This certainly makes it clear that Gardner considered himself to be such, and also that he was trying to gather material together. The letter is dated 24th December 1947, i.e. just over three weeks after Crowley had died. It says:

*... Aleister gave me a charter making me head of the O.T.O. in Europe. Now I want to get any papers about this that Aleister had; he had some typescript Rituals, I know. I have them, too, but I don't want his to fall into other people's hands, I'll buy them off the Executors at a reasonable price, together with any*

*other relics they may be willing to sell.*[69]

It was clear from this that Gardner hadn't really got to grips with things. For example, he referred to Crowley in his letter as 'Aleister', effecting a presumed familiarity, but one which seems at odds with how others closer to Crowley actually referred to him, usually as 'A.C.'. Gardner seemed to know very little about the O.T.O. and its history and was trying to find out what material there was.

It is also clear that Gardner was keener on collecting papers and other material than he was on reading and understanding them. He was certainly, as usual, concerned about information falling into the wrong hands, or rather wanting to consolidate his position and become the main source of information.

Kwaw states that: *After Crowley's death, Gardner wrote to Crowley's solicitor claiming that as "Head of the OTO in Britain" he, Gardner, was rightful heir to Crowley's goods and papers.*[70] Nothing came of this, however.

Geoffrey Smith states:

*In order to be "Head" of the OTO ("in Europe" [sic] or anywhere else) Gardner would have had to be a X[degree] at least (i.e. a National Grand Master) - but there was no such post! (i.e. a continental 'Head')*[71]

## The Enthusiasm Wanes

It appears that Gardner was really getting out of his depth. He was asking others for papers and suchlike, but he really didn't have any idea what to do and, following his return to England in March 1948, things ground to a halt. He didn't have the enthusiasm for the O.T.O. rituals and philosophy, insofar as he understood them, and, I imagine, was not prepared for the discipline and flexibility which working with other members of the O.T.O. entailed. Gardner wrote to John Symonds:

*I tried to start an order, but I got ill, & had to leave the Country, After his death word was sent to Germer that I was head of the order in Europe, & Germer acknowledged me as such. But owing to ill health I so far havent been able to get anything going. I had some people interested, but some of them were sent to Germany with the Army of Occupation & others live far away & so far nothing has happned. Actually, I havent all the rituals. The K.T. ritual has been lost, Gerald York thinks it may never have been writen. I have up to Prince of Jerusalam. You dont know about the lost degrees I suppose?* [72]

Gardner claims in this letter to be head of the order in Europe (not just in Britain), but also makes it clear that he was never active in setting anything up, probably partly due to his health. Bracelin quotes Gardner as saying: "I had neither the money, energy nor time"[73]. Gerald Yorke confirmed that "Gardner never opened a camp"[74].

Geoffrey Smith says:

*Gardner ... had not time to run the O.T.O. 'camp' authorised by Crowley and when the then O.H.O. Germer got a request* [in 1951] *for a charter from Kenneth Grant, he, after checking that Gardner had no intention of activating his 'camp', gave Grant a charter also allowing him to work the first three degrees of the O.T.O. system..*[75]

## The Book of Shadows

It has been a persistent rumour that Gardner paid Crowley to write his Book of Shadows for him. Francis King says unequivocally: "He ... hired Crowley, at a generous fee, to write elaborate rituals for the new 'Gardnerian' witch-cult ..."[76] But really, there doesn't seem to be any evidence for this.

Probably Gardner paid Crowley for the Charter and for various books and papers, but that is all. There is little in the Book of Shadows that 'smacks of Crowley', to use Gardner's phrase, which cannot be identified in one or other of Crowley's published works. In other words, there is no evidence that Crowley wrote anything specifically for Gardner, which is not to say that there is no Crowley material in the Book of Shadows.

Doreen Valiente [77] recalls that Gerald Yorke had told her "Well, you know, Gerald Gardner paid old Crowley about £300 or so for that." Now, this is probably the equivalent of upwards of £5000 today, which undoubtedly Gardner could well afford. This amount has been queried, for example by Morgan Davis who, knowing that Crowley left only £18 on his death apart from his property and effects, argues: "It would have been an impressive feat for an ill old man to spend £300 in a matter of six months just before his death ..."[78] However, it is clear from his diary entries that he was relying on contributions from his supporters in order to buy drugs: £300 from Gardner would thus have been very welcome and enough to permit any "bending of the rules" that might have been required. Nevertheless, whilst Crowley was meticulous in his diary entries about noting down these contributions, there is no mention of £300, or indeed any amount, from Gardner, so the story must be doubted on those grounds alone.

Valiente also says:

*It has been alleged that a Book of Shadows in Crowley's handwriting was formerly exhibited in Gerald's Museum of Witchcraft on the Isle of Man. I can only say I never saw this on either of the two occasions when I stayed with Gerald and Donna Gardner on the island. The large, handwritten book depicted in Witchcraft Today is not in Crowley's handwriting, but Gerald's...*[79]

In fact, rather surprisingly knowing his public persona, Crowley's handwriting is actually not very distinctive at all: it doesn't stand out in any way. Gardner's script, in contrast, particularly when he was writing out rituals to be seen from a distance or, indeed, the Charter, is very distinctive.

What might have happened is that someone saw the Charter on display at the museum, noted the distinctive character of the writing and, not unreasonably, assumed that it had been written by Crowley. Also on display was Gardner's Book of Shadows in the same script and the individual concerned therefore quite reasonably, but wrongly, deduced that Crowley had also written the Book of Shadows. And that is how rumours start!

The descriptive pamphlet for the Museum of Magic and Witchcraft says:

*The collection includes a Charter granted by Aleister Crowley to G.B. Gardner (the Director of this Museum) to operate a Lodge of Crowley's fraternity, the Ordo Templi Orientis. (The Director would like to point out, however, that he has never used this Charter and has no intention of doing so, although to the best of his belief he is the only person in Britain possessing such a Charter from Crowley himself; Crowley was a personal friend of his, and gave him the Charter because he liked him.)*[80]

This distancing of himself from Crowley is something which Gardner did increasingly over several years, as interest in witchcraft and the museum grew. As Greenfield puts it:

*The explanation for the curious wording of the Text, taking, as Dr. Gardner does, great pains to distance himself from*

31. Part of the Crowley exhibit at the Museum of Magic and Witchcraft (courtesy of Nicholas Culpeper)

*Crowley and the OTO, may be hinted at in that the booklet* [museum guide] *suggests that this display in the 'new upper gallery' (page 24) was put out at a relatively late date when ... Gardner was making himself answerable to the demands of the new* [sic] *witch cult and not the long-dead Crowley and (then) relatively moribund OTO* [81]

This story of his involvement with Crowley and the O.T.O. illustrates how Gardner's enthusiasms could wax and wane very quickly. The latest interest took all his energy until something else arrived to take it over.

## Conclusion

I think Gardner wanted to meet Crowley when the opportunity arose because he was impressed by what he had read of Crowley's writings.

At their meeting, Crowley clearly "buttered Gardner up", probably partly because he saw in him someone who might revive the O.T.O. in England, but perhaps also because he felt he could persuade Gardner to part with money which he needed badly for drugs. Gardner liked the idea of being "Head of the O.T.O. in Europe" and agreed to whatever Crowley suggested, in the way of financial contributions.

However, Gardner was unrealistic and when he realised that he would have to do some work organising an O.T.O. encampment, he wasn't prepared for it. Indeed, he still had a very hazy understanding of O.T.O. beliefs and practices. As time went on, it became clear that Gardner had neither the will nor the ability to solve the numerous problems which he encountered. This may have been in part because of his illness and subsequent convalescent trip to America.

Gardner and Crowley were two very different personalities and working within a magical order would never have suited Gardner. To start with, Gardner was not happy working within an existing structure where he was not free to indulge his own fantasies. He was certainly not prepared for the disciplined study which was needed to fully familiarise himself with the O.T.O. teachings. He was far too eclectic and mercurial. He was also not prepared to be given work to do - the organisation of an encampment was really beyond his ability. I also suspect that he contrasted what seemed to him to be the male orientation of the O.T.O. with the greater emphasis on the feminine which the Wica had shown him.

He began to feel increasingly uncomfortable with the O.T.O. and I guess that on his return to England in March 1948, particularly following his meeting with Germer, he took no more active part in it. By the time he returned to England, Crowley was dead and it became obvious that Gardner would do nothing further in connection with the O.T.O. organisation.

His sights turned towards his next project - a novel which had as its theme the beliefs and practices of the witches themselves.

## Chapter 10

# High Magic's Aid

### Back to the Witches

Gardner returned to England in March 1948 probably rather disillusioned with the reality of what involvement with the O.T.O. would mean. Crowley was dead and his attraction, for Gardner, seemed to die with him. During his stay in America, Gardner had had time to think. Why was he getting involved in a magical order whose rituals and practices seemed to be leading him in a direction away from his natural inclinations? After all, he had a tradition of his own - the Craft of the Wica - and he had a witch's cottage to perform rituals in. His enthusiasm for witchcraft returned and a book which he had been writing, off and on, for several years, took on renewed importance.

When he first asked the witches (in reality probably just Edith) whether he could write about what she had told him, Gardner met with a straight refusal. But he was up in London, and Edith and the others in Highcliffe were not exactly dynamic. He needed more people, younger people, and his mind turned again to the blank refusal his suggestion for publicity had met in the early days. Perhaps he should try again.

As Patricia Crowther says:

*...having been a close friend of Gerald's, I knew he could be very persuasive and convincing in his ideas. ... he had not*

*wanted to see the Craft die out. And how were people to become interested in it, if they did not know it still existed?* [1]

The idea of fiction as a medium to put over certain principles of the Craft probably came to Gardner after the initial refusal. He had some experience of writing fiction - *A Goddess Arrives* had been published in 1939 and it is highly likely that he would have given each of his new friends a copy, so they were familiar with his skills in that direction, which were considerable. Also, he had written about witchcraft in *A Goddess Arrives*, although this was written about a period when animal and human sacrifice took place, and he was now anxious to write about the witches as he knew them.

Gardner had probably secretly started work on what became *High Magic's Aid* at odd moments throughout the war years. He wasn't sure at that stage how much he would be allowed to say about the witches' beliefs and practices, but he had, I suspect, quite a good idea of the story and got quite a bit of writing done before he got permission to go ahead and publish it.

He had a freer hand in a work of fiction to give details of witch beliefs and practices without it being obvious that they were other than pure invention. Unless the hint was given that it was something more, the book could be read as a simple historical adventure story with elements of magic and witchcraft woven into it. At the same time, it could perform the function of an introductory guide to the 'Craft of the Wise' - the only one available - and Gardner would be prepared to give copies to those whom he thought ready to receive it.

In a letter to John Symonds, Gardner wrote about *High Magic's Aid*: *A.C. [Aleister Crowley] read part of the M.S. & highly approved. He wanted me to put the Witch part in full.* [2]

This must have been no later than June 1947, the last time that Gardner met Crowley, so parts at least of the manuscript must have been in a state to read at that date, over two years before publication.

The interlude with Crowley, the O.T.O. and Gardner's illness (see Chapter 9) took up most of the year from April 1947 to April 1948. It is my guess that it was in the Spring of 1948 that he took up the as yet unnamed manuscript again. And in May that year, Rosamund Sabine died. I don't think Edith told Gardner of this, since five years later he thought her death had been 'recent', but it clearly affected Edith's attitude to publicity, as she seems to have relented somewhat and Gardner finally got the permission he wanted:

*So, against their better judgement, they agreed to let me write a little about the cult in the form of fiction, an historical novel where a witch says a little of what they believe and of how they were persecuted.*[3]

This permission was certainly qualified, as Gardner told Symonds: ... *I was only given permission to publish things as fiction, & they* [i.e. the witches] *could cut out what they liked.*[4] In fact, by the time he got this permission, it seems likely that the book was actually substantially complete.

Yet, what had Gardner been allowed to say? Edith had been very strict about what could and couldn't be included, as Gardner makes very clear in a letter to a Mr. Gordon B... in America which Patricia Crowther quotes in her Foreword:

*...Actually, I wanted to write about a witch and what she'd told me, and she wouldn't let me tell anything about witchcraft, but I said why not let me write from the Witch's point of view. You are always persecuted and abused ... So she said I might if I didn't give any Witch's magic, and it must only be as fiction. So, as I had to give some magic, I simply copied it from Jewish Ritual Magic, chiefly "The Key of Solomon the King". It was thought that King Solomon could*

command the spirits and make them work for him. And if you know these words and sigils you could do the same. This key is usually in Latin or Hebrew, but there is an English translation by MacGregor Mathers. But personally I don't believe that it works. It's all very difficult and complicated ...[5]

Gardner obtained a manuscript copy (probably in facsimile) of *The Key of Solomon the King* from Gerald Yorke in June 1947, and I think it was following this, and probably mainly in 1948, that he incorporated material from it into his book. In addition, this provided an obvious name for the book, *High Magic's Aid* describing very clearly much of the theme.

Fred Lamond states: *...Don Frew ... claims to have seen a letter, sent by Gerald to a friend around 1948 explaining why he had used a kabbalistic initiation ritual in his description of a witch's initiation in High Magic's Aid: "I don't like it and find it too heavy and ceremonial for a witch's initiation. But what can I do, since I have been forbidden to reveal the actual initiation rite!"* [6] However, the first and second degree initiation rituals in *High Magic's Aid* are not overtly kabbalistic in content, so did Gardner, in the end, get permission to put the genuine witch rituals in the book?

He certainly tried to put the genuine 3rd degree ritual in because he tells Symonds: I wrote the third degree of the Witch Cult, but they went up in steam, & cut it out entirely.[7] He continues:

*... of course things have been changed a little in the ritual, but Ive got it as nearyl as thay do it, to the great scare of the publishers, but no one has objected in the slightest so far.*[8]

If Gardner had tried to put the genuine 3rd degree ritual in the book, it is, I think, reasonable to assume that he would also have tried to put the genuine 1st and 2nd degree rituals in as well (in terms of the story as much as anything else).

The fact that it was only the 3rd degree about which they "went up in steam" implies that they allowed the genuine 1st and 2nd degree rituals to be included.

Also, even assuming that they weren't the genuine rituals, Gardner would surely have used the proper ones in any actual (and secret) initiation rituals that he carried out. Yet we have the evidence from the works of Patricia Crowther and Doreen Valiente, plus Charles Cardell's *Witch*, that the rituals included in *High Magic's Aid* were, in essence, the rituals that he actually used.

Perhaps having written a "heavy and ceremonial" kabbalistic initiation ritual for the book and the strength of his feeling that it wasn't right, he approached Edith again and finally persuaded her of the need to include the genuine initiation rituals, subject to certain alterations and omissions. He may have tried to slip in the 3rd degree as well, presumably without agreement, which is why she "went up in steam".

## The Theme of the Book

But what did Gardner want to say in the book? He was already an accomplished author, with a very competent novel, *A Goddess Arrives*, under his belt, and there is, I suspect, once one has had one book published, the strong desire to write another one - it is certainly true in my own case! On one level, Gardner wanted to write a story, and what more natural than to use as a theme the Craft into which he had been initiated? In one way, it was an advantage to be writing a work of fiction. As Dion Fortune says: *Writers will put things into a novel that they daren't put in sober prose, where you have to dot the Is and cross the Ts.* [9]

Theoretically, Gardner was not limited to what the witches had told him: he could embellish and add exactly what he wanted to. He could make things up, alter traditions and beliefs and the reading public would be none the wiser. They would think of it as a good (or not so good!) story and that would be that. But he wasn't satisfied with this. He wanted to use the medium of this latest book to tell something of what the witches that he had met believed and did.

Since it had to be a work of fiction, he couldn't actually say that witches still existed, however much he might have wanted to, so it had to be set at some time in the past. However, he would be able to include something about witch beliefs and practices, although no witch magic. This restriction probably gave him one of the main themes for the book, as well as its title. He included ceremonial magic and the title of *High Magic's Aid*, probably fairly late in the process because he wasn't allowed to put in any witch magic. So Gardner used magic derived from various grimoires, including the *Key of Solomon*, turning the restriction into a key theme, that of "High Magic's Aid", in other words how ceremonial magic can help the simpler magical techniques of the witch.

Or rather, it is perhaps an example of "mutual aid", for, despite its title, one essential theme of the book is how witchcraft can assist 'High Magic' rather than the other way round. The protagonists are wanting to carry out magical working, which they can only do with the aid of a witch's consecrated tools and, indeed, the witch herself. As Gardner told Symonds, High Magic needed a medium to make it work, "which is best obtained from witches"[10] The presence of the witch character in the book, Morven, allows Gardner to introduce some witch philosophy, rituals and other witch practices in the guise of fiction.

## The Story

An advertisement which appeared in *The Occult Observer* described the book as follows:

*Here is a book of medieval witchcraft and magic in fiction form. The author has made thorough investigations into the rituals and ceremonies of magic circles with formulae and invocations. It is exceedingly readable and many have expressed their appreciation of its approach to the study of this fascinating subject. It is an exciting tale carrying the reader through an historical period when worship of the secret witch-cult was practised in spite of the persecution of the Church.* [11]

*High Magic's Aid* is an adventure story set in 13th Century England, of which the central theme is the use of magic and witchcraft to recapture land and property which had been usurped by a Norman baron. It has been described as a pastiche of Sir Walter Scott's *Ivanhoe*.

The young heroes, Jan and Olaf, are seeking to reclaim the land stolen from their father, Edgar Bonder, by the hated Norman Fitz-Urse. They seek the help of Thur Peterson, a medical practitioner, or 'leech', who is also adept at ritual magic, having learnt this at Cordoba in Spain.

The main magical theme is that in order to work their magic they need properly consecrated tools, which can only be made with other consecrated tools. They thus needed to find either another ritual magician or a witch. An elaborate ritual, based on *The Key of Solomon the King* is enacted, which results in the message "Seek the Witch of Wanda".

They search for the hamlet of Wanda and find Vada, a young half-starved and persecuted woman living on her own whom Thur recognises to be a witch from certain comments which she makes. The witch-hunt are following close, however, and the four have to depart in haste, just giving Vada enough time to dig up her mother's ritual knives which had been buried for safety in the garden. They have a narrow escape and are forced to keep under cover during the day, travelling only at night. To protect her identity, Vada takes on her witch-name of Morven and gradually assumes a rounder appearance through better nourishment.

After a stay in London, where it was easier to mingle with the crowd, Thur returns to his home town of St. Clare-in-Walden, with Morven, who assumes the identity of his niece whom he has taken under his wing following the death of her parents. Morven sets up home in Thur's house under the eye of Alice, Thur's housekeeper.

Further magical rituals take place to consecrate the necessary magical tools, but Jan is keen to raise an army to claim his inheritance. To help in this, Morven travels with the brothers to their home village wearing the red garters which indicate a high position within the Craft. These act as a sign to those who are members and she is invited to speak before a gathering which is assembled in the forest at the next full moon. She introduces Jan and he is accepted by those assembled as leader of a force to win back the castle usurped by Fitz-Urse. Later, magical ritual is again used to find the one individual, Even Gull's Egg, who knows the way into the stronghold.

In the meantime, Thur, Jan and Olaf are initiated into the first degree of witchcraft by Morven, and then Thur and Jan are taken through the second degree initiation.

The story ends with Fitz-Urse being defeated, the castle and lands being won back, and with the death of Thur in battle.

The one historical figure in the story is Stephen Langton, who seems to have been sympathetic to the Craft and who, perhaps by magical means, became Archbishop of Canterbury overnight from being an "utterly unknown man", according to Gardner.

*High Magic's Aid* should not be judged by its literary qualities: its importance lies in its author and what he revealed through it. But accepting this, there is a wide range of opinions about the book. Francis King [12] called it "long and almost unreadable", whereas Patricia Crowther has referred to it as "An exciting atmospheric novel ...its author...has encapsulated fascinating magical rituals which draw the reader into the scenes, as though actually experiencing them"[13] I certainly found it a good story and vividly written, although I am not competent to comment on its historical accuracy.

## The Witch Parts

Patricia Crowther has told me that the words of the witch rituals given in *High Magic's Aid* and which have generally been used since the book was published, whilst genuine, are not complete, and she has noted several important omissions, in order that certain things were deliberately concealed.[14]

But if the main reason that Gardner wrote *High Magic's Aid* was to give an indication of what witches believed and did, which parts of it provide that information? Bracelin states that: *...only the words used by the witch who is its heroine were claimed to be truly authentic.* [15] Patricia Crowther, commenting on this, says: *This is interesting in view of what Gerald said when he presented me with a copy of "High Magic's Aid" in 1960, "Darling, take notice of Morven's words, they will teach you much."*[16] It is interesting that he said this, even after *Witchcraft Today* and *The Meaning of Witchcraft* had been published, so there must be something revealed in Morven's words which are not in the other two books.

We may expect that Gardner would put a description of the beliefs and practices of the witches into the mouth of the witch who features in the story, and an examination of Morven's words does indeed give a picture of what Gardner calls 'the witch cult' in terms of its history, the powers of a witch, and numerous insights into the rituals which form part of the story.

Referring to *High Magic's Aid*, in a letter to Symonds[17] Gardner wrote: *The witchcraft parts are chap XIV Dearleap, & XVII The Witch Cult.* And, in *Witchcraft Today*, Gardner states: *They* [i.e. the witches] *showed me one queer trick with music which I described in my novel High Magic's Aid, in the chapter called 'Music Magic'.*[18] So, taking into account these three chapters, plus Morven's words where they occur throughout the book, what can we deduce about what Gardner wanted to convey about witch beliefs and practices?

The story Morven tells is of a young girl brought by her mother into a thriving faith where the members have magical and mystical powers. There are themes which are repeated in Gardner's first non-fiction book on witchcraft, *Witchcraft Today* - an emphasis on rebirth, the hereditary principle and nudity. Another is that the Craft came originally from the East. Also, the witches believed their gods were not all-powerful.

They believed in rebirth: *"Why," said she, "having rested for a while in the lovely country on the other side of life, we come back again, and are reborn on this earth. We ever progress, but to progress we must learn, and to learn oft means suffering. What we endure in this life fits us for a better existence in the next, and so we be heartened to endure all the troubles and trials here, for we know that they but help us to higher things. Thus the gods teach us to look forward to the time when we be not men any more...but gods!"*[19]

## Witches' Magic

Gardner seems to some extent to have ignored Edith's ban on the mention of any witch magic, as there are actually some very interesting magical and divinatory techniques described which are not repeated in his subsequent non-fiction books.

Morven speaks about a range of magical techniques as practised by the witches, which contrasts markedly with the ceremonial magic which also features prominently. These include divination by Drawing Down the Moon, the use of herbal cures, the scourge, trance mediumship, scrying and 'psychological' techniques such as those for invisibility.

The main magical theme of the book is that Thur, the magician, needs some tools that have been properly consecrated, particularly the knife. He is told to seek out a witch for these, which he does, but he finds that she herself can act as a catalyst for magical workings. Gardner has her saying: "... they said that I helped by giving power from my body. My coming was likened to the opening of the sluices of a water-mill for the power it gave to work marvels." [20]

Their divinatory techniques seemed to have a shamanic element. Morven is quoted as saying:

*"They also said that the witches' learning came secretly from these same old gods [Greek]. The Greek witches could draw down the Spirit of the Moon." "Artemis?" She flashed him an admiring glance. "Truly you are a learned man, Thur. Yes, Artemis. She could reveal the future and help gain the love of men. We used to invoke Ardrea, the daughter of Artemis." "How was that done?" "By sitting in a circle with a little drum we used for dancing. This was placed in the centre, and we laid our fingers lightly on the skin and asked questions of Ardrea. She answered Yes, or No, by tilting the drum. We had warnings of danger and much good advice that way."* [21]

A well-established witch divinatory technique is scrying, as indicated in the following passage, which also reveals Gardner's attitude to spiritualism:

*"Some witches there were who could read the hour of death on the face, or the future fate. Always they promised me sorrow, to*

*be followed by joy...and sorrow I have had aplenty. ... Others there were who would fall into a sleep and the spirits would enter their bodies, speaking with the lips but not the voices of the sleepers. Women would speak with the voice of a man, and men with a woman's pipe."* "Ah," cried Thur more hopefully, "and what said they?" She shrugged. *"Little, I fear. Warnings of danger or sorrow. What they foretold would come to pass, but methinks how to avoid direness would have been more to the purpose. When they wakened they knew naught of what they had said. ... Some there were who would look into a pool of water or a magic stone, and see visions of what was happening at a distance, and so we would be warned of approaching danger. ..."*[22]

There were also techniques of the mind, or what we might loosely call 'psychology':

*"Many of the farm folk who see us may be 'of the brotherhood'. Let us each wear a bit of white cloth behind us, like rabbits' scuts. ... Any brother who sees us wearing them will know that we wish to travel unseen, and even under torture will swear that they saw nothing but four rabbits on the road. Long ago we found that if a man swore under torture that he saw none, his eyes betrayed him, but if he believed that in some mystical way we are transformed into rabbits, he will maintain that he saw naught but rabbits to his death! Aye, 'tis queer, but 'tis so."*[23]

There is also a section on the way that witches became invisible, which is largely the matter of having the confidence to play a part convincingly:
*"Thus do we witches, ever bearing in mind that invisibility is not a lack of sight in all beholders, but lack of observation. Any but the blind may see, but he who carries the spell is not marked by all about him."*
*"Your witchcraft, it seems, is very much a thing of the mind...the dominance of the witch's mind over her*

*surroundings."*

*"Truly. A thing of much accurate observation, and knowledge of what people do, and may do in certain events. The witch holds the mind of those she would influence. 'Tis simple. An old woman with a load may come and go unnoticed, so long as her behaviour is that of an old woman with a load.."*

*"So if she hurry, or stop to glance about her, she would be marked?"*

*"Yes, always one so disguised wears the charm of the Talisman with such confidence that she knows none may note her. As she sees herself in her own mind, so do others see her. But if she trusts not in the powers she wears and lets fear taint her mind, then does she impart fear to those about her. They see her furtiveness, mark her, remember her, question her, and take her."* [24]

Gardner also gives a hint of the relevance of Chapter XI "Music Magic", when he writes in *Witchcraft Today* that it was based on something which happened to him:

*They showed me one queer trick with music which I described in my novel High Magic's Aid, in the chapter called 'Music Magic'. They told me they could make me fighting mad; I did not believe it, so they got me to sit, fixed in a chair so that I could not get out. Then one sat in front of me playing a little drum; not a tune, just a steady tom-tom-tom. We were laughing and talking at first ... it seemed a long time, although I could see the clock and knew it was not. The tom-tom-tom went on and I felt silly; they were watching me and grinning and those grins made me angry. I did realise that the tom-tomming seemed to be a little quicker and my heart seemed to be beating very hard. I felt flushes of heat, I was angry at their silly grins. Suddenly I felt furiously angry and wanted to pull loose out of the chair; I tugged out and would have gone for them, but as soon as I started moving they changed their beat and I was not angry any longer.*

*I said: 'It is just suggestion,' but they insisted it was something more - that it was an old secret and could be used to make men fighting mad before a charge.*[25]

## Dearleap

Chapter XIV is entitled "Dearleap", the title of which refers to a place in the forest where the witches met. Gardner describes it thus:

*... they saw an outcrop of high rocks at one end of a big clearing. On closer view it proved to be a natural amphitheatre, grass grown, wide at the base, upon whose boulder-strewn sides many people were assembled.*[26]

This is clearly not in the New Forest, as there are no rock outcrops of any sort, and it seems to be a product of Gardner's imagination - a sort of ideal meeting-place, perhaps, that many of us might fantasise about.

Neither does 'Dearleap' appear on any Ordnance Survey map, as far as I am aware, but 'Deerleap' does, and it seems to make more sense as well, as deer are apt to leap. One suspects a spelling error on Gardner's part which never got corrected! There is certainly a Deerleap Inclosure on the north-eastern edge of the forest not far from Lyndhurst and it may well be that Gardner was telling us indirectly to look closer at it, or perhaps he just liked the name! De Crespigny and Hutchinson say the following:

*Deer-Leap, not far from Lyndhurst, owes its name to an incident recorded by Gilpin. A stag was shot, and in its dying effort made so great a bound, that the distance was deemed worthy of being recorded by two posts planted in the ground -*

*the one at the spot from which the stag took off, the other at the spot on which he landed. The measurement from post to post is eighteen yards.*[27]

There are further such recorded 'leaps' in other parts of the country. In Lincolnshire, for example, is Byard's Leap, where a local legend involving a witch relates in part to the great leaps of a horse of that name which are to this day commemorated in sets of horse-shoes fixed into the ground.

This chapter is about a large gathering of the adherents of the Old Religion in the woods at night at which Morven speaks to those so assembled. There are certain elements which seem significant because they have become part of the modern Craft. Firstly the gathering is held at Full Moon. Margaret Murray does not appear to mention this, but it is certainly prominent in Leland's *Aradia*. Secondly, nudity is much in evidence and Morven appears naked amongst the assembled gathering. Other motifs that feature in this chapter are the use of the athame (the witches' ritual black-handled knife), chanting and harps (something which has not generally survived into the modern Craft) and a follow-my-leader dance, which Gardner also refers to in *Witchcraft Today*.

## The Witch Cult

The most remarkable section in the book, Chapter XVII consists of Morven taking the male characters through the first and second degree initiation rituals, which she calls the triangle and the pentagram respectively. The rituals are familiar to those who are practising Gardnerians and those of derivative traditions, plus others who have read of them in the books of the Farrars, Doreen Valiente, and Patricia Crowther. It is striking, to those who are familiar with the form of Craft initiations, to find the first printed versions of them in virtually the same wording that is often still used.

Even to those approaching them for the first time, they seem strangely mature for what, on the surface, is merely a chapter in a story. There is a certain richness about the text which leads me to suppose that it was taken wholesale from another source, presumably a witch's book. And, apart from the general influence of masonic practice, probably from Co-Masonry, and the Golden Dawn, the only known source of any part of these rituals is the *Key of Solomon*. This theme will be explored further in Chapter 13.

I believe that what we have here is the basic structure of pre-Gardner rituals. I am not claiming that these are ancient - I suspect that they date from no earlier than the 1920s, but I am reasonably clear that they were not invented for the purpose of one chapter in *High Magic's Aid*.

The third degree ritual is barely hinted at in the book, presumably all that Gardner felt able to write after the witches 'went up in steam':

*"There is but one degree more," she said. "Where you take an oath and are made to use the working tools, but after that, there is what is called a degree. There is no oath, and all who have taken the second degree are qualified to work it, but 'tis the quintessence of Magic, and 'tis not to be used lightly, and then only with one whom you love and are loved by, may it be done, all else were sin."* [28]

## The Creative Re-use of Material

Morven says much that subsequently appears (often in virtually the same words) in *Witchcraft Today* where Gardner claims to be quoting what the witches told him. This does not necessarily imply any deception on his part: it could reasonably be argued that he had accumulated material and statements on what the witches believed and experienced which he incorporated into *High Magic's Aid*, but that when he could write more openly about it all, in *Witchcraft Today*, he made use of the same material, and was able to give it in a more straightforward way and in a factual context. I suspect he took the passages from a notebook into which he put various things as they mentioned them to him.

In any case, they are obviously important passages to him. To quote just two:

*We worship the divine spirit of Creation, which is the Life-spring of the world, and without which the world would perish ... To us it is the most sacred and holy mystery, proof of the God within us whose command is: 'Go forth and multiply'* [Morven in *High Magic's Aid*][29]

The quotation is identical in *Witchcraft Today* up to "holy mystery". It then goes on:

*... proof that God is within us whose command is: 'Go forth and multiply'. Such rites are done in a holy and reverent way.*[30]

In the second passage, Morven is saying:

*When the brotherhood was strong, they ever picked out those who had a little natural power and they were taught, and practised one with another, and they developed their powers.*[31]

*In Witchcraft Today*, this passage is as follows:

*Another* [witch] *said: 'We ever pick out those who have a little inherent power and teach them, and they practise one with the other and they develop these powers.*[32]

I think what probably happened was this. Gardner had jotted down in a notebook what are some very evocative pieces from what the witches told him. Years later, he put them into his archaicised form of English and into the mouth of Morven in *High Magic's Aid*. After having written *Witchcraft Today*, he remembered these passages and, because they were genuine things that the witches told him, he added them to the text. It is perhaps significant that they are all in the same section of the last chapter of *Witchcraft Today* - Chapter 13 - "Recapitulation", almost as if, after Gardner had written the book, he realised that he still had quite a lot of material that the witches had told him which he hadn't included (perhaps he found that long lost notebook!) and so he tried to put it all into one extra chapter. Certainly there is a much higher proportion of 'relevant' material in this chapter than in any of the others, some of it also appearing in later versions of the Book of Shadows.

Other passages cannot be so easily explained. *The Moon Endureth* by John Buchan, originally published in 1912, is a collection of stories, one of which is entitled *"The Grove of Ashtaroth"*. It is a story of a sacred grove in Africa, where, following his part in its destruction, the hero finally realises that there is some virtue in the old beliefs and practices. The final line of the story goes: "And then my heartache returned, and I knew that I had driven something lovely and adorable from its last refuge on earth."

On reading the story, certain phrases struck me as being strangely familiar. I will quote certain extracts. I have underlined the relevant phrases:

*"As I sat and mused my glance fell on the inscrutable stone birds. They knew all those <u>old secrets of joy and terror.</u> And that moon of alabaster!"*

*"The calm face of Nature broke up for me into wrinkles of wild knowledge. I saw the <u>things which brush against the soul in dreams,</u> and found them lovely. There seemed no cruelty in the knife or the blood. It was a <u>delicate mystery of worship,</u> as wholesome as the morning song of birds."*

These phrases occur both in *High Magic's Aid* and in *Witchcraft Today*. In *High Magic's Aid*, in a conversation between Morven, Jan and Thur, Morven starts by saying:

"... I think you will never advance, if you feel not the <u>old secrets of joy and terror</u> 'tis useless for you to go on."
"I would go on", said Jan, "I felt <u>things which seemed to brush against my soul</u>, how was't with you Thur?"
"I know not, but there seemed there was some <u>mystery of worship, delicate, but as a dream</u>, the queer thing is, I can scarce remember what happened, I was as if in a trance, but I think of it with joy."[33]

In *Witchcraft Today*, Gardner claims that he is reporting what a witch of his acquaintance has said to him:

"It is a strange mystical experience. You feel a different person, as if much dross were sloughed off. There is some <u>strange mystery of worship, delicate as a dream</u>. It is as if I were in a trance during the rites; I can scarcely remember what happened; <u>something seems to brush against my soul</u> and I ever think of it with excitement - the <u>old secrets of joy and terror</u> quicken my blood."[34]

It is clear that these phrases were obtained from Buchan and subsequently used by Gardner in *High Magic's Aid* and *Witchcraft Today*. This could be deliberate plagiarism, but it is quite possible to imagine Gardner or someone else copying those phrases down because they liked their striking imagery. Subsequently Gardner used them in *High Magic's Aid* - undoubted plagiarism, but it could quite reasonably be that he wrote them down and later forgot where he got them from and perhaps thought either that he wrote them himself (I have done this myself before now!) or that they actually were the phrases that the witch had told him.

It is perhaps significant that 'Wood Magic', the poem with which Buchan concludes the story, was copied by Gardner into

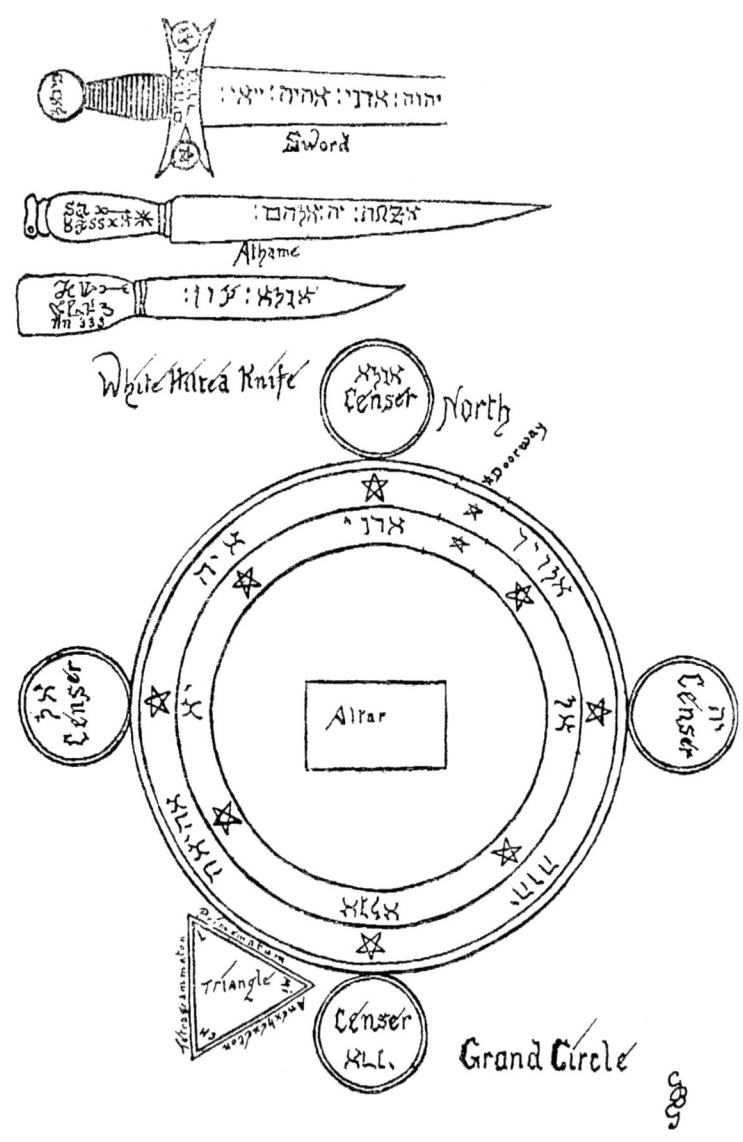

32. Endpaper to Gardner's "High Magic's Aid" (1949)

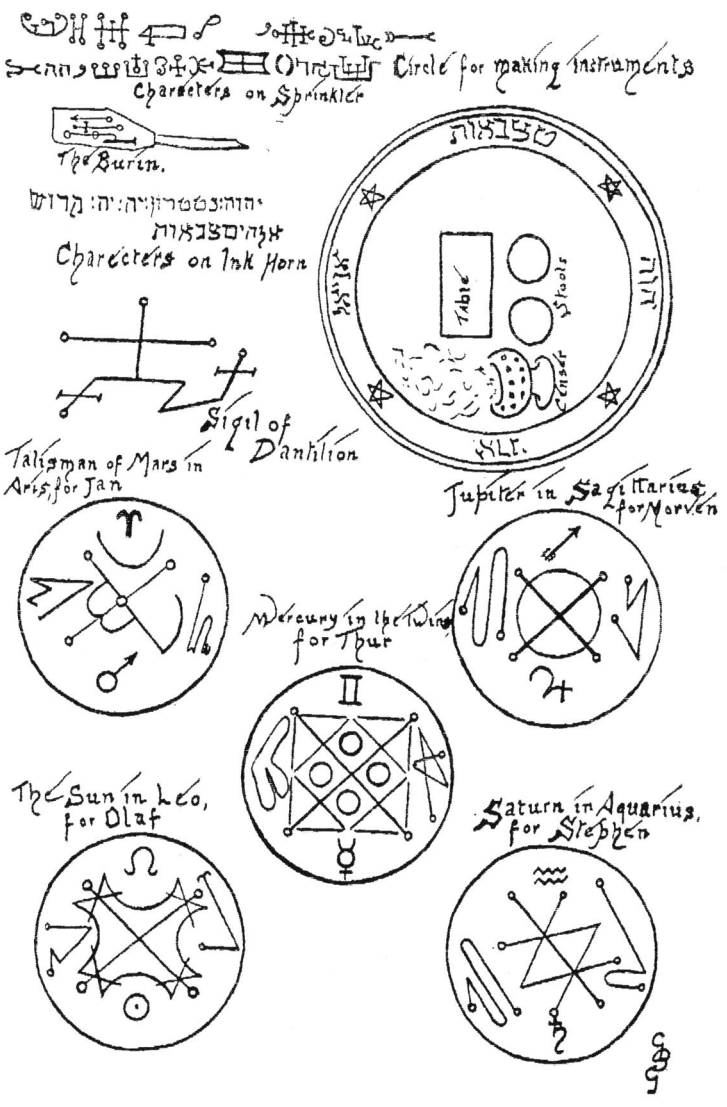

33. Endpaper to Gardner's "High Magic's Aid" (1949)

the volume known as 'Text A'.

## The Illustrated Endpapers

The endpapers of *High Magic's Aid* are clearly drawn by Gardner in his neatest calligraphy and consist of illustrations of the following: the sword; the athame; the white-hilted knife; the layout of the Grand Circle; the burin; characters on sprinkler; characters on the ink horn; the layout of another circle; the sigil of Dantilion; Various talismans, including Mars in Aries for Jan, Jupiter in Sagittarius for Morven, Mercury in the Twins for Thur, the Sun in Leo for Olaf and Saturn in Aquarius for Stephen. Gardner has signed each leaf with his "monogram" (see Illustration 32 and 33).

These drawings essentially derive from Mathers' edition of *The Key of Solomon*, published in 1888, and Barrett's *The Magus*, published in 1801. There are, however, minor variations which may be significant.

The drawing of the sword is clearly based on Mathers but there is no central disc, the inscription (which is in Hebrew and appears to be identical) is directly on the double-crescent hilt, the handle is hatched across rather than what looks to be a spiral and the discs between the crescent moons are inscribed with pentagrams.

The differences correspond to the sword referred to in Chapter 4, which suggests that Gardner already had the sword in his possession, or at any rate had seen and was familiar with it, prior to illustrating *High Magic's Aid*.

What Gardner calls the Athamé is essentially the same as that which Mathers calls 'The Knife with the Black Hilt'. It is, however, a different shape. The symbols on the handle are in a slightly different order, and only half of the symbols on the blade are reproduced.

The White Hilted Knife is also slightly different in shape and layout of the symbols, which are otherwise the same. The illustrations of the characters on the Ink Horn correspond with those illustrated by Mathers in Fig. 85 - the Inkstand. However, Gardner seems to have misread Mathers with regard to the characters on the Sprinkler. Instead of copying Mathers' Figs 82 and 83, he has copied Figs 83 (which does relate to one side of the sprinkler) and Fig 84, which relates to the engraving on a candle.

Two circle layouts are given, which are adapted from those given by Mathers. Gardner shows a smaller circle entitled "Circle for making instruments". It is clearly based on Mathers' "Circle for consecrating Pentacles etc.". The Hebrew characters and the pentagrams around the circumference of the circle are identical, and Gardner's Censer is clearly based on Mathers' "Vessel for Incense". However, Gardner includes a rectangular table within the circle and two circular stools.

What Gardner entitles the Grand Circle is based on a drawing by Mathers, but differs in several respects, the main ones being the replacement of various symbols with pentagrams; the addition of a rectangular altar in the circle; the addition of a "triangle of manifestation" to the south-west of the circle, which appears to be based on a drawing in Mathers' *Goetia*; and mention of a "doorway" at the north-east on the circumference of the circle.

The various illustrated talismans (planetary sigils) are adapted from illustrations in Barrett's *The Magus*. To these Gardner has added the traditional planetary glyphs for the Sun, Mercury, Mars, Jupiter and Saturn and those for the zodiacal signs that they are traditionally supposed to rule.

The endpapers demonstrate, as does the whole book, that Gardner was still heavily influenced by ceremonial magic.

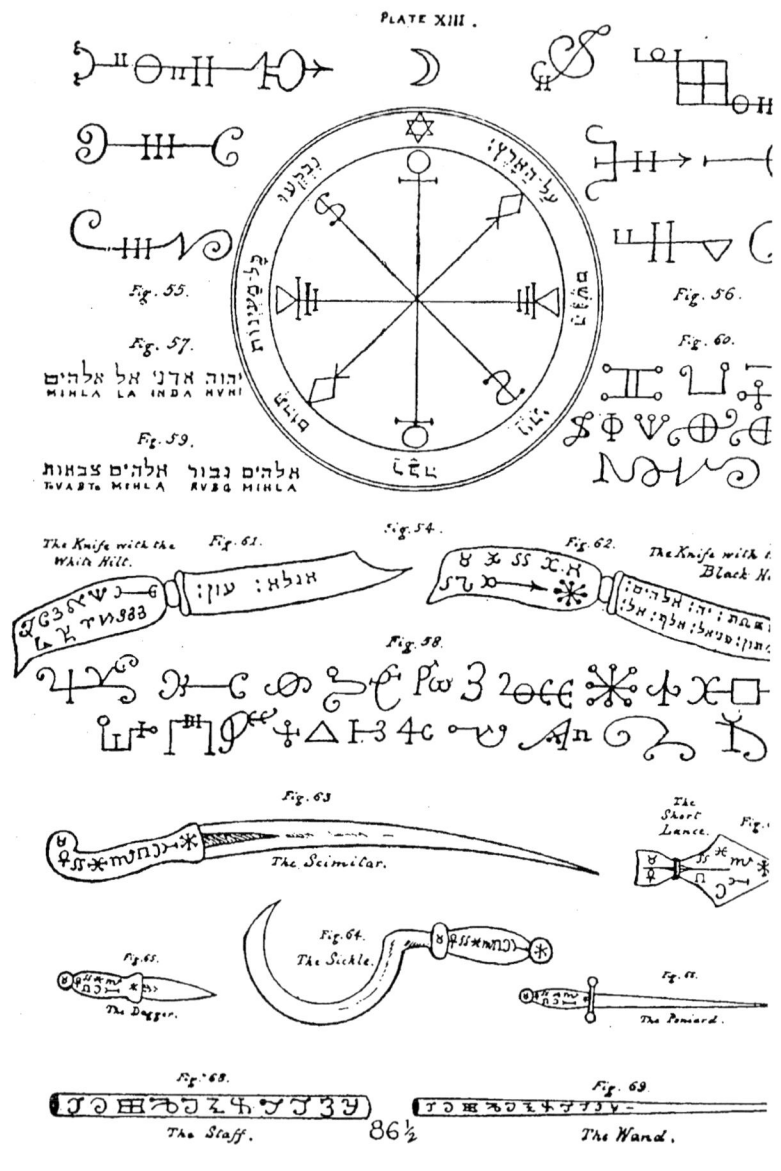

34. Illustrations from Mathers' "Key of Solomon" (1888)

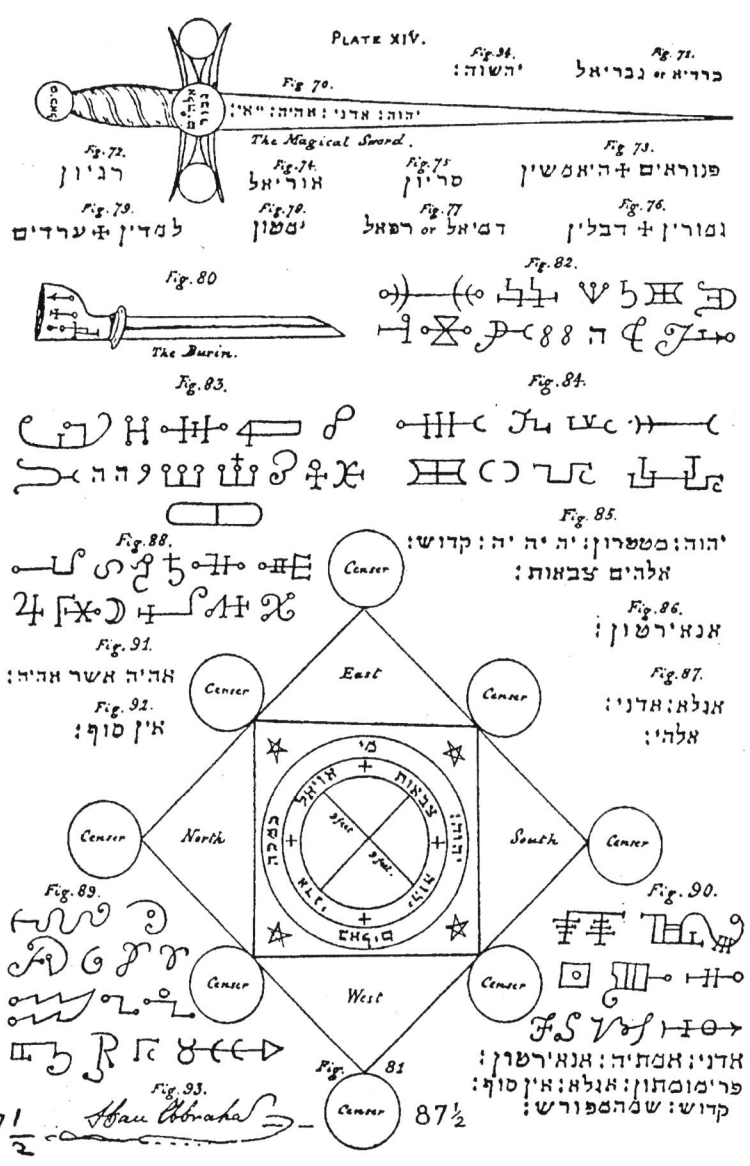

35. Illustrations from Mathers' "Key of Solomon" *(1888)*

However, there are differences from the source material as given by Mathers and Barrett and these are quite revealing as possibly reflecting some of the practices of the witch tradition into which Gardner was initiated. There is the introduction of pentagram symbols, rectangular altars in the circles, including two circular stools in one. Also, astrological symbols of the planets and zodiac signs are given on the talismans. All of this suggests an influence, either direct or indirect, from the Golden Dawn.

## Names

Gardner rarely did anything without there being a very particular purpose behind it, and he drops various hints throughout the text giving information in a rather obscure and roundabout way.

He has included names of people and places, either in a recognisable form or subtly altered. They rather suggest a pointing towards significant places for those who were "in the know" - places associated with witchcraft activity. First of all, the place where the witch lived was called 'Wanda' and the name by which she was known was 'Vada'. Combining these two names, I was reminded irresistibly of 'Vanda', who is mentioned by Patricia Crowther when she is writing about her husband, Arnold:

*... Gerald once took him to the home of a lady called Vanda. She frequently held soirees where various artistes, intellectuals and writers, were able to commune with their equals and let down their hair by 'peeling off', as Gerald put it, and sitting around sky-clad.* [35]

Was the introduction of variations on her name a subtle indication that Vanda had been a witch?

The name 'Morven' is equally interesting. It could have occurred to Gardner because of his contacts with Alexander Keiller, the archaeologist who had carried out excavations at Avebury and Windmill Hill. Keiller's Morven Institute was named after his family home in Aberdeenshire.

Incidentally, one of Keiller's interests was witchcraft, particularly the study of 16th Century witchcraft in Scotland, though he disagreed with Margaret Murray's findings. His biographer, Lynda Murray, writes:

*... in the 1930s, one Halloween night found him leading a small group of associates out into the garden of the Manor at Avebury. He carried before him a phallic symbol, and bowing three times before the Statue of Pan, he chanted 'witchlike' incantations.* [36]

Several places in the vicinity of Christchurch are mentioned by name. Morven says:

*"I have heard that the people of the Witch Cult band together at St. Catherine's Hill, and that is but a league beyond thy mother's farm.";* and *"... so say that you will ride with me to St. Catherine's Hill (as they call it now, though better is it known as Kerewidens Hill) and I will risk the night there."* [37]

In the last chapter of the book, almost as if Gardner was trying to cram all the names in that he could, the Abbot says:

*"Mind you, I think we must charge special fees for holding the Court at such short notice. Those farms at Southridge, for instance, and the mill at Walkford ... If you want money, I will give you a good price for Highcliffe Farm or Sumerford."* [38]

Southridge was the name of Gardner's house in Highland Avenue and Highcliffe was the village he lived in. Although there was never a Highcliffe Farm as such, it enabled him to mention Highcliffe without having to refer to a particular location. Somerford was the location of the Rosicrucian Theatre where Gardner claimed to have first met the witches.

There was never a mill at Walkford, but there was one on the Walkford Brook - Chewton Mill. We have, of course, already come across this: it is none other than the Mill House, the home of Dorothy St. Quintin Fordham! Was this a subtle indication that witches met there as well, somewhere that Doreen Valiente would later reveal as being the place where Gardner claimed to her to have been initiated?

Other places are also indicated, but not quite so clearly. In searching for the Witch of Wanda, Thur, Jan and Olaf stopped for the night at a hamlet called Eyeford. It is surely more than coincidence that the next village over the River Stour from Christchurch is called Iford. Indeed, the River Stour itself is also mentioned by name.

The town in which much of the story is set is 'St. Clare-in-Walden'. Some have attempted to identify it with Christchurch, but Gardner may well have had East Anglia in mind, where the towns of Clare and Saffron Walden are to be found, only 15 miles apart. Andrew Collins [39] has drawn our attention to the significance of the St. Clare family in that it was the St. Cleres who helped to gain the throne of England for William Rufus in place of the rightful heir, Robert, and they were implicated in the assassination of Thomas a Becket. They also had a long involvement with Freemasonry. There is also St. Paul's Walden in Hertfordshire, not too far from the 'Hertfordshire Nuderies'.
Other names seem totally invented by Gardner, like the etymologically unlikely Hurstwyck.

## Going Public

At some stage in the production of the manuscript, Gardner had to approach the problem of getting it published. It is highly likely that he had paid for the publication of *A Goddess Arrives* out of his own pocket. He was not short of money and I doubt if he would have been inclined to approach many orthodox publishers over *High Magic's Aid* and almost certainly be faced with a series of rejection slips, for it was not of the literary standard of most books published then. It was long and there was still a paper shortage.

After considerable negotiation with Edith as to what he could and couldn't include, Gardner was ready, towards the end of 1948, to look for a publisher. It was obvious that none of the mainstream publishers was interested, and Gardner chose the occultist, Michael Houghton, who was the proprietor of Atlantis Bookshop. Gardner almost certainly knew Houghton already, probably by visiting Atlantis on a regular basis.

Atlantis Bookshop is situated in Museum Street, very close to the British Museum, and is reputed to be the oldest occult bookshop in the world. It was founded in 1922 by Houghton, a refugee from eastern Europe, who wrote under the pen-name of Michael Juste. He ran the shop until his death on 2nd June 1961 at the age of 64.

It is fascinating to speculate whether Gardner visited Atlantis Bookshop during his leave in England in 1927 and 1932. As he had a reader's ticket to the British Museum in 1927, it is very likely that he did and, I am sure, became a regular visitor following his retirement. He probably knew Houghton sufficiently well by the late 1940s for him to agree to publish *High Magic's Aid*.

Atlantis Bookshop had become, in the words of Philip Carr-Gomm, a "... kind of salon to the occult intelligentsia of the 1940s and 50s".[40] It seems to have been used for formal and informal meetings of various kinds, and regular visitors included Aleister Crowley, Dion Fortune, Paul Brunton, Gerald Yorke, W.B. Crow, Ross Nichols, Cottie Burland and

John Hargrave.

Out of this emerged several enterprises. Houghton ran one of the first occult correspondence courses, as well as a magical lodge called 'The Order of the Hidden Masters' from the basement which, according to Caroline Wise:

> ... was turned into a temple, dedicated, rumour has it, to a Sumerian dog-headed goddess. Murals in a Near-Eastern style decorated the walls. It was here the order taught, following Golden Dawn-type rituals and ran a healing group.[41]

However, the writer, Charles Beatty, considered that the Order consisted of a "most sinister, hard-headed bunch of occultists" who "aimed at power over people - preferably in high places".[42] Gardner had wanted to be a member of this order, as Doreen Valiente's notebook entry for 8 December 1964 relates: *S... L... was a member of the circle which met at Michael Juste's. So were Gerald Yorke and John Symonds. Gerald Gardner had wanted to join, and so had Madeline Montalban, but they had been refused membership.*[43]

Another enterprise to emerge from Atlantis Bookshop was a magazine entitled *The Occult Observer*. Although only surviving regularly for six issues between 1949 and 1950, it was extremely influential, having some excellent writers and providing a focus for much of the occult revival which took place in the 1950s, not least the modern witchcraft revival.

Houghton was editor and Ross Nichols was appointed Assistant Editor. I get the impression that the various regular visitors to Atlantis were called upon to contribute, including Julian Shaw, W.B. Crow, John Hargrave, Gerald Yorke, Mir Bashir, Bernard Bromage, Dion Byngham, John Heath-Stubbs and John Cowper Powys.

The character of *The Occult Observer*, which had the sub-title 'A Quarterly Journal of Occultism, Art and Philosophy', was intellectual rather than sensational and the aim seems to have been to attract high quality writing from experts in their respective spheres. It hoped to 'publish and review such subjects as may disentangle the vast phantasmagoria misnamed occultism and bring a sense of proportion to these secret sciences of the illuminated'. In some ways, it could be seen as the journalistic equivalent of the Fouracres Club - certainly at least Cottie Burland and Dion Byngham were associated with both.

After the sixth issue, in 1950, production ceased. Possibly sales were not as great as had been expected or the work involved in producing it was more than Houghton and Nichols could cope with. Fortunately, after a gap of many years, *The Occult Observer* still continues as an occasional publication.

Houghton was also a book publisher, but on rather a small scale. Since 1935, when he had published a volume of his own verse under the imprint of the Atlantis Bookshop, he had published an average of one book every two years. At 352 pages, *High Magic's Aid* was by far the longest book he had ever published. Printing and binding costs alone would have been considerable and it is virtually certain that Gardner paid the bulk of the costs of production.

Gardner had difficulty with spelling, and so Houghton introduced him to someone who could edit his manuscript - Dolores North (also known as Madeline Montalban), who had been a journalist. Doreen Valiente confirms that Dolores North typed out the manuscript of *High Magic's Aid* for Gardner[44], or, more probably, for Houghton prior to publication. Indeed, Gardner implies that she worked for Houghton in a letter he wrote to Cecil Williamson:

*It's very funy. Mrs. North is 'Delores'. She used to work at the Atlantis Bookshop, + she typed + put the spelling right in High Magics Aid. She makes a living at Astrology + love philtres, on the quiet. I know she claimed to be a Witch; but got evrything wrong. But, she knows High Magics Aid + has a lively imagination.*[45]

However, Doreen Valiente claims that Gardner told her that he had first met Dolores North in London during the war, when she had been wearing the uniform of a WRNS officer, so perhaps she had been associated with Atlantis Bookshop for some time.

*High Magic's Aid* was published in July 1949, at a price of ten shillings and sixpence. It was a finely produced hardback volume, printed by Edgar G. Dunstan & Co., Drayton House, Gordon Street, London WC1. It was in page size 7.25 ins x 4.75 ins and was 352 pages in length. The dust cover has a very striking illustration, in black and lime-green on white, showing the main four characters of the story next to a censer from which much smoke is issuing forth (see Illustration 36). I do not know the identity of the artist, who is identified merely by the initials 'HD' or 'DH'.

The title page indicates the author as "Scrire O.T.O. 4=7 (G.B. Gardner)". "Scrire" is almost certainly Gardner's mis-spelling of "Scire", his magical name (Latin for "to know" and one of the four powers of the sphinx) which is spelt correctly on the dust-jacket. This suggests that Gardner was not that familiar with the name, which is likely to have been conferred on him by Crowley. It has also been pointed out that 4=7 is not an O.T.O. degree. Its use supports my conclusion in the previous chapter that Gardner did not understand the O.T.O. or its degree system.

The book did not sell well initially. Francis King puts this more bluntly: "The book seems to have been a resounding flop - five years later I saw the publisher's shelves still groaning under the weight of unsold copies"[46] This was probably because there was no way for potential readers to realise the

*36. The cover of the original edition of "High Magic's Aid"*

significance of the book, beyond that of a story of magic and adventure set in 13th Century England. Certainly distribution of the book does not seem to have been particularly effective, and it must have been given a low profile even within the shop itself if a tale recounted by Gardner in 1951 is to be believed. He was going into Atlantis, just as a man was leaving. The shop assistant was saying "No, there aren't any books that tell you how to do it." On enquiring what he had wanted, Gardner was informed that he had requested books on how to work magic. "What about *High Magic's Aid*?" said Gardner. The assistant replied that she hadn't thought about that! [47]

Those who bought or subscribed to *The Occult Observer* would have known about the book and some may have contacted Gardner as a result, perhaps particularly those who may have belonged to an existing witchcraft tradition.

## Significance

It was only after Gardner had started selling the book from the Museum of Magic and Witchcraft on the Isle of Man that he made it quite clear that witches still existed and that he was one himself. The notice that was on display there gives a good indication of his motives in writing the book:

*Though it is a novel it is the only book that tells how High Magic, Ritual or Kabalistic was worked & how the tools you see upstairs were used. It also gives things from the Witches point of view & tells all about Witchcraft that is permitted to be made public.* [48]

And it was really only after Gardner had "come out" following the publication of *Witchcraft Today* in 1954 that the book could be put in its rightful context, for in the very first chapter of *Witchcraft Today* Gardner admits that:

*... as it is a dying cult, I thought it was a pity that all the knowledge should be lost, so in the end I was permitted to write, as fiction, something of what a witch believes in the novel High Magic's Aid.*[49]

But the very book which revealed the significance of *High Magic's Aid* also put it "in the shade" because in *Witchcraft Today* Gardner was telling of witchcraft's survival - a work of non-fiction which claimed that witches still existed and which rather stole the thunder from a mere story set in mediaeval times.

And yet we have already noted that Gardner gave a copy of *High Magic's Aid* to Patricia Crowther in 1960 telling her to look at Morven's words particularly, so he must have considered it to be still relevant even after the publication of *Witchcraft Today* in 1954 and *The Meaning of Witchcraft* in 1959.

What was Gardner's intention in writing *High Magic's Aid*? I think really it was only to get something published, even though few who initially bought the book would have realised its significance. Perhaps he hoped that readers might decide independently to revive the Craft, based purely on the details given in the book. Or, more likely, he began to see it as purely an interim exercise, hoping all the time that he would be able to get a non-fiction book about the Craft published one day.

# Chapter 11

# Covens Old And New

Apart from his sometimes extensive 'winterings abroad' Gardner had been living permanently in London since 1945 and, as we have seen, actively participating in a variety of activities, including naturism, the Ancient British Church, and the Folk-Lore Society, amongst others.

But what about witchcraft activity? The existence of a witch coven is, even today, not usually publicised, even secret, so it is hardly surprising that we are rather vague about the situation over 50 years ago. However, we can make certain deductions based on what Gardner and others have written.

I have been unable to find any evidence that Gardner was involved in any witchcraft activity in the London area before *High Magic's Aid* was published in July 1949. Yet surely his intention behind the re-erection on a piece of secluded woodland in early 1946 of a building that had previously been displayed as a 'witch's cottage' was to use it for the purposes of witchcraft rituals?

There are, however, hints in his letters that he went down to Highcliffe for at least some of the seasonal festivals, performing rituals with Edith, and possibly others.

And we have already seen that his progressive interests in the Ancient Druid Order, the Ancient British Church and in Crowley and the O.T.O., followed by work on *High Magic's Aid*, effectively kept him busy for several years from 1946 to

1949.

I am sure that the main driving force behind writing *High Magic's Aid* was not just the desire to make known the existence of what Gardner called "the witch cult", but to recruit suitable members and to encourage the formation of new covens. It was only after its publication, and probably as a direct result, that there are hints of a coven being established in the London area. I think this was probably formed some time in 1950, from those who had read the book and then contacted Gardner, together with fellow members of Spielplatz and Five Acres.

In an interview with Barrie Harding in April 1951 about his forthcoming museum of witchcraft on the Isle of Man, Cecil Williamson made reference to "a coven of witches practising in the south of England". The article continues:

*Who are these witches? One is a woman school-teacher, another a Civil Servant. "I know of one very attractive girl in the coven" says Mr. Williamson ... "At certain times in the year they observe the fertility rituals, prancing and dancing in the nude. It is rather pathetic in a way, because some of them are quite old".* [1]

This is likely to be the coven meeting at or near Highcliffe. Williamson was obviously relaying what Gardner had told him about them: I doubt very much whether Williamson had met them himself, although later he did claim to have met Edith Woodford-Grimes.

And the same newspaper in an article in October 1951 [2] states: *I learned of a nudist camp where at midnight rites were performed with nude devotees of both sexes.* The implication of this report is that there was something going on at Five Acres, at least by October 1951.

251

37. ] *A ritual area (complete with cauldron) adjacent to the Witches' Cottage*

Certainly, writing about her initiation in 1953, Doreen Valiente says: *Later in the year Gerald invited me up to his London flat to meet the rest of his coven. There were about eight or ten of them, mostly people who were fellow members with Gerald of a naturist club he was interested in.*[3]

This confirms that by the end of 1953 there was a coven meeting in the London area with which Gardner was associated; that it had about eight or ten members; and that most of them were members of a naturist club (presumably Five Acres). A full account of this coven must await the appropriate time and further research.

## Gilbert and Barbara Vickers

One early member of the group was Barbara Vickers, as Doreen Valiente told Michael Howard, editor of *The Cauldron*:

*When I knew Gerald and first started working with him, there was a very pretty blonde girl in his coven called Barbara Vickers, whom Gerald had evidently known for quite some time. He told me that she and her husband had been members of a coven in Cheshire ...*[4]

In her notebook, there is an entry for November 1975, which states: Gerald used to know two people in the Craft who came from Cheshire, and belonged to the Craft there - Gilbert and Barbara Vickers.

Doreen mentioned Barbara to Michael Howard: ... *the HPS [High Priestess] of the traditional Cheshire coven ... Gardner apparently attended some of their meetings in Cheshire and Doreen met the HPS as she used to convene at St. Albans in the early 1950s.*[5] *Doreen also told Howard that Barbara had seemingly separated from Gilbert and come to live in London.*

Writing in 1954, Gardner referred to Barbara and Gilbert as having been willing to initiate Cecil Williamson, presumably not long after the two men had met, probably late 1950 or early 1951, though Williamson declined the offer, saying that his wife would not approve.[6]

The implication of this is that Williamson must have met Gilbert and Barbara on at least one occasion and that therefore they were probably in London at the time. Also, Gilbert and Barbara were obviously part of an established initiatory tradition at a time when Gardner was not, or rather that he had no conveniently available High Priestess who could initiate Williamson.

The only individuals of the right names and age that I have been able to find are Gilbert Hedley Vickers (age 37) and Barbara Kathryn Blake (age 22) who were married on 23rd December 1944. They lived at Kenry House, Kingston Vale, Surrey, the former residence of the Earl of Dunraven, and now part of the University of Kingston.

Gardner refers, in a letter to Williamson in March 1951[7], to Barbara having a 'Monomark' address, which is similar to a P.O. Box number, and frequently used by occult magazines, organisations and practitioners. This suggests that she may have been involved in some sort of commercial enterprise.

Apart from confirming that there had been a coven in Cheshire, Doreen Valiente seems to have known nothing about Gilbert and Barbara, though she got the impression that Gardner had worked with them[8] She confirmed to Howard, however, that it was this coven that she was referring to in an incident which she described in Chapter 3 of her book *Witchcraft for Tomorrow*, about a group of witches who met in the Cheshire region:

*...at a lonely crossroads on a heath, for the purpose of holding a Sabbat dance in the nude. It was such a remote spot that they thought it unlikely anyone would come by at night, so they threw off their clothes and were dancing a merry round, when to their horror they saw the headlights of a lorry approaching. Fortunately, they were provided with black cloaks, so they hastily covered themselves and fled.*[9]

Certainly Cheshire has a reputation for traditional witchcraft. Bob Clay-Egerton has written of how, when staying at his family's country retreat near Alderley Edge, as a 10-year old boy, he followed his mother's maid into the woods and, hidden behind a tree, watched as she "met a small group of men and women who greeted her by kissing her". The next time it happened he was caught and sworn to secrecy. Two years later, in the spring of 1943, he was initiated into the group, which dated back to at least the 1860s.[10] This is a tradition which deserves a full study in its own right, which may or may not be the same as the tradition known as the Tuatha de Cornovii, which is said to have originated in Cheshire, or the group which Janet and Stewart Farrar, in their book *The Life and Times of a Modern Witch*, refer to as 'The Cheshire Traditionals'.[11]

## Barbara's Television Non-appearance 1951

Gardner had certainly known Barbara for some time before February 1951, because that month Cecil Williamson had been approached by the BBC who were interested in producing a 10-minute television programme about witchcraft. Gardner had in turn approached Barbara about taking part, asking her to contact Williamson direct. He wrote to Williamson:

*If she fails me I have another one who I think I can get but she doesn't look as good as B. But her speaking voice will be good.*[12]

This is interesting in that it seems to indicate that Gardner was probably only in contact with two female witches at the time. The other one was probably Edith, who was 63 years old and was an experienced actress and teacher of elocution. Whether Edith would have been as willing to appear as Gardner seemed to think is open to considerable doubt.

In a letter to Gerald Yorke, Gardner gives details of the intention of the programme:

*The idea was we, Williamson and self, would talk about the Museum, & witchcraft, ending with "Would you like to see a witch? Well, here's one." Id arranged with a very pretty one, who was rather thrilled, the conditions being they'd not let any reporters know, & would see she got away immediately afterwards, & was not followed.*[13]

However, there were problems, as Gardner recounts:

*A few days after they rang up saying, unfortunatly, Roman Catholicks were so strong in the B.B.C. they wouldent allow it at any price, & would I go on alone. I refused, then they worried & worried, they wanted me, & got on to Donna. Williamson wanted publicity for the Museum, so I did it...*[14]

A letter to Williamson confirmed the decision not to have Barbara on the programme but was rather circumspect as to the reason:

*We are not having the lady from the north as there are difficulties which you will appreciate and which I have explained to the good Dr.*[15]

The programme was broadcast live on Saturday 14th April 1951 and, whatever the reason for the BBC not wanting Barbara to appear (and it may well not have been quite as Gardner surmised), in the event Gardner went on alone, being interviewed by Leslie Mitchell and Joan Gilbert and showing various witch tools.

### The Bicycle Shop

In an article in *Insight* magazine, Michael Howard stated:

*Following the publication of* [High Magic's Aid]*, Gardner parted company with the New Forest Coven & founded his own group which met in his flat above a bicycle shop in Finchley, North London.*[16]

I am endeavouring to track down where this flat was and when Gardner occupied it. He certainly had a relatively luxurious flat in Central London until at least mid-1939 and acquired another in early 1945. However, this flat above the bike shop could have been a sort of 'pied-de-terre' that he rented during the war. It was certainly his habit to have a modest London flat even when living away, and he could certainly afford it. Also, his frequent visits to Spielplatz during the war certainly suggest that he had somewhere nearer to stay than Highcliffe.

## The Hen House and the Three Covens

Cecil Williamson, who, as I shall demonstrate in Chapter 16, was not just unreliable but very good at making up stories, has this to say about the land which Gardner had leased or bought from Wellbye:

*On this he had a large ark type hen or chicken house, seven feet high at the apex but only four feet at the sides. On the land was also the famous Elizabethan 'witches cottage' ... There were three covens making use of the two buildings and were not seeing eye to eye on various matters. ... Coven A used the hen house and were there long before the 'witches cottage' arrived on site. This coven drew its members from the naturist club and most of their rites took place outside the chicken house. They had to for the space inside was cramped to say the least. So the bonfires, the leaping and the ring dancing took place on the well protected scrubland. They were homey folk mostly of retirement age and Sun lovers. Covens B and C used the 'witches cottage'. They started as one group with shared rituals and experienced practitioners of the Craft. Their numbers grew rapidly and it was decided to form two covens. As things turned out this was a mistake. Soon there was trouble in the camp and although Gardner tried to bring peace to the warring factions both covens packed up and went their separate ways. ... Coven A had already decided that the whole place was getting overcrowded and had left some time earlier.*[17]

It is difficult to know whether to put any credence on this statement. It hints at the possibility of some sort of witchcraft activity occurring before 1946, when the cottage was erected, but as yet I have no corroborative evidence of any sort, so the question must at present remain open. It is possible that someone like Dion Byngham may have initiated something at Fouracres which continued throughout the war, perhaps with a membership of such people as Cottie Burland.

Certainly Williamson, writing about when he first met Gardner in Atlantis Bookshop, states: *Gardner, always the extrovert, was holding forth centre stage about the trials and tribulations of his newly formed covenstead at St. Albans Brickets* [sic] *Wood adjoining the well known nudist club.* [18] This ties in with the suggestion that the two men probably met in the summer or autumn of 1950. Reference to the "covenstead" as being "newly formed" suggests that a date of late 1949 or early 1950 for the formation of a coven at Bricket Wood would be reasonable.

## Covens at Highcliffe and Bricket Wood

It certainly seems as if there was something going on in the London area as a direct result of the publication of *High Magic's Aid*, but exactly what, and where, and when, we can't be sure.

For the 1951 to 1954 period, however, we do have an invaluable resource which provides an insight into what witchcraft activity Gardner was involved in during that period. This is Gardner's side of his correspondence with Cecil Williamson in the archives of the Museum of Witchcraft at Boscastle, which I look at more generally in Chapters 15 and 16.

In a letter dated 8th February 1950 (almost certainly actually 1951 - Gardner put the previous year out of habit, as people sometimes do) Gardner, who was part-owner of the Five Acres Club, was trying to persuade Williamson to buy the Club and open a museum there. He writes: *"Being a Nudist Club no one could object to nude dances & Rites only the actual ceremonies would have to be kept secret. But this is all in the air & any breath of it would make them refuse to sell ..."* [19]

In late February, Gardner wrote another letter to Williamson, still advocating the museum idea, but adding: "If it could be managed, we could I think get a good and strong cult going."

It seems to me that the implication of these comments is that there was no witchcraft activity going on at Five Acres at that time. Yet, there were witches around, since Gardner wrote in his 8 February letter: "By the way, the Cult are very angry about my talking to the reporter."[20] This was in the context of articles which were supposed to have appeared in the *Sunday Dispatch* and at least one other paper, though research has so far failed to unearth these. This was clearly, I would suggest, not a group of people that he had brought in to the Craft, because they would be fairly new and unlikely to be so vehemently opposed to Gardner talking to the press (although in later years, of course, they did, as Doreen Valiente records). I suspect that this was Edith Woodford-Grimes who had read the articles in the papers and complained to Gardner.

Gardner's next relevant letter to Williamson, although undated, was almost certainly written on 1st May 1951, for it says:

*There was a very nice little May Eve Rite down here last night, but the people are not at all pleased with me or with a cutting about you that appeared in a Sunday paper a little time ago. I'd not seen the cutting and they can't tell me the paper. ... I'm trying to get one of them to come up to the Isle of Man with me & see the place for herself ... What I'm after is to borrow some of her things.*[21]

As I shall mention later, we know that Edith lent some things for the Museum, and it is clear that Gardner is referring to her. Now, it seems to me that the implication of saying "There was a ... May Eve Rite" rather than "We had ..." and that they were not at all pleased with Gardner is that this was an established group of which Edith was a member and Gardner was a guest rather than something which he had only recently set up himself. The fact that he is trying to persuade "one of them" to go to the Isle of Man and wanting to borrow her things also suggests to me a group of which Gardner was not a regular member, certainly not a leading light.

In June 1951, Gardner wrote:

*... the Witch wants me down to talk to the Coven. They're angry about things & I must soothe them down & incidentally try & get some more out of them .... I saw the Witches Daughter the other day. She says mother is better but still not come up to the Island, couldn't say why. So I must go down & try & find out what is the matter.*[22]

He also wrote: *The Witch is sending a car to Fetch me on Tuesday, so I have to go down & sweeten the coven. Will come to the Island as soon as I can.*[23]

It is interesting that Gardner is writing about "the Witch", for he claimed to know several as well as being one himself. The first witch that he met, the one that he had known for longest, had kept in touch with and had become very intimate with, was Edith. It is clear to me that when Gardner is referring to "the Witch" he means Edith: there is really no other candidate for such a description. This is emphasised by his reference to "the witch's daughter" for he knew Edith's daughter, Rosanne, very well also.

It is clear from this letter that Gardner was not writing from the Island but from London. The Witch is sending a car to fetch him and he is going down to see the coven. This clearly isn't Bricket Wood, as he journeyed there fairly regularly, and it could hardly be described as "down". It was a special journey. I have heard from Patricia Crowther that at a later date Eleanor Bone used to drive Gerald down to see Edith fairly regularly. I don't see that this can be anywhere other than Highcliffe, where Edith was living at the time, and where there was clearly what Gardner describes as "the coven".

I had always thought it unlikely that Edith was involved in the activity at Bricket Wood, but Ronald Hutton says: *...a coven flourished there under the leadership of Dafo and Gerald by the opening of the 1950s* [24] and Doreen Valiente, in the letter to Michael Howard quoted earlier, says: *I have the impression ... that the connection between Brickett [sic] Wood and the Craft goes back for some time before I met Gerald, because he and Dafo used to go there.* This is interesting and may even suggest that Edith met Gardner at a naturist club pre-war, which is what I hinted at in *Wiccan Roots*. However, Patricia Crowther informs me that Eleanor Bone, who knew Gardner and Edith well and who used to drive him down to see her fairly regularly, confirmed that Edith was never involved with the witchcraft activity at Bricket Wood.

## The Southern Coven of British Witches

The name "Southern Coven" first occurs in correspondence between Gardner and Williamson in May 1951 in the context of a loan of items by the coven to the Museum, but its first published mention seems to have been in July of that year in an article in the *Isle of Man Examiner* [25]. It is also referred to in an article by Allen Andrews entitled '*Witchcraft in Britain*' which appeared in the magazine *Illustrated* on 27th September 1952:

*... on the night of the first of August (Lammas) 1940, when an invasion of Britain seemed imminent; ... an extraordinary*

*summons was sent out to members of the Southern Coven of British Witches. It brought seventeen men and women to a clearing in the New Forest.*[26]

From the material given in the article, it is clear that Andrews had interviewed both Williamson and Gardner. Whether the name "Southern Coven of British Witches" was what they actually called themselves, it is clear that it was being applied to a group that was in existence in 1940 and who met in the area of the New Forest.

This was not a group of which Gardner was any longer a regular member. In a letter to Williamson dated 1st August 1953 he writes: "The Southern Coven lent you certain things of great value to them, at my request ..." There is the implication, by the use of the word "them", and "at my request", that Gardner was not part of such a coven. This is confirmed by his letter to Williamson on the following day, which distances himself from the 'Southern Coven' still further:

*As you know, I am only the mouthpiece, of others whome I induced to lend you things. I have been protesting on their behalf the whole of April and May the whole of June & the whole of July, & as you know, I received definite orders to remove their entire collection ... I posted your letter to the Coven on Saturday they will have to meet before they decide anything.*[27]

On 5th August 1953 there is (contained in an envelope postmarked "Christchurch") a document sealed by Dafo in the Theban alphabet which states: "We, of the Southern Coven, lent these articles ...". This confirms that Dafo (Edith Woodford-Grimes) was a member of what she and Gardner called 'The Southern Coven' and that this coven met in the Christchurch/Highcliffe area.

To call something "The Southern Coven" does imply at least one other coven, from another point of the compass, and indeed Gardner does refer to such (see below). It seems to me to be a name of convenience given by Gardner to a group which previously might have had no name at all, or perhaps a secret name known only to its members. Indeed, in the 5th August 1953 letter referred to above, Gardner refers to two covens:

*...I worked so hard to get the one coven to lend you things, & they lent you fifty two articles, by, your list. Another coven promised you things, were put off by what you put in the papers ...*

The first coven is clearly the one referred to as The Southern Coven: the other one is likely to be the one referred to below as "The North Coven".

In September 1952, after interviews with Gardner and Williamson, the following appeared in an article:

*... in addition to a number of places around the south coast, groups of witches are operating at Liverpool, at Barnet and in Cumberland.*[28]

It is likely that the Cumberland coven was the traditional one into which Eleanor Bone was initiated; the Barnet one was Williamson's mistake for Bricket Wood (for the witch's cottage was formerly at Barnet); the Liverpool one was probably the same as the Cheshire one with which Gilbert and Barbara Vickers were associated (also known as the "Northern Coven"). 'The number of places around the south coast' is very vague, but could well include Highcliffe, as well as a reputed coven at Chanctonbury in Sussex.

By October 1953, Gardner was writing to Williamson as follows: *Your information is wrong on many points. I am for instance not the High Priest of 3 covens. I am a member of 3 covens.* [29] Obviously by this time there was a coven established in the North London/Hertfordshire area which may well have been meeting in the Witch's Cottage. The other covens are, presumably, the Southern and Northern covens.

Also, in *Witchcraft Today*, published in November 1954, he writes:

*... I must make it clear - I am a humble member of a coven. I am not its head or leader in any way, and I have to do what I am told. People often speak as if I owned a coven and could call it up to perform for them in public. I can and have occasionally introduced people to a witch, when the witch was willing and agreeable. More than this I cannot do.* [30]

This is emphasised in a letter from Gardner to Williamson dated 23 December 1953:

*I had known ... that they always kept a few strings of beads at Headquarters in case a girl turned up without one, but never thought much about it, but last March I was at a meeting when a girl turned up wearing a small string of pearls & was told "you know you can't do that dear" & she was made to take them off & put on a proper necklace of big beads. They can't give me any reason, just "its always been so."* [31]

Clearly Gardner was not the instigator of what was going on here. It suggests a pre-existing coven with its own established way of doing things. The use of the word 'Headquarters' is very strange, but accords with this view of things. P.G. Wodehouse uses the word to mean Aunt Agatha's house in *The Inimitable Jeeves*, which, in view of the suggestion I make in Chapter 4, is interesting. This story is subsequently told in *Witchcraft Today*.

It is interesting to speculate whether the "girl" Gardner mentions was, in fact, Doreen Valiente. She had first met

Gardner and Edith in November 1952 and was initiated at Midsummer 1953. It could well be that her first meeting with the 'Southern Coven' in Highcliffe would have been around March 1953.

In support of the proposition that there was a pre-existing movement that Gardner joined, Gareth Medway makes the following comments:

*Gardner's repeated protestations that he is not a leader, but only a coven member who has to take orders, are important in view of the continuing allegation that Gardner created the cult himself... It is a fact to which I can think of no real exceptions that the founder of a religion or sect will remain in charge of it until his or her death. It has been suggested to me that Gardner put a High Priestess in charge because he enjoyed being dominated by women, but there is not the slightest evidence that he was a masochist, and a great deal against it. In Document 33 [32], for instance, he says "it is not my nature to take orders, but I have to do it." If he had really liked dominant women he would not have married a meek clergyman's daughter.* [33]

In late 1953 or early 1954 Gardner wrote to Williamson: *As you know I agreed to lend you my Collection & tried to get other people (the North and South covens) to lend you stuff for Exhibition...* Gardner here refers to the covens as "North" and "South", rather than as "Southern" as previously. This supports the idea that these were merely "Names of Convenience" rather than their actual names.

From the above, sometimes conflicting, evidence we may draw the following tentative conclusions:

(a) In early 1951, Gardner had the Witch's Cottage at Five Acres Club but was not using it for rituals and, in fact, offered it to Williamson, either on site or removed.

(b) Gardner was in regular contact with Edith Woodford-Grimes, who was living in Highcliffe. He went down to see her fairly regularly. He participated in seasonal rituals occasionally. There was a group there which he calls a coven. They can be identified with what he refers to variously as "The Southern Coven", "The South Coven" and "The Southern Coven of British Witches". They got upset with him when he engaged in what they saw as unwise publicity. They lent some items to Williamson's museum, with Gardner as the intermediary.

(c) Gardner was in contact with at least one other coven (probably the one which he refers to as "The North Coven"). This seems to have been one in Cheshire, probably not far from Liverpool, of which Gilbert and Barbara Vickers were members, until Barbara moved down to London.

## The Collections

The items which were lent to the Museum by the Southern Coven were listed on a schedule, probably, to judge from the spelling, by Gardner himself. An examination of this list is quite revealing. There are some 52 items in total, which can be classified as follows:

Preparation of Herbs: Brass-handled knives; Brass pestle and mortar; Steel balance; Brass 14-section filter; Pewter filter vase; Pewter measures; Earthenware candle oven with bars; Ivory spatula.

Storage: Inlaid fitted wooden box with secret drawers; Boxwood and pewter boxes; Round horn ointment box; Small 8-sided incense box.
Items for use in Rituals: Dwarf wooden candlesticks; Incense burners; Gong, beater and ring; Candle snuffer.

Magical Items: Pinchbeck love charm; Necklaces (jet and amber); Wooden hand mirror.

Miscellaneous: Tinder boxes (wood and ivory and silver); Silver spoons; Pottery bowl; Pewter dish.

This suggests that the cutting, preparation, weighing, grinding, filtering, heating and storage of herbal concoctions, ointments and incenses was a major activity.

The major magical tools, such as swords, athames and wands, are missing from this collection, and it is probable that these, if they existed, were in constant use and/or considered too valuable to lend. There are, however, several of what might be called the subsidiary magical tools, or items for use in ritual such as the candlesticks and snuffer, incense burners, gong, bowl and dish.

Cecil Williamson gives his own colourful description of these items, which differs to some extent from the list compiled at the time. Probably his memory was at fault, or he was muddling the display up with other items in the museum:

*I expect you have met with or know an arty crafty potter. Well by and large the stuff looked like that kind of thing. There were pots, pans, dishes, vases, bowls, bottles and such like. All glazed earthenware, dark brownish in colour, some grey and all streaked or flecked with lighter colours. Many had Oghma type signs in black on them. There were a range of Gardner type black and white handled knives and daggers, home made wands and necklaces - from stone type beads to hunks of marked pottery or wooden bits strung on leather thongs. There were candle holders to guard the flames from the wind, small wooden boxes worked from tree branches, some sheets of art class parchment with Oghma type symbols or script, some old plain earthenware pots, antique wooden spoons and some old two pronged forks. All of which looked as if they had come from local antique shops. All put together a brave gay little display filling a free standing showcase 8ft 2' long and wide.* [34]

The Museum Guide in 1958 described this material as follows:

*A collection of objects used by witches, lent by an existing coven of witches. Naturally, they have only lent articles which they are not using, hence the collection consists chiefly of implements for the making of herbal cures and charms; there is, however, one very fine ritual wand, and a curious old desk containing seven secret drawers, in which they used to hide some of their possessions.* [35]

These appear to be largely the same items which were lent by the 'Southern Coven' some six years previously. Whether they were actually ever physically returned to the Southern Coven or merely kept by Gardner is not clear, but certainly after Gardner had taken over the museum they (or most of them) were on display in their own case (see Illustration 36).

Patricia Crowther gives a more detailed description of one of the items in this photograph:

*One case in the museum was of great interest to me. Among other items it contained a large wooden box with a mirror inside the lid and paintings of the God and Goddess on either side. It held a miscellany of vials, charms, talismans and knives, and the latter had curious signs incised on them.* [36]

The guide book description tells us, or at least strongly suggests that the Southern Coven was still in existence in 1958, that it previously had members who made herbal cures and charms, but that they no longer had such members, who had presumably died or left the coven, or those members who had previously been involved in such activity had ceased their involvement for some reason.

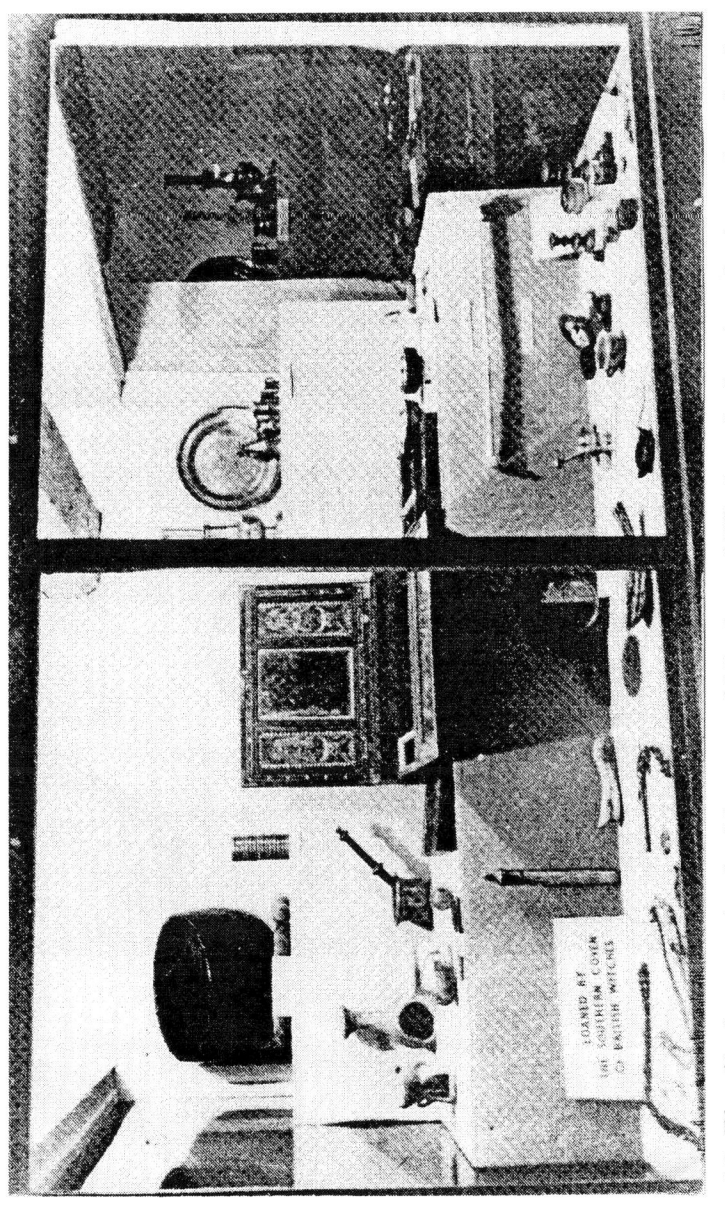

38. *The display case in the Museum of Magic and Witchcraft showing the items lent by the Southern Coven of British Witches.*

The "curious old desk containing seven secret drawers" sounds very much as if it is the same object as the "very nice little cabinet of little draws" that Gardner had acquired which had originally belonged to "Mother Sabine". However, Gardner claimed that he had only recently acquired that cabinet in December 1953, whereas the desk was in the 'Southern Coven' loan material given in 1952, so this identification must remain doubtful.

Gardner claimed to have received loan material from the 'Northern Coven' as well. The only possible mention of these items is from the 1958 Museum Guide where the description of the items in Case No. 14 includes the following: *This case ... contains another collection of objects lent by another coven of witches. This includes a horned helmet as used by the male leader in certain rites.* [37]

These items were almost certainly dispersed following the sale of the museum collection to Ripleys in the 1970s, but the fact is that they certainly did exist and were photographed.

## Scourge and Charm

In the Museum of Witchcraft at Boscastle there is on display an item with the following caption in Cecil Williamson's handwriting: *Ash Seed Wings charm. Boxed. Spray Bound with Red Wool. Presented by G.B. Gardner. Obtained From New Forrest* [sic] *Coven 1943.*

Doreen Valiente left many ritual tools and regalia. But there is only one item said to have belonged to the New Forest Coven, and that was a scourge. This is particularly interesting in view of the fact that many have accused Gardner of introducing the scourge into the Craft. The handle is made of rough pine, which is fairly knobbly where the twigs have only been roughly taken off, suggesting that it may have been collected "in the wild", quite likely in the New Forest itself. This handle has been painted green and is topped with a silver cap which may have come from another source rather than having been specially made. I have not yet been able to look and see if this cap has a hall-mark, as that would identify its age and manufacturer. The "working end" of the scourge consists of knotted thin rope or cord which has been dyed green. There is a photograph of the scourge on page 79 of *Charge of the Goddess* [38].

There is also, interestingly, a mythic connection between the scourge and 'Mother Sabine'. Raven Grimassi tells the story thus:

*... after the Sabine women had been raped they were left sterile. The Sabines then went to give prayer and offerings to the goddess Juno. Juno spoke through the sound of the winds rustling the trees, and told them their women must willingly submit to intimacy with a goat in order for their fertility to be restored (the goat was one of Juno's sacred animals). Lacking the desire to do as Juno had decreed, the Sabines turned to the Etruscans who were famous for their occult knowledge. One of the Etruscan priests told them to bring a goat offering. He then slew the goat and offered it to Juno. The priest cut the hide into straps and had the women appear before him and bare themselves. Then the priest had each woman pass by him as he lashed her across the back and buttocks with the goat strap. The lash penetrated the skin and thus were the women joined in intimate contact with the goat. Juno's decree was thereby honored and fertility was restored to the Sabine women.* [39]

## The Bricket Wood Coven

The coven that was formed by Gardner and his associates in the late 1940s or early 1950s at Bricket Wood still exists, though there have, of course, been numerous changes of membership over more than 50 years. Yet it is nearer our own time and it is important to respect the privacy of these individuals, several of whom are still living, so the time for writing a full history of the Bricket Wood Coven is not yet upon us.

# Chapter 12

# The Book of Shadows

One of the most useful books in the study of the origins and development of modern witchcraft is one that was never intended for publication. It is a book of rituals and magical techniques that each newly-initiated witch copies from that owned by their initiator. Known from the early 1950s by the evocative name of 'The Book of Shadows', its various versions are potentially very revealing of the sources of and influences on the Craft.

Witchcraft, and paganism generally, is a religion where experience is primary - the written word, whilst useful, is very much secondary. It is important to remember this when focusing on the Book of Shadows. This is no Holy Writ, upon which the Craft's beliefs are based. It is more like a cookery book - and, moreover, a handwritten one where each individual puts down their favourite recipes.

To give an account of the development of the Book of Shadows in the depth which it deserves would require a substantial book in itself. All I can attempt in this chapter and the next is to present an overview with a few insights of my own and to present some preliminary conclusions. I have unashamedly drawn on the work of others, who have in some cases carried out very detailed textural analysis. Pride of place, because he was one of the first to attempt anything of this nature, must go to Aidan Kelly.[1] Whilst I have criticisms of some of his conclusions, his pioneering work must be acknowledged for what it is. I have also drawn heavily on the work of Ronald

Hutton[2], Janet and Stewart Farrar[3], Doreen Valiente[4], Roger Dearnaley[5], Gareth Medway[6], Adrian Bott[7] and Rikki La Coste[8] concentrating on their conclusions rather than their detailed analysis.

## The Book

A secret book, the contents of which are copied afresh by each newly-initiated witch, is now fairly universal amongst many branches of the Craft, particularly those which derive, directly or indirectly, from Gardner. Such a book contains theology, philosophy, seasonal and other rituals, spells, ways of raising power, and numerous other matters. Surely if we could find one of these belonging to the old witches who initiated Gardner we could find out about their beliefs and practices. Unfortunately, things are not quite what they seem. It is significant that Morven, in *High Magic's Aid*, only takes her mother's athame and white-handled knife when fleeing: no book is mentioned at all.

A modern *Book of Shadows,* consisting of both rituals and details of magical techniques, has evolved over time. Each one is likely to be unique, as each coven or tradition evolves their own distinctive ritual elements and practices. There is therefore no such thing as *the* Gardnerian Book of Shadows.

Keeping a book in which one wrote things that one found significant or interesting is not and never has been an activity limited to witches. In the days before public libraries, photocopiers or accessible books on all conceivable subjects, let alone the internet, many people (at least amongst those who could read and write) would have had a 'commonplace book' into which they would have copied verses or prose that they admired or things that they thought might come in useful. We have in our own field Dorothy's "diaries" mentioned earlier and Doreen Valiente's notebooks, which she kept for over 30 years and which consisted of a mixture of rituals, instructions for lighting the boiler (not much difference between these two!), shopping lists, reviews of and extracts from books she had read, plus what might be called "gossip" about members of the Craft.

Witches who had books would have kept them secretly, but as well as being something which was painstakingly copied word for word from another witch's book, they would also gradually be added to over the years. Books such as this were never intended to be "carved in stone" for all time, and certainly Gardner didn't think so, as Fred Lamond, a member of Gardner's Bricket Wood coven, recalls:

*Gerald was always at pains to tell us: "The 'Book of Shadows' is not a Bible or Koran, but a personal 'cookbook' of spells that the individual witch has found to work. I (Gerald) am giving you my book to copy to get you started: it contains the spells and rituals that worked for me. As you gain in experience, add the successful spells that you have made up, and discard those that didn't work for you!"*[9]

Each Book of Shadows is very much a personal statement as well as the transmitter of a tradition. And, as a result, no two books were ever the same. They were constantly evolving, with old material being left out and fresh material added.

## The name "Book of Shadows"

However, we can say something about the phenomenon that goes by the collective name 'Book of Shadows' and we can start by looking at that name. In the pages of *The Occult Observer* (see Chapter 10) is a two part article by the well-known Indian palmist, Mir Bashir, about an ancient Sanskrit manuscript which described how one could foretell a person's destiny by measuring their shadow. The title of the article was 'The Book of Shadows'.[10]

This connection was first noticed by Doreen Valiente, who speculates:

*... did Gerald see this hitherto unknown (in Britain at any rate) and striking term for a magical manuscript and seize upon it as a good name for a witches' secret book?*[11]

However, whilst it is a term now commonly used, it does not appear in Gardner's published writings. Indeed the first mention in print for such a term to describe a witch's book, as far as I can determine, is not until 1969. [12]

## Secrecy and Oaths

On their initiation, Gardnerian witches take an oath not to reveal "The Secrets of the Art". So, as a Gardnerian initiate, am I able to write this chapter and be true to my oath? I think there are various points to make here. Firstly, "The Secrets of the Art" do not necessarily reside in the wording of rituals. Secondly, I am not revealing anything that I have been told under oath. The material I am discussing has either been made widely available through publication or is of purely historical interest. Also, I do not intend to publish a detailed textural analysis but to present the results of such analyses, by myself and others. My main purpose is to find the sources of Gardner's Book of Shadows and to determine what there might have been prior to Gardner's involvement.

## Published Sources

The Book of Shadows is by its nature secret and therefore unpublished. However, over the years, various versions and extracts have been widely available. Some of these are as follows:

*High Magic's Aid* (1949) [13] - Gardner incorporated various items of ritual, including the first and second degree initiations, into his novel, *High Magic's Aid*. We discussed the likelihood of these being the genuine rituals in Chapter 10 and came to the conclusion that they probably were.

*Witchcraft Today* (1954) [14] Gardner's first non-fiction book about the Craft contains several extracts from the *Book of Shadows*.

*Witch* (1964) [15] A copy of the *Book of Shadows* which was obtained from one of Gardner's initiates was published by Charles Cardell shortly after Gardner's death in an attempt to discredit him.

*Eight Sabbats for Witches* (1981) [16] and *The Witches' Way* (1984) [17] Janet and Stewart Farrar attempted the first analysis of the contents of the *Book of Shadows* and published a version which has become widely used today.

*Crafting the Art of Magic* (1991) [18] Aidan Kelly attempted in this book the first textural analysis of various versions of the *Book of Shadows*. It includes extracts from that important manuscript - 'Ye Bok of Ye Art Magical'.

## Unpublished Sources

Because of what the Book of Shadows is, there is also a very large number of unpublished versions, probably as many as there are initiated witches.

The earliest versions that we know of that are still in existence are Gardner's own, though it must be remembered that he neither called nor thought of them as Books of Shadows the way we do today, in that apart from ritual and magical elements, they are also used as "commonplace books", with much copying from published sources. One he called 'Ye Bok of Ye Art Magical' and the other has been referred to by the Farrars as Text A, so I shall refer to it by that name. I have been fortunate enough to have been able to study the text of these in detail.

There are other existing versions of Gardner's Book of Shadows. For example, Ronald Hutton writes: Gardner's own last Book of Shadows, kept in the Isle of Man after his death and recently added to the Toronto Collection, contains invocations and a wedding ceremony found, in my knowledge, nowhere else.[19] Doubtless there were other versions that have been lost, destroyed or stolen, and I speculate on one such in Chapter 13.

My aim in studying the Book of Shadows as it is represented in these various sources has been initially to identify the literary origins of much of the material as a first stage to identifying surviving older material, for I was not prepared to take at face value assertions like that of Aidan Kelly, who states that the major published sources from which the rituals had been constructed accounted for everything in the rituals.[20]

## The Contents of the Book of Shadows

In general, most *Books of Shadows* contain sections on Rituals and Magical Techniques.

The rituals almost invariably include instructions for casting and closing a magic circle; procedures for invoking the Goddess into the body of the Priestess (known as 'Drawing Down the Moon'), and the well-known 'Charge of the Goddess'; and procedures for the consecration of magical tools. Rituals for initiation into the 1st, 2nd and 3rd degrees are included as are rituals to be performed at the seasonal festivals.

There are also passages on a variety of what might be called psychic development and ways of magical working. They are likely to include details of the various methods of working magic, how to become more clairvoyant ("To Get the Sight") and how to travel astrally. There is also guidance on spells.

Many present-day *Books of Shadows* include what are referred to as the Craft Laws, frequently said to be an invention of Gardner in response to a criticism of his publicity seeking. I will not comment on them now, except to say that I consider them to be worthy of detailed study, beyond the scope of this book. I have a feeling I will return to them at some stage in the future.

## Ye Bok of Ye Art Magical

This manuscript book, now in the possession of the Wiccan Church of Canada, is in Gardner's handwriting and was found hidden in the back of a cabinet when Ripleys were examining the contents of the Museum of Magic and Witchcraft after they had acquired them from Monique Wilson to whom Gardner had left the Museum and its contents in his will.

Allen Greenfield describes his first impression of it:

At first glance it appeared to be a very old book, and it suggested to me where the rumours that a very old, possibly mediaeval *Book of Shadows* had once been on display in Gardner's Museum had emerged from.[21]

In fact, the leather cover had originally been on a book about Asian knives[22] but the original title had been crudely scratched out and the new title tooled in. There is also on the front cover a pentagram with a triangle above - the symbol for a third degree witch.

The book itself, according to Aidan Kelly, "consists of almost 150 large sheets, folded and sewn into signatures". The pages are approximately foolscap in size (8ins x 13ins). They were then handbound into the cover. Kelly adds "not very skilfully". I have not seen the book itself, but as Kelly refers to approximately 300 pages (and this is confirmed by other sources) I am wondering if he means that there are some 75 folded sheets rather than 150.

It was in Gardner's handwriting and had initially been prepared with blank pages between the original text. The book had been gradually added to by putting additional material on those pages. By looking at the pattern, and also the neatness of the writing, Kelly was able to determine the approximate order in which things had been written or copied into the book. It had originally been intended (as its title suggests) as a book of ceremonial magic, with material taken from Mathers' version of the Greater Key of Solomon, published in 1888 23. A large part of 'Ye Bok' is an abbreviated transcript of *The Goetia, The Lemegeton, The First Book of the Lesser Key of Solomon the King*, copied by S.L. MacGregor Mathers from manuscripts in the British Museum. The 'Bok' seemed to originate from a time when Gardner was still very interested in ceremonial magic.

This copying out was a great feat in itself, presumably because Gardner felt that it was important, and that he couldn't acquire an original copy of that text. It probably wasn't that he couldn't afford it, but that he wasn't prepared to wait until a copy became available.

Knowing Gardner, it is almost certain that he never tried to use this material in rituals or magical workings. He was aware of the old mediaeval grimoires and, as he was going through his 'ceremonial magic' phase, he attempted to construct something similar, and this appears to have survived in the guise of this volume.

It was only later that Gardner copied witch rituals and other witchcraft material into it as well. Much of this is in a large and very ornate script intended to be seen at a distance during the performance of rituals. There are some idiosyncratic spellings, of which Ronald Hutton says: ... *the aberrant spelling seems to have been part of the attempt to give the contents an archaic appearance.*[24] I do not agree that there is any significance in this apart from the fact that Gardner was just bad at spelling. This was probably partly at least because he was self-taught. He had never been to school and he tended to spell words phonetically.

By the early 1950s, it seems as if 'Ye Bok' was merely being used to record rough notes for a new book, which latterly came into the possession of Doreen Valiente. This, for the first time, was known as The Book of Shadows.

### 'Text A'

Gardner gave one manuscript volume to Doreen Valiente, who used it in compiling her own *Book of Shadows*. It is now in the collection of her books, papers and magical tools which are in storage pending the establishment of a permanent archive and museum to commemorate Doreen's life and work. I have had the privilege of seeing and handling this book and studying it in detail.[25] Janet and Stewart Farrar have referred to it as 'Text A'.

It is a mass-produced blank ledger book of foolscap size, i.e. 7.6 ins wide x 12.65 ins high, ruled wide feint in pale blue and with vertical red lines. It consists (at present) of 93 leaves, has covers of fibre-card, and a red cloth binding on the spine to a depth of 0.6 ins.

I am no expert on the history of stationery, but it appears to me to be of wartime or immediately post-war production. Even as late as 1951, Gardner could not manage to get a blank book to produce a grimoire for a museum display [26]. Paper was in short supply during that period and it is clear that he used whatever he could find - a book with vertical ledger lines, rather than what he might ideally have wanted for what was essentially a ritual item.

It is difficult to see 'Text A' as a unity, as it seems to have performed three totally different functions. It was originally intended as a working document to be used in rituals. Later Gardner copied out other material, mostly poetry from someone else's collection, what he described elsewhere as "a witch's book". Later still he used it as a book to copy relevant extracts from books he had borrowed, plus drafts of his own talks, articles, etc.

There are basically three styles of writing in the book representing, I believe, these three periods of entry (see Illustrations 39 and 40). Firstly, there are the rituals, which are written in large, ornate lettering. A double-page spread from this is reproduced in Doreen Valiente's *The Rebirth of Witchcraft* [27]. The lettering is large, ornate, distinctively coloured in green, red, blue and black, and is clearly intended to be seen from a distance in a ritual supported by a stand.

The ritual material is similar to that which has already been published by the Farrars and Aidan Kelly and contained in Gardner's *High Magic's Aid*. There are the usual blessings and rituals for casting the circle, together with the first, second and third degree initiations, which are similar but not identical to those in '*Ye Bok*'.

Text A is similar to 'Ye Bok' in that the ritual material is spaced out throughout the book. Gardner has numbered the pages from 1 to 187, page 1 being the inside front cover. The ritual material is on pages 2, 9, 37-54, 77-81, 153-155 and 173-175.

*Top: 39. The highly ornate caligraphy of the ritual passages in 'Text A' intended to be read from a distance during rituals. Bottom; 40. A further extract from 'Text A', the upper four lines in neat writing have probably been copied from another witch's book. The lower passage has been added later by Gardner when the book was used a s anotebook.*

Interspersed between these pages are pages with neatly copied verse and some prose. This is in neat and usually readable handwriting, which is nevertheless distinctively Gardner's. I have identified much of the verse, with the invaluable help of internet search engines, and it includes at least five poems by Kipling, and others by Crowley, Tennyson, Yeats, Masefield, Buchan, Nathalia Crane and 'Fiona McLeod' as well as traditional verse such as *'Tom O'Bedlam's Song'* and *'The Hills of Ruel'*.

There are also some poems which I have not yet been able to identify. This may be because they have obscure sources or because they have never been published and thus may have been by acquaintances of Gardner or even by Gardner himself. There are also brief items of regional folklore and what Gardner describes as 'General Maxims'. My overall impression is that these have been copied from at least one other person's 'Commonplace Book', where pieces of interest were noted in the days before photocopiers.

Also included is the poem *'Hymn to Fire'*, which I believe to be an early version of *'The Witch Remembers her Last Incarnation'*, which appears in *Witchcraft Today* [28]. Gardner stated that he found this in a witch's book, so it is at least possible that some of the other poems were found in the same book and copied at the same time. Indeed, if one compares the printed versions of the published poems with the versions in Text A, it seems obvious that Gardner copied them from a handwritten source, since the errors made are those which are consonant with such a situation.

As well as poems there are certain ritual elements written in this style, such as the "Blessed be..." sequence. There is a variety of material, some of which seems relevant to witchcraft, but there is a lot which does not even have any sort of magical 'flavour'. It seems to me that much of this was copied from other handwritten sources (presumably other people's commonplace books) without a great deal of thought as to its relevance.

The third category consists of pieces written in Gardner's usual handwriting, which is very difficult to read. These fill up most of the book and it is clear that they were written last as they fill in the blank spaces, with the same piece being split up between what were obviously gaps that could be filled in. They consist in the main of extracts from, or paraphrases of parts of, published books, presumably those that he didn't own. People didn't buy as many books in those days, even someone as affluent as Gardner, and esoteric books in particular were often difficult to obtain. This was before the days of photocopiers and people therefore copied out perhaps extensive extracts from books that particularly struck them, or that other people recommended or that they thought might come in useful. Some sections I have yet to identify and may be copied from previously unpublished works (perhaps an earlier Book of Shadows) or essays by Gardner himself. They include considerable extracts from Crowley's work, together with that of C.G. Leland, J.S.M. Ward, C.W. Olliver and Mathers *"Key of Solomon"*. Some may be Gardner's own work. By the time Gardner was including these passages, it was being used merely as a notebook rather than as what we would now consider a *Book of Shadows*.

There are also what appear to be extracts from books which I have so far been unable to identify, on a variety of magical subjects including the Kabbalah; The Great Mother; Initiation of the Knights Templar; Moon Worship; Egypt, Celts and Witchcraft; Thomas à Becket and Witchcraft, Ceremonial Magic and the Effect of Invocation. I am sure that in most cases these are just passages which Gardner found interesting from books which he had borrowed and are significant only in that they shed light on his interests of that period.

There are certainly extracts from Hugh Ross Williamson's *The Arrow and the Sword* (published 1947)[29] and Robert Graves' *The White Goddess* (published 1948)[30] as well as notes for a talk on Amulets which Gardner gave to the Folk Lore Society in June 1946. Professor Ronald Hutton confirms this when he writes:

*I would date much of it to the year 1948, for two reasons. First, in the section on amulets it mentions an encounter with a commando regiment guarding the beach at Highcliffe, 'when I was living' there 'four years ago'. Now, the obvious time for a front-line attack force like a commando regiment to be patrolling that beach would be in 1944, in the massive build-up of troops on the south coast before Operation Overlord. This tentative dating is given further circumstantial support by the quantity of material on the Templars in the manuscript, quite irrelevant to what Gardner wrote later, which suggests to me that he was still in his OTO phase and identifying with those knights.*[31]

He also pointed out to me that there is a picture from a magazine dated February 1950 pasted over the contents page and he takes this to be the date by which the book was completed. Whilst this is probably true, it is also possible that the book was completed quite some time previous to that date, and the picture pasted later. Alternatively, the picture may have been in Gardner's possession for some time before it was pasted in the book.

As an insert to Text A, there is a stapled folded foolscap (8ins x 13ins) lined booklet which contains further extracts plus some of Gardner's own writing.

My impression of Text A is that it was not really a Book of Shadows as we would recognise one today. It was a book which Gardner used, first of all, for some of the rituals to be read within the circle. Secondly, he used the blank pages to copy from some as yet unknown volume, which he described elsewhere as "a witch's book". Thirdly, he used the remaining pages to copy passages of interest from books which caught his eye. This confirms to me that it was written at a time when paper was in short supply - the immediate post-war period.

## 'The Witch Remembers her Last Incarnation'

In *Witchcraft Today* Gardner quotes a poem at the end of Chapter 10 entitled 'The Witch Remembers her Last Incarnation'[32]. He writes that he found them in a witch's book that he possessed, but which had no indication of who wrote them. There is in Text A what seems to be an earlier version of this poem in Gardner's own handwriting and I suspect that the difference between the two versions is due largely to careless copying on Gardner's part. If we take him at his word that he copied the verse out of a witch's book, then the earlier version might be of some interest.

Hymn to Fire [Original Version as in Text A]

> *I remember, O Fire,*
> *How thy flames once enkindled my flesh,*
> *Among writhing witches caught close in thy flame woven mesh*
> *How tortured for having beheld what is secret,*
> *We were flung to the fire for the joy of our sabbath*
> *But to those who who had seen what we saw,*
> *Yea, the fire was naught,*
> *Ah, well I remember*
> *The buildings ablase where burned*
> *In the fires we lit, and smiled to behold the flames wind*
> *About us, the faithful, among the faithless and blind.*

*To the chanting of prayers the frenzy of Flame,*
*We sang hosannahs to the, O strength giving fire:*
*Pledged love to thee from the pyre!*

There are at least 13 differences between these two versions, the most obvious, of course, being the title. The phrase "Hymn to Fire" occurs in both Hindu and Zoroastrian writings, suggesting that the verses may have been written by someone familiar with those traditions. Lines and phrases have been altered and missed out in the published version, including the vivid concept of "flame-woven mesh", which is surely worth including. If one compares the two versions it seems obvious that Gardner copied them from a handwritten source. Gareth Medway believes this poem to be by Victor Neuburg. If his authorship could be confirmed, this would be a very significant step in our research.

My conclusions are that both 'Ye Bok' and Text A were being compiled at roughly the same time (the late 1940s) and that the rituals and certain other material were copied from a third document or documents perhaps no longer extant. Gareth Medway agrees with this conclusion and points out that:

*The initiation ceremonies seem to be in an earlier form in Text A, and were probably copied from there into Ye Bok; on the other hand ... the Key of Solomon material was entered into Ye Bok first, then later into Text A. This further suggests that the two books were co-equal. If indeed the two books were compiled at about the same time, notice that at first Ye Bok contained ceremonial magic material, but no Witchcraft; while Text A contained the initiation ceremonies but not the Charge of the Goddess or some other basic Witchcraft rites. These latter, then, were for some time not in either book. This does suggest that there must have been another book that did contain them. And, of course, if there had been a coven in existence by 1939, one would expect at least some of their rituals to have been written down even then. Most likely, then, Text A and Ye Bok both date from the period when Gardner was starting to run his own coven, i.e. after the war.*[33]

# Chapter 13

# An Exercise In Creativity

Even a cursory examination of a present-day Book of Shadows will reveal passages which are taken from already published sources, many of which are well-known in their own right. Gardner acknowledged that this was the case, although even he was probably reluctant to admit the extent of the borrowings, though he may genuinely not have been aware of it all.

Fred Lamond has said: *Everybody in the coven knew that Gerald and Doreen had put the Book of Shadows together on a scissors and paste basis ...* [1] Indeed, it seems likely that the *Book of Shadows* currently in use by most present-day Gardnerians is a much more elaborate document than anything which may have existed when Gardner was initiated. Those who have looked into it, including Doreen Valiente, Ronald Hutton, Aidan Kelly, Roger Dearnaley, Gareth Medway and others, including myself, have identified sources from which parts of the Book of Shadows have been derived.

And there are, indeed, many different sources. Internet search engines have been very helpful in identifying far more than had previously been the case, and I acknowledge my gratitude to those who invented such a valuable research tool. An examination of these sources might enable us to learn something of the interests of those who compiled the Book of Shadows, the extent of their library and some narrowing down of the dates when such compilation may have taken place.

Apart from any surviving older material, we can say that there are six main sources or traditions from which specific parts of the Book of Shadows material are derived.

Firstly, the form and structure of the rituals owe a lot (as most modern mystery traditions do) to Masonic practice and ritual and particularly Co-Masonry.

Secondly, the consecrations, an important part of the ritual, are derived from *The Key of Solomon*.

Thirdly, certain ritual elements are derived from Golden Dawn material.

Fourthly, some of the most powerful invocations and much of the poetry and evocative language are from the works of Aleister Crowley.

Fifthly, from the works of Charles Godfrey Leland come parts of the evocative *Charge of the Goddess*, which have become such a well-known element in the rituals of the modern Craft.

And lastly, there is material, sometimes just minor phrases or names, from a wide range of other writers.

We shall be looking at these in more detail, but, when all this material is identified, there are parts of the ritual which do not seem to derive from any known source and which could therefore either be old material or modern creations.

## Freemasonry and Co-Masonry

Probably because of its relative longevity, there has been an inevitable influence by Masonic practice on a variety of esoteric movements, both direct and indirect. We know that Gardner was a member of the Sphinx Lodge in Colombo (No. 113) shortly after he took his first job in Ceylon at the age of 16 [2]. He was only an 'Entered Apprentice' [3] - the lowest grade -

and there is no evidence that he was an active member again, either during his working life or during his retirement in England.

However, there is a separate Masonic tradition which admits women as well as men, known as International Co-Freemasonry, or Co-Masonry for short, and we know that several of Gardner's friends, notably the Mason family from Southampton and Edith Woodford-Grimes ('Dafo') were members of the Harmony Lodge (No. 25) in that city. There is a rumour that Gardner was also a member, but the Co-Masons' records have been destroyed and I have been unable to find independent evidence for this. However, I quote below from an e-mail dated 27th August 1993 from Khaled to Brian Downs, which was provided by Michael Howard: *Gerald's involvement* [with Co-Masonry] *is confirmed by letters addressed to him concerning the splitting of some English Comasons from their Paris HQ in 1935 and dated June and July of that year.* I have so far been unable to track this down, but it would be a significant advance in our research and might well indicate that Gardner met Edith Woodford-Grimes via the Co-Masons whilst he was still in London in the 1936-37 period, if not before.

Whilst the Masonic rituals are supposed to be secret, they have been published, for example in Walton Hannah's *Darkness Visible*[4]. An examination of this shows that there is much in Wiccan ritual which appears to be taken from Masonic practices, and several researchers, including Gareth Medway[5], Steve Wilson and Steve Jones have identified many of the key elements.

(1) Masonic rituals are oriented according to the four points of the compass. Medway quotes C.W. Leadbeater as saying: ... *the usual system of invoking the four elements in the four quarters seems to have been brought to England from India and first practised in Co-Masonic lodges.*[6]

(2) Ritual circumambulation (walking or dancing round in a circle) is a feature of both.

(3) The similarity in the two traditions is most striking in the initiation rituals. In both, there are three degrees, the candidate, being 'properly prepared', is blindfolded and is ceremonially bound with a 'cable tow' placed round the neck and has cords at the right ankle and left knee. The candidate is admitted at the point of a sharp instrument and then takes an oath. The 'working tools' are then presented.

(4) There are several other similarities, such as the same terminology, including "The Craft", which is used for both Freemasonry and witchcraft, although this may have come into common use after Gardner's time, for as recently as 1960 he referred to "The Craft" as meaning Freemasonry:

*He has always had a very soft spot for the Craft, and nowadays feels that there are close similarities in the craft of the Witches; in fact he goes so far as to say that Witchcraft is the original Lodge.* [7]

As Steve Wilson writes:

*Imitations of Freemasonry became common throughout Britain, usually these orders were for Health Insurance. This spread the sword-point initiation idea to the lower classes, along with the phrase 'so mote it be'. An early Masonic song includes the phrase 'merry meet and merry part and merry meet again'.* [8]

Both 'so mote it be' and 'merry meet etc.' are popular phrases in modern witchcraft.

## The Key of Solomon

In an article which appeared in the magazine Illustrated in September 1952, the author, Allen Andrews, says that the 'Southern Coven': ... *base their ritual on instructions handed down from the elders, eked out with the Clavicles of Solomon, an obscure book which changes hands at some sixty guineas a time.* [9] The implication of this is that the material from the Key ("Clavicles") of Solomon was some of the first to be added to what we may surmise was the original ritual material.

*The Key of Solomon* consists largely of details about the right time to carry out workings, personal preparation and discipline; how to form a magic circle, prayers and conjurations; how to make and use pentacles, magic garters and carpets; how to consecrate a variety of magical instruments, water salt and incenses; and a variety of magical techniques such as divination and invisibility.

Gareth Medway [10] notes that: "It is fairly clear that the *"Key of Solomon"* was a legendary title, and hence given arbitrarily to several different magical works." He has examined the various texts now known by that title and is of the opinion that it was first written in Latin by Italian Catholic writers. He bases this view on the authors' lack of knowledge of Hebrew, the presence of numerous buried Christian references and the fact that the blessings of water, salt, etc. are similar to those used in the Catholic Church. As it uses material from Cornelius Agrippa's *Occult Philosophy*, published in 1533, it seems to date from the 16th Century.

Mention of the cost of obtaining a copy of *The Key of Solomon* in 1952 (the equivalent of over £1500 in today's money) shows the rarity of the volume, which had not been reprinted since 1909.

By the end of his life Gardner had an original 1888 edition of Mathers' translation in his library, as well as a facsimile of a handwritten manuscript [11]. There were also various handwritten copies (or probably in some cases just extracts) in circulation, of which Gardner had three in his library. How he acquired these I do not know. Perhaps manuscript versions were actually fairly common, as I suspect there was a lot of copying of manuscripts or particular parts thereof, perhaps at 2nd, 3rd or 4th hand from the British Museum and other originals, copying errors creeping in in the process.

Gerald Yorke, in an inscription in his own copy of Gardner's *High Magic's Aid* writes: *He takes his magic from a MS Clavicula which I gave him and his witchcraft from a secret society dealing with witchcraft of which he is a member, but whose name I do not know.*[12] By this, Yorke may have meant the Gollancz facsimile, published in 1914, mentioned above.

The fact that Gardner borrowed *The Key of Solomon* from Yorke does not necessarily mean that the extracts from that work in 'Ye Bok' and Text A were copied from this, as Hutton alleges [13]. Gardner may just have needed it for writing *High Magic's Aid* and the quotations in 'Ye Bok' and Text A may have been copied, at a time when he had no access to an original, from a witch's book which, in its turn, had been copied directly from *The Key of Solomon*.

Roger Dearnaley has made a study of this and has come to the same conclusions:

*... the Key of Solomon material in the published version of High Magic's Aid does not come from Ye Bok of Ye Art Magical - they contain different material with different copying errors in it - but was separately copied from Mathers, which is also evidence supporting the theory that the latter could have been copied from a manuscript derived from Mathers rather than directly from a printed copy.*[14]

In comparing the *Key of Solomon* material in 'Ye Bok' and

Text A, I found that there are several quotations which appear in both. They are all from the second part of *The Key of Solomon*, which is referred to as 'Book Two'. They are all 'conjurations' or exorcisms, what we would probably today call consecrat-ions.

They involve:

> The Benediction of the Salt
> The Bath
> Of the Light and of the Fire
> The Conjuration of the Sword
> The Needle and Other Iron Instruments
> Of Wax and Virgin Earth

The passages in *Ye Bok* and Text A are generally quotations from *The Key of Solomon*, although they are in some cases adaptations. Some passages have been added that are not in the *Key of Solomon*. For example, in Ye Bok, the section on The Bath has added at the end: But ever mind, the water *prifieth the body, but tis the scurge that purifieth the soul and increth the inner sight*. And in Text A, the section on the Sword includes the statement *Magus and helper shall be as naked as a drawn sword and purified*. These clearly seem to be additions by someone, possibly but not necessarily Gardner, who wanted to emphasise nudity and scourging.

The passages in Ye Bok and Text A are in all cases shorter than the originals in *The Key of Solomon*, i.e. some sections have been missed out. For example, the section on 'Reciting Psalms' is always left out of both Ye Bok and Text A.

In some cases, the passages in *Ye Bok* and Text A are identical, both differing from the original in *The Key of Solomon*, suggesting that one was copied from the other, or both from a third source independent of *The Key of Solomon*.

What seems to have happened is that someone (possibly Gardner) made copies of parts of the Mathers edition of *The Key of Solomon* particularly relating to consecrations of tools. There was a certain degree of selection in this, such as omitting reference to the saying of Psalms, plus a general shortening of the 'introductory' passages (as opposed to the actual 'conjurations'). This was itself copied (probably with some amendment) into Ye Bok when Gardner was wanting to create a 'grimoire', and, at a different time, into 'Text A'.

## *Aleister Crowley*

One source from which a lot of the *Book of Shadows* has been taken is repeatedly mentioned: the works of the occultist, Aleister Crowley (1875-1947). There is a considerable amount of material taken from Crowley's writings, much of which is generally recognised to be some of the finest occult or esoteric poetry of the 20th Century. Gardner met him in 1947: I tell of this meeting and what emerged from it in Chapter 9.

We know from Doreen Valiente that Gardner introduced Crowley material into the *Book of Shadows* himself. In *Witchcraft for Tomorrow* she writes:

*That these rituals contain phrases from Crowley's published works is ... undoubtedly true. Gerald told me that the rituals he recorded were fragmentary. He had to augment them in order to make them workable; and he used some quotations from Crowley's works because he recognized the magical power and beauty inherent in Crowley's writings, though he had no great admiration for Crowley as a man.*[15]

In a letter to Allen Greenfield she writes:

*... there is no doubt that Crowley had a great influence on Gerald Gardner. He proclaims his membership of the O.T.O. on the title-page of "High Magic's Aid". In a way, this influence*

*was a great pity, because I think Gerald fell under Crowley's spell for a while, as many people did, and incorporated much O.T.O. material into the "Book of Shadows", possibly displacing older rituals to make way for it, with the idea of bringing the Old Religion into Crowley's new "Aeon of Horus". Not being quite as be-glamoured by Crowley as Gerald was, I did my best to sling this stuff out again - as I have explained to Janet and Stewart Farrar.* [16]

In *The Rebirth of Witchcraft* she writes:

*As time went on, I had in practice become Gerald's High Priestess. He had got over his discomfiture at realizing that I could spot all the Crowley material in the rites we used. He explained this to me by saying, firstly, that as the holder of a Charter from Crowley himself to operate a Lodge of the OTO, he was entitled to use it; secondly that the rituals he had received from the old coven were very fragmentary and that in order to make them workable he had been compelled to supplement them with other material. He had felt that Crowley's writings, modern though they were, breathed the very spirit of paganism and were expressed in splendid poetry. That was why he had used them.* [17]

It has been suggested that Gardner's statement in Witchcraft Today that there are: ... *certain expressions and certain words used which smack of Crowley* [18] was deliberately duplicitous, the implication being that Gardner knew perfectly well that they came from Crowley because he had incorporated them himself.

I think there is another explanation. Someone else, prior to Gardner, had incorporated some Crowley material into the rituals. Gardner had looked through *Magick in Theory and Practice*, a copy of which Arnold Crowther had given or lent him, and incorporated some of it into the rituals, but may well have been unfamiliar with most of Crowley's other works, even after he had met him. It was only after Doreen Valiente tackled Gardner that he began to realise how much Crowley material had already been incorporated into the Book of Shadows. This may be why Gardner said that some parts "smack of Crowley". He was not denying his own Crowley additions, but may not have been sufficiently familiar with the rest of Crowley's work to positively identify them.

There is indeed much Crowley material in 'Ye Bok' and Text A and Doreen Valiente did remove much but not all of this when she and Gardner produced a revised Book of Shadows in the mid 1950s.

Gareth Medway and Roger Dearnaley have done some remarkable and detailed detective work and they have determined that all the Crowley extracts in 'Ye Bok' could have been obtained from only two works - *Magick in Theory and Practice* and *The Blue Equinox.*

The bulk of the Crowley material in the *Book of Shadows* comes from his Gnostic Mass, which incorporates extracts from his sacred text, "*The Book of the Law*". This material is included mainly in the sections of the Book of Shadows dealing with the 1st, 2nd and 3rd degree initiations, the Sabbat rituals, and the elements of ritual known as 'Drawing Down the Moon' and 'Lifting the Veil'.

Gareth Medway has looked at the Crowley content in the *Book of Shadows* and has found that some of the quotations are not from the most readily available of Crowley's works. For example, one quotation is taken from his essay The Law of Liberty rather than directly from Liber Legis (*The Book of the Law*). He says:

*It is essential to notice that the quotations from The Book of the Law in the Book of Shadows are all at second hand from The Law of Liberty and The Gnostic Mass. The only explanation that makes sense is that the Book of Shadows was drafted by someone who did not possess a copy of The Book of the Law.*[19]

An analysis of the Crowley material in 'Ye Bok' has been carried out by Roger Dearnaley[20]. Firstly, he identified the Crowley passages in *'Ye Bok'*. He found that these were all derived from a limited number of Crowley's works, namely *The Law of Liberty*, the *Gnostic Mass*, *Liber Cordis Cincte Serpente* and *Khabs am Pekht*.

These passages happened to be all included in an edition of Crowley's journal *The Equinox*, published in Detroit in 1919 and which is commonly known as "The Blue Equinox", so that all the Crowley content of the Book of Shadows could be obtained from that one volume alone.

Significantly, it would not be necessary for the compiler to have had access to Crowley's sacred text, *'The Book of the Law'*. Indeed, there is much excellent poetry there which would fit well into the context of the *Book of Shadows* which is not used. It is therefore highly likely that the compiler was not an O.T.O. member, since they would have received a copy on becoming a member. As Dearnaley says:

*... whoever did* [compose the Wiccan rituals]*, while they took some material from a few of Crowley's published works, was evidently not very familiar with Crowley's writings, and seems very unlikely to have even been an O.T.O. initiate.*[21]

Also, the writer takes liberties with the text of *'The Book of the Law'*, which an O.T.O. initiate would never do, because of its sacred nature.

I don't think that Gardner had read much of Crowley's work - probably just *Magick in Theory and Practice* which Arnold lent him and, at a later date, *Book 4*, which he refers to in correspondence with Cecil Williamson. In particular, I don't think he was familiar with most of the contents of *The Blue Equinox*, although he later acquired a copy. He could therefore say truthfully that there were phrases which "smack of Crowley" but which he could not identify. In other words, they were present in the rituals as he received them from Edith.

It has been suggested by some [22] that Gardner paid Crowley to write the rituals for him. A moment's thought will disprove this. There is nothing in the Book of Shadows which "smacks of Crowley" that has not been positively identified as being from one or other of Crowley's published works. And if they are from Crowley's published works, then clearly he did not write them specifically for Gardner's Book of Shadows. In other words, if Crowley had written something for Gardner's Book of Shadows it was in a style totally alien to his usual writing. Quite clearly in my view he did not! It seems obvious to me that at some stage someone (not necessarily Gardner) incorporated material from Crowley's published works into the Book of Shadows.

## Rosicrucianism

There is little evidence that Gardner was directly affected very much by the philosophy and rituals espoused by the Crotona Fellowship during the two-year period (1938-40) that he attended their meetings in Christchurch.

If there is any Rosicrucian material in the Book of Shadows then it was probably introduced through Edith Woodford-Grimes, who was a prominent member of the Crotona Fellowship, or, I suspect, Rosamund Sabine, who may well have been also. Certainly there was much interchange between esoteric movements of the period and the Crotona Fellowship rituals which I have seen seem very Masonic.

Some members of the Crotona Fellowship were certainly

aware of, and used, a variety of magical techniques such as weather magic and positive thinking and it is a little unclear in which tradition Gardner's friends who claimed to be of 'the Wica' as well as the Crotona Fellowship - Edith Woodford-Grimes and the Mason family - developed their powers. In fact, it is likely not to be that clear-cut.

## The Golden Dawn

In Chapter 3 we saw how Rosamund Sabine had been involved in Golden Dawn-type activities, and it has certainly been noticed that the Book of Shadows contains material similar to that in the Golden Dawn rituals. Gareth Medway has confirmed this when he writes:

*... the borrowings in the Wiccan rituals strike me as being of the kind that would be made by someone who had been familiar with both Co-Masonry and the Golden Dawn ... system for years beforehand.*[23]

He has noted some of the similarities as follows:

*... tracing of Pentagrams in the air is a G.D. practice ... Chapter 15 of "High Magic's Aid", "Charging the Pentacles", involves a variant of the method of the G.D. "Z" documents, and is a much shorter form of the ritual given in Israel Regardie, The Golden Dawn Book 3, pp195-211. Gardner owned Regardie's book, but the version in "High Magic's Aid" does not look as if it was derived directly from Regardie. It may be pertinent that in each case - the initiations, the Pentagrams and the consecration - the Wiccan method is much shorter and simpler than that of the Golden Dawn.*[24]

Aidan Kelly has identified many similarities and correspondences between the 1st degree initiation ritual in the Book of Shadows and the Golden Dawn Neophyte ritual[25]. Some of what Kelly suggests as similarities are in fact not so, but the following certainly are:

> Purification by sprinkling and censing the temple to the four quarters
> Circumambulation
> The candidate is blindfolded
> There is an oath of secrecy
> The candidate is given a new name
> The candidate is shown various secrets

A lot of this is clearly based on masonic ritual, but there is some that is distinctively Golden Dawn.

## Minor Sources

Researchers have identified a variety of other sources, often just an odd reference, but indicative of the wide reading which those who compiled the *Book of Shadows* had carried out. These include:

Brodie-Innes, J.W. *The Devil's Mistress* 1915
Cahagnet, L.A. *Magnetic Magic* 1898
Frazer, Sir James *The Golden Bough* 1890
Fuller, J.F.C., *The Black Arts* in *Occult Review* 43 1926
Graves, Robert, *The White Goddess* 1948
Grillot de Givry, Emile, *Witchcraft, Magic and Alchemy* 1931
Harrison, Jane E. [various works]
Ithel, Rev. J.W. *Barddas* 1862
Kipling, Rudyard, *Puck of Pook's Hill* 1906
Leland, Charles Godfrey *Aradia* or *The Gospel of the Witches of Tuscany* 1890
R.Lowe Thompson - [various works]
*The Merry Order of St. Bridget*
Woodroffe, Sir John ('*Arthur Avalon*') *Shakti and Shakta*

This list is very incomplete, but gives an indication of the rich variety of sources from which evocative passages and phrases have found their way into Wiccan rituals.

## Evidence for an Earlier Book

On reading through 'Ye Bok' and Text A it gradually became clear to me that much of the ritual and other material was copied from an earlier manuscript book. For example, on examining the initiation rituals in both I found numerous examples where each included words or phrases not found in the other.

For example, in the section relating to the consecration of the wine (Kelly does not identify the origin except to say that the sources are "clearly Judaeo-Christian") "conjoined" is missed out of Text A and "Hands and ..." is missed out of 'Ye Bok', suggesting that they were both copied from a third document.

A comparison of the first, second and third degree initiation rituals in Text A and 'Ye Bok' reveals a considerable number of differences. The Text A version is usually shorter and less formal than 'Ye Bok'. But each contains words that are omitted in the other, such as the following:

Text A: *Domains of the Dread Lords; perish misrably; With oil, wine and lips; They go out to P(ostulant) and give this warning; Vultis flagellari in discendo?*
Ye Bok: *Time is ashamed, the mind bewildered; plessent abodes; Be Pleased to Kneel; and perform Ritual of Pentagram; Tho hast obeyed the Law; twice consecrated and Holy.*
These do not have the appearance of additions but integral parts of some text which Gardner, with the careless copying which was almost his trademark, left out of one of the two versions. I strongly suggest that these passages were both copied (or adapted) from a third, earlier document which may no longer be in existence or at least not publicly known. There is what I would describe as an undefinable maturity about the rituals. It seems clear to me that they had evolved over some,

perhaps considerable, time and that the versions which appear in 'Ye Bok', Text A and in *High Magic's Aid* are unlikely to be the earliest - they appear to be the result of an evolutionary process.

Gareth Medway also makes the comment that:

*Such phrases as the "Domains of the Dread Lords" are not in Gardner's style. This is important, because some other parts of the Book of Shadows, e.g. The Warning, are in Gardner's distinctive pseudo-archaic style. It seems reasonable to suppose that those passages not in his style were not composed by him, but copied from somewhere else.* [26]

There is also some anecdotal evidence for the existence of an earlier book. Doreen Valiente, in an interview with Michael Thorn in 1991 stated:

*... Cecil Williamson ... said that Gerald had an old book which was not a very big book. It was a manuscript book, and he used to keep this very carefully. Unfortunately, one day when he was showing visitors round his museum in the Isle of Man, this book was stolen ...* [27]

Williamson gives further details in a letter written to Michael Howard in 1982:

*How well I remember that little book ... it never left his side and it is a true fact that he even took it to bed with him ... tucked into the Book of Shadows Gerald had two large sheets of carefully folded very thin air-mail type paper. These were covered from top to bottom in closely-spaced hand-writing done with a pen and a fine steel nib. Much of it was like blank verse and the rest descriptive instruction. One sheet had the Crowley symbol ... in the bottom left-hand corner ...*

*Well, on that fateful day there was Gerald putting on the*

*charm ... he left his table to take a small party of French ladies upstairs to see. His only exhibition stall was a showcase near the head of the stairway in which were displayed the Loan Collection of artifacts as used by the New Forest coven.*

*This was around three o'clock on a Friday afternoon. Lunch was over and the staff had not reset the tables for the cream tea trade. Being Gerald, and being in charming company he did his stuff and treated his party to an extended tour of the Museum. In due time they descended and departed - Gerald was provided with his usual afternoon tea, and later gathered up his gear to go back to his house. Only then was it discovered that his beloved "Book of Shadows" was missing. It was quite clear that some visitor had drifted in, browsed around and pocketed the "Book of Shadows" as a souvenir. All rather sad.*[28]

From clues in this account we can date the loss of the book as probably 1952.

Gardner's excessive protection of it suggests strongly that it was not originally his, in other words that it pre-dated his own Book of Shadows.

Gardner mentions witches' books in *Witchcraft Today* : *The faith of the cult is summed up in a witch's book I possess which states that they believed in gods who were not all-powerful. ... In this book are the following verses, but no indication of who wrote them:*[29] There then follows the poem, 'The Witch Remembers her Last Incarnation', which I quote in Chapter 12.

It seems clear that this book was originally somebody else's but that it had come into Gardner's possession by the time he was writing *Witchcraft Today* in 1952-53, though he might have acquired it far earlier. He may have been given the book or inherited it. We have to remember that by 1954 he was

Director of the Museum of Magic and Witchcraft and it is quite conceivable that it might have been given to him or left to him in a will because of the role that he occupied.

The only other mention in his writings of a witch's book are the following:

*I found these verses in a witch's book. The owner did not remember where they were copied from or if they were ancient or modern, if they were by someone who had seen the dance or simply by someone with a vivid imagination. So, with acknowledgement to the unknown author and congratulations on a good bit of description or imagination, I give them:*

> *Twilight is over, and the noon of night*
> *Draws to its zenith, as beyond the stream*
> *Dance the wild witches, fair as a dream*
> *In a garden, naked in Diana's sight,*
> *Flaming Censers on the sweet altar, light*
> *Gleams on the waters, drifting vapours teem,*
> *Laughter and swaying white shoulders gleam,*
> *Oh joy and wonder at their lovely sight!*

The author of this evidently had no faith in the foul old witch story.[30]

It is not clear whether this is the same book as the above, for Gardner talks about discussing it with the witch. Perhaps it did not leave the witch's possession, but he was allowed to copy it.

Gareth Medway has drawn my attention to the fact that this verse is actually an adaptation of Crowley's poem *By the Cam*, which was published in his *Songs of the Spirit* in 1898 and in his *Collected Works Vol 1* in 1905.[31] The equivalent in the last four lines in Crowley's original reads:

> *Foul censers, altars desecrated, blight*
> *The corpse-lit river, whose dank vapours teem*
> *Heavy and horrible, a deadly stream*
> *Of murder's black intolerable night.*

Crowley's verse emphasises the image of the "foul old witch" and Gardner's last comment rather suggests that he was aware of that fact. And yet, the adaptation does not seem to be by Gardner. If the witch were telling the truth about not knowing the origin of it, then it must have been copied from another book, perhaps owned by somebody with a poetic nature who may have felt inspired on reading Crowley's poem to write something based on it which put the witches in a more positive light. It is also remotely possible that the poem dates back to the 19th Century and it was actually Crowley who did the adaptation.

I think it is significant that two out of the three extracts from witches' books that Gardner quotes are poetry. In this context, it is interesting that *'The Witch Remembers Her Last Incarnation'* appears in Text A (as *'Hymn to Fire'*) along with several other poems, and the "Blessed Be..." sequence, all apparently written at the same time and, from internal evidence, copied from a manuscript source. So perhaps these items were in the same witch's book. Indeed, perhaps this is what witch's books largely consisted of - a mixture of verse copied from elsewhere or newly-written, plus recipes of various sorts, but with, in addition, sections on witch ethics, ways of working, old spells, etc.

It is generally accepted, and I think I have demonstrated in the earlier part of this chapter, that much of the Book of Shadows in use today originates from known literary sources. This is not, however, the same as saying that Gardner invented it all, because, firstly, there is quite a lot remaining in the rituals with no known source and, secondly, even for those sections of known provenance, we do not have to assume that they were introduced by Gardner.

I have also found a tendency to state that individual elements "come from" a particular source when in fact they have only a slight resemblance to it. To give just two examples, let us take what is perhaps the most distinctive piece of ritual in the whole of the Book of Shadows - that which is known as The Fivefold Kiss. It is a well-known and loved part of modern Gardnerian ritual, where it is accompanied by a physical fivefold kiss. There are slightly different versions: the one in Text A is as follows (I have, as usual, preserved Gardner's spelling):

> *Blessed be thy feet*
> *Which have braught the in these ways*
>
> *Blessed be thy knees*
> *That shall kneel at the sacred Alter*
>
> *Blessed be thy Womb (or orgen of generation)*
> *Without which we would not be.*
>
> *Blessed be they Breasts*
> *Erected in beauty and in strength*
>
> Blessed be thy Lips
> Which shall utter the Sacred Name.

This is in the same neat writing which much of the poetry is in. It has subsequently been 'written round' to fill up the page. '*Hymn to Fire*' was copied from a witch's book, so perhaps this was as well. The 'Ye Bok' version, apart from the inclusion of one phrase - 'the Fount of Life', which is from Crowley - seems less polished, perhaps from Gardner's memory. No one has identified its origin. Although some have claimed that it has echoes of the Five Points of Fellowship in Masonic ritual, the two are almost completely dissimilar.

In Text A the wording of the challenge, which is given to all candidates for initiation, is:

*O thou who standeth on the threashold between the pleasent world of men and the Domains of the Dread Lords of the Outer Spaces, Hast thou the courage to make the Assey? (Placing sword point on Postulants Heart) For I say verily It were better to rush on my sword and perish than to attempt it with fear in your heart.*

Apart from the use of the sword, which is in Masonic ritual, this does not seem to be derived from any known source. Most initiation rituals include some such challenge. This wording, however, seems unique to the Gardnerian Craft, as does the method of admitting the candidate to the circle. To quote from *High Magic's Aid*:

*... going behind him she blindfolded him, then clasping him from behind with her left arm around his waist, and pulling his right arm around her neck and his lips down to hers, said: "I give you the third password: 'A kiss'." So saying she pushed him forward with her body, through the doorway, into the Circle. Once inside she released him, whispering "This is the way all are first brought into the Circle." She then carefully closed the doorway by drawing the point of her Athame across it three times, joining all the circles.*[32]

The phrase "by thy rosey love" occurs in the Lammas ritual in 'Ye Bok'. It is an unusual phrase and suggests some special significance for roses and for the rose. We have already seen that the one article we know of written by Rosamund Sabine was entitled *'The Rose of the World'*, and have noted possible links to the Fellowship of the Rosy Cross and the Rosicrucian connections of some of the witches that Gardner met.

## Concluding Remarks

It is now generally recognised that the Book of Shadows in common use today derives from quite a number of identifiable sources plus material written by Gardner himself and Doreen Valiente. I suspect that in his non-fiction books *Witchcraft Today* and *The Meaning of Witchcraft* and the later Books of Shadows to which Aidan Kelly refers, dating from 1957, Gardner felt increasingly able to put in some of the material which the witches he knew had told him, but which he was reticent about in *High Magic's Aid*. The Book of Shadows and particularly 'Ye Bok' and Text A are worthy of much closer investigation than I have given in this chapter, which, I suspect, would reveal the heart of the ritual which is distinctive to the Craft.

# Chapter 14

# The Cunning Man and the Temple of the Muses

Gerald Gardner ran the Museum of Magic and Witchcraft at Castletown on the Isle of Man for almost ten years, from April 1954 until his death in February 1964. He described it, probably with justification at the time, as being the only museum of its kind in the world. Even though it closed in the 1970s and its contents dispersed, it played an important role in the modern history of the Craft and, as such, its story is worth telling.

Its importance lay in three directions. Firstly, it was a point of contact for journalists and others wanting to write about witchcraft. Gardner being the sort of person he was, they knew they could rely on him talking to them, and he gained much publicity as a result - for the Museum, for his books, and for the Craft itself.

Secondly, any museum is an attraction of attention, both from interested visitors and from those who are able to provide information. As Gardner says in the very first sentence of *The Meaning of Witchcraft*:

*My Directorship of the Museum ... brings me a great deal of correspondence from all parts of the world; some interesting, some abusive (a very little, just enough to enliven matters), some fantastic, and some funny in all senses of the word.* [1]

But a museum also attracts exhibits. There were clearly many people who had items, perhaps bequeathed by a relative, who were looking for a "good home" for them. A museum devoted exclusively to magic and witchcraft would in many cases seem to fit the bill, and so Gardner gradually accumulated items with which to expand the museum. And he also made contacts - a lot of them, including a variety of people who either claimed to be witches or wanted to become one.

The story of how Gardner came to be in the self-styled position of Director of such a museum needs to be looked at in some detail, particularly as it includes collaboration with someone who is never mentioned by Gardner in his published writings - Cecil Williamson.

Museums were probably in Gardner's blood. Bracelin[2] records how he bought a knife in the Canary Islands with his first pocket money at the age of seven, and his fascination for collecting went on from there. *Gerald Gardner Witch* includes a photograph of Gardner's wife, Donna, in their Johore bungalow in front of a wall on which all sorts of weapons are displayed. This developed into a detailed study of the Malay *kris* - the local magical weapon - which culminated in the publication in 1936 of Gardner's first book, *Keris and other Malay Weapons.*[3]

It seems likely that Gardner had had the idea of a museum of witchcraft at the back of his mind possibly as early as 1939 when he acquired the box of witchcraft relics about which he wrote the article for *Folk-Lore* journal. We know from this article that by 1939 Gardner was also in contact with J.S.M. Ward and was therefore undoubtedly familiar with his Abbey Folk Park, which opened in 1934. I am sure that Gardner would have approved of this pioneering venture in a form of display which has now become virtually universal.

During the war, Gardner retained his interest in history by joining the Historical Association and in June 1944 was elected co-President of the Bournemouth and Christchurch branch. The following month, he gave a talk to the local Adult School on "A Museum for the Borough of Christchurch". At that date, Christchurch had no museum: Druitt, the local notable, had opened one at his own expense at the Red House, but this had closed.

Gardner described the typical museum of the time. Of Gardner's experience of the one in Bournemouth, the *Christchurch Times* reported:

*His first impression had been that there was "no decent system of labelling: no one to tell you anything: a doorkeeper, whose answer was, "look what the label says." If there wasn't a "label", or the label was upside down or on the wrong article, it didn't then seem to be anybody's business to put it right."*[5]

He went on to say: *Museums, called by the Greeks, "The Temples of the Muses", ... should be places to foster love of learning and beauty, the love of country and liberty: places which would inspire youth to defend these things.*[6] He was obviously pleased with this pronouncement because it is reproduced in Bracelin.[7]

He contrasted this with the museum at Salisbury, which he said was:

*... beautifully run. They concentrate on local things and, with the aid of models, showed exhibits in a way that were easy to understand. "It is possible to see, at a glance, how beautiful and well designed many things were in the past: and you realise that houses needn't be ugly or ill-planned," he said, adding that he could not imagine a boy who had been interested in Salisbury museum designing or allowing to be put up a badly designed house.*[8]

Gardner's talk caused a certain amount of correspondence in the local paper. In a letter to Councillor Donovan Lane, he made the following points:

*Mrs. Woodford Grimes has raised the question of a Museum at several of her lectures to various women's societies in Christchurch (the women's branch of the British Legion among others) and they had all said the same thing, viz. they didn't want museums, because the only thing they were interested in was in getting better houses built, and that the local museums were so uninteresting. So I took this for my theme, showing that local museums were only uninteresting because they were put in charge of a doorkeeper who was only interested in drawing his pay and who, sure of a fixed job, discouraged visitors; people coming in meant answering questions and being bothered. No people meant no work and steady pay. So they made the place uninteresting while, where museums were made interesting, they were full of people and children, and were so good for education: and that if a museum was properly organised to show the local types of buildings by models showing good and bad construction, they would be able to get the good houses they were clamouring for and not get the bad types of construction they were complaining about.*[9]

There are at least two points to be made about this. This letter, in the *Christchurch Times*, is from Donovan Lane, who is quoting from a letter written by Gardner, presumably to Lane himself. Gardner must therefore have known Lane reasonably well and it has been rumoured locally that Lane may have been a naturist, although no evidence has been forthcoming. Secondly, Edith Woodford Grimes was clearly still very closely involved with Gardner.

Gardner was unable to do much more of a practical nature to encourage the re-establishment of a museum in Christchurch as, particularly when the war had come to an end, he was spending more and more time in London. However, the Red House is once more a museum and one, I am sure, of which Gardner would have approved.

*41. Gerald Gardner in 1951.*

He was therefore obviously very interested, when he had a chance encounter at that centre of the occult scene, Atlantis Bookshop, with someone who was wanting to set up just such a museum. Atlantis Bookshop was a favourite meeting place in the immediate post-war period when interest in such topics was much rarer and less well accepted than it is today, and it seems to have been the custom for free coffee to be made available to customers, some of whom may have travelled a considerable distance.

Some time following the publication of Gardner's *High Magic's Aid* in July 1949, probably in the summer or autumn of 1950, Gardner was paying a not infrequent visit to the shop to enquire about sales when there entered a character whose life was to be closely bound up with his for the next few years

- Cecil Williamson.

His story is important enough to devote a chapter to it, and I have taken its title from an article about him written by Michael Howard in his journal, *The Cauldron*.[10] In fact, his life was exciting and significant enough to merit a full-scale biography in its own right.

## Cecil Williamson (1909-1999)

Cecil Hugh Williamson was born at 9am on 18th September 1909 at Paignton in Devon. His father had had a long and distinguished career in the Royal Navy and had later joined the Fleet Air Arm. One of the family homes was Newlands Manor, at Everton, between Highcliffe and Lymington, so there was a definite connection with the New Forest area. The other home was Carrington House, Shepherd Street, in the prestigious Mayfair area of London. Previous occupants had included Nell Gwynn and Lord Nelson and, according to Williamson, there was "a sad female ghost and an overactive poltergeist".[11]

Cecil's first contact with witchcraft was at the age of seven when he was spending the summer with his uncle, the Reverend William Russell-Fox, Vicar of North Bovey, on the edge of Dartmoor. One afternoon, there was the sound of uproar on the village green. Cecil found four or five farm-workers tormenting an old woman. He tried to protect her, but was subject to kicks and punches himself until his uncle appeared. Apparently the workers thought that their cattle had had a curse put on them and that the old woman was a witch and was responsible. After getting drunk, they attacked her, saying they were "looking for the devil's teat". A week or so later, Cecil met the old woman again. She befriended him and taught him a lot of practical skills, like tickling for trout, as well as folklore and witchcraft, for she was indeed a witch.

Cecil's next experience of the power of magic was when he was a resident at Norfolk House Preparatory School, near Beaconsfield in Buckinghamshire. Being rather bullied by the older boys, he used to escape by helping in the garden. One day he saw an old woman picking up twigs who seemed to know that he was not very happy. He told her about the bullying, particularly by a boy named Bulstrode [12]. She showed him how to make a swing on a branch hanging over a bonfire. He sat on the swing and, in time to its movements, he intoned "Go away Bulstrode!" He repeated this several times during the term. Bulstrode did not return for the winter term - he had been badly injured in a skiing accident.

Cecil's grandmother lived at Thurloe Square, South Kensington (which, incidentally, was where, later, Dorothy Fordham had her town house), in a residence which she shared with the astrologer, Mona Mackenzie. They were friends with Madame de la Haye, a medium, palmist and Tarot reader. At her seances, Cecil used to dress up in white and stand very still until she asked him questions to "put to the spirit world". "Then she would move something, like a little bell, to show me whether I was to answer 'Yea' or 'Nay'. That was all I had to do. And I also got paid!" [13]

There was a family expectation that Cecil would be going into the Navy, but at that time Dartmouth was not taking any more pupils, so he went to Malvern College, of which one previous pupil had been Aleister Crowley.

One experience which widened Cecil's experience of life was the Docklands Settlement in Canning Town, London. This was sponsored by Malvern College and run by Kennedy Cox. Cecil volunteered working in a soup kitchen, dropping off bread. He saw tremendous poverty, but he met many people, including those who described themselves as witches and wise women. He said: "They were good people, who gave of their skill free, for nobody had any money ... in the middle of the city, you had this back-street cult of wise women and people who told fortunes and this and that". [14] Alec Gill [15] has found a similar tradition in the fishing community of Hessle Road, in Hull.

When he left Malvern College, his father decided that Cecil should go to Southern Rhodesia (now Zimbabwe) to learn to grow tobacco. Cecil's "houseboy" was Zandonda, a retired witch-doctor, who taught him a lot about what he called the secret world of "never-never land".

Returning to England in the early 1930s, Cecil was attracted to the growing popularity of the film industry. He worked for several studios as a film producer, the most notable episode of which was, he says, "helping to have Broadway Melody dubbed into forty seven languages". In 1933, he married his co-director's niece, Gwen Wilcox.

During this time in London, he built up contacts with individuals in the occult world. The list reputedly included Aleister Crowley, Montague Summers, Harry Price, Wallis Budge, Margaret Murray and James Laver, as well as practitioners of rural witchcraft - the characters he called 'Auntie Mays'.

In 1938, as war loomed, Col. Maltby, an old family friend, who worked for MI6, the Secret Intelligence Service, invited Cecil to meet him. He had learned of Cecil's knowledge of the occult and wanted him to find out the names of Nazis in the German military and government who were interested in the occult. To carry out this task, Cecil created the Witchcraft Research Centre, together with headed notepaper and visiting cards. He then made several visits to Germany under the guise of a folklore researcher, compiling a list of 2000 Nazi officials who were interested in astrology and the occult.

When the war started, Col. Maltby sent Cecil to work for Richard Gambier-Parry, who ran what later became the

Political Warfare Executive, one of the objectives of which was to broadcast programmes on wavelengths near those used by German transmitters, so that some misinformation could be fed to those listening. At first, this was in Whaddon Hall and Wavendon Towers in Bedfordshire, but in 1942, the most powerful transmitter in the world, known as 'Aspidistra', was installed in Ashdown Forest in Sussex. Williamson lived nearby, in Gorse Cottage, Chuck Hatch.

He continued to live there throughout the war, although later Cecil became involved in Operation Fortitude, which fed misleading information to convince the Germans that the 1944 Normandy landings were merely a diversion from a major attack which was to take place in the Pas de Calais.[16] Various methods were employed, including artificial airfields with papier-mâché aircraft! Cecil's role was to set up in a truck in the New Forest making broadcasts which simulated Army manoeuvres which gave the impression that they were concentrating their forces in Essex for a possible invasion from that location.

When the war ended, Cecil was demobilised: *I was without a job. My assets were a little cash in hand from wartime pay, and a large data file on the occult and the supernatural.*[17] He decided to go back to the film industry, and in 1948 he was filming Trophy Island in the Isle of Man, which set the scene for the 1949 TT Races, including a piece featuring the last native speaker of Manx Gaelic.

However, Cecil sold his interest in the film company and was looking for another way of making a living. Like Gardner, Williamson seems to have been a born collector and friends who were connected with London museums commented to him that his "stuff ought to be seen by the public as it was too good to be tucked away".

He was undoubtedly at a crossroads in his life and open to new ideas when he made that fateful encounter with Gardner in Atlantis Bookshop in the summer or autumn of 1950.

## Chapter 15

# The Witches' Mill

The setting up of the witchcraft museum on the Isle of Man is an important part of Wiccan history, and its story reveals insights into the characters of both Gerald Gardner and Cecil Williamson.

We are fortunate in that Gardner's letters to Williamson, during the 1951 to 1954 period, are preserved in the Museum of Witchcraft archives at Boscastle in Cornwall. But it is an inevitable fact that correspondence only takes place when individuals are apart - letters are not usually written to the same extent when people are in daily contact. And, at the time (late 1950), Williamson was living (or at any rate working) at 2 Wardour Mews, D'Arblay Street, Wardour Street, London W1, and Gardner was at 47 Ridgmount Gardens, which were less than a mile apart.

The first item of correspondence between them is dated 4th January 1951, a note from Gardner which refers to Williamson as "Mr. Wilkinson", which suggests that they had not been acquainted long! Indeed, the way in which Gardner addresses Williamson is interesting and helps to date some of the letters. The earliest note calls him "Mr. Wilkinson", as mentioned above; then he is referred to as "Mr. Williamson" (i.e. Gardner gets the surname right); then as "Cyril" (in other words, on first name terms, but he gets the name wrong); then, finally, as "Cecil"!

So, the early discussions between Gardner and Williamson following their meeting in Atlantis Bookshop are not recorded or, at any rate, any correspondence does not appear to have survived. It certainly seems as if many different ideas were being discussed, and they mostly seemed to focus around the Witch's Cottage.

It seems that Williamson started his search for somewhere to display his exhibition material back in May 1950, for in the guide booklet issued at the opening of the museum, he writes: *... after nine months of persistent but fruitless endeavour the idea of trying to open in England was abandoned.*[1] We don't know exactly what efforts Williamson made, but they seem to have been tied in with the Festival of Britain.

## Celebrating the Festival of Britain

1951 was the year of the Festival of Britain - the centenary of the Great Exhibition of 1851 and an opportunity to publicise the cultural and industrial life of Britain emerging from the austerity of the Second World War.

Gardner and Williamson clearly had the idea of capitalising on the interest surrounding this event by making the Witch's Cottage available as an exhibition centre to show something of the history and practices of witchcraft. The idea was to dismantle the cottage and re-erect it temporarily, for the duration of the summer of 1951 (the Festival ran from 1st May to 30th September that year) wherever it was wanted. I don't think any detailed costings had been worked out and in practice the cost of moving and re-erecting it would undoubtedly have proved prohibitive, as Williamson was eventually to realise.

The main Festival of Britain site was on the South Bank in London, but there were also numerous local events taking place that summer. Williamson had written to several local Festival committees offering the cottage and an accompanying exhibition, which probably hadn't, at that stage, been put together. At the end of January 1951, he received rejection

42. Cecil Williamson in the doorway of the Witches' Cottage in 1951.

letters from Chelsea and Canterbury. It seems, however, as if Warwickshire did not dismiss the idea out of hand, as the Birmingham *Sunday Mercury* reported:

*Mr Williamson has searched the country for a suitable site on which to erect his museum, which will also incorporate exhibits on all aspects of magic, including voodooism. After consulting the Town and Country Planning authorities he has decided upon Warwickshire - preferably near to Warwick itself.*[2]

The following week, the *Daily Herald* was reporting things more definitely:

*"Mr. Williamson favours Warwickshire, always a witches' stronghold, "where there are seven or eight most charming witches". And he has found a site which foreign visitors could get to easily."* [3]

## Stratford-on-Avon

The mention of foreign visitors suggest that Williamson had Stratford-on-Avon in mind, about which he says the following:

*...I had met a very nice doctor in Stratford on Avon, one of whose pet interests was collecting apothecary jars. This doctor's house and surgery was quite close to the church at Stratford where the bard was buried. During the war a considerable part of the doctor's very large garden had been taken over by the Fire Brigade who had cut all the trees down and put concrete down and built a lot of block garages. When the war finished, he asked the Fire Brigade to take them away but no one took the slightest bit of interest. So he said to me, "would they be any use to you to open up and put your showcases in and have a little exhibition. Four walls and a roof and plenty of parking space". So I said "Yes, rather!" and set about quite happily. Everything was doing nicely, setting*

up a museum in his back garden until the press got hold of it and did an article on it, all about tourism and so on. The Tourist Board was quite interested but then the locals got to hear about it and I was run out of town so fast it was nobody's business!*[4]*

We know that Williamson never actually moved the Witches' Cottage, but could his enterprise at Stratford on Avon actually have been as late as 1951? He may well have been negotiating with the doctor and the Tourist Board in the months leading up to February that year. Williamson himself admits he was 'run out of town so fast it was nobody's business'. Indeed, the exhibition may never have formally opened, and by the end of the month he was already turning his sights elsewhere - to the Isle of Man.

## A Museum at Five Acres?

During January and February 1951, Gardner was out of the country, wintering abroad, as was his custom, this time in Gibraltar, staying at the prestigious Rock Hotel. In his absence (and he usually went on his own, not with Donna), he left Williamson a note dated 4th January 1951, which stated, unambiguously: *To Whom It May Concern: I have give the Witch's Cottage to Mr. Wilkinson* [sic] *to Remove when he can get transport. G.B. Gardner.* This tells us that they expected that things would go fast and that the cottage might be needed for removal while Gardner was away.

There was quite a lot of correspondence between Gardner in Gibraltar and Williamson. He had obviously told Gardner about the rejections from Chelsea and Canterbury (and possibly elsewhere) because, in a letter dated 8th February 1950 (almost certainly actually 1951) Gardner makes the suggestion to Williamson that he puts in an offer for the half share in Five Acres Club not owned by Gardner and his friends and that he opens it as a museum and witchcraft study centre. He says:

> ... *there is a Row on at the Club where I took you that day, & one section say sell the damned place. There are supposed to be 5 acres there, & another 2 acres for £200/- some income from parts leased to people who own the Huts, a good Club House, which you saw. I'd value the land at £100/- per acre, Club House at say £300/-/-. Say £800/- more or less for the place, & an additional 2 acres for £200/-. The Club House wd make a lovely museum & Refreshment Room, Caretaker in adjacent Hut. Leave the Witchs Cottage where it is this year, take people to museum first, then to cottage by the entrance they came in. Move Witchs Cottage next year. We then could have the centre for a Study Group, who could stay out there in Huts if they liked. Being a Nudist Club no one could object to Nude Dances & Rites only the Actual Ceremonies wd have to be kept secret. But this is all in the air, & any breath of it would make them refuse to sell, & no mention of my name, or there be trouble, but think it over & see how it strikes you.*[5]

Whilst Gardner was trying to persuade Williamson to make the cottage at Bricket Wood into a tourist attraction, there is the first indication, at the end of February, that Williamson had turned his sights elsewhere. Gardner says:

*Do I understand that you will open the museum in the Isle of Man, & do you want to transport the Witches Hut up there?*[6]

## The Isle of Man

Williamson had learnt from his experiences in Stratford. He began to look elsewhere for somewhere where the environment for opening his exhibition might be more congenial. It would have to be a tourist area, but he had been rather discouraged by the bureaucracy involved with local government in England, particularly the need to get planning permission which had been introduced universally four years previously in 1947.

His thoughts began to be directed towards the Isle of Man, where he had directed the publicity film for the Tourist Department and had kept in touch with some of the staff. He approached them informally and they were enthusiastic about his project. Perhaps in part because of his established contacts, Williamson found the attitude of the authorities on the Isle of Man much more positive than in England, and he received help and encouragement from the Castletown Board of Commissioners and the Chief Executive Officer of the Publicity Board. Anticipating objections, and with the wisdom of hindsight, Williamson recounted:

*This time I took good care to play down all mention of that awful word witchcraft. All the documents concerned with the project bore the style "The Folk-lore Centre of Superstition and Witchcraft".*[7]

He drew their attention to the relative absence of displays on witchcraft, magic and superstition in national and municipal museums.

He went over to the island to look for suitable premises. Those in Douglas proved to be too expensive and so he spread his net wider. He finally found what he was looking for in Castletown, the ancient capital of the island.

## Windmill Farm, Castletown

Williamson's eye was caught by Windmill Farm, on the outskirts of Castletown, a ruined mill, with a collection of outbuildings which seemed fairly sound. The farm, or rather the farmstead and immediate curtilage, consisted of approximately four acres, which was probably the old farmyard and gardens. It was off Arbory Road, in the vicinity known as Red Gap, next to the present-day Castle Rushen

Secondary School, and it appeared to have been disused for some years. It consisted of a dwelling house, two former millers' cottages, several stone barns each over 40 feet long, another large range of detached stone outhouses, a large 3-storey limestone granary and a 60 foot high derelict windmill tower open to the sky.

Williamson could see the potential of the place, which was available on lease at a price which he could afford. The dwelling house was habitable and the granary would be ideal for the museum. There was also a large area suitable for car and coach parking.

The site had an interesting history. The first mill on the site was certainly in existence by 1611, for Gardner quotes a Court Record for that date:

*'Thomas Moore of the Mill was fined two muttons (i.e. two sheep) for not turning out with the Watch and Wand'* [sic - actually 'Watch and Ward'] *(a kind of local defence corps). Millers were excused from this duty; but the court held that his father was the miller, so Thomas had to turn out in future.*[8]

Windmills are rare on the Isle of Man, possibly because watermills were cheaper to build and also because of the frequency of very high winds and gales which make their operation impractical. There are records of only 12 having existed on the Island. The Castletown windmill dates from 1828, though its history, right from the start, was full of misfortune. Qualtrough recounts that:

*... on the Saturday prior to the mill being officially declared open it was decided to see if the mill was in proper working order. The new sails were hoisted and the arms began slowly to turn, causing the two pairs of French and two pairs of Greys millstones to be set in motion. All seemed well and in working order, so it was decided to secure the mill by having the break*

wheel operated. This break wheel prevented the top of the mill from rotating freely. Normally, if the wind veered the top of the mill would move around to take full advantage of the change in direction of the wind. On that eventful Saturday evening the wind suddenly shifted, and before the break wheel could be released and thus allow the top of the mill to move, the sails backfilled and the sail arms were blown off and destroyed. In their fall they passed through the roof of the threshing mill which adjoined the windmill and, as a consequence, considerable damage was done.[9]

A few months later, a severe gale caused the brake-chain to snap and the vanes were destroyed. And in 1848, the mill was destroyed by fire. There is some uncertainty about whether it was rebuilt immediately, because Jenkinson, in his guide of 1874, describes it as "an antique ruin damaged by fire some years hence." Gardner, in his museum guide, writes:

*The Mill got its name because the famous Arbory witches lived close there, and the story goes that when the old mill was burned out in 1848 they used the ruins as a dancing-ground, for which, as visitors may see, it was eminently suited; being round inside to accommodate the witches' circle, while the remains of the stone walls screened them from the wind and from prying eyes.*[6]

I have so far been unable to find any independent verification of this story, so I can't give any opinion as to whether this was anything more than Gardner's fantasy of what he would have liked the history of the mill to have been, though it seems as if he did at some stage make contact with an old witchcraft tradition on the island.

Certainly, when Williamson took over the mill and buildings in 1951 the farm had been abandoned for several years, probably since before the war. His strategy in approaching the authorities seemed to work, because all the necessary permissions were granted. He then proceeded to convert the buildings into a museum and living accommodation. He moved to Castletown and started work on the buildings in April 1951. The property included a small house, which he renovated and occupied, probably in early May 1951, followed by his family later the same month.

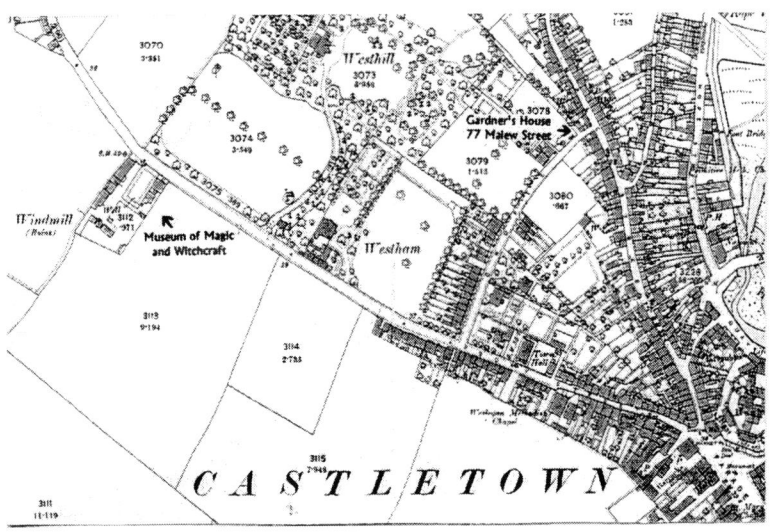

43. *Castletown showing the Museum and Gardner's house.*

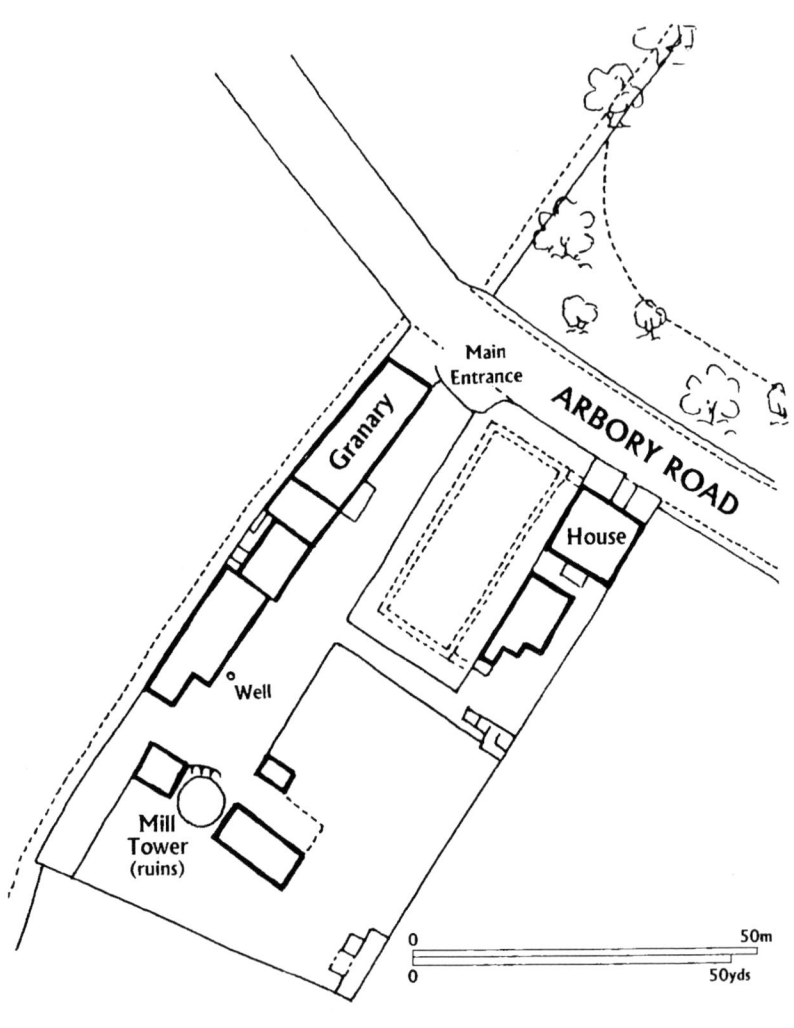

44. *The Museum of Magic and Witchcraft, Castletown.*

45. Windfall Farm buildings in early 1951 before occupation by the Museum.

## Gardner becomes involved

Williamson only told Gardner that he was interested in opening a museum in the Isle of Man in late February 1951. Gardner got back from wintering in Gibraltar on 6th March 1951 and immediately made arrangements to meet Williamson on the island. These seem to have been rather loose arrangements, at least on Williamson's part, since Gardner sent a telegram from the Isle of Man to Williamson at his home in Herne Bay in Kent saying "At George till Tuesday. Are you coming?" [11] Whether they ever did meet at that time, I do not know!

A witchcraft museum was something which combined two of Gardner's greatest interests and at some stage he had probably had a similar idea himself. He clearly didn't want Williamson to beat him to it, so I suspect that on the spur of the moment he decided to get closely involved in Williamson's project.

Williamson had obviously asked Gardner about his box of witchcraft relics, for Gardner wrote: Of course you can have Mat Hopkins Box & anything else you want. [12] Williamson took him up on this, and clearly arranged with Gardner that the bulk of his collection should go to the museum.

Not everyone was as enthusiastic, notably Walter Hildburgh, long-standing member of the Folk-Lore Society, and Gardner's sponsor in his application for membership back in 1939. Gardner wrote to Williamson in March 1951:

*"Donna told Dr. Hildburgh I was giving my collection to a museum in the Isle of Man & he's furious "They mustnt be allowed to leave England, etc. etc." Donna said, England has known about Them & won't let them be Exhibited, so what!!!* [13] ...

It is clear that Gardner kept a keen eye on how things were going, offering advice by letter and coming over to the island on several occasions, usually staying at the George Hotel in Castletown.

## The Witches' Kitchen

Williamson thought that the granary was the most promising building for the exhibition, but he had been carrying out research into what factors helped a museum to be successful, and started by planning a restaurant. This was his wife's suggestion, for *...on inquiring into the ways and means of the museum trade had hit on the hard fact that, whereas there were about 700 museums in the British Isles, not more than a score of them showed a profit or paid their way. As my wife wisely suggested, "At least we will be able to eat on the firm." This restaurant we called "The Witches Kitchen". It was to prove an instant success and the revenue from it allowed me to stay in business with the museum in its first unprofitable two years.*[14] And so plans were prepared to open the restaurant at the same time as the exhibition.

When it first opened, it was known as "The Folklore Restaurant", though it very quickly changed to "The Witches' Kitchen". It was located on the ground floor of the granary building and is described as being 'primarily for the enjoyment and refreshment of the visitors to the Centre'. But there were other aims as well, for it was intended to *'bring back and offer to the public many of the old country dishes associated with the numerous feast and festival days which are found throughout the calendar'*. Particular emphasis was to be given to old Manx dishes and *'those of a superstitious nature'*.[15]

It is uncertain whether this aim was realised, as a menu card, which is reproduced in Illustration 46, has nothing which would be out of place in most ordinary cafes of the period. It

## Menu

| | |
|---|---|
| Morning Coffee and Biscuits | 9d |

| | |
|---|---|
| Grilled Steak, Tomato and Chips | 4/6 |
| Grilled Lamb Chop, Tomato and Chips | 3/6 |
| Bacon, 2 Eggs and Tomato | 3/6 |
| Fried Eggs and Chips | 2/6 |

| | |
|---|---|
| Ham and Salad | 4/6 |
| Cold Tongue and Salad | 3/6 |
| Cold Stuffed Roast Pork and Salad | 4/6 |
| Crab Mayonnaise | 3/6 |
| Egg Mayonnaise | 2/- |

| | |
|---|---|
| Apple Tart and Cream | 1/- |
| Trifle | 1/- |
| Jelly and Cream | 10d |

## Menu

| | |
|---|---|
| Strawberries and Cream | 2/- |
| Strawberry Sundae | 2/- |
| Fresh Peach Melba | 2/6 |
| Raspberries and Cream | 2/6 |
| Ices | 6d. & 1/- |
| Coffee | 6d. |

**Afternoon Tea**     2/-

(Tea, Bread and Butter,
Scone & Butter & Jam,
Cakes.)

**Devonshire Tea**     3/-

(Tea, Boiled Egg, Bread and Butter,
Scone, Butter, Jam and Cream,
Cakes.)

*46. The Witches' Kitchen daytime menu card.*

is, however, possible that the menu card was for daytime only and that the fare in the evenings was more elaborate, for in the first season the premises stayed open from 10am until midnight.

A poster for the restaurant produced shortly after its opening stated "We are famous for our superb Home Baked Cakes in the old Manx farmhouse style", adding "To Drink? What better than the Original Witches Brew?" This was said to have a rum base. Whether it was ever made, or whether the establishment ever actually got a licence for the sale of intoxicating liquors, I don't know. Certainly, after Gardner took over, it didn't, much to his regret.[16]

*47. The Witches' Kitchen*

From the evidence of surviving photographs, the restaurant appears to have had a very strong atmosphere with large beams and simple but heavy timber furniture (see Illustration 47). Teare describes it as follows:

*"... blackened beams bedecked with relics from the past ... solid unpolished wooden tables, a feature in themselves, spotlessly clean with their uneven contours following the shape of the tree*

*trunks from which they have been hewn."* [17]

The restaurant paid its way during the crucial first season, vindicating the decision to open it along with the exhibition. Of course, nowadays no self-respecting museum would be without a cafe area attached, but the Williamsons' step in opening the restaurant was pioneering at the time.

### The Exhibition

When Williamson took over the building, there was no staircase between the ground and first floors, probably because there had been an external timber staircase that had been removed when the granary closed down, perhaps for use elsewhere. In his view, the upper floors would be ideal for the exhibition, so he pondered on where to put the staircase. Gardner, in a letter dated 17th April 1951 strongly advised an internal staircase:

*Would it not be better to have the staircase inside, instead of outside the building? It will be warmer. Also, if it comes on to rain, People won't want to go out in the Rain to go to the Museum, or from the Museum to the restaurant. What is wanted is for People from the Restaurant to think 'Oh, it's showery. I'll go up to the Museum for an hour till it's over...'* [18]

In the end, this is what happened: the staircase rose from the middle of the restaurant up to the exhibition areas on the upper floors.

Williamson intended to start on a fairly modest scale in the first season, with an exhibition on the first floor. The central feature was to be a reconstruction of the magic circle as used by the Elizabethan magician, Dr. John Dee:

*The main feature will be Dr. Dee's magic circle, of which he produced carefully drawn plans. The circle must be constructed to a complicated formula of dimensions and there are constituents involving an altar carved with innumerable cabalistic signs each with a separate significance; inscriptions of the names of Hebrew gods; nine candlesticks each in the form of a different symbol; black earth (to be specially imported), the eye of Horus; the magician's wand and cup and four white swans' wings.*[19]

It is clear that Williamson wanted the circle to be "live", as he described it, "not just a waxworks". He intended to invite witches to the island to use it: "When it is completed, members of the only sect in the world who can endow the circle with power are coming here to do so."[20] He involved the local community in this work, not just in obtaining construction materials from local contractors, but in commissioning the Douglas School of Art:

*In the preparation of Dr. Dee's magical circle, Mr. Williamson encountered difficulty in having a series of brightly coloured and extremely intricate emblems - which are an essential part - executed. Commercial firms would not tackle the job, and he was stumped until the students of the Douglas School of Art stepped in. By arrangement with Mr.W.H.Whitehead, the principal, the students carried out the work very successfully - they painted the Hebrew characters and Thebian* [sic] *outlines perfectly, completing the Tree of Life, Calvary Cross, the seals of Saturn, Luna and Mercury, and the Devil's Head without fault. It is probably the strangest job they will ever have.*[21]

As part of this exhibit there was the matter of the "black earth" from the banks of the River Ronce in France: *They tried to get permission to bring over a couple of hundredweights of specially spooky black earth from France - but the superstitious island authorities said. 'No.'*

At the time he was being interviewed, in April 1951, Williamson clearly still had hopes of bringing the Witches'

Cottage to the Island for a period, though he gives a rather romanticised view of its history, for he says that it is: ...*a genuine Elizabethan witches' hut in which the cult of witchcraft has been practised since the 16th century.*[22]

Apart from the centre-piece of the circle, the main exhibits were from Gardner's and Williamson's existing collections. Williamson's material consisted of magical items from a variety of cultures in all parts of the world, particularly talismans and items designed to protect from the 'evil eye'. Gardner had lent the contents of his box of witchcraft relics together with assorted vessels and knives, including what was reputed to be a "500-year old sorceror's sword". There was also a shrine to the memory of those who had died as a result of witch persecutions over the years.

Gardner worked closely with Williamson during this period, collecting and making appropriate items for display as well as advising on where certain items might be acquired. His skill at making ritual items and his contacts with likely manufacturers were acknowledged and appreciated by Williamson. Gardner had been trying unsuccessfully to get a copy made of one of his ritual swords and, in the end, offered to make a wooden one. He had some larger items which were obviously in the witch's cottage at Bricket Wood which he was trying to arrange transport for. He offered to make a crown and a silver bell, and made suggestions as to where Williamson might obtain an appropriate lamp and chain. He was also painting a picture of a witch-burning for the Sanctuary.

By May 1951, Gardner was promising Williamson various items on loan from the Southern and Northern Covens (i.e. from Edith Woodford-Grimes and Barbara Vickers). He went up to the Island on 10th July 1951 bringing quite a lot of material up with him. Meanwhile he had been busy making and collecting material for the ground-floor display which Williamsom wanted:

*I've been to sevral more Theatrical People, but none of them will make the sword, so Ime bringing up 2 swords for you to see, & I think we can fake them up. Ive made the Unicorns Crown, & got some chain - will have to burnish it ... I have a Bacon Spit of my own Ill bring. Ive made the picture for the shrine, & I have written out a lot of the grimoire ... I think it will look quite imposing when its stuck up. Binding it is a trouble, but will fake up somthing. It seems absolutely impossible to get a Blank Book anywhere nowadays. They say Government prohibit these being made, excepting Printed Account Books. So I got an old album, nice paper but the covers were impossible. ... Re Silver Bell. Ime told that to get Silver to Ring, it must be Cast. Ive got a Dentist who thinks he could cast one. Only, I cant remember what the bell in Book 4 looked like. You say a flat bell, is that like a Cow Bell? We could send him drawings & trust to luck, or there are Bell founders. I dont know if they would take a small job on. Do you need Robes for show? The Theatrical People can make them. But, they say, it takes time nowadays. I sent off the Golden Dawn book before I left. Hope they arrived OK & you can get what you want out of them. The man who works the Golden Dawn Rituals, showed me a lovvely manuscript coppied from some of Dee's. But he won't sell. Ime bringing 2 Daggers up to choose from, & a lot of other stuff.* [23]

I am not sure of the extent to which Williamson had solicited Gardner's advice, as he was a film-maker of considerable experience, but he did appreciate Gardner's knowledge of weapons and his expertise in making things that were needed but not readily available in the post-war period. The dentist referred to was probably Edith's son-in-law, Alfred Maguire.

Gardner also gave his advice, at a distance, on Williamson's idea of converting part of the property into a theatre. Having talked to Edith about it, Gardner was putting forward the practicalities: the need for plays to be staged properly and convincingly with, perhaps, out-of-work movie actors, and the need to work out the costs of conversion.[24] In the end, Williamson did not go further in this direction.

## Gardner Moves to the Island

Gardner had had the idea of taking more permanent accommodation in the Isle of Man as early as April 1951, when he wrote to Williamson: ...*if theres any sort of small house or flat or cottage for rent or sale please let me know & Ill come up.*[25]

This had been made more definite by 1st May 1951 when he wrote: *I want to see about getting a cottage or somewhere to stay, where my wife can come. If there's anything reasonable for sale or leese or of course lodgings. Furnished rooms would do, but they're sure to be full for the summer.*[26]

He kept in touch with Williamson by letter and on his return seems on a sudden whim, probably mid-May 1951, to have arrived unannounced on the Williamsons' doorstep:

*In the spring of the following year* [i.e. 1951] *he suddenly appeared without warning; I turned around to find him standing in my doorway. He had arrived on a flying visit "to see how things were going" - with his overnight things stuffed into an old, battered music case. Gardner planned to return to London a couple of days later, but what he saw changed all that! When he left for London it was to make final arrangements for moving his home to a house in Castletown's Malew Street, a mere stone's throw from the museum.*[27]

During that visit, Gardner definitely began to look seriously for a place to live. Initially he did not find it easy, as house prices were very high. It must not be forgotten that Gardner was by birth a Lancastrian, and the Isle of Man has a particular fascination for inhabitants of that county, particularly for those who live or have lived on the coast. It acts as a sort of 'Shangri-La', 'El Dorado' or 'Tir-na-nOg' - that ultimate destination in the west that is ever strived for. To visit was something which had to be undertaken, like the Muslim's pilgrimage to Mecca: to live there was to reach that which was attainable only by the very few.

*Leasing a house in the Island was next to impossible. Prisoners of War, people who had come to avoid the bombing on the Mainland, people looking for a place with less irksome restrictions than England, seemed to fill the place. Housing was at a premium - a few small houses here and there, at £6,000 apiece. People had paid these prices during the War, and now they wanted their money back. Some of them found that property in England was so costly that they would not be able to move away unless they made an exceptional bargain with their existing property.* [28]

Williamson claimed to have helped Gardner to find somewhere, which he may well have done as by that time he had undoubtedly built up many local contacts. Gardner eventually found somewhere which seemed ideal. It was vacant but the owner was unwilling to sell.

*There was a queer little place at a corner, and I had fallen in love with it. Stone-built; beamed, with lofts and an ideal workshop. I asked about it and was told that it belonged to someone who could have had any price during the war for it, but that he would not sell. 'He has loads of money and never spends any. It is no use asking him'.* [29]

Bracelin reports that Gardner then turned to his fellow witches, and magic, to help: *Gardner sent someone to ask the owner if he would sell, and got a savage No. ... He went to England and asked some witches to perform a rite, to enable him to have the house, "more as a joke than anything."* [30]

Gardner put it this way:

48. 77 Malew Street, Castletown - Gardner's home from 1952 until his death in 1964.

*My secret friends helped me to get my house in Castletown, Isle of Man. I could not find a house within my means on the island. I had to live in digs, apart from my wife. There was an empty cottage but the owner would not sell. He had refused every offer since its last occupant, his brother, had died.*

*Eight other witches helped me to cast a spell. We danced round a priestess of the Moon Goddess. Charcoal, herbs and incense burned in a cauldron. We chanted phrases and made signs handed down to witches for generations ... A strange spirit filled the circle ... I trembled, lost all sense of time as the power radiated from my body ...* [31]

The result was certainly striking, as is recounted in Bracelin:

*Gardner arrived back one afternoon on the Island at three-thirty. At four o'clock, he relates, a man came around to his lodgings. "The owner says he'll sell to you. Come and see him before he changes his mind". Gardner went over to see the old man. Someone, he said, needed a holiday, which would cost so much. If Gardner was willing to pay that, he could have the house.* [32]

Gardner added: *The owner was quite resigned to selling the cottage ... he had quite suddenly CHANGED HIS MIND. It took us only 10 minutes to clinch the deal.* [33]

In a letter to Williamson probably dating from June 1951, Gardner is referring to his "new home" and to dealings with a house agent and lawyer, so it is likely that things moved quickly after Gardner's initial enquiry in April 1951 and that the events surrounding the acquisition of 77 Malew Street took place in May and early June that year. The house was probably bought in early June. However, Gardner records that he was still "trying to get the house ready" in December 1951, and he probably did not move in permanently until his return from wintering in Italy in March 1952.

Bracelin describes the 400-year old house, 77 Malew Street, when Gardner was living in it as follows:

[Malew Street] *runs, curving slightly, toward the edge of the little town. I'ts houses are brightened by restrained colour-washes - grey, or faint pink, or light green. An exception, one of the few, is a low, rough-stone house, built, L-shaped, at the corner of Malew Street and Crofts, a short road that leads into it.* [34]

Gardner quickly made himself at home there, with Donna joining him a short time later. In the context of acquiring 77 Malew Street, Gardner decided to relinquish his flat at 47 Ridgmount Gardens. However, he was reluctant to give up a place in London altogether, as he tells Williamson:

*We're trying to get a smaller flat. None to be had in the ordy. way, & we're trying to do a three legged swap (being a Manx man now it should come natural). It's an awful job packing, when you don't know where you're going.*[35]

He acquired a flat at 145 Holland Road, near Shepherd's Bush in West London. He described this as a "pied-de-terre", in other words a small flat that would enable him to visit London regularly without having to book accommodation. In this, he was carrying on a tradition which I suspect he kept up during the war.

Interestingly, Gareth Medway tells me that the Electoral Register entry for 145 Holland Road had a "John and Mary Gardner" living there. I strongly suspect that this was merely another example of Gardner's sometimes apparently pointless and inappropriate mystification. He frequently used "John" and "Mary" as archetypal names in the stories that he told.

Even though he was there only part of the year, the new flat in Holland Road didn't really suit Gardner. After only nine months he was writing to Williamson: *I get so damned tired it takes such a time to get anywhere these days, being out here is so different from Goodge Street.*[36] Goodge Street Station was the nearest underground station to his previous flat at Ridgmount Gardens. It must be remembered that Gardner was 68 when he wrote that letter.

Gardner settled in to Malew Street very easily and it seemed to most who visited him as if he belonged to the house and had grown old with it. Various descriptions have been given of Gardner at home, those by Bracelin and Teare being remarkably similar:

*Inside, the difference between this house and its neighbours is ... marked, for the walls of the low rooms, of the narrow staircase, of the huge study upstairs, are covered, encrusted with swords, spears, daggers, pikes; clumsy mediaeval blades and bright Toledo rapiers stand side-by-side with curved Saracen scimitars and snakelike kris from Malaya. This is the harvest of a lifetime's interest. Between dull or gleaming steel, books lean and lie in untidy groups - books on folk-lore, on archaeology, on weapons, on the Far East, on psychical research, on Magic, witchcraft, extra-sensory perception, secret societies.*[37]

*The walls were covered with swords, spears, daggers, cutlasses and pistols, the harvest of a collector's lifetime. There were books in every room, on folk-lore, on weapons, on the Far East, on archaeology, on magic, witchcraft, secret societies and suchlike, but these were not contained in show-cases; they were used for daily reference.*[38]

There was a barn leading back from the main building, the upper floor of which Gardner used as his magical temple or ritual area. Access could only be obtained via the bathroom in the main house. Patricia Crowther gives a vivid description of this:

*A small door in the bathroom connected the house to a barn comprising of two stories. The top floor of the barn held Gerald's Magic Circle as well as hundreds of books which lined the rough stone walls. An ancient carved sideboard fashioned with many cupboards and secret drawers occupied a position between the small door and one of the windows, while old swords and pieces of armour decorated any available space on the walls. Beautifully wrought incense burners and lamps from distant lands hung from the great beams, and the aroma of incense permeated everything in this unique chamber.*[39]

Gardner's friend, the writer Alasdair Alpin MacGregor, whom he had met at meetings of the Folk-Lore Society, writes about a ghost which Gardner and a female friend saw when they were performing a ritual. MacGregor only identifies her as 'Miss A', but Doreen Valiente confirms that she was the witness concerned. The ghost of a woman walked across the room without entering the magic circle, eventually vanishing through a wall. Gardner's wife, Donna, also saw a woman of the same description some weeks later sitting on a chair by the fireside. [40]

## The Official Opening

July 1951 was a particularly appropriate time to open a museum devoted to witchcraft, since the last of the witchcraft acts had been repealed the month before: it was no longer illegal to proclaim oneself to be a witch or to practise witchcraft.

Of course, at the time when the exhibition was first being proposed, witchcraft, strictly speaking, was still illegal, under the Witchcraft Act 1735. This was not just of theoretical and historic interest. As recently as 1944, the spiritualist medium Helen Duncan had been sentenced to nine months imprisonment, prosecuted under the 1735 Act for carrying on her normal mediumship activities.

There was outrage at this sentence, from more than just Spiritualists, and as a result of pressure on Members of Parliament, the Fraudulent Mediums Act (14 Geo VI, cap. 33) was passed, and became law on 22nd June 1951. This Act abolished the Witchcraft Act of 1735 and, instead, made it an offence for anyone to "act as a spiritualistic medium or to exercise any powers of telepathy, clairvoyance or other similar powers" with intent to deceive. It also prohibited the use of any "fraudulent device". Thus did the law for the first time recognise genuine mediumship and distinguish it from deliberate deception.

This was very important for the witches. For the first time in many hundreds of years they could practise their Craft without fear of prosecution. The fear of persecution did, however, remain, and most witches preferred to continue to practise their religion in secret.

So, by the time the Folklore Centre opened, in July 1951, it was no longer illegal to be a witch, which was just as well as Williamson made much in the publicity to the fact that he knew witches and that a witch would perform the opening ceremony.

Williamson was a good publicist. He had supplied both national and local papers with material for several months before the opening. Two pieces appeared in the *Sunday Pictorial*. On 29th April 1951, was an article by Barrie Harding entitled *He Plans a Jamboree for the Witches of the World* [41]. The emphasis of the article is very much on Williamson's plan, which is described as "an international gathering of witches, wizards, sorcerors and witch-doctors" On 29th July 1951, the same paper published an article by Allen Andrews entitled *Calling All Covens* [42], which made mention of the Grand Opening that same day of what was called The Folklore Centre of Superstition and Witchcraft. The opening ceremony was to be performed by Gardner, who is described as "the resident witch". Articles also appeared in the local *Isle of Man Examiner* with an interview of Williamson on 20th April 1951 and a piece about Gardner entitled "Introduction to a Witch" on 20th July. The Grand Opening was set for Sunday 29th July 1951 and the place opened to the public the following day. The Isle of Man Examiner reported the event as follows:

*Dr. Gerald Gardner, 67-year-old, white-haired "resident witch" at the witches' den at the Old Windmill Farm, Red Gap,*

*Castletown, performed the first ceremony in the magic circle of power on Sunday. Three young women, first visitors to enter the magic circle, knelt before him as he read part of the ritual contained in his grimoire (textbook of witchcraft practice) to promote a spell of good fortune for them. ... Dr. Gardner stood by the altar in the centre of the mystic circle to perform the initial rites. He held a witch's "thaim" - ceremonial dagger - in his hand as he read from his grimoire.*[43]

Gerald had been staying with Edith in Highcliffe for a 3-week period in late June and early July. He had managed to persuade her to lend some items for the museum and she had agreed to come up to the Island about the middle of July.

Gardner stayed with the Williamsons for a prolonged period and, in the meantime, helped in the museum selling copies of his book:

*He became the 'resident witch' at the museum during the summer season and entertained old and young ladies in the teashop with colourful stories of his adventures in the Far East.*[44]

Williamson paints a vivid picture of the following (1952) season:

*Every day he would toddle over to the Museum around 11.30am, have coffee, chat up the tourists, lunch on the House. He had his own special table located on the left hand side of the wide set of steps leading up from the main entrance. He was decorative, looked the part of a Magician, and of course he was happy, and on to a good thing, for he was selling his book "High Magic's Aid" and of course signed every copy he sold. You can picture the scene - Gerald at a large elm wood Rustic Table, stacks of books, and a litter of letters, papers etc.*[45]

The sign Gardner prepared to advertise that *High Magic's Aid* was available for sale is still in existence, in the possession of the Museum of Witchcraft, in Boscastle in Cornwall, and I quote it on page 248.

## The Second Season

The Restaurant and Exhibition were only open during the relatively short tourist season in the Isle of Man. They closed at the end of September 1951 for the winter.

In January 1952, Williamson had written to Gardner reporting that the enterprise was not doing at all well financially and that he needed some money urgently to continue to pay the rent to Barclays, who were acting on behalf of the owner, J. J. McArd of Port Erin. Gardner, who was wintering in Italy at the time, wrote to Williamson sympathising:

*This is bad news indeed. I was dubious about any customers in Winter. Unless, as we have often talked about, if people can dance & enjoy themselvs somhow they will come, but they won't come out in the cold simply & have lunch & then go home again. ... I'll write to Mr Moore* [Gardner's solicitor]... *asking him to see if he can fix up somthing. Funnily enough, Edith* [Woodford-Grimes] *wrote me two days ago asking about you. Saying that of course you couldent possibly make a place like that pay in the Winter unless there was some attraction. ... She also said why dosent he contact the teachers? School, Elocution, & Music, & suggest that they should give Recitals, & possibly they could link up with their local Drama League. Something to attract the Local Talent. ... Edith speaks as if there are lots of stray Music Teachers & Elocaution Teachers about, not in schools but in private practice. I don't know if there are. Anyhow, good luck & see what Mr Moore can fix.*[46]

Gardner wrote further on 20th February 1952 saying that he would arrange for £200 to be forwarded to Williamson as soon as possible. Gardner also reported that his bank had suggested that he purchased the Windmill Farm buildings and that he offered them to Williamson on a mortgage. He also wrote that his bank would be willing to forward £400 to Williamson and would be amenable to forwarding further sums if the money was spent on buildings and land.

This is a very different picture from that presented by Williamson in his various accounts of the relationship, and shows that, at least initially, Gardner was the benefactor whose actions enabled the museum to remain open.

Williamson obviously agreed to this, because on 29th February 1952 Gardner wrote to his solicitors asking them to prepare a mortgage for £2100. The money was transferred to Williamson at the end of June 1952. The interest was to be at 4%, but Gardner had the discretion to charge 5% if payment were more than one month in arrears. The mortgage was repayable with 6 months' notice on either side.

Williamson was more enthusiastic when he wrote to Gerald Yorke in August 1952:

The formation of this "shop window" was deliberately planned to act as a magnet to draw to one those interested. The place was chosen because it suited my overall plan. So it is that now a year is passed. I look back and see the results of my efforts. These one time, and some what extensive Ruins are now well on the way to re-establishment. The Restaurant is well established. The Museum or Exhibition call it what you will is launched and as such is successful. In short then the entire project is under way and in being...[47]

There was much enthusiasm on the part of both Williamson and Gardner to expand the exhibition into the top floor of the granary with a lot more exhibits for the following season. What is described as the 'upper hall', or upper gallery, of the granary was a fine room, with the roofing timbers on display. There were some 17 display cases (airtight, made by Gardner and Williamson) arranged around a central circulation area (Illustration 49). There were also two "tableaux", representing the interior of a 17th Century witch's cottage and the temple of a ceremonial magician.

Williamson had accumulated quite an extensive collection of amulets and talismans and a large proportion of the exhibits consisted of these. A guidance sheet, which was sold or given to those looking round the exhibition, was largely devoted to an explanation of the philosophy underlying amulets and talismans. It stated:

*Our aim is to please you with Good Food and Pleasant Surroundings and to interest you with our Exhibition of Superstition Magic and Witchcraft. So that together these two things combine to make your visit one that you can look back upon with pleasure.*

*The Exhibition is limited to the study of three subjects, namely: Magic, Witchcraft, and Superstition. Oddly enough, for one reason or another, these subjects are either completely ignored or at the best only lightly touched upon by National and Municipal Museums. One wonders why?*

*Small as it now is, a start has been made to bring together, for the first time in one place, matters relative to this purpose. We have been here but a few months; our aim is to have over three thousand exhibits on display within three years. Behind the scenes we hold a mass of printed and written material. The whole combining to form a solid base from which in time future generations of research workers in this field, may build upon with confidence.*[48]

*49. The Upper Gallery, Museum of Magic and Witchcraft*

The leaflet was undersigned by Cecil H. Williamson and Gerald B. Gardner, indicating that by that stage Gardner had become part of the establishment, as it were.

Williamson was intending to set up some form of membership organisation based on the museum, possibly what was later known as the Witchcraft Research Centre, but initially just called 'The Folklore Centre':

50. *Witch's Cottage display at the Museum of Magic and Witchcraft*

*Anyone is welcome to apply for membership to the Centre. Election is subject to suitable references and payment of the small annual subscription. Members will receive periodically, a journal compounded of current news regarding the activities of the Centre; detailed descriptions of new additions to the collection; articles on a variety of subjects both from members and non-members; answers to members correspondence queries. Members will have free use of the Centre's library (postage extra). Members will be encouraged to help in extending the scope of the collection by themselves gathering items of interest from their own location, whether it be within the British Isles or in any other part of the world. Members may join the study group. The function of the study group is to examine in a practical way, the methods alleged to have been employed for the working of magic. Members will be invited to attend the Centre's annual "Witchcraft convention" held on June 24th of each year at the Folklore Centre, Castletown, Isle of Man.*[49]

I have no evidence that such a membership organisation actually started or that the witchcraft conventions were ever held.

## A Living Museum

It is clear that during the whole of the 1951 season, Gardner and Williamson had not discussed the ritual practices that each were carrying out. In a December 1951 letter, Gardner writes:

*How exactly are you working, what system I mean? You speak of getting results, & answers, somhow it seems as if Ive never had a yarn with you since weve been on the Island, always too busy, or somthing. I know its proberbly my fault. Ime always on the rush, trying to get the house etc ready, next year Ill have more time.*[50]

In an article published in September 1952, Williamson claimed that he had followed a very elaborate spell, including burning the bodies of three toads, a rat and a cock, in order to bring torment to someone, and there are photographs of him carrying out these procedures.[51]

Whilst it is quite possible that this is just another one of Williamson's stories (see Chapter 16), it is clear that neither Gardner nor the witches were happy being linked with what can really only be called 'black magic' and, from that moment on, the relationship between Gardner and Williamson began to deteriorate.

It is clear that Williamson was also interested in the practice of ceremonial magic. His headed notepaper and the first introductory guide for visitors include sigils and quotations from Dee's *Of Spirits and Apparitions*: "Who so bears this sign about him, all spirits shall do him homage" and "Who so bears this sign about him, let him fear no one but fear God".

In a letter to Gerald Yorke dated 7th August 1952, Williamson wrote about forming some sort of magical group. He claimed to have received a message from Crowley, though he was anxious to distance himself from spiritualism. He seemed to be in the process of developing rituals for his group and wanted Yorke to lend him some of Crowley's books to assist in that. I doubt whether this ever amounted to anything: nothing else that I have seen of Williamson's refers to it further, and I can only suppose that it was overtaken by events. It does, however, belie Williamson's future claims that he was only actively interested in the "village wise woman" type of witchcraft.

Gardner liked the dramatic and putting over ideas to people in an attractive way, using what we might today call "multi-media presentation", as we can deduce from his earlier comments about Salisbury Museum. And witchcraft and magic in particular cannot be fully comprehended by static displays: they involve activity and ritual. Gardner and Williamson had obviously discussed the possibility of incorporating special events, including live rituals, into the Museum programme, and in a letter to Williamson on 20th February 1952, Gardner makes some perceptive comments about the difficulties of performing rituals in public:

*... the trouble with them* [Rites] *is, no one will perform the Rites of anything of which he is a member, in public, but they will often go through the Rites of a society of which they are not members.*[52]

In preparation for the second season, Gardner makes the suggestion that Druid ceremonies might fit the bill, probably because they were more public than witchcraft rituals, and therefore could be performed without compromising oaths of secrecy. As we have seen (Chapter 4), Gardner had been a member of the Ancient Druid Order since at least 1946 and knew the Order's Chosen Chief, Robert MacGregor Reid, well. An undated note signed "RMR" (Robert MacGregor Reid) states:

*Re the Isle of Man Druid Lodge. It wants a Founder. That is yourself. And three who are interested. We will assist in all other matters except - at present - financial. It wants a Name and a date for its inauguration meeting, at which you could defect the Mother Lodge.*

Gardner wrote to Williamson in November 1951:

*I have been trying to get a Charter from the Druids. Apparently they will give me one if I can get 3 other members to make a start. Now do you know any likely people? And is there anything in this neighbourhood where we could perform any ceremonyes? I could take it on, then resign and hand it over to you if you like. Being a Crowned Druid, they will give me a Charter to start with, and that gives us some sort of legal standing, so to speak.*[53]

Williamson obviously replied positively because in an undated letter, probably written in December 1951, Gardner states:

*I wrote to Macgregor Reid, asking him to come & see me as soon as I got your letter. It was waiting for me when I got back. but have had no reply yet, only four days so not much time yet, I asked him to grant me a Charter, & to get me copies of the Rituals. They are always so Piso* [I don't know what this word means. The letter is typed, so there's no scope for misreading. In the context it seems to mean something like "secretive"] *about them. I tried to get copies before & they wouldent let me, but if Ime to have a Charter, I must have them.*[54]

In fact, there is a copy of a Druid initiation ritual dated 1948 filed away with the correspondence Williamson received from Gardner, so it looks like he managed to get something!

Gardner went on to express a certain degree of disillusionment with the Ancient Druid Order rituals, for he says:

*Actually, Ive a very poor opinion of what Ive seen. but, we must have somthing to start on, I think we can rewrite them to cut all the false Christanity & silly sentiamality out of them & get some of the truth that is behind it out to the light, if its been cut out, we can put some back.*[55]

He had ideas about the sort of performance that could be put on; which didn't seem to involve too much input from the Druids:

*I dont think the Druids would expect much of our Lodge, we may have to pay some small sum to be in communication with them. They're very hard up, so will be content with anything, if we can make up some sort of show that they can boast about.*[56]

Williamson had suggested to Gardner that the inside of the derelict windmill be used as a 'dancing ground'. This appealed to Gardner, who later perpetuated what was probably a myth that the Arbory Witches used the burnt-out tower for that very purpose in the mid-19th Century.

As far as I have been able to discover, nothing came of the proposed Isle of Man Druid Chapter and it remains just one of the many ideas which never came to fruition.

# Chapter 16

# Conflict

Williamson was still very much involved in the Museum in the summer of 1952 and was planning for the future. However, the season had not been particularly successful financially, and whilst numerous stories and allegations have grown up over the years, there definitely seems to have been a clash of personalities between Gardner and Williamson. Suffice it to say that, by late 1952 or early 1953, Williamson, quoting the short length of the tourist season on the Isle of Man, decided to go back to England, although, as we shall see, financial and legal matters were probably the determining factors.

### The Southern Coven Loan

The loan of certain items in the ownership of the 'Southern Coven of British Witches' for display in the museum seems to have been first mentioned back in April 1951, at Gardner's request. The provenance of the name 'Southern Coven of British Witches' and details of the items loaned were examined in Chapter 11. Suffice it to say here that arrangements were made, with Gardner acting as a go-between, for Dafo to send up 52 items for display and that these were exhibited, probably at the opening of the 1952 season.

At first, all went well and the items were exhibited in a display case all to themselves, with an appropriate caption.

Apparently, some members of the 'Southern Coven' visited the museum and were happy with how their material was being displayed.

However, after a few weeks, what seems to have happened is that Williamson rearranged things, using some of the items in other displays and taking other items out of the exhibition altogether. Gardner was not pleased with this course of action, and this seems to have been the source of the first conflict between himself and Williamson which got more acrimonious as time went on. He obviously informed Edith, who requested the return of the items in April 1953. After what seems to have been repeated requests, Williamson finally packaged up the items for return to her in July of that year. They were obviously received safely, for on 5th August 1953 a receipt for the returned items was typed and sealed 'Dafo' in Theban script and posted in Christchurch[1].

Williamson's account of the incident suggests that Gardner had deliberately chosen the middle of the summer season to request their return, to make things awkward for Williamson. However, Gardner's letters make clear that the first request had been made back in April. In any case, by his own account Williamson had plenty of material in storage to replace the display.

### Other Disagreements

There also seems to have been a disagreement which arose through a misunderstanding of the basis on which Gardner allowed some of his own exhibits to be displayed. On 1st August 1953, Gardner wrote to Williamson:

*With reguards to my collection, it was offered to you & accepted on the clear understanding that it was a collection, & would be treated with the customary courtesey, & would not be broken up, but shown as a whole, this was in Donnas presence in London. It was to show the public what magic & witchcraft realy is, & not as ignorant & intrested people conspire to make people think it is. You promised it would have a room to itself, with my portrait, called the Gardner room. Yesterday you complained that the case was so empty. I suggested that you should either return the many things that were formerly in this case which were removed without my knowledge or consent, or else you should put the various magical books of mine which you have put into another case in to fill up this case & make a good show such as it formerly enjoyed & you were not willing to do either. If you will only tell me clearly what you are aiming at, possibly I could help you, but it must be true, I will not co-opperate in making a ... pack of lies. As you long ago agreed upon, my collection is only of value if unbroken, so I cannot sell any part ...*[2]

He went on:

*As you said you did not wish me to show people round the Museum this year, I have kept away. If you wish my co-opperation in future I shall always be happy to assist you, but I must be allowed to understand what you are intending to do, a little discussion beforehand would have perhaps prevented this unhappy business with the Southern Coven, which has taken away nearly all the Scientific value of your Museum.*[3]

In a letter, probably of 2nd or 3rd August 1953, Gardner says:

*I gather you now have a very large collection of your own & wish to exhibit this. This was all along understood. My stuff should have a room to itself, & yours should be the main museum, but this did not include my and my friends stuff being put away, or hidden, or mixed up to make it inchomprehensible. Anyhow, if youll explain to me what your new ideas are, we may agree that it is better that as space is limated it is better that your collection alone should be on show for a year or two, as I gather mine does not intrest the man in the street. I quite understand this, & agree to it.* [4]

And on 5th August 1953 he wrote:

*As you know, I have always been very dissatisfied with the presentation (from the museum point of view) because the things were not explaned. But I knew it was your museum, & realise you did not wish the things to be explained, so said little.* [5]

As so often seems to be the case, it was in the financial arrangement between Gardner and Williamson that the relationship became fraught. The 1952 season was not a success financially and at one stage Williamson discussed with Gardner the possibility of moving the museum to Douglas, to see if that improved matters, but in the end nothing was done.

In December 1952, in reply to a query from Williamson, Gardner made clear his views on the future of his collection. He wanted it to be available for the public to see, but said he couldn't afford to donate it to the museum, as he wanted something to provide an income for Donna should he die first:

*I think the Museum should have the stuff when we pass on. We've no children or anyone dependant on us. Otherwise I think you cant blame me if I get a good offer from some Museum or from America, if I let the stuff go. But I'd be very sorry for it to go to America. Only Donna must be made secure she's about 60 now, so it's really a life interest for her. Of course I know so well you simply cannot do anything in the next two or three years, the top floor must be got open, & in working order, & if possible, the place made a centre for like minded people to meet.* [6]

It is clear from this that Gardner intended that his share of the collection should generate an income for Donna when the museum started to make a profit, but that it would be left to the museum after they had both died. The comment "... Id be very sorry for it to go to America" is rather poignant in view of the final destination of much of the museum's contents.

One event which did not help matters was a severe storm on 17th December 1952, where winds reached 130 mph on Snaefell. In a letter written the same day, Williamson reported to Gardner how it had affected the museum buildings:

> ... it has been too much for the roofs. They have been breaking up all day long. There is a huge hole in the Museum Roof and the Big Barn on the left of the windmill tower is a shambles. [7]

The relationship deteriorated during the 1953 season, partly because of the saga of the Southern Coven's artifacts, mentioned above, and in September 1953 Gardner's solicitors served formal notice on Williamson that repayment of the mortgage would be required in 6 months' time, as interest had not been paid on it.

It is obvious that by this time Gardner was determined to extract all he could from Williamson because, when Williamson paid the due interest at the end of September 1953, Gardner insisted on it at the 5% rate because it was not paid on time. In addition, he also asked for £19.15s for items that he bought in Africa in 1951 and £9 for swords that Williamson wanted to acquire. Gardner was wanting to make life difficult for Williamson: the relationship had obviously deteriorated seriously in the course of the previous year.

All Gardner's grievances against Williamson seemed to surface in a series of letters which he wrote in the early months of 1954. He complained that, for the previous 18 months, Williamson had not kept a promise to pass all those who were enquiring about the Craft to Gardner. Williamson was obviously generating a lot of ideas for making the museum more financially viable, none of which seemed to Gardner to be very sensible. He was not very keen on Williamson's ideas about changing the restaurant into a 'Road House', organising a travelling exhibition, or turning it into a plaster cast factory!

Gardner certainly expected Williamson to move imminently, perhaps back to London. To end his letter of 7th February 1954, from Africa, he wrote: *If you have moved on before I get back, let me know where to as I'd like to see your show.*[8]

## Gardner Takes Over

At the expiry of the period of notice, in March 1954, Gardner's solicitors reminded Williamson that repayment was required or proceedings would be taken. Gardner also informed Williamson, via his solicitors, that Edith Woodford-Grimes would be willing to take over the property with vacant possession for the amount due to Gardner on the mortgage. Williamson's solicitors warned him that this was less than the property was worth.

Two days before the deadline, Williamson sent a telegram to Gardner asking him to withhold legal action and requesting a telephone conversation. Gardner replied, telling Williamson not to worry and immediately came up to the Island for discussions. We don't know exactly what was agreed, but on 7th April 1954, Gardner wrote a note accepting that Edith would take over the mortgage and stating that he would instruct his solicitor to draw up the necessary agreement.

Williamson claimed that Gardner carried on all the negotiations via Edith, trying to hide the fact that he wanted to take over the museum. But Williamson also gives the impression that he was the one who wanted to move and he knowingly and voluntarily sold the museum to Gardner:

*By the second year I had decided that I would go back to England. Gerald was very keen on the place so I told him that he could buy the place if he wanted to ...* [9]

Williamson moved out some time in April 1954. He later wrote that Gardner had expected him to leave some of the exhibits. However, Williamson makes it clear [10] that none of the exhibits were included in the sale. Much of the material that was previously owned by Gardner had been bought some time previously by Williamson under pressure from Gardner, whose own collection was far from sufficient to provide enough material for a viable museum. According to Williamson, Gardner pleaded with him to let him have some material to fill the cases and that, after Donna's intervention, he agreed to let Gardner have his collection of talismans and amulets.

There were subsequent disagreements following the move. Williamson had, according to Gardner, removed certain items that should have remained, and Gardner wanted the purchase price adjusted to take account of this. Williamson tells an unlikely story about removing the witch logos from the plates in the restaurant because Gardner wouldn't pay anything for the goodwill and that when Gardner found out what he had done he tried to stab Williamson with his athame. [11]

Lois Bourne told me:

*When he sold his property to Gerald he made so many difficulties and when Gerald and Donna took possession they found that every toilet and wash basin had been smashed and damage done to other parts of the property which had to be repaired and which cost quite a lot of money.* [12]

I suspect that fundamentally the conflict arose because of a difference of approach between the two which did not surface initially because of the excitement of the whole thing and the activity of setting the museum up. It was only when cold financial consideration came into play that the differences surfaced. Gardner stepped in and bailed Williamson out. This is always a difficult circumstance and so it proved in this case. Williamson was the one who found the site for the museum and set it up. However, Gardner must have felt that his financial support gave him certain rights over the displays, as we can tell from the saga of the 'Southern Coven' artifacts, and his daily routine. It seems as if Williamson responded by making life difficult for Gardner, not just in re-arranging the exhibits but by keeping back information about enquirers and so on.

It is clear that Williamson was more of a showman than Gardner. He wanted to emphasise the more sensational aspects of witchcraft, whereas Gardner tried to be more academic, giving more explanation of the exhibits. It was really inevitable that, as the financial crisis came to a head, they would go their own ways, with Gardner taking over the museum, and Williamson taking his exhibits, eventually finding a permanent home for them at Boscastle, which still houses them.

## Williamson's Subsequent Museums

Following his split with Gardner, and certainly by mid-1954, Williamson was living at 106 Royal Avenue, Onchan, north of Douglas. He had formed what he called the Anti-Torture League, of which he was the Principal (and, I suspect, the only member), and he had opened a Torture Exhibition at Onchan Head.

I have no idea how long this lasted, but certainly by late 1954 Williamson had turned back to witchcraft and was in the process of arranging to open a museum in Windsor. The Museum of Witchcraft opened in Windsor for the 1955 season.

However, the establishment did not take kindly to something of that sort right opposite the gates of Windsor Castle, and Williamson was persuaded to move. His next museum opened in Bourton-on-the-Water in the Cotswolds on Easter Sunday 1956 and ran for several years, not without opposition from local people. In 1960, Williamson's collection became too large for one museum and he opened another one in Boscastle, in Cornwall. He ran this very successfully until his retirement in 1996 at the age of 87, when he sold it to the present owner, Graham King.

## Aftermath

For the 1954 season, Gardner had taken over the museum at Castletown completely. And, as if to seal the change, the name had become "The Museum of Magic and Witchcraft".

Gardner continued to run the Museum for the rest of his life, but this is not the place to write of the twists and turns of publicity, good and bad, that accompanied him during that period.

He continued to suffer with his asthma and, to help relieve the symptoms, took a boat to Lebanon during the winter of 1963/64. He was returning on the *S.S. Scottish Prince* in the Mediterranean when, on the morning of 12th February 1964, he had finished his breakfast and was reading a book when he died of a heart attack. The ship called in at Tunis, where his body was buried.

In his final will, which was only signed a month before his death and witnessed by the British Vice-Consul in Beirut, Gardner left the museum to Monique Wilson. She was one of his newest High Priestesses and, together with her husband, Campbell, ran the museum for several more years. By 1973, however, they were in financial difficulties and did the very thing that Gardner hoped would never happen - they sold the collection, including 3000 books from Gardner's library, to America, with the Ripley 'Believe it or Not' company buying it for £120,000. Many of the items were subsequently exhibited at their Museum of Witchcraft and Black Magic at Fisherman's Wharf, San Francisco. That museum closed in the late 1970s and the items were sold and dispersed, though some continue to come up for sale from time to time. However, many of Gardner's papers were acquired in 1987 by the Wiccan Church of Canada in Toronto.

Michael Howard gives details of the recent history of the Witches' Mill buildings as follows:

[the mill] *is on the market for rent or lease. Apparently after the Wilsons sold its contents the building was sold and resold*

51. Gardner at the entrance to his Museum of Magic and WItchcraft

several times. It was finally purchased by a property developer in 1995 for £225,000 and has now been restored at a cost of £1 million. The mill tower has been converted into a three-bedroom dwelling with a Victorian spiral staircase. The adjoining granary has been converted into flats and the former farmhouse, offices and workshop are now two-bedroom cottages.[13]

As I have said, any museum attracts items and information to it and, for the present, our greatest hope must lie in the Museum of Witchcraft at Boscastle in Cornwall. The present owner, Graham King, has made various improvements and is intending to make more. I have great hopes that it will act as a focus for the accumulation of artifacts and archives connected with the history of witchcraft and, as such, is very much worthy of all the support it can get. Certainly these chapters could not have been written without it.

### Cecil's Stories

In published and unpublished articles, letters and interviews, Williamson tells a variety of stories about Gardner, usually to his detriment. The fact that they rarely tie up with anything else and the animosity which Williamson held towards Gardner following their break-up, means that there are serious problems with taking these stories at face value. To be frank, Williamson was making a lot of them up. After all, it had been his job! Firstly in the film industry, then with Operation Fortitude during the war, making up convincing stories had been his stock-in-trade. So we should not be surprised that he had got into the habit of it! However, there are elements of truth in at least some of his stories, so to dismiss them all might be to ignore some vital clue, but they do need to be taken with at least a small dish of salt.

What were these stories? This is not the place to recount them in full. Williamson was an interesting enough person to deserve a biography to himself, containing a full analysis of his character. However, a selection of some of his more colourful stories might be in order, with an assessment of the degree of truth contained therein.

In telling stories, there are certain techniques used in convincing people, and Williamson seems to have employed these in great measure. Firstly, the story is rarely completely made up, but a mixture of truth and falsehood. Secondly, quite a bit of circumstantial detail, even if totally spurious, is scattered in to the story to make it sound more authentic. I'm not claiming that Williamson consciously made up stories about Gardner and others: I believe that they just flowed naturally at a time in his life when he wasn't able to employ such talents in his work.

There is a whole range of stories, some of which I have already mentioned. They include writing the Book of Shadows together with Williamson at Gardner's house on the Isle of Man; Margaret Murray introducing Gardner to Williamson; that Gardner didn't own the land on which the witch's cottage was situated and that Gardner had told him that the cottage had previously been owned by George Pickingill, the Essex "cunning man".

I refer to some of these stories elsewhere in this book and show how they are unsupported and inconsistent with the evidence from other sources.

I shall limit myself to recounting just four stories: they could be expanded many times. It is often true that we accuse others of our own proclivities, and it is certainly true that Williamson seemed particularly interested in sex and several of his Gardner stories are in that vein.

In one, the New Forest coven's "Cone of Power" ritual was supposed to consist of the High Priestess masturbating one of the male members into a chalice to which spirit alcohol was added and then ignited.[14] However, Williamson told an identical story about a group that he participated in that met many years before at Dinard in France.[15]

He also tells the story of Gardner's first group in the witch's cottage being involved in sexual intercourse on old army mattresses placed on a Morrison shelter in the middle of the floor, claiming that women were not interested as a result.[16] This seems highly unlikely, knowing what we do about the contents of the rituals.

Another example of Williamson's elaboration of the truth, this time not involving Gardner, is in his account of the circumstances surrounding the closure of Ward's Abbey Folk Park. He writes:

*... there was a case where somebody complained that their charming young daughter, who had been enrolled as a sort of nun, had been involved in fornications of various kinds. It then got into the national press and he got a lot of publicity about it. Then Ward did a stupid thing and tried to sue the News of the World or the Daily Express but he lost the case and had enormous costs ...*[17]

As usual, Williamson introduces a sexual element into the matter, whereas there is no mention whatever of this in the court reports. Also, I have no evidence that Ward ever sued a newspaper - the case which resulted in bankruptcy was of the girl's father suing Ward (see Chapter 6).

There is also a story about Aleister Crowley, with whom Williamson claimed to be on good terms. He wrote that Gardner would not pay Crowley for the lessons he had not received and took some of Crowley's paintings. Many years later (according to Williamson it was 1945 or 1946) Gardner asked Williamson to take him down to see Crowley and make it up with him. Crowley then apparently asked Williamson if he would like a ring for his museum.[18]

Now, apart from Williamson never being mentioned in Crowley's diaries, the chronology is all wrong. Not only did Gardner first meet Crowley in 1947, and did not meet Williamson until 1950, but Williamson's museum was not started until 1951, four years after Crowley's death.

## Conclusion

Both Gardner and Williamson were colourful characters and, although each had flaws in their personalities, between them they built up what was a major showcase for witchcraft - a religion emerging from the shadows of illegality.

The Museum achieved a lot in the way of publicity and it paved the way for an event which, more than any other factor, achieved Gardner's long-cherished hope that the Craft of the Wica would not die but gain new adherents: it was the publication of his non-fiction book, *Witchcraft Today*.

## Chapter 17

# "Witchcraft Today"

Whilst Gardner achieved a lot of what he wanted to with *High Magic's Aid*, he was obviously limited because it was a work of fiction, and he couldn't therefore make the statement that he wanted to make - that witches still existed and moreover that he was an initiated witch himself - though those visiting the museum on the Isle of Man would get a very clear idea about that. Some of the exhibits were specifically captioned as coming from present-day witch covens, and the notice that was on display at the table where Gardner was selling *High Magic's Aid* makes it quite clear that witches still existed (see page 249).

The turning point was the publication of Pennethorne Hughes' book *Witchcraft* [1] in 1952. Hughes, a former teacher who had worked for many years with the BBC, had written extensively on historical and anthropological subjects, though this was his first book on witchcraft. The witches were incensed by the way his book gave a totally distorted view of their beliefs and practices, and this led them to support Gardner's book project more enthusiastically, but still subject to certain things which could not be mentioned: "This [Hughes' *Witchcraft*] made some of my friends very angry, and I managed to persuade them that it might do good to write a factual book about witchcraft, and so I wrote *Witchcraft Today*" [2]

There are probably several reasons why the witches got angry about the book. The following is a typical passage:

> *... witchcraft, as a cult-belief in Europe, is dead. As a degenerate form of a primitive fertility belief, incorporating the earliest instructive wisdom, the practice is over. Conjurers, wisewomen, palmists, and perverts may be called witches, but it is using an old stick to beat a dead dog.*[3]

One can well imagine how being equated with degeneracy, perverts and dead dogs would not enamour the witches with Hughes, and may be why Gardner writes in the Foreword to *Witchcraft Today*:

> *I have been told by witches in England: "Write and tell people we are not perverts. We are decent people, we only want to be left alone, but there are certain secrets that you mustn't give away". So, after some argument as to exactly what I must not reveal, I am permitted to tell much that has never before been made public concerning their beliefs, their rituals and their reasons for what they do ...*[4]

It is clear that the witches themselves wanted to be very much in the background, as can be seen in their response to an article which appeared in *Illustrated* in September 1952 and which was not looked on favourably by them.[5] The following month Gardner wrote:

> *I may somtime be able to persuade some [witches] to come forward, but the publicity that has happned, things like what was in Illustrated for instance, makes them angry, & they want to keep out of it.*[6]

Now, it is clear that both Williamson and Gardner were interviewed for the *Illustrated* article, so it was likely to be Williamson's contribution, which, as we have seen, seemed to link witchcraft to 'black magic', that the witches objected to. Gardner had probably been working on a book quite a while before being given formal permission in 1952. There are, for example, some notes in Text A that appear to be roughs for parts of *Witchcraft Today*. In a sense, his whole life, and his interest in and wide reading around a large number of topics, had been preparation for what in many ways would become his 'magnum opus'.

So, Gardner got what he wanted, but there was some negotiation with the witches as to what he could and couldn't include:

*... I soon found myself between Scylla and Charybdis. If I said too much, I ran the risk of offending people whom I had come to regard highly as friends. If I said too little, the publishers would not be interested. In this situation I did the best I could.*[7]

In fact, we know that they did not want Gardner to give details of any rituals which were definitely magical, nor did they wish it to be known how they raised power.[8] Anyway, within these guidelines, we can imagine that Gardner started work on the manuscript of a book which was initially to be entitled *"New Light on Witchcraft"*.

However, he probably found fairly quickly that merely giving the witches' beliefs and non-magical practices resulted in a very short manuscript. The problem was that what the witches told him tended to slip through his fingers. Much was non-verbal and he probably forgot a lot. And by late 1952 and early 1953, when the bulk of the book was being written, he was living in the Isle of Man, away from regular contact with Edith, whom I suspect to be the only one of the original group that he was still in touch with. Anyway, it became clear that he needed to supplement the text with other material. And Gardner was far from short of material. Here was a blank canvas on which he could speculate.

In one sense, the lapse of time also had its effect. When he started writing the book it was 13 years since he had been initiated and Old Dorothy and Mother Sabine had died. The link with the 'old people' had gone and he perhaps felt free from the shackles that had kept him in check for over a decade and able to mention things which he had not thought appropriate to include in *High Magic's Aid*.

Gardner always needed help in bringing a manuscript to the stage where it would be suitable for publication. Betty Lumsden Milne polished his classic text on the Malayan kris that was published in 1936. Three years later, I suspect that Edith Woodford-Grimes performed a similar function for *A Goddess Arrives*. And in 1949, Dolores North edited and typed the manuscript of *High Magic's Aid*.

Gardner realised that he needed help with 'New Light on Witchcraft' and I suspect that he approached his old friend Ross Nichols, who had acted as Assistant Editor for *The Occult Observer* and had also edited and revised a 19th Century French work, Paul Christian's *The History and Practice of Magic*, which was published in two volumes by the Forge Press in 1952.

Nichols took on the job enthusiastically and also approached Gerald Yorke, whom he had met through *The Occult Observer* and who worked for the well-respected publishers, Rider and Co., who specialised in books on the occult and mysticism. Riders offered Gardner a contract and Nichols was appointed in 1953 to edit "*New Light on Witchcraft*" for publication. Francis King implies that Nichols' role was an important one in making the book what it is, when he writes:

*... not at all a bad book, for the reader responsible for its acceptance, himself an occult scholar of distinction, managed to blue-pencil most of the more rubbishy passages.*[9]

It is possible that King was referring to Yorke rather than Nichols, but I do not know on what basis he was able to make such a statement. It would certainly be interesting to see the original version, partly to check the rejected passages to see whether they were as "rubbishy" as King suggests, as I suspect that they may actually have contained some of the most interesting material.

Gardner certainly seems to have been involved in quite a lot of negotiation about the draft manuscript, with Yorke on the one hand and with the witches on the other. Ross Nichols was also undoubtedly closely involved in the whole process.

An indication of the matters which were covered in this negotiation is provided in a surviving letter from Gardner to Yorke. Gardner had obviously submitted a draft of the manuscript for comment, which Yorke had made, and this was Gardner's response. The topics covered in the letter which I have seen included yoga, a hallucinatory drug called soma, the Knights Templars and certain details of the witch rituals. Gardner had obviously included quite a lot about yoga, which Yorke had persuaded him to cut out, presumably because it was not directly relevant to the subject.

I am sure that there must have been other correspondence between Yorke and Gardner, although much may have been carried out indirectly via Nichols. One thing that changed was the title, almost certainly at the suggestion of the publishers, from *"New Light on Witchcraft"* to the more punchy and informative *"Witchcraft Today"*.

Margaret Murray agreed to write the Foreword to the book. Gardner had known her since before the war and was certainly well aware of her work on witchcraft. He usually called the Craft "the witch cult" following her usage of the term.

By late 1952, Gardner was clearly fully committed to the Craft. He was the author of the only book in existence (*High Magic's Aid*) which gave present-day witches' beliefs and practices, albeit in the unrecognised guise of historical fiction. And although not yet running it, he was also spending a lot of time at the Museum at Castletown and had moved there earlier in the year. He had also met someone who would not only help him with his forthcoming book but would become his High Priestess and make her own contribution to the development of the Craft - Doreen Valiente.

We can imagine, perhaps, that this new spirit of optimism encouraged Gardner to look again at what material he had been given by the witches. The 13 years since his initiation had perhaps given him some sort of perspective so that he was able to see things more clearly when writing about what he was told and shown.

He was also probably being given material all the time. In Chapter 13 we saw how he kept a manuscript book close to him until it was stolen. He also refers to at least two other witches' books, so there were sources of information available to him which he probably didn't have initially. He also undoubtedly met witches who made contact with him following the publication of *High Magic's Aid*, most notably Barbara Vickers. And, of course, museums always attract information and contacts, which Gardner would have followed up where possible.

## *Contents*

*Witchcraft Today* is not just an account of Gardner's contact with the witches and of their beliefs and practices. It isn't even mainly about that: in fact, probably less than 10% of the book is about the thoughts and activities of the witches that Gardner claimed to have met. I think the problem was that, when he came to write about what the witches told him, he found it difficult because it had been in no sense a structured course of learning - more things told at odd times in a strange order and he wasn't very good at remembering. Anyway, he set things down as best he could.

Nevertheless, there wasn't enough material to make a book on its own, so Gardner gave himself a free hand to write about his own ideas and theories about the development of witchcraft, including much historical material. The information about the witches he had met was scattered about the book like plums in a pudding. In fact, just as plums might tend to sink to the bottom, so much of this material seems to be included in Chapter 13 - Recapitulation - which is almost an afterthought, as if Gardner suddenly realised that there was material on the witches that he had forgotten about and hadn't included and that therefore he had to cram it in the final chapter, probably at the last minute.

What comes over very strongly in what Gardner writes about the witches that he knew is their character - the sort of people that they were - simple and direct, and capable of attracting great loyalty.

In *Wiccan Roots* I looked at the parts of *Witchcraft Today* where Gardner writes about their beliefs and practices, in particular examining what he had to say about their rituals, the function of the magic circle, how they raised power, magical and divinatory abilities and how to develop them, initiation, incenses, herbs and poisons. It seemed to me that Gardner was describing people whose religion was one of experience rather than being taken from books. They were practical and their feelings and emotions were important in how they performed their rituals. They knew that they had psychic ability and that their magic worked and it was therefore important to keep their methods secret.

Despite their confidence in their ability to work magic, they were modest in their lives, freely admitting their ignorance on many subjects raised by Gardner, such as the history of their tradition. They seemed to inspire confidence, affection and loyalty. As Gardner said when he had only known them a little while: "... I would have gone through hell and high water even then for any of them".[10]

Their rites seem to have been simple and spontaneous, based on casting the circle in order to keep the power raised from their bodies within a small area so that it could be focused into what they called a Cone of Power.

The bulk of the book is really a summation of Gardner's reading on witchcraft and allied subjects over a number of years. What I think he was aiming to do was to provide an outline history of witchcraft, from the Stone Age onwards, at the same time showing the connections that certain religious or other groups may have had with the Craft. This gave him the opportunity to write about many of his favourite topics, including the Druids, the 'Little People', the Knights Templars, Ancient Egypt, the Greek Mysteries and much more besides. In many ways, *Witchcraft Today* is a record of Gardner's phases of enthusiasm, some of which I have chronicled in earlier chapters of this book.

*Witchcraft Today* was published in November 1954. It sold well, his first book to do so, and it made Gardner's name. The difference was that for the first time he had not paid the costs of production. Moreover, a mainstream publisher such as Riders had a good distribution system, which is always a key ingredient in sales figures.

It certainly achieved reviews in several of the journals of the organisations of which Gardner was a member. These reviews were rather mixed. That in *Folk-Lore*[11] is unsigned and refers to the book as 'an apology for witchcraft' and considers that it

52. Gerald Gardner in 1954.

'can hardly be regarded as a serious contribution to a very complex and highly controversial subject".

The reviewer for the *Journal of the Society for Psychical Research*, Geoffrey B. Riddehough, takes up this theme, saying "Somehow, the apology is not quite convincing". He continues "Some of his historical assertions resemble those of Dr Murray's in that they ignore other interpretations of a fact than the author's own". The reviewer concludes by saying "... it is greatly to be regretted that in what is in many ways a pleasant and interesting book there are so many slips, typographical and otherwise. ...One can only hope that when Dr Gardner and his witch-colleagues recite their incantations they prudently maintain a higher standard of accuracy". [12]

Despite the mixed reviews, the book has been included in the permanent collections of most major public libraries in Britain and throughout the world, and for a generation was likely to have been an enquirer's first taste of the subject. It is still, for many, a classic text.

# Chapter 18

# Heritage Of The Wica

In a detective story, the last chapter usually contains the dénouement, where all the loose ends are tidied up and the true culprit is revealed. This book is not like that at all! The loose ends have multiplied luxuriously and I am still not in a position to give even a bare outline of the true story.

What I hope I have succeeded in doing, however, is pushing the boundaries of our knowledge back to the early 1920s, if no further. If the "old coven" referred to in *Gerald Gardner Witch* had a longer lineage then it is for the moment lost in the mists of antiquity.

How did it all start? Did any of the participants that we have identified come from a surviving hereditary witch tradition? Rosamund Carnsew from Cornwall - a land rich in tradition? Or George Sabine from Ireland - ditto? Or the Clutterbucks from Hertfordshire? Or perhaps the Oldmeadows from Cheshire, a county we have already identified as probably having several traditional witch groups?

What I have failed to do so far is to find any convincing evidence of a surviving witchcraft tradition in the New Forest itself. None of the participants whom I have identified were born or brought up anywhere near the Forest. They grew up elsewhere and only moved to the area in adulthood.

The only individuals involved where there is any evidence at all of an earlier tradition are the Mason family from

Southampton, whom I wrote about in *Wiccan Roots*, but they were the ones who discovered the 'old coven' already in existence, so it was clearly not them.

## Witch Blood

Whilst I admit that there may well have been a surviving tradition that further research could uncover, there is also another possibility. This is that Rosamund Sabine, in 1921 or 1922, already an experienced occultist, probably a Golden Dawn initiate and possibly a Co-Mason as well, read Margaret Murray's *The Witch Cult in Western Europe*[1], which had just been published. I can imagine that she could well have had what she felt were memories of a previous lifetime as a witch, and thus read the book with great enthusiasm. She was then not just convinced that she had been a witch in a previous lifetime but believed that this was sufficient to make her a witch in the present lifetime.

There is certainly now a strong belief amongst some witches that not only is there such a thing as 'witch blood', a direct physical inheritance through a hereditary tradition, but also what Michael Howard calls 'the spiritual lineage of witch blood' where one knows inwardly that one is a witch and may well be able to remember previous lifetimes as a witch, or be firmly convinced that they had occurred.

Reincarnation was clearly an important subject to the witches that Gardner knew. In one sense, this is not surprising, since anyone who is prepared to look at the evidence is highly likely to be convinced of its reality. However, in the 1920s and 1930s, acceptance of its existence was much less common, except amongst occult and esoteric groups. We know that the witches whom Gardner first met at the Crotona Fellowship held reincarnation to be important because it was the topic of conversation which convinced them not only that Gardner had witch ancestors but that he had been a witch himself in a previous lifetime and should be initiated. As they said: "You belonged to us in the past - why don't you come back to us?". [2]

Many of the incidents recounted by Gardner in *Witchcraft Today* are just the sort of things that might be remembered (or thought to have been remembered) from a previous lifetime as a witch, rather than being handed down through several generations. So let me put forward just one possibility, one which seems to be consistent with most of the facts, but nevertheless just an idea, though I think a fruitful one.

At some stage, Rosamund came to the realisation that she had been a witch in a previous lifetime. She may well have "got through" certain details which she was convinced were how the witches used to do things. It seems from what we know of their personalities and interests that Rosamund was the instigator of whatever was going on and that George went along with it, including the belief in having been a witch in a former lifetime. They realised, or believed, that they had previously been lovers and had been drawn together again in the present life. And when they met Edith, and the Mason family, they also remembered, or thought they remembered, being together as a coven of witches in the past.

We do not know where Rosamund and George were living before they moved to Highcliffe in 1924, or why they moved. But they did call the house 'Whinchat' when they moved in, so, if I am correct about the derivation of the name, Rosamund already considered herself a witch by that date, belonging to what she called "the Wica". If it were a modern invention, then it would at least have acquired a name - the 'Wica' - between 1921, when *The Witch Cult in Western Europe* was published, and 1924, when the Sabines named their house 'Whinchat'. Rosamund may then have gradually developed the rituals and magical techniques, perhaps from a surviving tradition or from her own imagination and her considerable occult knowledge, including information which she felt that she had 'brought through' from a previous lifetime.

Some time in the following year or two, Rosamund probably met Katherine Oldmeadow on Chewton Common through their mutual interest in herbs.

What I suspect is that Katherine Oldmeadow and her friend and near neighbour, Dorothy Clutterbuck, had already been performing pagan rituals by the stream in the grounds of Mill House. It seems to me highly likely that Katherine would have performed barefoot some variant of the rituals which she mentions in her books. Her love for Chewton Glen and its fairies and her friendship with Dorothy would, I imagine, have almost certainly brought Dorothy into performing rituals with her. Indeed, judging by her poetry, this partnership may have started with Dorothy's mother, Ellen, and even her companion, Elizabeth Slatter. As Ronald Hutton has mentioned, these 'performances' were not that unusual, though I have no evidence to suggest that they took place.

I have argued elsewhere [3] that Dorothy was not usually present at the witchcraft rituals. Following her move in 1932, I suspect that she allowed the coven to use Mill House. She knew what was going on, though perhaps not completely, but she didn't get actively involved.

## Gerald and Dafo

The other important question is how Gardner fits in to the picture. I don't know the answer, but I'm pretty sure that it lies in naturism.

I know that we wouldn't have heard of Gardner unless he had met the witches, but nevertheless it seems a remarkable coincidence that, when moving out of London, he chose a house right in the heart of an area where a group of people, some of whom called themselves witches, were living. It really is too much of a coincidence that Gardner moved to Highcliffe in 1938 to live within half a mile of Dorothy Fordham, Katherine Oldmeadow and the Sabines. He must have known someone before he moved and that person directed him to Highcliffe. It was someone whose influence was strong enough for Gardner to move out of London to be near. And I have speculated that this individual was a naturist who was a member of the New Forest Club.

Why did Gardner move to Highcliffe? Bracelin says: "The only place in England where he had friends was the region of the New Forest..."[4] This is little enough to go on, but the friends were obviously sufficiently close to him for the friendship to affect where he wanted to move to.

How did he meet and cultivate these friends? Presumably through some organisation that he belonged to in London, the most obvious of which was the Fouracres Club.

This presumption is strengthened by the use of the phrase "the region of the New Forest", almost as if the friends weren't actually living in the New Forest, just somewhere near. This is, indeed, just the sort of phrase which might be used in connection with the New Forest Club, which was in the vicinity of but not actually within the New Forest.

I have only a hunch to go on, but I think that the driving force leading Gardner to move to the New Forest area was that he had fallen in love with one of the members of the Fouracres Club, who also had strong links with the New Forest. If so, there is in my view only one person it could be: Edith Woodford-Grimes.

It is all very much speculation, but I think it possible that Gardner met Edith at Fouracres in 1936 or 1937. Her marriage had not been a success and it was about this time that she left her husband. Might she not have ventured up to the naturist clubs in the London area, and been attracted particularly by the philosophy of Fouracres?

Gardner was naked at his initiation. I suspect that he liked this because it fitted in with naturism and may then have introduced it for all rituals. Edith seemed to go along with this and it is possible that she was already a naturist herself.

When Gardner suggested moving down to be near her, Edith may have suggested Highcliffe to live because she already knew of the coven in that vicinity and was contemplating moving there herself, which she did in 1940.

And what of Gardner's other contacts through naturism, particularly the Dionysians? If I am right about Edith, then had Dion Byngham influenced her, either through contacts at Fouracres or at the New Forest Club? If so, then was it Edith who introduced ritual nudity into the Wica?

For the moment, such questions are unanswerable.

Ian Stevenson, the Highcliffe local historian, is quoted by Ronald Hutton as confirming that the social worlds of Dorothy and Gardner never overlapped. Hutton writes:

*She was a well-known and well-loved figure at the centre of the community's life, while his friends visited from outside it and he was regarded in Highcliffe as an exotic, mysterious, and rather sinister figure.* [5]

Yet it is interesting that Gardner, when talking to Doreen Valiente many years later referred to Dorothy by her surname of Clutterbuck. Now, she started to be known locally as Mrs. Fordham in 1935, whereas Gardner didn't move to Highcliffe until 1938. He must have known someone who had been in Highcliffe since at least 1935 in order to know that her previous name was Clutterbuck. Now, Edith didn't move to Highcliffe until 1940, so it must have been some other Highcliffe resident: I suspect that it was Rosamund Sabine.

I think that Gardner and Edith went through the same sort of process as Rosamund and George. They talked about rebirth: they both accepted it and remembered incidents from their previous lifetimes. Then, somehow, they realised that they were remembering the same incidents when they had been lovers in a previous lifetime. This would explain the comment in *Gerald Gardner Witch*:

The day came when one said: "I have seen you before". Gardner, interested, asked where: "In a former life". Then all gathered around and agreed that this was so. What made it all remarkable to Gardner was that one of the number proceeded to describe a scene "exactly like one which I had written in *A Goddess Arrives*, which was due to be published any day then, and which in fact came out the following week". Then someone said, "You belonged to us in the past - why don't you come back to us?" [6]

Since Gardner admitted that *A Goddess Arrives* was inspired by his memories of a former lifetime in Cyprus, the fact that one of the witches (very likely Edith) described a similar scene would undoubtedly suggest strongly that they had been together in that lifetime. This is, of course, all speculation, but it would explain the particular emphasis on being reborn amongst one's friends.

There is certainly a suggestion that Edith had other memories of being a witch in a previous lifetime. In Chapter 12 we looked at the poem "The Witch Remembers Her Last Incarnation", which is reproduced in Gardner's *Witchcraft Today* [7]. Gardner wrote that this was contained in "a witch's book that I possess" and I pointed out that an earlier version of this poem, entitled "Hymn to Fire", occurs in 'Text A', very likely copied from a witch's book.

Why did Gardner change the title for publication? It suddenly occurred to me that the use of the term 'The Witch' was very interesting. Surely 'A Witch' would be expected, unless one was referring to a particular witch. I remembered that Gardner had used the term 'the witch' previously in correspondence with Cecil Williamson where he was referring to Edith. Could the use of the same phrase be a strong indication that Edith was the author of the poem? If so, then she may have considered it to have been a memory of her own former lifetime as a witch, and her death at the stake.

## Herbs, Psychology and Roses

Can we, at this length of time, get any idea of what the particular interests or emphasis of the coven were?

We have already noted that herbs were a strong theme, particularly herbal remedies, for both Rosamund and Katherine, and the nature of the items in the Southern Coven loan collection (see Chapter 11) backs this up.

The scent of the rose seems to permeate everywhere. I wrote in *Wiccan Roots* that the evidence in her diaries indicated that Dorothy seemed to be obsessed with roses and I speculated that this suggested some connection with the Rosicrucians. The information which I have accumulated about Mother Sabine gives additional support to such speculation. She seems to have chosen the name 'Rosamund' (meaning 'Rose of the World') for herself and later written an article with the same name. Indeed, the Co-Masons, members of which included Edith and the Mason family, seemed to have an equal fascination, as is evidenced by Aimée Bothwell-Gosse's book, *The Rose Immortal*. And I have already noted that unusual phrase, "by thy rosey love", in the Lammas ritual as recorded in "Ye Bok of Ye Art Magical".

Why the rose should be so important to the witches perhaps lies in its significance both in the esoteric field and in the realm of nature, the combination of which is particularly important to those in the Craft.

According to Gardner, the witches seemed to be experts at applied psychology, or, as he put it, "witches are good leg-pullers". We have already noted the Sabines' playing with the words 'Whinchat' and 'Vacuna' and the tale about the first and last house. I think it quite clear that Gardner was highly practised at this sort of thing himself, his attitude being summed up by what he says about Joan of Arc:

*It is evident from her trial that Joan did not like telling a direct lie, but that she was an adept at evasion; she could dodge about like a lawyer.* [8]

There seems to have been an interest in yoga, which was sufficiently great for Gardner to think for a while that the secret that his new friends might have was yoga rather than the still-unsuspected witchcraft. Bracelin writes:

*He felt sure that they had some secret, there must be something which allowed them to take the slights at the theatre without really caring. He still thought that they might be mooting Yoga, or something of that nature.* [9]

This suggests that they had at least mentioned yoga to Gardner as one of their interests, and we have seen in Chapter 17 that Gardner included quite a lot about yoga in the draft version of *Witchcraft Today* which was subsequently removed.

Indeed, the interest in yoga might explain how Edith acquired the witch-name of 'Dafo', which I suspect started out as a little joke on Gardner's part. One of the meanings of 'Dafo' is a large statue of Buddha, one of the largest in the world, carved out of a rocky cliff in China. Could it be that Edith was interested in yoga and that when she adopted the lotus posture she appeared to Gardner to resemble the classic statues of Buddha, particularly if she was sky-clad and as she seems to have been somewhat over-weight.

## The Crotona Fellowship

Bracelin says of the witches that Gardner met at the Crotona Fellowship meetings (and I think I demonstrated in *Wiccan Roots* that these were Edith Woodford-Grimes and the Mason family, from Southampton) that they had "discovered an old Coven, and remained here because of that".

Now, how could Edith and the Masons have met Rosamund and the others? The most obvious place is at the Crotona Fellowship meetings. The Masons and Edith lived in Southampton and had to travel 25 miles to the meetings. They probably wouldn't have had the time or opportunity to get to know anyone well enough for them to reveal that they belonged to an "old coven" unless they were also present at the Crotona Fellowship meetings.

Rosamund's name does not appear in any of the reports of theatrical performances, sales of work, etc. by the Fellowship (and neither, incidentally, do those of Katherine Oldmeadow or Dorothy Fordham), but nevertheless it is quite possible that she was associated with it because of her demonstrated interest in the rose lamen of the Golden Dawn. She was the same age as Catherine Chalk, who was a prominent member of the Crotona Fellowship and a Co-Mason, who donated land for the Fellowship's Ashrama and who came to live at Somerford in 1925 or 1926. It is quite likely that the two may have come into contact with each other through their joint interests quite a while before the Crotona Fellowship moved to Somerford. Indeed, I have always thought it possible that Catherine Chalk may have been a member of the coven.

Whether there was anyone other than Rosamund and George involved through the 1920s and early 1930s, I do not know. There are so many uncertainties, but, if I am right in my suggestion in Chapter 3 that Rosamund was a Co-Mason and was friendly with Catherine Chalk and that she could therefore have been a member of the Crotona Fellowship, particularly following the movement of the centre of activities to Somerford in 1935, then we have a way in which Edith and the Mason family could have met the "old coven". It is plausible and, indeed, even likely, but I have so far no proof.

I think it highly likely that Gardner really did believe it was an ancient cult and tried to find evidence to reinforce this belief. I also suspect that Edith, whilst convinced of the line of continuity via the Mason family, realised early on that Rosamund's connection was only via a firmly-believed-in previous lifetime. So, Edith may well have been rather ambivalent in what she told Gardner and got rather embarrassed when he started to publicise the Craft, withdrawing into the background.

I put the foregoing outline forward merely as a possibility. I must stress that I am by no means sure about it, nor addicted to it. I am quite prepared to change my mind at a moment's notice if contrary evidence comes forward. I welcome any research or information on these matters.

I hope I have succeeded in filling in some of the chronology of Gardner's lifetime and given considerably more detail than has previously appeared in print about his links with naturism, the establishment of the coven which met in the witch's cottage, his meetings with Aleister Crowley and his partnership with Cecil Williamson in establishing the museum on the Isle of Man. This material will act as a contribution towards my full biography of Gardner which is in course of preparation.

Yet I am still a long way from carrying out the task of examining critically the various influences on Gardner and on the development of the Craft during the immediate post-war period. There are several fruitful lines for further research, apart from finding out more about Rosamund Sabine and the 'old coven', including the origins of the various elements which make up the modern Craft, not just the contents of the Book of Shadows but symbolism, beliefs, techniques and practices, looking into when and where they first appeared.

It is my belief that some knowledge of our spiritual roots is beneficial and in no way detracts from the essential mystery of direct experience of the divinity inherent in the universe. I hope that this book has been a contribution towards the history of a craft/religion to which a growing number of people belong.

# Appendix A
# Acknowledgements

It is very much in the nature of a work of history or biography that the author relies on information from others as the basic raw material for the book being written. It is certainly true with this current volume. Indeed, the number of people to whom I am indebted is so great that, as with my previous book, *Wiccan Roots*, they have an appendix all to themselves.

**Professor Ronald Hutton** has always been encouraging and supportive of my researches, offering both valuable information and constructive criticism. I am grateful to him for agreeing to write the Foreword to this book.

**Gareth Medway** is truly a fellow researcher of the finest quality. He has provided much information and exciting new leads as well as valuable comment on my ideas.

**Patricia Crowther**, who is a High Priestess and a Grand Mother of the Craft, has always encouraged my researches. As someone who knew Gardner well, she has provided many valuable insights into his life and I am most grateful to her.

Highcliffe's local historian, **Ian Stevenson**, has played a crucial role in the researches which resulted in the chapters on Katherine Oldmeadow and 'Mother Sabine'. He is an invaluable source of information about the Highcliffe of Gardner's time and of the people that he knew.

**Graham King**, of the Museum of Witchcraft at Boscastle has been most hospitable in allowing me access to the museum's archives for my investigations, as well as helping in numerous ways. It is a most valuable resource which is in very capable hands.

**John and Julie Belham-Payne** were also generous in their hospitality and in giving me access to the wealth of books and papers formerly owned by Doreen Valiente. I was able to look at only a small proportion of this material and I hope that their vision of a permanent archive where researchers can carry out their studies will one day come to fruition.

**Michael Howard**, the editor of the long-running Pagan journal, *The Cauldron*, has been most supportive of my efforts by providing useful snippets of information and suggesting valuable contacts. I am immensely grateful for his obvious enthusiasm for the history of witchcraft.

**Philip Carr-Gomm**, Chief of the Order of Bards, Ovates and Druids, has co-operated fully with me in trying to unearth, amongst other matters, the origins of Gardner's friendship with Ross Nichols. We have helped each other in our researches, which are still continuing.

British Naturism's archivist, **Michael Farrar**, gave of his time and made me most welcome, guiding me through the wealth of information for which he is the guardian.

I will long remember visiting **Iseult Weston** and her sister, **Cosette**, at Spielplatz. It was most generous of them to make time to talk to me and I am most grateful to them for the valuable knowledge of the early years which I gained.

**Melissa Montgomery** and **Rufus Harrington** allowed me access to Doreen Valiente's many scrapbooks of press cuttings and made me most welcome whilst studying them.

Archivists and librarians have been, without exception, most helpful and willing to delve into their sources of information to find what I was looking for, even when I didn't quite know what it was myself! I could never have completed this book without their help. They are M.Y. Ashcroft, County Archivist, North Yorkshire County Council; The staff at the London Borough of Barnet archives; Lesley Barton, Office of National Statistics; Simon Bennett, Assistant Archivist, University of Glasgow; Roger Bristow, Information Services Librarian, Hastings Library; the staff at the British Library; Anne Dacre, Administrator, Braziers Park; Alan Franklin, Assistant Librarian, Manx National Heritage Library; Simon Green, Gareth Watkins and staff at the Hull Central Library; M.A. Hayes, Principal Librarian - Local Studies, Worthing Library; John Hopkins, Archivist, Chester; Beryl Housley, Librarian (Local Studies) St. Albans Central Library; Claire James, Information Librarian, Stratford-upon-Avon Library; Richard Knight, Camden Local Studies and Archives Centre; the staff of the Lansdowne Library, Bournemouth; Miss J. Middleton, Chichester Reference Library; Alan Moorhouse, St. Albans Planning; Andrew Robertson, Hertfordshire Archives and Local Studies; Jean Rose, Library Manager, The Random House Archive and Library; W.F. Ryan, Warburg Institute; George Schrager, Octagon Press Ltd.; Elizabeth Silverthorne, Archivist, London Borough of Bromley; Andrew Stoodley, Archives Assistant, Hampshire Record Office; Helen Thorne, Assistant Library Supervisor, County Library, Lymington; and Cerys Williams, Companies House.

The officials of voluntary societies have, on very limited budgets and time constraints, been equally helpful. They include Dr. Phyllis Croft, International Co-Freemasonry; Lalita du Perron, Royal Asiatic Society; Beverley Emery, Royal Anthropological Institute; William Mullan, The Royal Inniskilling Fusiliers Regimental Museum; Joy Piper, Theosophical Society; Mrs. W. Poynton, Librarian, Society for Psychical Research; Carol Price, Membership Secretary, Royal Automobile Club; Martin Westlake, Chieftain, The Order of

Woodcraft Chivalry; and Nicky Westwood, The Herb Society.

I would particularly like to thank the Honorary Archivists of the Folklore Society, Mrs. Jean Tsushima and Mr. George Monger, for permission to consult materials in the Society's archives and to Dr Caroline Oates, the Society's Information Officer and Librarian, for her time and help in locating relevant items.

But perhaps it is the private individuals from all walks of life who have enthusiastically provided me with information to whom I am most grateful. They include Mike Allen; Paul Atkin; Helen Bassett; Adrian Bott; Lois Bourne; Francis Cameron; Keith Chisholm; Marilyn and Trevor Clark; Jerry Cornelius; Nick Culpeper; Morgan Davis; Roger Dearnaley; Peter Dickens; Jani Farrell-Roberts; John Ferguson and Chris Wallis; Ben Fernee; Robert Gilbert; Clive Harper; Martin Hinchcliffe; Michael Hodges; Prudence Jones; Steve Jones; Aidan Kelly; Ray and Lynda Lindfield; Carey Littlefield; Catherine Lloyd; Nagia Lombardo; Beverly Lyon Clark; Lucas Mellinger; Levannah Morgan; Sue Newman; Andy Norfolk; Caroline Robertson; Dr. Geoffrey Basil Smith; Tony Steele; Jonathan Tapsell; Kevin Tingay; Sibyl Webster; Roy and Grace Wheadon; Caroline Wise; and John Yeowell.

Many thanks also to the members of the North London coven who allowed me to examine and photograph their sword and who made me most welcome.

I have used the Google search engine extensively in my researches, and numerous times it has come up with some reference that I would otherwise almost certainly not have found. The power of such a technology is awe-inspiring and I wish to thank those who created it.

To conclude, I will repeat what I wrote in *Wiccan Roots*: I am sure that I will have missed someone! This is no reflection on their contribution, but more on my failing memory and the fact that so many were willing to help. I apologise in advance!

# Appendix B
# References

*Notes: The page numbers quoted are those in the original edition of the work, except where otherwise stated.*

*The "Document Nos." quoted are those of the archives of the Museum of Witchcraft in Boscastle.*

### Introduction
[1] Gardner, G.B. *Witchcraft Today* (Rider 1954)
[2] Heselton, Philip *Wiccan Roots - Gerald Gardner and the Modern Witchcraft Revival* (Capall Bann 2000)
[3] Thorn, Michael - *Interview with Doreen Valiente* in *Fireheart 6* (1991); [reproduced in http://www.earthspirit.org/fireheart/fhdv1.html]
[4] Carr-Gomm, Philip *I am Tough, Fantastic and Old - The Life of Ross Nichols* (unpublished manuscript 2001) 56

### Chapter 1 - From The New Forest
[1] Heselton (2000)
[2] Gardner's year of retirement is usually given as 1936, but I have reason to believe that it was actually 1935, which would enable the events recounted in *Wiccan Roots* and the present book to have occurred over a longer period. People are often very vague about dates, even of events which seem to have been highly significant in their lives, and I have learnt in the course of my research to treat given dates as approximate at best or even totally wrong! I have relied more on dated documents, the most reliable being newspaper cuttings where the printed date is visible. Even letters written near the beginning of a year may have the previous year's date on them, particularly in Gardner's case!
[3] Bracelin, J.L. *Gerald Gardner Witch* (Octagon 1960) 166
[4] Ibid. 159
[5] Ibid. 159

[6] Ibid. 164-165
[7] Ibid. 165
[8] Valiente, Doreen *'The Search for Old Dorothy'* - Appendix A to Janet and Stewart Farrar - *The Witches' Way* (Hale 1984) 283-293
[9] Hutton, Ronald *The Triumph of the Moon* (Oxford 1999) 212
[10] Bracelin 165
[11] Heselton 179
[12] Heselton 262-268
[13] Bott, Adrian *'The Great Wicca Hoax?'* in *White Dragon* (Lughnasa 2001) 13-15
[14] letter from Ronald Hutton to the author 28th August 2001
[15] Bracelin 166
[16] I am grateful to John Belham-Payne for permission to quote from Doreen Valiente's notebooks.
[17] Sumner, Heywood *Cuckoo Hill - The Book of Gorley* (Dent 1987) 111

## Chapter 2 - Katherine Oldmeadow - Children's Author

Note: Whilst her first name is clearly "Katherine" on her birth certificate, her publishers, Collins, usually spelt her name "Katharine", which explains the variations in the following references!
[1] Oldmeadow, Katharine L. *Princess Elizabeth* (Collins 1926)
[2] Stevenson, Ian - Accompanying notes to the exhibition 'Costumes and Characters' held at Highcliffe Castle 2001.
[3] Oldmeadow, Katherine *The Folklore of Herbs* (Cornish Bros. 1946) 65-66
[4] Carpenter, Humphrey and Prichard, Mari *The Oxford Companion to Children's Literature* (Oxford 1984)
[5] Oldmeadow, Katharine L. *Madcap Judy* (Collins 1919) 41
[6] Ibid. 223
[7] Oldmeadow, Katharine L. *Ragged Robin* (Collins 1920) 22
[8] Oldmeadow, Katharine L. *Princess Charming* (Collins 1923) 199
[9] Oldmeadow, Katherine (writing as Pamela Grant) *The Fortunes of Billy* (Collins 1925) 60 and 108
[10] Oldmeadow, Katharine L. *The Pimpernel Patrol* (Collins 1925) 178
[11] Ibid. 179
[12] Oldmeadow (1923) 256-257
[13] Oldmeadow (1926) 9
[14] letter from Ian Stevenson to the author 5th December 2000
[15] Oldmeadow, Katharine L. *'The Witch of Whitestones'* in *Hulton's Girls' Stories* (Allied Newspapers 1926) 144
[16] Stevenson (2001)
[17] Oldmeadow (1923) 83
[18] Ibid. 92-93

[19] Ibid. 94
[20] Ibid. 278-279
[21] Allan, Mabel Esther *'Ragged Robin Began It'* in *Folly* No. 5 (January 1992).
[22] letter from Ian Stevenson to the author 5th December 2000
[23] Oldmeadow (1919) 273
[24] Oldmeadow (1923) 101
[25] Ibid. 142-143
[26] Ibid. 144 and 152
[27] Oldmeadow (1919) 276 and 278
[28] Ibid. 284
[29] Oldmeadow, Katharine L. *Princess Anne* (Collins 1925) 200-201
[30] Ibid. 211
[31] Ibid. 212-213
[32] Ibid. 214
[33] Ibid. 215-216
[34] Oldmeadow, Katherine (writing as Pamela Grant) *The Fortunes of Billy* (Collins 1925)
[35] letter from Katherine Oldmeadow to Mabel Esther Allan 19th October 1950
[36] Oldmeadow (1946)
[37] Oldmeadow (1919) 179
[38] Oldmeadow (1946) 46
[39] Ibid. 47
[40] Ibid. 63
[41] Ibid. 1
[42] Ibid. 6
[43] Ibid. 6
[44] Ibid. 24
[45] Ibid. 44-45
[46] Ibid. 9-10
[47] Oldmeadow (1926) 171-172
[48] Oldmeadow, Katharine L. *Princess Candida* (Collins 1922) 228-237
[49] Oldmeadow, Katharine L. *Princess Anne* (Collins 1925) 248
[50] Oldmeadow, Katherine (writing as Pamela Grant) *The Fortunes of Billy* (Collins 1925) 58
[51] Oldmeadow (1926) 150
[52] Ibid. 154-156
[53] Oldmeadow, Katharine L. *The Fortunes of Jacky* (The Children's Press 1957)
[54] Oldmeadow, K.L. *When George The Third Was King* (Hutchinson 1934)
[55] Oldmeadow (1919) 58
[56] Ibid. 59

[57] Oldmeadow (1920) 122
[58] Oldmeadow (1919) 74
[59] Ibid. 59
[60] Ibid. 71
[61] Ibid. 73
[62] Oldmeadow, Katherine (writing as Pamela Grant) *The Fortunes of Billy* (Collins 1925) 213
[63] letter from Ian Stevenson to the author 5th December 2000
[64] Oldmeadow (1919) 229
[65] Oldmeadow (1926) 53
[66] Oldmeadow (1922) 257
[67] Oldmeadow (1923) 247
[68] Oldmeadow, Katherine (writing as Pamela Grant) *The Fortunes of Billy* (Collins 1925) 159
[69] Oldmeadow (1923) 229
[70] Oldmeadow, Katharine L. *The Pimpernel Patrol* (Collins 1925) 260
[71] Oldmeadow (1919) 221
[72] Ibid. 225
[73] Oldmeadow (1923) 306-308
[74] Oldmeadow, Katherine *The Three Mary Anns* (Cassell 1948)
[75] Oldmeadow (1919) 148
[76] Ibid. 151
[77] Oldmeadow (1920) 22
[78] Ibid. 93
[79] Oldmeadow, Katharine L. *Princess Anne* (Collins 1925) 156
[80] Ibid. 214
[81] Oldmeadow, Katharine L. '*The Witch of Whitestones*' in *Hulton's Girls' Stories* (Allied Newspapers 1926) 144
[82] Ibid. 148
[83] Oldmeadow (1920) 144
[84] Oldmeadow (1948) 104
[85] Oldmeadow (1946) 24
[86] Ibid. 15
[87] Oldmeadow (1934). This volume is very rare. Even the British Library does not have a copy. The date is taken from an article in *Dorset Life* magazine entitled 'Weymouth Writers' dated November 2001.
[88] Oldmeadow (1934) 22-24
[89] Ibid. 61
[90] letter from Ronald Hutton to the author dated 11th August 2001

## Chapter 3 - Mother Sabine - Matriarch Of The Coven?
[1] Gilbert, R.A. *The Golden Dawn Companion* (Aquarian 1986)
[2] McIntosh, Christopher *The Rosicrucians* (Weiser 1997) 104-105

[3] letter from Gareth Medway to the author 15th July 2002
[4] letter from R.A. Gilbert to the author 6th March 2003
[5] Holt, T.G., SJ *'Burton Park: A Centre of Recusancy* in *Sussex'* in *Recusant History Vol 13* (1975-1976) 106-122
[6] *Christchurch Times*, 20th October 1928
[7] I am indebted to John Yeowell (letter to the author 5th November 2002) for this information.
[8] *Christchurch Times* 6th July 1940
[9] letter from Gerald Gardner to Cecil Williamson 23rd December 1953 (Document 89)
[10] letter from Gareth Medway to the author 29th November 2002
[11] letter from R.A. Gilbert to the author 6th March 2003
[12] letter from Dr. Phyllis G. Croft, OBE to the author 9th November 2001

## Chapter 4 - Druidry, Aunt Agatha And The Sword Of Nuada

[1] Medway, Gareth *The Ancient Druid Order: a preliminary survey* (unpublished manuscript)
[2] Ibid. 2
[3] Colquhoun, Ithell *Sword of Wisdom* (Neville Spearman 1975) 124
[4] Ibid. 118
[5] Ibid. 128
[6] Ibid. 117
[7] Ibid. 129-130
[8] Medway, op. cit. 3
[9] Nichols, Ross *The Book of Druidry* (Aquarian 1990) 109
[10] letter from Gareth Medway to the author 29th November 2002
[11] Ibid.
[12] Ibid.
[13] *Christchurch Times* 2nd, 9th and 16th October 1937
[14] Medway, op. cit. 5
[15] Colquhoun 126
[16] letter from Gareth Medway to the author April 1999
[17] Mannix, Daniel P. *'Witchcraft's Inner Sanctum'* in *True Magazine* (August 1959) 78
[18] Gardner, G.B. *The Museum of Magic and Witchcraft - The Story of the Famous Witches' Mill at Castletown, Isle of Man* (1958) 17
[19] Luhrmann, Tanya M. *Persuasions of a Witch's Craft* (Blackwell 1989) between pages 230 and 231
[20] Mathers, Samuel Liddell MacGregor *The Key of Solomon the King* (Clavicula Salomonis) (George Redway 1888)
[21] letter from Gareth Medway to the author August 1999

[22] Gardner, G.B. *The Meaning of Witchcraft* (Aquarian 1959) 124
[23] Gardner (1958) 16-17
[24] Mannix 78
[25] Bracelin 166
[26] Gardner (1954) 130-131
[27] Ibid. 54

## Chapter 5 - Gymnosophists And Dionysians

[1] Cinder, Cec *The Nudist Idea* (The Ultraviolet Press 2001) 425-426
[2] Wellbye, Rex (writing as 'Ancton Tuqvor') *'The Story of Nudism II - The Birth of English Nudism'* in *Verity* (September 1949) 52
[3] The Constitution and Customs of the Moonella Group (1925) 2-4
[4] Cinder 432
[5] Burland, Cottie *Time Will Tell* (1963) (manuscript in the archives of British Naturism) 2
[6] Ibid. 2
[7] Wellbye, Rex (writing as 'Ancton Tuqvor') *'The Story of Nudism IV - How it Spread'* in *Verity* (March 1950) 32
[8] Bracelin 151
[9] Ibid. 155
[10] 'The Fouracres Club - A Feminine Member's Impression' in Sun Bathing Review (August/September 1936) 73
[11] Advertisement in *Sun Bathing Review* (Spring 1936) 25
[12] 'The Fouracres Club' in Sun Bathing Review (Spring 1937) 34-35
[13] Wellbye, Reginald *The Roadfaring Guides No. 2 - South-East England* (Phoenix House 1954)
[14] Bourne, Lois *Dancing with Witches* (Hale 1998) 94-95
[15] Cinder 424
[16] Greer, John Michael and Cooper, Gordon *'The Red God - Woodcraft and the Origins of Wicca'* in *Gnosis 48* (Summer 1998) 51-58
[17] e-mail from Philip Carr-Gomm to the author 3rd December 2002
[18] Byngham, Harry 'Dion' 'Greeting!' in *Pine Cone* 1 (July 1923) 1-3; quoted in Edgell, Derek *The Order of Woodcraft Chivalry* 1916-1949 *as a New Age Alternative to the Boy Scouts* (Mellen 1992) 192
[19] Ibid. 251, quoting 'Religious & Festive Dress in the Order: A Forecast' by Byngham in *Pine Cone* 4 (August-September 1926) 207
[20] Ibid 278-279
[21] Ibid. 294
[22] Ibid. 212
[23] Ibid. 212-213
[24] Kelly, Aidan A. *Inventing Witchcraft - The Origins and Nature of Gardnerian Neopagan Witchcraft as a New Religion* (Art Magickal 1998)
[25] Wilson, Steve *Wicca: The Real History* (2000) [zee-list]

[26] Hare, Chris *Washington Story* (Washington Parish Council 2000) 62-77
[27] letter from Gareth Medway to the author 6th May 1999
[28] Neuburg, Victor *The Triumph of Pan* (The Equinox 1910)
[29] Neuburg, Victor *A Green Garland* (Young Cambridge Press 1908)
[30] Neuburg, Victor *Songs of the Groves* (The Vine Press 1921)
[31] Pragnell, Vera *The Story of the Sanctuary* (The Vine Press 1928)
[32] Edgell 198
[33] letter from Harry 'Dion' Byngham to Aleister Crowley 14th June 1947 (in the Yorke Collection, Warburg Institute)
[34] Byngham, Dion 'Cosmic Patterns and Spirals in *The Occult Observer* 4 (1950) 218-228
[35] Richardson, Iseult *No Shadows Fall - The Story of Spielplatz* (Coast and Country Naturist Publications 1994)
[36] letter from Iseult Weston to the author 8th December 2002
[37] Carr-Gomm 2001 footnote 28 532
[38] Carr-Gomm, Philip *In the Grove of the Druids - The Druid Teachings of Ross Nichols* (Watkins 2002)
[39] Carr-Gomm (2001) 35
[40] Nichols, Ross *Prose Chants and Proems* (Fortune Press 1941)
[41] Carr-Gomm (2001) 36
[42] Valiente, Doreen *The Rebirth of Witchcraft* (Hale 1989) 133
[43] Knight, Gareth *Dion Fortune & the Inner Light* (Thoth 2000) 307
[44] Alan Richardson, quoted in e-mail from Philip Carr-Gomm to the author 27th January 2003
[45] Ibid.
[46] Fortune, Dion *The Sea Priestess* (published by the author 1938)
[47] Clifton, Chas. S. 'A Goddess Arrives - The Novels of Dion Fortune and the Development of Gardnerian Witchcraft' in *Gnosis* 9 (Fall 1988); also on http://www.sacred-texts.com/bos/bos474.htm
[48] Hutton 231

## Chapter 6 - The Abbey Folk Park And The Ancient British Church

[1] I am much indebted to Keith Chisholm for much of the biographical detail about Ward.
[2] Ward, J.S.M. and Stirling, W.G. *The Hung Society - or the Society of Heaven and Earth* (Baskerville Press 1925)
[3] Tillett, Gregory 'Gerald Gardner: Some Historical Fragments' in *The Australian Wiccan* 14 [n.d.]
[4] Ward, J.S.M. *Freemasonry and the Ancient Gods* (Simpkin Marshall 1921)
[5] Ward, J.S.M. *Who was Hiram Abiff?* (Baskerville Press 1925)

[6] Ward, J.S.M. *Gone West: three narratives of after-death experiences communicated through the mediumship of J.S.M. Ward* (Rider 1917)
[7] Ward, J.S.M. *A Subaltern in Spirit Land* (Rider 1920)
[8] Bracelin 156
[9] Ward, J.S.M. *The Kingdom of the Wise - Life's Problems* (Baskerville Press 1929)
[10] Bracelin 156
[11] Gardner (1959) 58-59
[12] Ward, J.S.M. *The Orthodox Catholic Church in England* (*Showing its History and the Validity of its Orders*) (1944) 37-38
[13] Ibid. 39
[14] Davis, Morgan *From Man to Witch* - Gerald Gardner 1946-1949 (www.geraldgardner.com 2002)
[15] http://www.angelfire.com/ca/redgarters/gbglibidx.html
[16] Tillett, op. cit.
[17] *Fellowship of the Holy Grail* (British Church, n.d.)
[18] Tillett, op. cit.
[19] Ward (1921)
[20] Gardner, Gerald B. '*Collectanea - Witchcraft*' in *Folk-Lore* 50 (June 1939) 188-190
[21] Marlowe, Eveline '*Barnet's Folk Park*' in *Hertfordshire Countryside* (1981) 32
[22] Ibid. 32
[23] http://www.abbeymuseum.asn.au/abbey1.htm
[24] Ward, J.S.M. '*The Abbey Folk Park, New Barnet*' in *East Herts. Archaeological Society Transactions* Vol IX Part III 1936 320
[25] Cobban, Jennie '*The Witch's Cottage (Part I)* in *Hendon and District Archaeological Society Newsletter* 245 (1991)
[26] Ward (1936) 322
[27] Mee, Arthur *The King's England - Hertfordshire* (Hodder and Stoughton 1939) 77
[28] Ward, J.S.M. '*Homes of Our Ancestors From Mud Hut to Victorian Parlour*' in *Homes and Gardens* (August 1939) xviii
[29] Marlowe 32
[30] Marlowe 32
[31] Gentle, C.A. Letter in *Hertfordshire Countryside* Vol 26 No 149 (September 1971)
[32] *The Times* Law Reports 1st-5th, 8th, 11th, 12th, 15th, 16th and 19th May and 20th September 1945
[33] Gentle, op. cit.
[34] *The Times* Law Report 19th May 1945
[35] e-mail from Keith Chisholm to the author 1st April 2002
[36] *The Times* 20th September 1945
[37] Cobban, Jennie '*The Continuing Saga of the Witch's Cottage*' in

*Hendon and District Archaeological Society Newsletter* 249 (December 1991) 2
[38] The Abbey Art Centre and Museum (1963)
[39] Orthodox Catholic Leaflet No. 4 (The Catholic Apostolic Church 1945) 4
[40] e-mail from Keith Chisholm to the author 1st April 2002
[41] Pevsner, Nikolaus *The Buildings of England - Hertfordshire* (Penguin 1953) 176

## Chapter 7 - The Witch's Cottage In The Woods
[1] letter from Rex Wellbye to Hugh Shayler 11th August 1954 (in British Naturism archives)
[2] I am indebted to Iseult Weston and Philip Carr-Gomm for this information.
[3] 'Survey of the Sun Clubs 1946' in *Sun Bathing Review* (Spring 1946) 15
[4] 'Survey of the Sun Clubs 1947' in *Sun Bathing Review* (Spring 1947) 16
[5] I am indebted to Philip Carr-Gomm for this information.
[6] letter from Gerald Gardner to Cecil Williamson 8th February 1951 (Document 49)
[7] letter from Gerald Gardner to Cecil Williamson 27th February 1951 (Document 38)
[8] letter from Rex Wellbye to Ernest Virgo 13th January 1951 (in British Naturism archives)
[9] Lamond, Frederick *Religion without Beliefs* (Janus 1997) 164-165
[10] Bourne 24
[11] e-mail from Morgan Davis to the author 10th February 2002
[12] Ibid.
[13] Hutton 214
[14] Cobban, Jennie 'The Witch's Cottage Part 2' in *Hendon and District Archaeological Society Newsletter* 247 (October 1991) 7
[15] Ibid. 6
[16] Bishop, Peter "Now I will lose my job' says girl who revels in nude rites' in *The People* 11th January 1959
[17] e-mail from Lesley Barton of the Office of National Statistics to the author 22nd October 2001
[18] Bourne 23
[19] Ibid. 23
[20] Crowther, Patricia *One Witch's World* (Hale 1998) 46
[21] Cobban, Jennie 'The Witch's Cottage Part 2' in *Hendon and District Archaeological Society Newsletter* 247 (October 1991) 6

## Chapter 8 - Folk-Lore And Other Societies

[1] I am indebted to Roger Dearnaley for this information.
[2] letter from Beverley Emery, library representative of the Royal Anthropological Institute to the author 4th October 2001
[3] Gardner, G.B. *'Notes on Some Ancient Gold Coins from the Johore River'* in Journal Malayan Branch Royal Asiatic Society Vol XI Part II 171-176
[4] Gardner, G.B. *'Notes on Two Uncommon Varieties of the Malay Kris'* in *Journal Malayan Branch Royal Asiatic Society* Vol XI Part II 178-182
[5] Gardner, G.B. *'Ancient Beads from the Johore River as Evidence of an Early Link by Sea between Malaya and the Roman Empire'* in *Journal Royal Asiatic Society* 1937 467-470
[6] 'Minutes of Meetings - Wednesday 15th March 1939' in *Folk-Lore* Vol 50 No 2 (June 1939) 113-114
[7] Gardner, G.B. *'Collectanea - Witchcraft'* in *Folk-Lore* Vol 50 No 2 (June 1939) 188-190
[8] Smyth, Frank *Modern Witchcraft* (Macdonald Unit 75 1970) 28
[9] Gardner, Gerald Brosseau *'British Charms, Amulets and Talismans'* in *Folk-Lore* Vol 53 No 2 (30th June 1942) 95-103
[10] Ibid. 95
[11] Ibid. 103
[12] Gardner, G.B. *Keris and Other Malay Weapons* (Progressive Publishing Company, Singapore 1936)
[13] letter from Caroline Oates, Folklore Society Librarian, to the author, 11th April 2001
[14] letter from John Yeowell to the author 12th September 2002
[15] Smyth 32
[16] Hole, Christina letter to *Man, Myth and Magic* quoted in Smyth 32
[17] letter from Gardner to Gerald Yorke 24th October 1952 (Yorke Collection, Warburg Institute)
[18] letter from Gardner to Cecil Williamson 1st May 1951 (Document 48)
[19] Her address in the List of Members published in the November 1938 issue of *Folk-Lore* is given as "c/o The Westminster Bank, Boscombe".
[20] Begg, E.J. *'Collectanea - Cases of Witchcraft in Dorsetshire'* in *Folk-Lore* Vol 52 (1941) 70-72
[21] letter from Gardner to Cecil Williamson 23rd December 1953 (Document 89)
[22] Buddicom, Jacintha *Eric and Us - A Remembrance of George Orwell* (Leslie Frewin 1974)
[23] Ibid. 74-75
[24] Ibid. 72
[25] Hutton xi

[26] letter from Gardner to Cecil Williamson 14th December 1952 (Document 76)
[27] Gardner (1954) 139

## Chapter 9 - Aleister Crowley And The O.T.O.
[1] Valiente (1989) 58
[2] Patricia Crowther - personal communication with the author
[3] Symonds, John *The Great Beast - The Life and Magick of Aleister Crowley* (Rider 1951)
[4] letter from Roger Bristow, Information Services Librarian, Hastings Library to the author 7th February 2001
[5] Patricia Crowther - personal communication with the author
[6] letter from Gareth Medway to the author 20th February 2001
[7] Laver, James *Museum Piece or the Education of an Iconographer* (Andre Deutsch 1963) 227-228
[8] Sabazius $X^0$ and AMT $IX^0$ *History of Ordo Templi Orientis* [http://www.otohq.org/oto/history.html]
[9] e-mail from Adrian Bott to the author 14th August 2001
[10] Greenfield, Dr. Allen H., DD 'Wicca and the Ordo Templi Orientis' in *Lashtal* Vol 1 No 1 (1988) 47
[11] King, Francis *Ritual Magic in England* (Neville Spearman 1970) 159-161
[12] Culling, Louis T. *The Complete Magick Curriculum of the Secret Order*, G.B.G. (Llewellyn 1969)
[13] MSS 21-23 Gerald Yorke Collection, Warburg Institute
[14] Colquhoun 207
[15] Patricia Crowther - personal communication with the author
[16] Bracelin 174
[17] letter from Gardner to John Symonds 12th July 1950 in Scrapbook EE, Gerald Yorke collection, Warburg Institute
[18] letter from Gardner to Cecil Williamson 8th February 1951 (Document 49)
[19] Gardner (1954) 47
[20] Bracelin 174
[21] e-mail from Adrian Bott to the author 13th August 2001
[22] in a note on a statement by 'Ameth' (Doreen Valiente), Gerald Yorke Collection, Warburg Institute
[23] Hutton 218-221
[24] King 177
[25] Valiente (1978) 15
[26] MSS 21-23 Gerald Yorke Collection, Warburg Institute
[27] letter from Clive Harper to the author 17th June 1998
[28] Davis 27

[29] Greenfield, T. Allen *The Secret History of Modern Witchcraft* (1996)
[30] letter from Bill Heidrick to Clive Harper 9th September 1992
[31] Valiente (1989) 59
[32] Clive Harper - personal communication to the author 5th June 1998
[33] Ben Fernee - personal communication to the author 4th June 1998
[34] Davis 29
[35] letter from Geoffrey Smith to the author 15th May 2001
[36] Greenfield (1996)
[37] Clive Harper - personal communication to the author 5th June 1998
[38] Gerald Yorke collection, Warburg Institute
[39] Ibid. MSS 21-23
[40] Ben Fernee - personal communication to the author 4th June 1998
[41] letter from Doreen Valiente to Allen Greenfield 8th August 1986
[42] Ibid. and Symonds, John *The Magic of Aleister Crowley* (Frederick Muller 1958)
[43] e-mail from Adrian Bott to the author 14th August 2001
[44] letter from Jerry Cornelius to the author 12th September 1999
[45] Harper, Clive *'Gerald Gardner and the O.T.O. Part I - The Charter'* in *Nuit Isis* No 10 (1991) 9
[46] letter from Jerry Cornelius to the author 12th September 1999
[47] Greenfield (1988) 43
[48] e-mail from Adrian Bott to the author 13th August 2001
[49] Harper (1991) 9
[50] e-mail from Adrian Bott to the author 14th August 2001
[51] Clive Harper - personal communication to the author 5th June 1998
[52] Harper (1991) 9
[53] Greenfield (1988) 43
[54] letter from Jerry Cornelius to the author 12th September 1999
[55] letter from Bill Heidrick to Clive Harper 9th September 1992
[56] Clive Harper - personal communication to the author 5th June 1998
[57] Greenfield (1988) 43
[58] letter from Jerry Cornelius to the author 29th September 1999
[59] Sutin, Lawrence *Do What Thou Wilt - A Life of Aleister Crowley* (St.. Martin's 2000) 409
[60] Harper (1991) 9
[61] Davis 30
[62] Ibid. 40
[63] letter from Stein Jarving to Bill Heidrick 9th February 1993
[64] Bracelin 174
[65] Davis 34
[66] Bracelin 174
[67] *Thelema Lodge O.T.O. Newsletter* (November 1992)
[68] Ibid.
[69] Greenfield (1996)

[70] quoted in e-mail from Ben Fernee to the author 18th January 2000
[71] letter from Geoffrey Smith to the author 15th May 2001
[72] letter from Gardner to John Symonds 12th July 1950 in Scrapbook EE, Gerald Yorke Collection, Warburg Institute
[73] Bracelin 171
[74] inscription in front of Yorke's copy of *High Magic's Aid* in the Yorke Collection, Warburg Institute
[75] Smith, Geoff *Knights of the Solar Cross* (1981-83) 26-27. Geoffrey Smith has asked me to point out that following Grant's expulsion in 1955 there had been "only one person [Gardner] chartered to conduct a 'camp' of the order in England". He continues (in *Knights of the Solar Cross*): "I have been enabled to utilise the Gardner charter through the lineage involving Patricia [Crowther], for which I am most grateful". In a note accompanying a letter to me of 9th May 2001, he writes: "...because I was aware of the unused Gardner O.T.O. charter and that Pat Crowther was considered one of his main heirs - and since we both lived in Sheffield - I asked Pat if she felt it was permissible to finally utilise the old Gardner charter. I felt she was the one inheritor of his legacy MOST qualified to decide on this since it was, after all, HER late husband who had introduced Gardner to Crowley back in 1947. ... Pat Crowther, who had no real knowledge of the O.T.O. structure, went along with my suggestion of resurrecting the old charter out of the goodness of her heart at that time." So, although Smith does not own the physical charter, he considers that he validly possesses Gardner's succession.
[76] King 180
[77] letter from Doreen Valiente to Allen Greenfield 28th August 1986
[78] Davis 31
[79] Valiente, Doreen *Witchcraft for Tomorrow* (Hale 1978) 17
[80] Gardner (1958)
[81] Greenfield (1996)

## Chapter 10 - High Magic's Aid

[1] Crowther, Patricia Foreword to *High Magic's Aid* (Pentacle Enterprises edition 1993) 1
[2] letter from Gardner to John Symonds 12th July 1950 (in Scrapbook EE2, Gerald Yorke Collection, Warburg Institute)
[3] Gardner (1959) 11-12
[4] letter from Gardner to Symonds, op. cit.
[5] Crowther, op. cit.
[6] 'Robert' (Frederick Lamond) *Witness to Wicca* (manuscript copy in the Museum of Witchcraft archives, Boscastle) 3/5
[7] letter from Gardner to Symonds, op. cit.

[8] Ibid.
[9] Fortune, Dion *The Goat-Foot God* (Williams and Norgate 1936)
[10] letter from Gardner to Symonds, op. cit.
[11] Advertisement on inside cover of *The Occult Observer* Vol 1 No 3 (1949)
[12] King 180
[13] Crowther, op. cit.
[14] Patricia Crowther - personal communication with the author
[15] Bracelin 183
[16] Crowther, op. cit.
[17] letter from Gardner to Symonds, op. cit.
[18] Gardner (1954) 142
[19] Scire (G.B. Gardner) *High Magic's Aid* (Michael Houghton 1949) 84
[20] Ibid. 120
[21] Ibid. 118-119
[22] Ibid. 119-120
[23] Ibid. 77
[24] Ibid. 140
[25] Gardner (1954) 142
[26] Gardner (1949) 220
[27] De Crespigny, Rose C. and Hutchinson, Horace *The New Forest, Its Traditions, Inhabitants and Customs* (Murray 1895) 102
[28] Gardner (1949) 299-300
[29] Ibid. 120
[30] Gardner (1954) 140
[31] Gardner (1949) 297
[32] Gardner (1954) 140
[33] Gardner (1949) 299
[34] Gardner (1954) 141
[35] Crowther (1998) 18
[36] Murray, Lynda J. *A Zest for Life - the story of Alexander Keiller* (Morven Books 1999) 23
[37] Gardner (1949) 170 and 171
[38] Ibid. 348 and 349
[39] Collins, Andrew *The Knights of Danbury* (Earthquest 1985)
[40] Carr-Gomm (2001) 50
[41] Wise, Caroline 'A Pagan London Landmark - The Legendary Atlantis Bookshop' in *Pagan Dawn* 116 (Lammas 1995) 14
[42] Beatty, Charles *Gate of Dreams* (Geoffrey Chapman 1972) 178-179
[43] I am indebted to John Belham-Payne for permission to quote from Doreen Valiente's notebooks.
[44] Valiente (1989) 49
[45] letter from Gardner to Cecil Williamson June 1951 (Document 42)
[46] King 180

[47] letter from Gardner to Cecil Williamson late 1951 (Document 35)
[48] This notice is currently on display at the Museum of Witchcraft at Boscastle.
[49] Gardner (1954) 18-19

## Chapter 11 - Covens Old And New
[1] Harding, Barrie 'He Plans a Jamboree for the Witches of the World' in *Sunday Pictorial* 29th April 1951
[2] Hawkins, Peter 'Black Magic' in *Sunday Pictorial* 28th October 1951
[3] Valiente (1989) 47
[4] letter from Doreen Valiente to Michael Howard 24th March 1997 (in archives of the Museum of Witchcraft, Boscastle)
[5] letter from Michael Howard to the author 17th February 1998
[6] letter from Gardner to Cecil Williamson late 1953 or early 1954 (Document 29)
[7] letter from Gardner to Cecil Williamson 11th March 1951 (Document 37)
[8] letter from Doreen Valiente to Michael Howard 24th March 1997
[9] Valiente (1978) 49-50
[10] Clay-Egerton, Alastair R *'Pre-Gardnerian Witchcraft'* in The Bridge (1994); *'Crafty Ones'* in *The Cauldron* No 70 (1993) and *'Craft Teachings'* in *The Cauldron* No 81 (1996)
[11] Farrar, Janet and Stewart *The Life and Times of a Modern Witch* (Piatkus 1987)
[12] letter from Gardner to Cecil Williamson 27th February 1951 (Document 38)
[13] letter from Gardner to Gerald Yorke 24th October 1952 (Yorke Collection, Warburg Institute)
[14] Ibid.
[15] letter from Peter Hunt to Cecil Williamson 9th April 1951
[16] Howard, Michael *'The Gerald Gardner Story'* in *Insight* [n.d.]
[17] Williamson, Cecil *'Gerald Gardner - The Formative Years'* in *The Cauldron* No 36 (Samhain/Yule 1984)
[18] Williamson, Cecil *'The Wonderful World of Wicca'* (manuscript article in the archives of the Museum of Witchcraft, Boscastle)
[19] letter from Gardner to Cecil Williamson 8th February 1951 (Document 49)
[20] Ibid.
[21] letter from Gardner to Cecil Williamson 1st May 1951 (Document 48)
[22] letter from Gardner to Cecil Williamson June 1951 (Document 42)
[23] letter from Gardner to Cecil Williamson June 1951 (Document 46)
[24] Hutton 214

[25] Kinrade, E.W. *'Introduction to a Witch'* in *Isle of Man Examiner* 20th July 1951
[26] Andrews, Allen *'Witchcraft in Britain'* in *Illustrated* 27th September 1952
[27] letter from Gardner to Cecil Williamson 2nd August 1953 (Document 2)
[28] Andrews, op. cit.
[29] letter from Gardner to Cecil Williamson 30th October 1953 (Document 55)
[30] Gardner (1954) 138
[31] letter from Gardner to Cecil Williamson 23rd December 1953 (Document 89)
[32] letter from Gardner to Cecil Williamson 15th March 1954 (Document 33)
[33] letter from Gareth Medway to the author 15th July 2002
[34] Williamson, Cecil *'Gerald Gardner - The Formative Years'* in *The Cauldron* 36 (Samhain/Yule 1984) 4
[35] Gardner (1958)
[36] Crowther (1998) 27
[37] Gardner (1958)
[38] Valiente, Doreen *Charge of the Goddess* (Hexagon Hoopix 2000) 79
[39] Grimassi, Raven *The Witches' Craft* (Llewellyn 2002) 155

## Chapter 12 - The Book Of Shadows

[1] Kelly, Aidan A. *Crafting the Art of Magic, Book I - A History of Modern Witchcraft 1939-1964* (Llewellyn 1991) and *Inventing Witchcraft - The Origins and Nature of Gardnerian Neopagan Witchcraft as a New Religion* (Art Magickal Publications 1998)
[2] Hutton, Ronald *The Triumph of the Moon* (Oxford 1999)
[3] Farrar, Janet and Stewart *The Witches' Way - Principles, Rituals and Beliefs of Modern Witchcraft* (Hale 1984)
[4] Valiente, Doreen *The Rebirth of Witchcraft* (Hale 1989)
[5] Dearnaley, Roger *The Influence of Aleister Crowley upon "Ye Bok of Ye Art Magical"* (1999-2002)
[http://www.cyprian.org/Articles/CrowleyBAM0.html]
[6] Medway, Gareth *'Aradia's Children Parts 1,2,3 and 4'* in *Silver Moon* Vol 1 Nos 1,2,3 and 4 (June 1990, September 1990, December 1990, March 1991); *The Key of Solomon and the Book of Shadows* (unpublished manuscript)
[7] Bott, Adrian *'The Great Wicca Hoax?'* in *White Dragon* (Lugnasa 2001) 13-15
[8] La Coste Rikki *Thelema and Wicca* (2001)
[http://www.redflame93.com/Gardner.html]

[9] Lamond, Frederick *'Magicking the Art of the Craft'* in *The Deosil Dance* 34 (Imbolc 1993)
[10] Bashir, Mir *'The Book of Shadows'* in *The Occult Observer* 3 (1949) 154-161 and 4 (1950) 211-216
[11] Valiente (1989) 52
[12] Johns, June *King of the Witches: the World of Alex Sanders* (Peter Davies 1969)
[13] Gardner (1949)
[14] Gardner (1954)
[15] Cardell, Charles *Witch* (Dumblecott Magick Productions 1964)
[16] Farrar, Janet and Stewart *Eight Sabbats for Witches* (Hale 1981)
[17] Farrar, Janet and Stewart (1984)
[18] Kelly (1991)
[19] Hutton 248
[20] Kelly (1991) xvi
[21] Greenfield (1996)
[22] Ibid.
[23] Mathers (1888)
[24] Hutton 227
[25] I am grateful to John Belham-Payne for giving me access to this book and allowing me to quote from it.
[26] letter from Gardner to Cecil Williamson late June 1951 (Document 47)
[27] Valiente (1989) between pages 64 and 65
[28] Gardner (1954) 123
[29] Williamson, Hugh Ross *The Arrow and the Sword* (Faber 1947)
[30] Graves, Robert *The White Goddess* (Faber 1948)
[31] letter from Ronald Hutton to the author 16th January 2001
[32] Gardner (1954) 123
[33] letter from Gareth Medway to the author 29th November 2002

## Chapter 13 - An Exercise In Creativity

[1] Lamond (1993)
[2] Bracelin 35
[3] I am indebted to Geoffrey Smith for this information in his letter to me of 15th May 2001.
[4] Hannah, Walton *Darkness Visible - A Christian Appraisal of Freemasonry* (Augustine Press 1952)
[5] Medway, Gareth *'Aradia's Children: Part 2'* in *Silver Moon* Vol 1 No 2 (September 1990)
[6] Leadbeater, C.W. *The Hidden Life in Freemasonry* (Theosophical Publishing House 1926) 79
[7] Bracelin 35

[8] Wilson, Steve *Wicca: The Real History*
[9] Andrews, op. cit.
[10] Medway, Gareth *The Key of Solomon and the Book of Shadows* (unpublished manuscript)
[11] Gollancz, Hermann (trans.) *Clavicula Salomanis: a Hebrew Manuscript* - facsimile of handwritten MSS c. 1859 (published 1914)
[12] in the Yorke Collection, Warburg Institute
[13] Hutton 228
[14] e-mail from Roger Dearnaley to the author 22nd November 1999
[15] Valiente (1978) 17
[16] letter from Doreen Valiente to Allen Greenfield 8th August 1986
[17] Valiente (1989) 57
[18] Gardner (1954) 47
[19] Medway, Gareth *'The Origins of Wicca'* (to be included in a forthcoming book edited by Shelley Rabinovich)
[20] Dearnaley, op. cit.
[21] Ibid.
[22] King 180
[23] letter from Gareth Medway to the author 19th February 2001
[24] Medway, Gareth *The Ancient Druid Order - A Preliminary Survey* (unpublished manuscript)
[25] Kelly (1991) 64
[26] letter from Gareth Medway to the author 29th November 2002
[27] Thorn, Michael - *Interview with Doreen Valiente* in *Fireheart* 6 (1991); [reproduced in http://www.earthspirit.org/fireheart/fhdv1.html]
[28] letter from Cecil Williamson to Michael Howard about 1972 (in Museum of Witchcraft archives)
[29] Gardner (1954) 123
[30] Ibid. 143
[31] Crowley, Aleister *Songs of the Spirit* (Kegan Paul, Trench, Trubner and Co. 1898); *Collected Works Vol 1* (Society for the Propagation of Religious Truth 1905)
[32] Gardner (1949) 292

## Chapter 14 - The Cunning Man And The Temple Of The Muses
[1] Gardner (1959) 9
[2] Bracelin 15
[3] Gardner (1936)
[4] Gardner, G.B. *'Collectanea - Witchcraft'* in *Folk-Lore* Vol 50 No 2 (June 1939) 188-190
[5] *Christchurch Times* 29th July 1944
[6] Ibid.

[7] Bracelin 10
[8] *Christchurch Times* 29th July 1944
[9] *Christchurch Times* 12 August 1944
[10] Howard, Michael *'The Cunning Man'* in *The Cauldron* 95 (February 2000) 3-6
[11] Much of the biographical material on Cecil Williamson in this chapter is taken from a five-part series with the overall title of 'An Interview with Cecil Williamson' which appeared in Talking Stick between Summer 1992 and Spring 1994.
[12] The tapes of the interview give the boy's name as 'Bulstrode' whereas the printed version in *Talking Stick* gives it as 'Bentham'.
[13] *'Tales of the Unexpected'* - the fourth in the 'Interview with Cecil Williamson' series in *Talking Stick* XII (Autumn 1993) 33-34
[14] Williamson, Cecil *A Report from the Enquiring Eye of the Witchcraft Research Centre* (1991)
[15] Gill, Alec *Superstitions - Folk Magic in Hull's Fishing Community* (Hutton Press 1993)
[16] Hesketh, Roger *Fortitude - The D-Day Deception Campaign* (St. Ermin's Press 1999)
[17] Williamson (1991)

## Chapter 15 - The Witches' Mill

[1] The Folklore Centre of Superstition and Witchcraft - An Introduction to Visitors (1951)
[2] *'Witchcraft Back in the Midlands!'* in *Sunday Mercury* (28th January 1951)
[3] Fagence, Maurice *'Britain's Witches Want Corner at the Festival'* in *Daily Herald* (5th February 1951)
[4] 'An Interview with Cecil Williamson Part 5' in *Talking Stick* XIV (Spring 1994) 33
[5] letter from Gardner to Williamson 8th February 1951 (Document 49)
[6] letter from Gardner to Williamson 27th February 1951 (Document 38)
[7] Williamson, Cecil *'The Witchcraft Museums'* in *Pentagram* 6 (Candlemas 1967) 27
[8] Gardner, Gerald B. *'Witchcraft in the Isle of Man'* in *New Dimensions* (March 1964) 7
[9] Qualtrough, J.K. *'The Windmill, Castletown'* in *Proc IoM NH&ASoc* VII No 2 248-263
[10] Gardner (1958)
[11] Telegram from Gardner to Williamson 7th April 1951 (Document 24)

[12] letter from Gardner to Williamson 27th February 1951 (Document 38)
[13] letter from Gardner to Williamson 11th March 1951 (Document 37)
[14] Williamson (1967) 27
[15] The Folklore Centre of Superstition and Witchcraft - An Introduction to Visitors (1951)
[16] letter from Gardner to Williamson - Spring 1962 (Document 31)
[17] Teare, T.D.G. Folk Doctor's Island (Times Press, Douglas 1964) 192
[18] letter from Gardner to Williamson 17th April 1951 (Document 40)
[19] Kinrade, E.W. *'There's Something Brewing in Castletown!'* in *Isle of Man Examiner* 20th April 1951
[20] Ibid.
[21] Kinrade, E.W. *'Introduction to a Witch'* in *Isle of Man Examiner* 20th July 1951
[22] Kinrade (April 1951)
[23] letter from Gardner to Williamson late June 1951 (Document 47)
[24] letters from Gardner to Williamson 5th February 1952 (Document 34) and 20th February 1952 (Document 25)
[25] letter from Gardner to Williamson 17th April 1951 (Document 40)
[26] letter from Gardner to Williamson 1st May 1951 (Document 48)
[27] Williamson (1967) 28
[28] Bracelin 183
[29] Bracelin 184
[30] Ibid.
[31] Gardner, Gerald *'I Am A Witch'* in *Weekend* 24th-30th June 1957
[32] Bracelin 184
[33] Gardner (1957)
[34] Bracelin 7
[35] letter from Gardner to Williamson 24th March 1952 (Document 8)
[36] letter from Gardner to Williamson 14th December 1952 (Document 76)
[37] Bracelin 7
[38] Teare 197
[39] Crowther, Patricia *From Stagecraft to Witchcraft* (Capall Bann 2002) 142
[40] MacGregor, Alasdair *Alpin Phantom Footsteps* (Hale 1959) 154-156
[41] Harding, Barrie *'He Plans a Jamboree for the Witches of the World'* in *Sunday Pictorial* 29th April 1951
[42] Andrews, Allen *'Calling All Covens'* in *Sunday Pictorial* 29th July 1951
[43] *'The Witches' Den Opened'* in *Isle of Man Examiner* 3rd August 1951 4
[44] Howard, Michael *'Gerald Gardner - The Man, the Myth & the Magick - Part Two'* in *The Cauldron* 84 (Beltane/Midsummer 1997) 20

[45] letter from Cecil Williamson to Michael Howard about 1982 (in Museum of Witchcraft archives)
[46] letter from Gardner to Williamson 5th February 1952 (Document 34)
[47] letter from Cecil Williamson to Gerald Yorke 7th August 1952 (in Yorke collection, Warburg Institute)
[48] Williamson, Cecil H. and Gardner, Gerald B. The Witches' Kitchen, Castletown, Isle of Man (n.d., probably 1952)
[49] The Folklore Centre of Superstition and Witchcraft - An Introduction to Visitors (1951)
[50] letter from Gardner to Williamson December 1951 (Document 28)
[51] Andrews (1952)
[52] letter from Gardner to Williamson 20th February 1952 (Document 25)
[53] letter from Gardner to Williamson 6th November 1951 (Document 32)
[54] letter from Gardner to Williamson December 1951 (Document 28)
[55] Ibid.
[56] Ibid.

## Chapter 16 - Conflict
[1] letter from Dafo to Cecil Williamson posted 5th August 1953 (Document 1)
[2] letter from Gardner to Williamson 1st August 1953 (Document 30)
[3] Ibid.
[4] letter from Gardner to Williamson 2nd or 3rd August 1953 (Document 2)
[5] letter from Gardner to Williamson 5th August 1953 (Document 3)
[6] letter from Gardner to Williamson 14th December 1952 (Document 76)
[7] letter from Williamson to Gardner 17th December 1952
[8] letter from Gardner to Williamson 7th February 1954 (Document 27)
[9] 'An Interview with Cecil Williamson - Part 2' in *Talking Stick* VIII (Autumn 1992)
[10] letter from Williamson to Graham King 14th June 1997
[11] 'An Interview with Cecil Williamson - Part 2' in *Talking Stick* VIII (Autumn 1992) 20
[12] letter from Lois Bourne to the author 19th May 1999
[13] Howard, Michael 'The Witches' Mill - Past & Present' in *The Cauldron* 97 (August 2000) 34-35
[14] letter from Williamson to Paul T. Collins July 1986 (in Museum of Witchcraft archives)
[15] 'Tales of the Unexpected - An Interview with Cecil Williamson Part

4' in *Talking Stick* XII (Autumn 1993) 34
[16] *'Gerald Gardner - An Interview with Cecil Williamson - Part 2'* in *Talking Stick* VIII (Autumn 1992) 18
[17] Ibid. 19
[18] *'Aleister Crowley - An Interview with Cecil Williamson - Part 3'* in *Talking Stick* IX (Winter 1992) 24-25

## Chapter 17 - "Witchcraft Today"
[1] Hughes, Pennethorne *Witchcraft* (Longmans Green 1952)
[2] Gardner (1959) 12
[3] Hughes 217
[4] Gardner (1954) 13
[5] Andrews (1952)
[6] letter from Gardner to Gerald Yorke 24th October 1952 (in Yorke Collection, Warburg Institute)
[7] Gardner (1959) 12
[8] Gardner (1954) 26
[9] King 180
[10] Bracelin 165
[11] Review of *Witchcraft Today* in *Folk-Lore* Vol LXVI No. 2 (June 1955) 313-314
[12] Riddehough, Geoffrey B. - Review of *Witchcraft Today* in *Journal of the Society for Psychical Research* Vol. 38 No. 690 (December 1956) 378-379

### Chapter 18 - Heritage Of The Wica
[1] Murray, Margaret Alice *The Witch-Cult in Western Europe* (Oxford 1921)
[2] Bracelin 165
[3] Heselton (2000) 179-180
[4] Bracelin 159
[5] Hutton 211
[6] Bracelin 165
[7] Gardner (1954) 123
[8] Gardner (1959) 123-124
[9] Bracelin 165

# Appendix C

# Further Reading

For me, the inspiration for writing a book such as this is that there is nothing similar available. Indeed, there is much genuinely new material which is being published for the first time.

However, there are some books which will be helpful to readers who wishes to familiarise themselves with some of the background.

I will start with my own book, *Wiccan Roots - Gerald Gardner and the Modern Witchcraft Revival* (Capall Bann 2000), since in many ways the current book can be seen as a sequel. *Wiccan Roots* goes into a lot more detail about Gardner's time in Highcliffe during the crucial 1938-1940 period, as well as including extensive studies of the Crotona Fellowship and Dorothy Clutterbuck.

A most useful book is Professor Ronald Hutton's *The Triumph of the Moon: A History of Modern Pagan Witchcraft* (Oxford 1999). This looks at a much wider period, exploring the environment in which the witchcraft revival took place, continuing to the present day. It is a finely researched volume and is essential to any historian of the witchcraft revival.

The only biography of Gardner which is currently available is *Gerald Gardner: Witch* by J.L. Bracelin (Octagon 1960). Whilst, as I demonstrate in my books, this is inaccurate in part, it is nevertheless the only source of information on certain aspects of Gardner's story. I am currently carrying out research for what I hope will be a more fully comprehensive and accurate account of Gardner's life.

Gardner's own books, particularly *A Goddess Arrives* (Stockwell 1936); *High Magic's Aid* (Michael Houghton 1949); *Witchcraft Today* (Rider 1954) and *The Meaning of Witchcraft* (Aquarian 1959) are essential to any understanding of his ideas and ways of thinking. The first three have recently been reprinted by I-H-O Books, as has *Gerald Gardner: Witch*.

Books written by those who knew Gardner are valuable sources of information about his life and ideas. In particular, I would mention *One Witch's World* by Patricia Crowther (Hale 1998); *The Rebirth of Witchcraft* by Doreen Valiente (1989) and *Dancing with Witches* by Lois Bourne (Hale 1998).

The References section (Appendix B) gives useful books on the subject matter of each chapter. Books by Philip Carr-Gomm, Cec Cinder, Iseult Richardson, Janet and Stewart Farrar, Lawrence Sutin and Aidan Kelly immediately spring to mind.

Articles in journals and on the Internet by such authors as Gareth Medway, Roger Dearnaley, Michael Howard, Morgan Davis and others are also referred to in Appendix B and are valuable sources of information.

The well-respected and long-running journal, *The Cauldron*, which is well past its 25th birthday and 100th issue, frequently has articles on the history of witchcraft (including some by the present author!) and is always very interesting and informative to read. Details can be obtained from the editor, Michael Howard, BM Cauldron, London WC1N 3XX. He asks that you do not put pentagrams etc on the envelope. There is also a website at http://www.the-cauldron.fsnet.co.uk

# Index

'A Goddess Arrives', 216, 219, 243, 377, 390
Abbey Art Centre, 110, 153
Abbey Folk Park, 135, 145-146, 148-152, 160, 163, 313, 372
Abbey Museum, 152
Abbey of Christ the King, 138, 145
Africa, 71, 232, 364-365
Agape Lodge, 206
Agrippa, Cornelius, 294
Aiwass, 179
Alderley Edge, 254
Allan, Mabel Esther, 45, 49
America, 110, 145, 197, 205, 207, 213, 215, 217, 363-364, 369
Amulets, 170, 286, 353, 366
Ancient British Church, 86, 135, 139, 141-144, 153, 161, 164-165, 250
Ancient Crafts Ltd., 160
Ancient Druid Order, 80-83, 86-87, 90, 97-98, 250, 358-359
Ancient Orthodox Catholic Church, 138
Ancient Universal (Orthodox Catholic) Church, 139
'Ancton Tuqvor', 102, 106
Andrews, Allen, 261-262, 294, 349
Anglican Church, 135, 137-138
anthropology, 79
Anti-Torture League, 367
Antioch, 140, 142
Antrobus, Edward, 81

Apostolic Succession, 140-141
Arbory Road, 329
Arbory Witches, 330, 359
archaeology, 79, 152, 178, 347
Aristotle, 111
Armada, Spanish, 57-58
Armenian Church, 140
Arter, Wallace, 113
Arthur, Ivy, 85
Ashdown Forest, 320
Ashrama, 78, 393
'Aspidistra', 320
asthma, 196, 205, 368
Astrology, 52, 82, 107, 246, 320
Atlantis, 87
Atlantis Bookshop, 124, 243-246, 248, 258, 316, 321, 323
'Aunt Agatha', 24, 79, 95-98, 264
Australia, 152
Avalon, 131-132, 304
Avebury, 241
Avenue Road, Walkford, 65, 73-74
Avon Water, 30
Aztecs, 110

Banks, M.M., 170
Baptism, 140
Bards, Ovates and Druids, Order of (OBOD), 80, 127
barefoot, 46, 55-56, 387
Barlavington, 70
Barrett, Francis, 171, 236, 240
Bashir, Mir, 245, 275
Basque folklore, 168

425

Beaconsfield, 318
Beatty, Charles, 244
Beazley, Stuart, 26
Bedford, 34, 170
Bedfordshire, 23, 320
Beekeepers' Association, 24
Begg, Elspeth, 170, 174-175
Beirut, 368
Berashith Lodge, 83
Bergson, Henri, 111-112
Berrill, Roland, 103
Bethersden, 26
Birchington, 147
Bishop, Peter 165
Bishops, 86, 137-139, 141-144
Blackboy Wood, 104
Blair, Eric, 175
Blake, Barbara, 254
Blake, William, 80
Bloom, Ursula, 102
'Blue Equinox', 299-301
Boltwood, C.D., 85-86
Bone, Eleanor, 261, 263
Book of Shadows, 15, 185, 198, 209-211, 232, 273-279, 281, 285-286, 290-291, 297-303, 305-306, 309, 311, 371, 395
Booth, Harold Clare, 101-103, 109, 112-113, 120
Borneo, 18, 124, 168, 177
Boscastle, 258, 270, 322, 351, 367-368, 370
Boscombe, 174
Bothwell-Gosse, Aimeé, 391
Bott, Adrian, 186, 191, 195-196, 200, 274
Bourne, Lois, 110, 160, 164-165, 366
Bournemouth, 64, 75, 88, 171, 174, 314
Bourton-on-the-Water, 368
Bowers, Roy, 131

Boy Scouts, 113
Bracelin, Jack, 21, 27-28, 106-107, 136-137, 160, 189-190, 206-207, 209, 223, 313-314, 343, 345-346, 388, 392-393
Bradford, 68
Branford, Sybella, 109
Bricket Wood, 12, 90, 104, 107, 125, 130-131, 134, 156, 161, 163, 165, 258, 261, 263, 271-272, 275, 327, 340
Brisbane, 152
British Honduras, 135
British Museum, 82, 110, 154-155, 168, 243, 280, 295
British Orthodox Catholic Church, 139
Brodie Innes, J.W., 68, 82, 303
Bromage, Bernard, 245
Bromley, W. 85
Brunton, Paul, 244
Buchan, John, 232-233, 236, 284
Buckinghamshire, 130, 318
Buddha, 147, 392-393
Buddhism, 82
Buddicom, Jacintha, 170, 175-177
Budge, E.A. Wallis, 319
Burland, Cottie, 105, 110, 124, 153-154, 184, 244-245, 258
Burley Old Enclosure, 29-30
Burma, 135
Burton Common, 70
Burton Park, 72
Byngham, Harry 'Dion', 103, 111-117, 120-125, 130, 134, 245, 258, 389

Caboolture, 152
Caerleon, Bishop of, 140-142
Caerleon Declaration, 143
California, 206

Cambridge, 121, 127, 129, 135, 179, 191
Camp, The, 38, 102, 105, 125, 131-132
Canada, 151, 279, 369
Canary Islands, 313
Canning Town, 318
Cannon, Alexander, 177
Canterbury, 113, 222, 325-326
Canterton Glen, 57
Cardell, Charles, 219, 277
Carnsew, Elizabeth, 65
Carnsew, Henry, 65
Carnsew, Rosamund (see Sabine, Rosamund)
Carpenter, Edward, 112, 119
Carr-Gomm, Philip, 15, 126-127, 129-131, 133, 244
Carter, Sydney, 169-170
Cassels, Mr. Justice, 151
Castletown, 8-9, 174, 197, 312, 328-329, 331-332, 335, 342, 344, 350, 356, 368, 379
Catford, 111
Catholic Apostolic Church, 139
Catholic Church, 35, 65, 68, 70, 72, 139-140, 143, 294
Catholicate of the West, 138, 142
'Cauldron, The', 317
Ceylon, 18, 152, 168, 292
Chaldean-Uniate, 140
Chalk, Catherine, 21-22, 78, 393-394
Chalk, Gordon, 152
Chanctonbury, 120-121, 263
Charlotte, Empress, 61, 65
Charter (Druid), 358
Charter (O.T.O.), 195-199, 201-204, 207, 209-211, 298
Chaucer, 62
Chechemian, Leon, 142
Chellew, H., 85

Chelsea, 325-326
Cheshire, 34, 253-255, 263, 266, 384
Chester, 34-35, 398
Chewton Common, 76-77, 387
Chewton Glen, 39, 41, 43, 73, 77, 387
Chewton Glen Farm, 73
Chewton Mill House, 18, 22
China, 110, 135, 185, 392
Chisholm, Keith, 151-152
'Chong', 103
Christchurch, 18, 20-21, 27, 74, 80, 86, 88, 171, 241-242, 262-263, 302, 314-315, 361
'Christchurch Times', 74, 86, 314-315
Christian, Paul, 377
Christianity, 45-46, 50, 62, 69, 84, 112, 114-116, 119, 143, 176, 186, 294
Chuck Hatch, 320
Cinder, Cec, 102, 113
Clay-Egerton, Alastair, 254
Clee, John, 85
Clifton, Chas, 132-133
Clutterbuck, Dorothy (see Fordham, Dorothy)
Clutterbuck, Ellen, 22-23
Clutterbuck, Thomas, 22-23
Co-Masonry, 78, 194-195, 230, 291-293, 302, 385, 391, 393-394
Cobban, Jennie, 163, 167
Cochrane, Robert, 131
Collins, Andrew, 242
Collins, Eva, 187-188
Colombo, 152, 292
Colquhoun, Ithell, 81-83, 87, 184
'Comment', 121
Confraternity of Christ the King, 136, 144, 151

conservatism, 24, 116, 127
Coote Lake Medal, 174
Cornelius, Jerry, 198-201, 203
Cornwall, 65, 322, 351, 368, 370, 384
Corrall, Enid, 131
Cotswolds, 368
coven-tree, 30
Cowley's Wood, 125
Craft Laws, 279
Crane, Nathalia, 284
Cranemoor, 87-88
Crawford, Charles E.G., 112
cremation, 72
Crick, Molly, 117
Crotona Fellowship, 18, 20-21, 27, 78-79, 86, 301-302, 385, 393-394
Crow, W.B., 139, 204, 244-245
Crowan, 65
Crowley, Aleister, 68, 82-83, 115, 117, 120-121, 124, 172, 175, 177-217, 244, 246, 251, 284-285, 291, 297-301, 306, 308, 310, 318-319, 357, 372-373, 394
Crowther, Arnold, 180, 182, 184, 187-189, 240, 299, 301
Crowther, Patricia, 24, 97, 162, 164, 166, 180, 188-189, 215, 217, 219, 223, 230, 240, 249, 261, 268, 347
Culpeper, Nicolas, 77, 199, 201, 212
Culpepper, Nicholas, 75
Cumberland, 263
Cyprus, 144, 151-152, 160, 390
Cyrillic, 91

Dafo, (see Woodford-Grimes, Edith)
Dartmoor, 47, 317

Dartmouth, 318
Davies, Geoffrey, 109
Davis, Morgan, 140, 161, 192, 194, 205, 207, 210
'Dayonis', 27
de la Haye, Madame, 318
Dearleap, 224, 228
Dearnaley, Roger, 274, 290, 295, 299-300
Dee, John, 338-339, 341, 357
Deerleap, 228-229
Derbyshire, 105
Devil, 99, 303, 317, 339
Devon, 317
Dictionary of National Biography, 80-81
Dinard, 372
Dingwall, E.J., 177
Dionysianism, 101, 112-113, 115-116, 121-124, 130, 133-134, 389
divination, 52-53, 61, 77, 80, 225-226, 294, 380
Docklands Settlement, 318
Dorian, 141-142
Dorset, 175
'Double Circle, The', 86, 88, 90, 165
Douglas, C.H., 129
Douglas, Isle of Man, 177, 328, 339, 363, 367
Douglas School of Art, 339
Dowding, Mary, 80, 126
Downs, Brian, 292
Doyle, Arthur Conan, 136
Druidry, 77, 79-90, 93-94, 96-98, 126-127, 130, 250, 357-359, 381
Druitt, 314
Dublin, 70, 72
Duke of Edinburgh's Wiltshire Regiment, 71

Duncan, J.C., 85
Duncan, Helen, 348

Earle, Dennis, 122
East Barnet, 163
Edgell, Derek, 116-117, 122
Edinburgh, 68
Egypt, 110, 152, 179, 285, 381
élan vital, 112
Elan Vitalgart, 112
Eliot, T.S., 127
ENSA, 180
Essex, 102, 320, 371
Ethnography, 110
Eucharist, 140
Europe, 57, 196, 207-209, 213, 243, 375, 385-386
Eutrophia Society, 111
'Eva C.', 188
Evans, William, 85
Everton, 317

Farrar, Janet and Stewart, 230, 255, 274, 277-278, 281-282, 298
Federation of British Industries, 135
Felkin, R.W., 68
Fernee, Ben, 193, 195
Ferny Knap Inclosure, 30, 32
Ferrette, Jules, 142
Festival of Britain, 323
'Fflang', 103
Finchley, 107, 256
Firth, Violet M., 131, 134
Fisherman's Wharf, San Francisco, 369
Five Acres, 105, 111, 126, 130-132, 134, 136, 154-158, 161, 164, 166, 168, 251-252, 259, 266, 326-327
Flying Saucer Society, 178

folk-dancing, 107, 120
Folk-Lore Journal, 168-170, 175, 313
Folklore Centre of Superstition and Magic, 328, 349, 354, 356
folklore, 38, 48-49, 60, 62, 79, 130, 141, 145, 168-170, 172-175, 180, 250, 284, 313, 318-319, 328, 334-335, 347-349, 354, 356
Folklore Restaurant, 335
Folklore Society, 168-170, 172-175, 180, 250, 334, 348
Folkmoot, 116
Fordham, Dorothy, 18, 22-26, 28, 30, 34-36, 45, 56, 62-64, 73, 88, 96-100, 125-126, 242, 274, 318, 377, 387-389, 391, 393
Fordham, Rupert, 23, 99
Fortune, Dion, 23, 65, 131-134, 219, 244, 350
fortune-telling, 107
Fouracres, 104-109, 111, 113, 118, 120, 122-126, 131-132, 154-157, 184, 245, 258, 388-389
France, 339, 372
Fraudulent Mediums Act, 348
Frazer, James, 129, 303
Freemasonry, 72, 80, 135-136, 141, 143-145, 186, 194, 242, 292-293
'Freethinker, The', 121
Frew, Don, 218
Friar's Rest, 74
Fudge, Rosetta, 21

Gambier-Parry, Richard 320
Gandhi, 147
Garden House, 74
Gardner, Donna, 18, 106, 155, 161, 171-172, 187, 205, 210, 256, 313, 326, 334, 346, 348,

**429**

363-364, 366
Gardner, Douglas, 205
Gardner, Mimi, 161, 172, 205
Gardner, Miriam, 161, 205
'Gart', 103, 113
Gentle, C.A., 150, 189
George Hotel, Castletown, 335
Germany, 18, 35, 67, 91, 101-102, 112, 130, 186, 206, 209, 319-320
Germer, Karl, 193, 206-207, 209, 214
Gibraltar, 326, 334
Gilbert, Joan, 256
Gilbert, R.A., 65-66, 69
Gill, Alec, 319
Glass, Justine, 131
Glen House, The, 35-36, 41
Gnostic Catholic Church, 138
Gnostic Mass, 299-300
Gnosticism, 20, 186, 206
'Goetia, The', 237, 280
'Golden Bough, The' 129, 303
Golden Dawn, 65, 67-70, 82-83, 92, 94, 97-98, 179, 230, 240, 291, 302-303, 341, 385, 393
Goodge Street, 346
Grant, Kenneth, 209
Grant, Pamela, 37-38
Graves, Robert, 286, 303
Great Ballard, 86
Greece, 110
Greenfield, Allen, 187, 193-194, 197, 200-202, 211, 279, 298
Grimassi, Raven, 271
Grove of Ashtaroth, 232
Guy, William, 86
gymnosophy, (see naturism)
gypsies, 35, 49, 51, 56, 60

Hadley Hall, 136
Hambleden, 130
Hampshire, 18, 27, 122, 125
Hannah, Walton, 292
Harding, Barrie, 251, 349
Hargrave, John, 127, 129, 244-245
Harmony Lodge, 292
Harper, Clive, 192-194, 198, 200-202
Harris, Frieda, 207
Harrison, Jane, 112, 304
Hastings, 181-184
'Health and Efficiency', 111-112
'Healthy Life', 111-112, 120
Heard, Herbert J.M., 142
Heath Common, 118
Heath-Stubbs, John, 245
Hebrew, 91, 93, 218, 236-237, 294, 339
Heel Stone, 89, 93, 96
Heidrick, Bill, 193, 201
Hellas, 103
herbalism, 38, 48-51, 60-62, 74-75, 77, 96-97, 266, 344, 380, 387, 391
Herefordshire, 162
'Hermetic Journal', 111
Herne Bay, 334
Hertfordshire, 104, 125, 130, 153, 162, 242, 264, 384
Hidden Masters, Order of the, 244
'High Magic's Aid', 98, 164, 171, 193-195, 206, 215-216, 218-221, 223-224, 227, 230-237, 243, 245-251, 256, 258, 274, 277, 282, 295-296, 298, 302-303, 305, 310-311, 316, 350-351, 374, 377, 379
Highcliffe, 15, 18-19, 22-23, 27-28, 30, 35, 37-38, 73, 75-76, 79, 87, 100, 125, 127, 164, 169, 215, 242, 250-251, 257-258,

261, 263, 265-266, 286, 317, 350, 386, 388-390
Hildburgh, Walter, 169-170, 173-174, 334
Historical Association, 314
Hitler, Adolf, 18
Hole, Christina, 173, 180
Holland, 139
Holland Road, 346
Holy Grail, 142-143, 408
Holy Orthodox Catholic Church, 139
Hooper, W.G., 87-88
Hopkins, Matthew, 334
Horace, 72
Horniman, Annie, 68
Horticultural Society, 24
Houghton, Michael, 243-246
Howard, Michael, 253-254, 256, 261, 292, 306, 317, 369, 385
Hughes, Pennethorne, 374-375
Hull, 16, 319
Hutton, Ronald, 62, 132-133, 162, 177, 191, 261, 274, 278, 281, 286, 290, 295, 387, 389, 396, 402, 404, 407, 409-411, 415-419, 422-423
'Hymn to Fire', 284, 287-288, 308, 310, 390

'Illustrated', 261, 294, 375
Incas, 110
Independent Catholic Church, 138-139
Inner Light, Society of the, 131
Inniskilling, 70
'Insight', 256
invasion, 18, 35, 57-58, 61, 122, 262, 320
invisibility, 225, 227, 294
Iona, 140, 142
Ipswich, 86

Ireland, 70, 95, 139, 384
Isabella, Queen, 65
Isis, 68, 111
Isis/Urania temple, 68
Isle of Man, 88-89, 177, 197, 210, 248, 251, 259-261, 278, 305, 312, 320, 322, 326-329, 334, 342, 344, 349, 351, 356, 358-360, 371, 374, 376, 394
'Isle of Man Examiner', 261, 349
Italy, 72, 345, 351

Jansenius, 139
Jefferies, Richard, 112
Jesus, 23, 46, 62, 70, 140
Joan of Arc, 392
Johore, 168-169, 313
Jones, G.C., 82
Jones, Steve, 292
Juste, Michael, 243-244

Keiller, Alexander, 241
Kelly, Aidan, 117, 273, 277-278, 280, 282, 290, 303-304, 311, 399
Kelly's Directory, 64, 70
Kennedy Cox, 318
Kensington, 72, 318
Kent, 26, 147, 334
'Key of Solomon', 90, 93-94, 218, 220-221, 230, 236, 238-239, 280, 285, 288, 291, 294-297
Khaled, 292
Kibbo Kift Kindred, 127
King, Francis, 187, 209, 223, 248, 377-378
King, Graham, 368, 370
King, Peter, 153
Kingsley, Charles, 87
Kipling, Rudyard, 284, 304
Knight, Gareth, 131
Knight, Lilian, 152

Knightwood Oak, 28-29
kris, 169, 313, 347, 377

La Coste, Rikki, 274
Lake Cutilia, 72
Lamond, Frederic, 159, 218, 275, 290
Lane, Donovan, 315
Latimers, 23-24, 74, 87
Launders, 65
Laver, James, 110, 184, 189, 319
Lawrence, Col., 187
Lawrie, Arthur, 35
Lawrie, Edith, 35
Leadbeater, C.W., 293
Leamington Spa, 85, 179
Lebanon, 368
Ledbury, 162
Leland, C.G., 206, 229, 285, 291, 304
Liberal Catholic Church, 139
Lincolnshire, 229
Liverpool, 18, 21, 101, 263, 266
Local Defence Volunteers, 73-74, 329
London, 18-20, 34-35, 68, 90, 102, 106, 111-112, 122, 125, 127, 131, 141, 144, 150, 153, 155, 161, 168-173, 204-205, 215, 222, 246, 250-253, 256-258, 261, 264, 266, 292, 315, 317-320, 322-323, 342, 346, 362, 365, 387-389
'Lonecraft', 127
Lorelli, 103
Los Angeles, 87
Lotus League, 107, 125
Lough, Dorothy, 150, 152
Lough, Stanley, 150
Lower Lyes, 104
Luhrmann, Tanya, 90
Lymington, 35, 317

Lyndhurst, 228-229
Lyon-Clark, Irene, 80, 85-86

Macaskie, Charles, 125
Macaskie, Dorothy, 125
MacGregor, Alasdair Alpin, 348
MacGregor Reid, George Watson, 81-82, 84-85
MacGregor Reid, Robert A.F., 82, 85, 358
Machen, Arthur, 68
Mackay, Anne, 194
Mackenzie, Bishop Colin, 144
Mackenzie, Mona, 318
Maguire, Alfred, 341
Major, The, 105, 124, 155
Malaya, 18, 101, 124, 168-169, 177, 347
Malew Street, 9, 342, 344-346
Maltby, Col., 319-320
Malton, 27
Malvern College, 318-319
Man, Isle of, 88-89, 177, 197, 251, 259-261, 278, 305, 312, 320, 322, 326-360, 371, 374, 376, 394
Mannix, Daniel, 89, 96
Marholm, 142
Mark Ash Wood, 28-29
Marlborough, 169
Marlowe, Eveline, 145, 147, 149
Marryatt, Florence, 177
Masefield, John, 284
Mason, Ernie, 21-22, 99
Mason family, 18, 21-22, 27, 78, 99, 292, 302, 385-386, 391, 393-394
Mason, Rosetta, 99
Mason, Susie, 21-22, 99
Massey, Gerald, 80-81

432

Mathers, Samuel L. MacGregor, 67-68, 82, 90, 93-94, 218, 236-240, 280, 285, 295-297
Mathews, Alex, 21
Maxwell, Wilfred, 132
May Day, 46-48, 187
McIntosh, Christopher, 69
McLagen, A.C.A., 142
McLean, Adam, 111
'McLeod, Fiona', 82, 284
'Meaning of Witchcraft, The', 95, 223, 249, 311-312
Medway, Gareth, 69, 75, 80-81, 83-87, 94, 120, 184, 265, 274, 288, 290, 292-294, 299-300, 302, 305, 308, 346
Mee, Arthur, 148
Melchizedek, Order of, 87
Mellinger, Frederick, 207
Mellinger, Lucas, 181
Memphis, 205-206
Mexico, 110
Mill House, 18, 22-24, 35-36, 98, 242, 387
Mill House Players, 23
Millard, R., 85
Milne, Betty Lumsden, 172, 377
Minerva Café, 102
Minerval Degree, 192, 195, 197, 200, 202, 204-205
Mitchell, Leslie, 256
Montalban, Madeline, 244-245
'Moon Endureth, The', 232
Moonella, 102, 104-105, 109, 113, 118
Moonella Group, 102, 105, 109, 113, 118
Moore, Henry, 153
Moore, Thomas, 329
Morgan, R.W., 142
Morgen Rothe, Order of, 66, 68
Morven, 220, 222-225, 229, 231-233, 236, 241, 249, 274
Mother Sabine, (see Sabine, Rosamund)
Murray, Margaret, 57, 170, 173, 229, 241, 319, 371, 378, 383, 385
museums, 77, 82, 89-90, 95-97, 110, 141, 144-146, 150-155, 168, 174, 184, 197, 199, 206, 210-212, 243, 248, 251, 255-256, 258-261, 266-270, 279-282, 295, 305-307, 312-316, 320, 322-323, 325-335, 338, 342, 348, 350-357, 360-370, 373-374, 379, 394
Music Magic, 224, 227
mythology, 80, 123, 129-130, 176

Naked Man, The, 28-30
Naked Trust, Fellowship of the, 101, 112
Napoleon, 57-58, 61
Narnia, 62
'Nature Cure', 81
naturism, 20, 101-102, 105-109, 111-113, 115-116, 120, 122, 124-125, 129-134, 157-158, 161, 177, 184, 250-252, 257-259, 261, 315, 327, 387-389, 394
naturopathy, 81
Nazism, 319
Neil, H., 85
Nestorian Church, 153
Netherwood, 181-183
Neuburg, Victor, 115, 121-122, 288
New Barnet, 136-137, 147
New Forest Club, 20, 125, 388-389

New Forest, 13-15, 17-20, 28, 30-33, 39-40, 64, 117, 122, 125, 162, 164, 169, 228, 256, 262, 270-271, 306, 317, 320, 372, 384, 388-389
New Milton, 86
New Orleans, 206
New York, 206-207
Newlands Manor, 317
Nichols, Ross, 84, 89, 124, 127-130, 133, 158, 244-245, 377-378
Nietzche, 112
Norfolk House, 318
Norfolk, 86, 127, 318
Normandy, 320
North Bovey, 317
North, Dolores, 245-246, 377
Northern Coven, 263-264, 266, 270, 340
Nottingham, 87
NSPCC, 24
Nuada, Temple of, 83, 94, 97
nudism, (see naturism)
numerology, 52-53

O'Callaghan, J.B., 80
O.T.O. (Ordo Templi Orientis), 175, 179-180, 186-188, 192-197, 200-202, 205-209, 212-215, 217, 246, 251, 286, 298, 300-301
oakleaf crown, 89
Oakwood Road, 155, 161
Ober Water, 30
'Occult Observer', 124, 130, 221, 244-245, 248, 275, 377
'Occult Review', 69-70, 303
Ohly, W.F.C., 141, 152-153
Old Catholic Movement, 138, 140-142

Old Catholic Orthodox Church, 139
Old Pack, The, 103-104
Oldmeadow, Ann, 35
Oldmeadow, Annie, 34
Oldmeadow, Ernest, 35
Oldmeadow family, 34, 100, 384
Oldmeadow, Katherine, 28, 34-63, 77, 99, 387-388, 391, 393
Olliver, C.W., 285
Onchan, 367
Operation Fortitude, 320, 370
Operation Overlord, 286
Orchard, W.E., 119
Orthodox Catholic Church, 138
Orwell, George, 175
Ouless, C., 170
Ovate Og, 83
Ovid, 72
Oxford, 38, 175-176, 190-191
Oxfordshire, 130, 175

P.R.I., 73
Page, Jessica, 136
Paignton, 317
palmistry, 107
Pan, 41, 43-44, 46, 117, 120-121, 123, 133, 241
Paris, 68, 182, 292
Parkins, Mary, 115
Parsons, Jack, 206
Pas de Calais, 320
Peacock, Arthur, 84
Pembrokeshire, 57
'Pendragon', 82, 87
Peterborough, 142
Pettipher, Frank, 87
Pettipher, Grace, 87
Pevsner, Nikolaus, 153
Pickingill, George, 371
'Pine Cone', 115, 117, 122
Plato, 111

Plymouth, 175, 179
Political Warfare Executive, 320
Powell, Douglas, 157
Powys, 245
Pragnell, George, 119
Pragnell, Vera, 118-122
Preston, Hayter, 121
Price, Harry, 319
Prince of Jerusalem, 194, 200, 204
Psychical Research, Society for, 177-178, 347, 383
psychology, 226, 391-392

Qabalah, 82
Queensland, 152

Rectified Rite, 65, 67-70, 72, 75
Red Cross, 24
Red Gap, 329, 349
Red House, 314-315
Reuss, Theodor, 186
Rhinefield House, 29
Richardson, Alan, 131
Riddehough, Geoffrey, 383
Rider and Co., 377, 381
Ridgmount Gardens, 155, 322, 346
Ripleys, 197, 270, 279
Ripon, 101
Ronce, 339
Rose of the World, 65, 69-70, 311, 391
roses, 26-27, 36, 65, 67, 69-70, 83-84, 311, 338, 391-393
Rosedale, Ida, 172
Rosher, Charles, 82-83
Rosicrucianism, 18, 20-21, 67, 69, 78, 83, 86, 186, 242, 302, 311, 391
Royal Anthropological Society, 168, 174

Royal Arch, 187-188, 194
Royal Asiatic Society, 169
Royal Stuart Society, 172
RSPCA, 24
Ruskin, John, 112
Russell, Bertrand, 127
Russell, C., 187

S.S. Scottish Prince, 368
Sabine, George, 70-75, 384, 386, 388, 390, 392, 394
Sabine, Rosamund, 28, 64-78, 97-100, 217, 270-271, 302, 311, 377, 384-388, 390-395
Salisbury, 314, 357
San Francisco, 202, 369
Sanctuary, The, 118-121
Sandy Balls, 116
Sauders, M.S., 141
Scandinavia, 145
'Scire', 192, 196-197, 246
Scots Pines, 32
scourge, 54, 225, 270-271
secret societies, 54, 61, 104, 135, 347
Selsey, 140, 142
Seton, Ernest Thompson, 114-115, 127
Shah, Idries, 21, 98
Sharp, William, 82, 293
Shaw, Julian, 245
Shepherd, Annie, 34
Shepherd Street, 317
Shepherd's Bush, 346
Shiplake-on-Thames, 175
Sibley, J.C., 138
Singapore, 187-188
Slatter, Elizabeth, 23, 387
Smith, Geoffrey, 194-195, 198, 208-209
Smyth, Frank, 173
Snaefell, 364

Social Credit Movement, 129
Societas Rosicruciana in Anglia (S.R.I.A.), 67
Sociological Society, 109
Somerford, 78, 86, 242, 393-394
Sorensen, Harold, 102-103, 109
Sorensen, Helen, 103
Soul, Pat, 85
South Downs, 117-118, 120
Southampton, 18, 27, 292, 385, 393
Southern Coven of British Witches, 77, 261-263, 265-266, 268-270, 294, 360-362, 364, 367, 391
Southern Rhodesia, 319
Southridge, 241-242
Spenser, Edmund, 62
Spielplatz, 124-130, 132, 155, 157, 251, 257
spiritualism, 79, 107, 136, 177, 226, 348, 357
Sprengel, Anna, 67-68
St. Albans, 137, 163, 165, 253, 258
Steer, Allan, 85
Stella Matutina, 68
Stevens, C.I., 142
Stevenson, Ian, 25, 35, 37-38, 41, 43, 45, 55, 64, 73, 389
Steyning, 121
Stonehenge, 81, 83, 88-89, 96-97
Storrington, 118, 120
Stratford-on-Avon, 325-326
Stukeley, William, 80
Sullivan, G.A., 21-22, 27
Summers, Montague, 319
Sumner, Heywood, 31
Sun Tan Club, 157
'Sunday Referee', 121
Surrey, 198, 254

Sussex, 7, 70-71, 118, 121, 263, 320
Sutin, Lawrence, 203
Sutton, 70-71
Sword of Nuada, 84, 89-95
swords, 75, 79, 84, 87, 89-98, 149, 236-237, 286, 296, 310, 340-341
Symonds, Edmund Vernon, 183, 207
Symonds, John, 189, 196, 209, 216-218, 220, 224, 244
Syrian-Malabar, 140
Syro-Chaldean, 140

'Tablet, The', 35
Tantra, 186
Tarot, 82
Teare, T.D.G., 337, 346
Templars, 186, 286, 378, 381
Tennyson, Alfred, 284
'Text A', 170, 236, 278, 281-284, 286-289, 295-297, 299, 304-305, 308-311, 376, 390
'The People', 165
The Ridge, 183
Theban, 262, 339, 361
Theosophical Society, 81
Thomas, Dylan, 122
Thorn, Michael, 14, 305
Thorney Hill, 35
Thweng, 103
Tillett, Gregory, 135, 141, 144-145
toadstone, 175
Tob, 103
Tolkien, J.R.R., 62
Toronto, 192, 278, 369
Trelawny, C., 85
Trinity College, Dublin, 70, 72
Trinity Hall College, Cambridge, 135

'Trophy Island', 320
TT Races, 320
Tuatha de Cornovii, 255
Tunis, 368
Tyrrell, Walter, 57

Universal Bond, 80-81, 84
Universalism, 81-82, 84-85
Utrecht, 139

Vacuna, 72-73, 392
Vada, 221-222, 240
Valiente, Doreen, 14, 22, 27-29, 64, 74, 89-90, 95-97, 124, 131,179-180, 192-193, 195, 210, 219, 230, 242, 244-246, 252-254, 259, 261, 265, 270, 274-276, 281-282, 290, 297, 299, 305, 311, 348, 379, 389
Vanda, 240-241
Verwood, 175
Vibraclair readings, 88
Vickers, Barbara, 253-256, 263, 266, 340, 379
Vickers, Gilbert, 253-254, 263, 266
Vine Press, 121

Waite, A.E., 68-70, 78, 83
Walkford, 65, 73-74, 76, 242
Walsingham, 86
Wanda, 221, 240, 242
Ward, J.S.M., 86, 134-138, 141, 144-152, 154, 160-161, 163, 205, 285, 313, 329, 372
Warwick, 325
Warwickshire, 325
Washington, 118, 120
Waugh, Evelyn, 106
Wavendon Towers, 320
Wayland, 86

Wellbye, Reginald (Rex), 102-103, 105-106, 109-110, 124-126, 155, 157-159, 161, 257
Wells, Christine, 23, 35
Welsh folklore, 168
Welsh Harp reservoir, 106
Westcott, Wynn, 67-68
Western Orthodox Catholic Church, 139
Westlake, Aubrey, 113-114, 127
Westlake, Ernest, 113-114, 127
Weston-super-Mare, 68
Weston, Iseult, 107, 124, 126, 129, 132
Whaddon Hall, 320
'Whinchat', 73-75, 386, 392
Whitehead, W.H., 339
Whitman, Walt, 112
Wica, 18, 26, 73, 213, 215, 302, 373, 384, 386, 389
Wiccan Church of Canada, 279, 369
'Wiccan Roots', 16, 22, 26, 28, 63-64, 98, 261, 380, 385, 391, 393
Wick, 88
Wickford, 102, 104-105
Wilby, Basil, 131
Wilcox, Gwen, 319
Wilkinson, Louis, 191, 195
William Rufus, 57, 242
Williamson, Cecil, 74, 77, 89, 110, 158, 163, 174, 177, 189, 246, 251, 253-259, 261-267, 270, 301, 305-306, 313, 317-373, 375, 391, 394
Williamson, Hugh Ross, 286
Wilson, Campbell, 368
Wilson, Monique, 279, 368
Wilson, Steve, 117, 120, 292-293
Wiltshire, 71
Wilverley Post, 30
Windmill Farm, 328, 349, 352

Windsor, 368
Wise, Caroline, 244
Witchcraft Research Centre, 319, 354
'Witchcraft Today', 14, 90, 99-100, 173, 178, 190, 211, 223-224, 227, 229, 231-233, 249, 264, 277, 284, 287, 298, 307, 311, 373-376, 378-381, 386, 390, 392
Witches' Cottage, 90, 144, 148-149, 151, 155-156, 158, 160-164, 166-167, 189, 215, 250, 257, 263-264, 266, 323-324, 326, 339-340, 353, 355, 371-372, 394
Witches' Kitchen, 8, 335-337
Witches' Mill, 5, 322, 369
Wodehouse, P.G., 97
Women's Freedom League, 102
Woodcraft Chivalry, Order of, 113-114, 117-118, 123-124
Woodford, Rev. A.F.A., 67
Woodford-Grimes, Edith (Dafo), 18, 21-22, 25-28, 65, 73, 75, 77-78, 90-91, 98-99, 141, 158, 160, 164, 188, 215, 217, 219, 225, 243, 250-251, 255, 259-262, 265-266, 292, 301-302, 315, 340-341, 350-351, 360-361, 365, 376-377, 386-394
Woodford-Grimes, Rosanne, 26, 260
Woodlands, Dorset, 175
Woodman, W.R., 67
Woodside Close, 157
Woodside Road, 155

Ye Bok of Ye Art Magical, 93, 277, 279-282, 288-289, 295-297, 299-300, 304-305, 310-311, 391

Yeats, W.B., 68, 284
Yeowell, John, 73, 172
yoga, 378, 392-393
Yorke, Gerald, 173, 191-192, 195, 209-210, 218, 244-245, 255, 295, 352, 357, 377-378
Yorkshire, 27, 101

Zandonda, 319
'Zex', 103, 109
Zimbabwe, 319

# FREE DETAILED CATALOGUE

Capall Bann is owned and run by people actively involved in many of the areas in which we publish. A detailed illustrated catalogue is available on request, SAE or International Postal Coupon appreciated. **Titles can be ordered direct from Capall Bann, post free in the UK** (cheque or PO with order) or from good bookshops and specialist outlets.

Do contact us for details on the latest releases at: **Capall Bann Publishing, Auton Farm, Milverton, Somerset, TA4 1NE.** Titles include:

A Breath Behind Time, Terri Hector
Angels and Goddesses - Celtic Christianity & Paganism, M. Howard
Arthur - The Legend Unveiled, C Johnson & E Lung
Astrology The Inner Eye - A Guide in Everyday Language, E Smith
Auguries and Omens - The Magical Lore of Birds, Yvonne Aburrow
Asyniur - Womens Mysteries in the Northern Tradition, S McGrath
Beginnings - Geomancy, Builder's Rites & Electional Astrology in the
    European Tradition, Nigel Pennick
Between Earth and Sky, Julia Day
Book of the Veil , Peter Paddon
Caer Sidhe - Celtic Astrology and Astronomy, Vol 1, Michael Bayley
Caer Sidhe - Celtic Astrology and Astronomy, Vol 2 M Bayley
Call of the Horned Piper, Nigel Jackson
Cat's Company, Ann Walker
Celtic Faery Shamanism, Catrin James
Celtic Faery Shamanism - The Wisdom of the Otherworld, Catrin James
Celtic Lore & Druidic Ritual, Rhiannon Ryall
Celtic Sacrifice - Pre Christian Ritual & Religion, Marion Pearce
Celtic Saints and the Glastonbury Zodiac, Mary Caine
Circle and the Square, Jack Gale
Compleat Vampyre - The Vampyre Shaman, Nigel Jackson
Creating Form From the Mist - The Wisdom of Women in Celtic Myth and
    Culture, Lynne Sinclair-Wood
Crystal Clear - A Guide to Quartz Crystal, Jennifer Dent
Crystal Doorways, Simon & Sue Lilly
Crossing the Borderlines - Guising, Masking & Ritual Animal Disguise in the
    European Tradition, Nigel Pennick
Dragons of the West, Nigel Pennick
Earth Dance - A Year of Pagan Rituals, Jan Brodie
Earth Harmony - Places of Power, Holiness & Healing, Nigel Pennick
Earth Magic, Margaret McArthur

Eildon Tree (The) Romany Language & Lore, Michael Hoadley
Enchanted Forest - The Magical Lore of Trees, Yvonne Aburrow
Eternal Priestess, Sage Weston
Eternally Yours Faithfully, Roy Radford & Evelyn Gregory
Everything You Always Wanted To Know About Your Body, But So Far Nobody's Been Able To Tell You, Chris Thomas & D Baker
Face of the Deep - Healing Body & Soul, Penny Allen
Fairies in the Irish Tradition, Molly Gowen
Familiars - Animal Powers of Britain, Anna Franklin
Fool's First Steps, (The) Chris Thomas
Forest Paths - Tree Divination, Brian Harrison, Ill. S. Rouse
From Past to Future Life, Dr Roger Webber
Gardening For Wildlife Ron Wilson
God Year, The, Nigel Pennick & Helen Field
Goddess on the Cross, Dr George Young
Goddess Year, The, Nigel Pennick & Helen Field
Goddesses, Guardians & Groves, Jack Gale
Handbook For Pagan Healers, Liz Joan
Handbook of Fairies, Ronan Coghlan
Healing Book, The, Chris Thomas and Diane Baker
Healing Homes, Jennifer Dent
Healing Journeys, Paul Williamson
Healing Stones, Sue Philips
Herb Craft - Shamanic & Ritual Use of Herbs, Lavender & Franklin
Hidden Heritage - Exploring Ancient Essex, Terry Johnson
Hub of the Wheel, Skytoucher
In Search of Herne the Hunter, Eric Fitch
Inner Celtia, Alan Richardson & David Annwn
Inner Mysteries of the Goths, Nigel Pennick
Inner Space Workbook - Develop Thru Tarot, C Summers & J Vayne
Intuitive Journey, Ann Walker Isis - African Queen, Akkadia Ford
Journey Home, The, Chris Thomas
Kecks, Keddles & Kesh - Celtic Lang & The Cog Almanac, Bayley
Language of the Psycards, Berenice
Legend of Robin Hood, The, Richard Rutherford-Moore
Lid Off the Cauldron, Patricia Crowther
Light From the Shadows - Modern Traditional Witchcraft, Gwyn
Living Tarot, Ann Walker
Lore of the Sacred Horse, Marion Davies
Lost Lands & Sunken Cities (2nd ed.), Nigel Pennick
Magic of Herbs - A Complete Home Herbal, Rhiannon Ryall
Magical Guardians - Exploring the Spirit and Nature of Trees, Philip Heselton
Magical History of the Horse, Janet Farrar & Virginia Russell
Magical Lore of Animals, Yvonne Aburrow
Magical Lore of Cats, Marion Davies
Magical Lore of Herbs, Marion Davies

Magick Without Peers, Ariadne Rainbird & David Rankine
Masks of Misrule - Horned God & His Cult in Europe, Nigel Jackson
Medicine For The Coming Age, Lisa Sand MD
Medium Rare - Reminiscences of a Clairvoyant, Muriel Renard
Menopausal Woman on the Run, Jaki da Costa
Mind Massage - 60 Creative Visualisations, Marlene Maundrill
Mirrors of Magic - Evoking the Spirit of the Dewponds, P Heselton
Moon Mysteries, Jan Brodie
Mysteries of the Runes, Michael Howard
Mystic Life of Animals, Ann Walker
New Celtic Oracle The, Nigel Pennick & Nigel Jackson
Oracle of Geomancy, Nigel Pennick
Pagan Feasts - Seasonal Food for the 8 Festivals, Franklin & Phillips
Patchwork of Magic - Living in a Pagan World, Julia Day
Pathworking - A Practical Book of Guided Meditations, Pete Jennings
Personal Power, Anna Franklin
Pickingill Papers - The Origins of Gardnerian Wicca, Bill Liddell
Pillars of Tubal Cain, Nigel Jackson
Places of Pilgrimage and Healing, Adrian Cooper
Practical Divining, Richard Foord
Practical Meditation, Steve Hounsome
Practical Spirituality, Steve Hounsome
Psychic Self Defence - Real Solutions, Jan Brodie
Real Fairies, David Tame
Reality - How It Works & Why It Mostly Doesn't, Rik Dent
Romany Tapestry, Michael Houghton
Runic Astrology, Nigel Pennick
Sacred Animals, Gordon MacLellan
Sacred Celtic Animals, Marion Davies, Ill. Simon Rouse
Sacred Dorset - On the Path of the Dragon, Peter Knight
Sacred Grove - The Mysteries of the Forest, Yvonne Aburrow
Sacred Geometry, Nigel Pennick
Sacred Nature, Ancient Wisdom & Modern Meanings, A Cooper
Sacred Ring - Pagan Origins of British Folk Festivals, M. Howard
Season of Sorcery - On Becoming a Wisewoman, Poppy Palin
Seasonal Magic - Diary of a Village Witch, Paddy Slade
Secret Places of the Goddess, Philip Heselton
Secret Signs & Sigils, Nigel Pennick
Self Enlightenment, Mayan O'Brien
Spirits of the Air, Jaq D Hawkins
Spirits of the Earth, Jaq D Hawkins
Spirits of the Earth, Jaq D Hawkins
Stony Gaze, Investigating Celtic Heads John Billingsley
Stumbling Through the Undergrowth, Mark Kirwan-Heyhoe
Subterranean Kingdom, The, revised 2nd ed, Nigel Pennick
Symbols of Ancient Gods, Rhiannon Ryall

Talking to the Earth, Gordon MacLellan
Taming the Wolf - Full Moon Meditations, Steve Hounsome
Teachings of the Wisewomen, Rhiannon Ryall
The Other Kingdoms Speak, Helena Hawley
Tree: Essence of Healing, Simon & Sue Lilly
Tree: Essence, Spirit & Teacher, Simon & Sue Lilly
Through the Veil, Peter Paddon
Torch and the Spear, Patrick Regan
Understanding Chaos Magic, Jaq D Hawkins
Vortex - The End of History, Mary Russell
Warp and Weft - In Search of the I-Ching, William de Fancourt
Warriors at the Edge of Time, Jan Fry
Water Witches, Tony Steele
Way of the Magus, Michael Howard
Weaving a Web of Magic, Rhiannon Ryall
West Country Wicca, Rhiannon Ryall
Wildwitch - The Craft of the Natural Psychic, Poppy Palin
Wildwood King, Philip Kane
Witches of Oz, Matthew & Julia Philips
Wondrous Land - The Faery Faith of Ireland by Dr Kay Mullin
Working With the Merlin, Geoff Hughes
Your Talking Pet, Ann Walker

# FREE detailed catalogue and FREE 'Inspiration' magazine
## Contact: Capall Bann Publishing, Auton Farm, Milverton, Somerset, TA4 1NE